RESTRUCTURING POLITICAL POWER IN CHINA

RESTRUCTURING POLITICAL POWER IN CHINA
Alliances and Opposition, 1978–1998

AN CHEN

LYNNE
RIENNER
PUBLISHERS

BOULDER
LONDON

Published in the United States of America in 1999 by
Lynne Rienner Publishers, Inc.
1800 30th Street, Boulder, Colorado 80301

and in the United Kingdom by
Lynne Rienner Publishers, Inc.
3 Henrietta Street, Covent Garden, London WC2E 8LU

Library of Congress Cataloging-in-Publication Data
Chen, An, 1955–
    Restructuring political power in China : alliances and opposition,
1978–1998 / An Chen.
        p.   cm.
    Includes bibliographical references and index.
    ISBN 1-55587-842-3 (alk. paper)
    1. China—Politics and government—1978–   2. China—Economic
conditions—1978–   3. China—Economic policy—1978–   4. China—
Social conditions—1978–   5. Structural adjustment (Economic
policy)—China.   I. Title.
JQ1510.C483   1999
320.951'09'048—DC21   99-11103
                                                                  CIP
                                                                  Rev.

British Cataloguing in Publication Data
A Cataloguing in Publication record for this book
is available from the British Library.

Printed and bound in the United States of America

∞   The paper used in this publication meets the requirements
     of the American National Standard for Permanence of
     Paper for Printed Library Materials Z39.48-1984.

    5   4   3   2   1

To the memory of my father

Contents

Tables and Figures

Tables

Figures

Acknowledgments

In the decade of writing and revising this book, I received valuable help from a number of people, to whom I express my sincere gratitude.

My greatest intellectual debt is to Joseph LaPalombara, my chief adviser at Yale University. One of his comparative politics courses introduced me to Chinese politics, and he offered me important guidance in building the theoretical framework of this study: He taught me to approach China's political transformation in comparative perspective, placing it in a broad, world-historical context. I am also deeply grateful to James C. Scott, from whom I learned how to sharpen the focus of this work and to apply the methodology of social scientific analysis to the study of China as an Asian country.

I have profited greatly from the criticism, comments, suggestions, and encouragement offered by David Cameron, Edward Friedman, David Mayhew, Barrett McCormick, Mike Mochizuki, Kevin O'Brien, Jonathan Spence, John Starr, and John Watt. They were generous with their time and patience, reading all or parts of the manuscript. I also gratefully acknowledge the contributions of Frances J. Bassett, Chen Yizi, Deborah Davis, Ding Yuan, Trond Gilberg, Hong Yung Lee, Barnett Rubin, Shaoguang Wang, Timothy White, and Zhao Chenggen.

I wish to thank Shena Redmond at Lynne Rienner Publishers for guiding this book through the production process and Alice Colwell for her superb editing.

I appreciate the support and assistance of the Committee on International Relations Studies with the People's Republic of China (CIRSPRC), the Chinese Academy of Social Sciences, the Yale Center for International and Area Studies, the Standing Committee of the Wuxi Municipal People's Congress, the East-West Center in Honolulu, and the Department of Political Science, National University of Singapore.

Finally, I thank my wife, Shuhong, for the work she did for this book as well as for her understanding whenever I had to stay late in the office. I dedicate this book to the memory of my father, whose dream for a progressive and democratic China has been a major source of my inspiration and a driving force of my intellectual pursuits.

—*An Chen*

Author's Note

Except for a few names that are well known in other forms, I have used pinyin, China's official system of transliteration, throughout this book. I have given titles of Chinese books, journals, and newspapers in pinyin, with English translations in parentheses; I have indicated the titles of articles, chapters, and documents in English only. The reader may need to check both the English- and the Chinese-language parts of the bibliography to find the references cited in the notes.

"Party," with an initial cap, indicates the Chinese Communist Party (CCP). I use a lowercased "party" only in the term "party leadership," by which I mean the leadership position of the CCP.

1

Checks and Balances
Without Political Opposition

Social scientists usually find it safer to elaborate theories that explain why what has happened had to happen than to predict what is going to happen. More than a decade ago, the tide of democratization that swept much of the noncommunist world stimulated an explosion of academic enthusiasm about "transitions to democracy" as well as renewed optimism about the democratic prospects of the globe. Perhaps we had been too pessimistic when we had argued, referring to studies of the historical evolution of democracy, that certain prerequisites regarding political culture, socioeconomic development, historical legacy, and so on must be met for democratization to take place. During this period, we saw some conventional approaches challenged and many improvements made to existing democratic theory.[1]

The scholarly literature regarding the causes and origins of democratic transitions and the subsequent consolidation had been enriched to such an extent that any sort of democratic breakthrough in the contemporary world was not likely to come as a surprise. Yet the new theoretical elaboration again proved to have more explanatory than predictive power. The great democratic transformation in Eastern Europe and later in the Soviet Union in 1989 and 1990—which showed few clear signs before it occurred—caught many political scientists unprepared.[2] To be sure, it is not unusual to have history disprove judgments about the future. It is perhaps especially difficult and risky to predict the political development (or lack thereof) in communist countries. In retrospect we can see that this difficulty arose from two related factors. One is the nature of these states as closed societies in which the tight control of the population by the Communist Party in both political and economic areas dampens societal vitality and makes social progress, if any, extremely slow and hard to discern. Pervasive political terror also gravely impedes meaningful social science field research. Although outside observers could do little about this problem, the second factor is a more or less self-imposed intellectual constraint. A stereotyped conception in the intellectual community is that the communist state, unlike the authoritarian state, represents a totalitarian model that is ideologically and institutionally entrenched and resists any structural evolution in a democratic direction.[3] This rigid conceptualization and the alleged distinctiveness and incomparability of communist regimes resulted in little progress in social science research on these states.[4]

If we regard the democratization of Eastern Europe and the former Soviet Union as little more than historic accident, we will not sharpen our ability to predict regime changes in China. If anything can be learned from the unexpectedness of the events in the former Eastern bloc, it may be that the "organic" mode of democratization—a gradual societal transformation followed by a change in political regime, the first serving as a precondition of the second—works not only for capitalistic authoritarian regimes[5] but also to varying degrees for communist states, despite their seeming lack of the socioeconomic and sociopolitical changes perceived necessary for democratization. As some scholars noted in their retrospective contemplation, the internal changes in both political and economic relations in Eastern Europe and the Soviet Union did not receive due attention in the United States and the rest of the West: "With some exceptions most US area specialists failed to conceptualize or monitor explicitly these alterations in the structure of underlying power and production relations prior to the change in regime [in Eastern Europe and the former Soviet Union]—much less predict the magnitude of their impact upon regime persistence."[6]

Defying what Samuel Huntington calls the third wave of democratization, China still maintains a nondemocratic, one-party system. The Chinese communist regime's survival of "the Leninist extinction" and the fact that the Party monopoly of power in China was left intact by the global movement toward democracy seem to have become an anomaly, a cause for speculation.[7] Optimists believe that China's democratization is just at hand. Some appear to be so certain as to predict its exact timing.[8] The pessimists have been perhaps discouraged by the 1989 Tiananmen bloodshed and the apparent strong capability of the Chinese communists to hang on to power. In an article published in 1996, a seasoned political analyst includes China in a category of "most powerful and influential authoritarian states" that show "little or no prospect of democratization in the near term."[9]

As the stories of democratic transition in Eastern Europe and the former Soviet Union manifest, predictions of this kind do not make good sense unless they are based on a careful empirical study of the internal changes of China's society and government, in addition to relevant international factors. Because of China's large population and economy and its long-established political culture and strong political tradition, democratization is not likely to take place there all of a sudden. It will not come as a result of external blows, as may be the case in some small authoritarian states that desperately need democratic legitimacy for international financial aid. Chinese democracy must be mainly a product—though not necessarily an unavoidable one—of a certain stage of its internal socioeconomic and political-structural evolution. Given the broadness of the question concerning China's democratization, I will borrow from the method of Robert Dahl in *Who Governs?* and subdivide the general question into a number of more specific questions. Before we know when China will democratize, we need to know the following:

How undemocratic is China's current political system? Or put another way, if we see the political reform launched in 1978 as the beginning of a long march toward democracy, where does China stand now?

Is there any meaningful citizen representation in China's political process under the regime of Deng Xiaoping? Or is there any degree of genuine popular participation—not in the Maoist sense but through institutionalized channels—in government? If the answer is yes, what are its causes, motivations, implications, and possible consequences for political liberalization and democratization, defined at a minimum as political pluralism, a multiparty system, and free elections? If no, what have been the main obstacles to such participation? What is more important for our purpose, *have there been any differences concerning the extent of citizen representation between the national (central) and subnational (provincial, municipal, county, and grassroots) levels of government?*

Although these closely entwined questions constitute the focus of this study, my aim is not to predict the timing of China's democratization but to contemplate the specific and realistic way in which China is most likely to evolve toward a Western-type democracy. For without knowing *how* China's democratization will happen and what its dynamics are, one can hardly predict when it will occur. In this introductory chapter, I first discuss the distinctiveness of China within the comparative study of democratization. I then offer a preview of the main argument of this book. The final section presents a basic theoretical framework of this study, its research method, and organization.

A Comparative Framework of Democratic Transitions

The comparative study of democracy has advanced numerous relevant theories and arguments to generalize past democratic experience. But the explanations of democratization thus far still seem to be insufficient for an evaluation of China's democratic possibilities. "To explain a specific event," as Adam Przeworski and Henry Teune say, "is to state the conditions under which it always or usually takes place, that is, to cite general statements (laws) from which other statements concerning properties of specific events can be inferred with some reasonable certainty."[10] In practical application, however, the existing theories of democratization can hardly be valid across all social systems because there are too many intervening variables. It is especially so in the Chinese case. Long before the issue of democratic transition in communist states was placed on the agenda of scholarly research, most China scholars treated the Chinese political system as sui generis, different from that of a totalitarian, communist, or developing country.[11]

When we evaluate China's democratic prospects according to existing models of democratization, we face the same problem of Chinese uniqueness: Differences between China and most, if not all, democratized countries in terms of preconditions perceived as necessary for democracy seem to be too great for meaningful comparisons to be made. In the cradle of modern representative democracy in Western Europe, democratic transition was promoted by a unique combination of elements, none of which China has. They include the long-established principle of liberty that governed economic relations, the rule of law developed from the hallowed nature of business contracts,[12] the relative weakness of absolutist rulers and the power-limited minimalist state,[13] the small size of the peasantry and the turn toward appropriate forms of commercial farming at an early point, and Protestantism.[14]

The democratic experiences of many of the postwar democratized states are either irrelevant or inapplicable to China. In West Germany and Japan, democracy was imposed on defeated dictatorships by Allied occupation; their experience is unlikely to be repeated.[15] In southern Europe and Latin America, there had been a long history of alternation between authoritarianism and democracy. As a result, in the recent redemocratization the major task for democrats was not to build but to rebuild democratic institutions, not to create but to resurrect a civil society. Presumably, it was just these repeated though interrupted experiments with democratic rules that made the transition toward democracy, in which "traditional rulers remain in control . . . and use . . . compromise or force—or some mix of the two—to retain at least part of their power," more successful and of a less revolutionary nature.[16]

In recent cases of democratization, the areas that seem to bear the most contextual similarities with China are the former communist Eastern Europe, the former Soviet Union, and East Asia (South Korea and Taiwan). As a matter of fact, much of the optimism about China's democratic future, particularly among liberal Chinese intellectuals, derives from the recent transformation in these regions. Indeed, this transformation destroyed two myths regarding the possibility of democratization. First, a market economy, a strong bourgeoisie (or middle class), and a civil society (or social pluralism) had long been considered prerequisites for the development of a competitive political system. Given its highly centralized economy and totalitarian control of society, the communist system, by definition, had none of these conditions and so seemed an unlikely seedbed for democracy. The second myth lies in the alleged difficulty with which democracy grows out of an Asian context characterized by traditional paternalistic authority combined with Confucian culture.[17]

Whereas democratic transitions in Eastern Europe, the Soviet Union, and East Asia justify a favorable reevaluation of China's democratic prospects, a question remains: Despite the similarities in a few important aspects, are they really comparable? That is, from what has happened in those areas can we infer that the same thing will happen in the same way in China? Probably not. A careful comparative analysis suggests that there is no optimal combination of similarities and differences either between China and Confucian East Asia or between China and communist Eastern Europe.

The success of democracy in East Asia can hardly be used, as some scholars have done, to counter the argument that East Asia's political tradition and culture constitute a major obstacle to democratization.[18] Rather, it may be more appropriate to argue that democratic progress was made there because democratic forces had grown to such a magnitude as to overcome the impediments of tradition and culture. The following factors may have contributed to the growth of democracy in these regions: social pluralism (or what Robert Scalapino calls the "authoritarian-pluralist system"[19]), a market-oriented capitalist economy, high levels of economic development, urbanization, literacy and mass communication, the rapid rise of the proportion of the population who identified themselves as members of the middle class,[20] and international (mainly U.S.) pressure. By contrast, China stands in a substantially different environment. It is true that a certain, if not comparable, degree of social pluralism and civil society can be expected as China moves toward capitalism. But it is hardly guaranteed that the capitalist mode of production will become as dominant in China as in Taiwan and South Korea as long as the Chinese Communist Party remains in power. We may even imagine that China will catch up with Taiwan and South Korea someday—though with much greater difficulty—in terms of education, economic development, and mass communication. However, given China's huge population, a majority of which lives in the countryside, the middle class—which many Korean and Taiwanese scholars largely credit with their countries' shifts to democracy[21]—may never expand enough to constitute a driving force for democratization.[22] In addition, the United States was able to exert strong influence over the democratization processes in Taiwan and South Korea, to a significant extent because these countries relied so heavily upon the Americans militarily and economically. China's vast internal market and its potential for economic self-reliance make it less likely for exogenous factors of this kind to play a decisive role in China's choice of political systems.

China and communist Eastern Europe had quite similar political and economic systems. But they differed substantially in most of the independent variables that explain democratization.[23] Above all, the Eastern European countries were simply not politically independent states. As Valerie Bunce puts it, virtually every one of the East European transitions amounted to national liberation; as such, nationalism is central to the story of the collapse of communism, and nation-building and state-building are central to the story of postcommunism.[24] This is perhaps a convincing explanation for Eastern Europe's particular mode of transition—that is, mass mobilization—in contrast with the negotiated transitions in southern Europe and Latin America. To the extent it is politically relevant in China, nationalism—whether spontaneous or deliberately stirred up by the government—works against the West and hence most probably against democratic transition.[25]

The former Soviet Union may be most comparable to China. The political traditions of both countries are overwhelmingly authoritarian, with limited and twisted parliamentary experience: from the 1860s to World War I in Russia and from the republican revolution of 1911 to the military defeat of the Kuomintang regime in 1949 in mainland China, with many interruptions in between. If we compare the two countries at the beginning of reforms (that is, the USSR of 1985 and China of 1979), the relevant resemblance is even more striking. A powerful Communist Party with Marxist ideology maintained a firm hold over state institutions and society in both countries. Political terror and intimidation as an instrument of rule persisted.[26] Most important, faced with rapidly deteriorating economic performance, both countries needed to overhaul their centrally planned economic system and introduce market reforms, and in fact they did.

The two countries started to diverge at that point. In the Soviet Union, just as in China, the leadership initially agreed upon the need for economic reform, for the economic status quo was no longer tenable. But the leaders could not reach a consensus regarding the extent and direction of reform. In China this disagreement did not intensify into conflict within the central leadership circle, to a large extent thanks to Deng's unrivaled personal prestige and authority and his deeply rooted patron-client network, all of which Mikhail Gorbachev lacked.[27] To prepare for his relatively radical market-oriented reform plans, Gorbachev sponsored a freer exchange of information known as glasnost. But his conservative rivals in the Politburo exploited the fear of loss of power and privilege among a large proportion of the Soviet Party-state elite and rallied enough support to circumvent Gorbachev's reforms. Then Gorbachev turned to political reform. He needed some democratizing measures to undermine his opponents and secure his and his followers' positions, at the same time creating new power bases to execute reform policies.[28] Since the opponents of reform were entrenched in the Party apparatus, Gorbachev's strategy was to restructure and upgrade the Soviet legislative system and shift legislative control from the Party to a democratically elected legislature—a historic breakthrough toward political liberalization and democratization.[29] Because this pattern was replicated at the regional and local levels, radical democrats in the Soviet republics, including Russia, took the opportunity to seize more and more power from the center and non-Russians moved toward secession. The resulting tension culminated in an abortive coup in August 1991 and quickly led to the breakup of the Soviet Union and downfall of Gorbachev.

How relevant is the Gorbachev experience to China? Obviously, in twenty years of reform China has irreversibly embarked on a different path of transition. Nevertheless, the series of dramatic events in the former Soviet Union during 1985–1991 suggest a number of questions. The most perplexing is, Why could Deng succeed where Gorbachev failed? Or to be more specific, *Why has market reform without political democratization proceeded relatively smoothly in China if it did not in the Soviet Union?*

The Soviet experience perfectly confirms the conventional wisdom, derived from the failure of reforms in socialist systems during the 1960s and 1970s, that because of the Stalinist "fusion of politics and economics," sweeping economic and political reforms are inseparable.[30] The rationale may be summarized as this: The mechanisms of a command economy, characterized by central planning, state monopolies, and lack of competition, require an omnipresent and omniscient bureaucracy dominated by the Party. As such, if an established command economy is to be transformed into a market economy regulated by market forces, the power and size of the bureaucracy have to be considerably diminished. Party-state bureaucracies may reasonably be expected to block the implementation of reform policies to protect their power and privileges. Reformers have to marginalize the power-holders of the old system, most feasibly through democratic means, and create a new base of support for reform from outside. Gorbachev slipped in this shift of the locus of power, allegedly because he failed to create a lasting political base.[31]

To what extent does Deng's reform disconfirm this conventional wisdom? From the above discussion, one may recognize that successful economic reform without democratization in a communist system hinges on whether and to what extent reformers can compel Party cadres to implement willingly and faithfully reforms that contradict their own bureaucratic interests. Unlike Gorbachev, Deng was able to neutralize the expected opposition to his reforms from the Party-state bureaucracy and even transformed it, without a drastic reshuffle, from an obstructive into a more or less supportive force.

What was Deng's strategy, then? When we discuss the opposition to market reforms in China and the Soviet Union and contrast Deng's strategy with Gorbachev's, we should note a key difference: As the top leader and initiator of reform, Gorbachev had a power base that was much more precarious than that of Deng. First, vertically, as Russell Bova indicates, the USSR was a state that had not been able to forge a unified Soviet nation. Political energies released by Gorbachev for decentralization and liberalization were "diverted from the quest for democracy by traveling down the road of national separation instead."[32] Second, horizontally, as mentioned before, Gorbachev's position among Party elite was much weaker. He had never been as paramount in the Soviet Union as Deng was in China. His reforms faced the challenges posed by a powerful alliance that included the number-two Politburo member, Egor Ligachev, and a broad segment of regional and local Party leadership. In contrast, Deng's task was relatively easy. In a short period after economic reform started in 1978, Deng defeated Mao's successor, Hua Guofeng, in a power struggle and established his dominance in the Party-state hierarchy. Because of the historical cooperation and personal contact between Deng and his old comrades, the need to create a relaxed and amicable atmosphere in the Politburo following Mao's brutal purges, as well as their common suffering under Mao's extreme socialism, the whole Party leadership projected an image of unity behind Deng's reform efforts. Deng's main concern was how to cope with the expected opposition from local cadres, whose potential power was limited in that they, unlike their Soviet counterparts, could not find explicit or organizational support from the Party center. Even so, a strategy to co-opt local cadres and neutralize their opposition was critical to the success of reform, because it was local cadres who were responsible for implementing the reform policies across the country.

Economists and political scientists have tried various angles to explain Deng's success in winning cooperation from local cadres.[33] Their perspectives offer insights into the nature of China's economic reform and correctly caution against overestimating the extent of China's departure from the planning system. But they may be inappropriate in three respects. First, they tend to interpret the "decentralization"—which was indeed a major component of economic reform—as defining just the relationships between the central and local governments. In fact, this notion was also applied to the status of industrial enterprises and, to a lesser extent, to Chinese society at large vis-à-vis Party government. Second, because they do not analyze the balance between the "benefits" allegedly gained from the decentralization process and the losses suffered by local bureaucracy, they may have overestimated its willingness to be "bought off" and underestimated its resentment against even mild measures for marketization.[34] Third, they explain the outcomes of economic reform mainly through patterns of interaction inside the political elite in which the masses had no role.[35] Although I agree that China's market reform was structurally limited, I would argue that even this moderate reform met with widespread resistance from local bureaucracy from its very outset. That is to say, China was no exception to the logic of the Leninist system as fusing politics and economics. Deng could proceed with market reform largely for two reasons. On the one hand, as many scholars have pointed out, the damage done by the market reform to deeply entrenched local cadre interests was deliberately minimized to assure these cadres that the costs of opposing reform exceeded the costs of supporting it. On the other hand, Deng did use political reform—which went beyond a renunciation of Maoism and the justification of the market to reach the core of China's political institutions—to prevent and thwart local cadre obstruction of market reform.

The significance of Deng's political reform, it seems, has not received due scholarly attention, presumably because it was not the kind of political liberalization or pluralization, let alone democratization. Deng's political reform never made the communist one-party system an issue, as did Gorbachev's. But Deng's reform, probably against his own intentions and expectations, has prepared China for a smoother democratic transition not only because it developed an institutional and procedural basis for democracy but also, and more important, because it brought a certain degree of institutionalized citizen participation and representation into China's governmental process, particularly at local administrative and grassroots levels.

Dividing and Controlling the Party-State Bureaucracy

Neither Gorbachev nor Deng intended for his reform to introduce a capitalist system and Western-style democracy.[36] When they came to dominate the political agenda, they recognized the need to revitalize the economy and, less urgently, make the rules of the political game more humane—in the case of China in order to regain legitimacy badly damaged by the havoc of the Cultural Revolution. To humanize politics did not require structural changes, but to improve the economy did. Presumably amazed by the success of Western market economies and impressed by the positive results of his constrained experiments with capitalism in the early 1960s, Deng attempted to usher in some market mechanisms as complements to the command economy.[37] Hence China's reform started with a modest goal, structurally limited and basically economic. It was not based on any elaborate theories or official blueprints, nor did it follow any specific examples. Once started, however, the reform took on a life of its own and caused a chain reaction in China's intertwined economic and political systems.

China's political reform may be divided into two stages, 1978 to 1986 and 1986 to 1998, each with different origins and goals, and three levels: at the center, within regions, and at the grassroots. The first stage took off almost simultaneously with economic reform. At the government level, it was marked by the restoration, with some changes, of the election of people's deputies and the revival of the people's congress in 1979; direct elections of chiefs in industrial enterprises and some workplaces took place the same year. Only in industrial enterprises were economic and political reforms integrated from the very beginning, simply because management could not be revamped to improve economic efficiency unless power was restructured. But this both-or-neither situation did not initially emerge at government levels, where political and economic reforms were entirely separate and served different purposes.

The first-stage political reform was propelled by a combination of pragmatic considerations that differed from those of the second stage. In the first place, in his struggle with Mao's handpicked successor, Hua Guofeng, Deng exploited the mass protests against Maoist atrocities and social pressure for changes. But he had to pay a price for his assumption of supreme power: He had to abide by his promises for both economic and political reform, on which the legitimacy of his leadership lay. In the second place, Mao's death threatened to leave Chinese society in upheaval, and hence Deng's primary task was to restore social order and stability. But to reach this goal he could no longer exclusively resort to Maoist forms of political terrorism. And as the Cultural Revolution showed, the stability under Mao had been merely superficial because of what Marc Blecher refers to as the "contradictions involved in the Maoist state's emphases on both direct popular participation and strong statism"—not to mention Mao's charisma and personal prestige, which Deng and his colleagues lacked. [38] All these factors made it necessary for Deng to rebuild the Party-state bureaucracy and place social order under institutional control.[39]

Deng could not, however, simply restore the Party-state institutions of the 1950s, which had depended on a combination of successful indoctrination, political terror exercised largely by the "mass dictatorship,"[40] some degree of "legitimacy" deriving from the 1949 revolution, and Maoist mobilizational politics to maintain control and achieve policy goals. The mass disillusionment with Maoism and the communist ideology removed an important part of the foundation of the regime's "legitimacy." It made both citizen participation in and mass mobilization for political campaigns very difficult and also brought the "mass dictatorship" to an end. [41] In addition, Mao's stripping legitimacy from established political institutions during the Cultural Revolution shook the traditional Chinese awe of political authority. Therefore, Deng was confronted with not only the task of rebuilding political institutions but also reestablishing the authority of government institutions among the citizens, who had become more intractable and disobedient. Deng thus had to seek new sources of legitimacy for these institutions. In the third place, since Deng had to continue to justify Party domination by means of Marxism, he had to show equal respect for the Marxist "democratic principles" regarding citizen participation in government. These factors combined to contribute to a political reform drive to effect, to use Tang Tsou's words, a change from a politics of the masses to a politics of citizens.[42]

But during the early 1980s priority was given to the continuation of Party domination under changing circumstances, with little democratic intention. Despite the new institutionalized channels for the people's participation, such as elections, then, there were few real structural differences with regard to Party hegemony. During this period economic reform was limited mostly to the privatization of agriculture, large-scale opening to foreign investment, and some tentative measures to increase the autonomy of enterprises and encourage urban private economy. The reform had yet to have a recognizable impact upon the traditional structure of political power.

Political reform was forced to become more substantive when radical market reform began to unfold in urban areas in 1984 and rapidly approached its political structural bottleneck. Since market forces assumed increasing importance in the operation of the economy, the Party-state bureaucracy at all administrative levels was essentially deprived of much of its traditional authority over economy and society.[43] Even though they managed to keep their jobs, a large proportion of these bureaucrats lost much of their power and were left with little to do. This threat to deeply entrenched bureaucratic interests provoked desperate resistance of the sort that caused the failure of economic reforms in other socialist systems. It also placed the central leadership in a fundamental dilemma. Although Deng did attempt to replace old bureaucrats with new, reform-minded ones, he could do so only slowly, on a limited scale. Moreover, this approach could not be a panacea because reform infringed upon the well-being not just of individual cadres but of the institutional prerogative of the Party-state apparatus. In addition, Deng's initial efforts to reduce the size of the bureaucracy failed miserably partly because many of the old bureaucrats could not find suitable jobs for lack of professional training in fields other than economic planning and political control.

It was in such a predicament (around 1986) that Deng turned back to political reform, which thus far had remained more symbolic than substantial, and sponsored a significant restructuring of administrative powers. In this second stage, Deng did not, as did Gorbachev, adopt the strategy of political liberalization and pluralization that was inherently threatening to communist hegemony. Instead, Deng attempted to divide and control the Party-state bureaucracy by introducing some mechanisms of checks and balances in which ordinary citizens were allowed to play a role. Deng took two concrete measures. One was to separate the Party committee from the government (executive administration) and define their respective distinct functions; another was to establish the authority of the people's congress, in which citizen representation was supposed to increase through reform of the electoral system. To understand such an institutional rearrangement—its subjective intentions and aims, its possible impact upon the policy process, and its democratic implications—one needs to identify three major players and analyze their distinct interests in reform.

Party Cadres

Party cadres at subnational levels (province, municipality, county, township, and grassroots) usually constitute the mainstay of the bureaucracy in a communist system, and the communist party relies on them as tools to govern. [44] In China, Party cadres used to wield unrestrained power over the masses and enjoy numerous privileges. Many of them may have recognized the necessity of economic reform because it was expected to appease restless citizens and was therefore ultimately favorable to the consolidation of the regime in which they had great personal stake. But when it came to the concrete reform measures that directly jeopardized their power and privileges, broader issues such as system legitimacy and social stability were simply too remote to induce Party cadres to accept personal sacrifices.[45] It is logical to assume that any effort to alter the status quo must victimize the political forces and social groups who profit most from it. The whole Party, which held a monopoly on power, thus would stand to be the biggest loser in political reform; to initiate reform must have been a painful decision for Deng.

Although policymaking was a top-down process in China, reform was to be implemented in a bottom-up way. As central leaders stood at the top of the power pyramid and maintained almost complete control over the reform process, they made sure the hardships did not reach the highest level. Party cadres instead became the most immediate and miserable victims of reform. The leadership in Beijing needed their sacrifices to exchange for public support and its own legitimacy. Thus, the Party cadre opposition was targeted not just at reform but also at the Party center.[46] The alienation of local cadres from the leadership caused by reform would have to erode the organizational coherence of the Party and has actually tended to dissolve it, more vertically than horizontally, as a monolithic dominant political force.

The Subordinate Population

In all relevant aspects, ordinary citizens were the largest beneficiaries of economic reform. They embraced it with high hopes during most of the reform years simply because they believed nothing could make their material plight even worse. At the turn of the 1970s, Chinese peasants were the first to profit from the collapse of public economy and the traditional Party control system in the countryside. The entire Chinese society enjoyed a degree of freedom for socioeconomic and intellectual activities never seen after 1957. Until economic reform reached the level at which many citizens were upset by job insecurity and inflation, the mass public constituted the main base of support for reform.[47] They shared interests with the central elite in ensuring reform success (measured by a higher standard of living) and were ready to give any credit for that success to party leadership.

Although the leadership's serious efforts at economic restructuring complicated popular attitudes toward the Party, making it an increasingly abstract notion, the reform process exposed what amounted to a zero-sum power relationship between Party cadres and the masses. The subordinate population benefited equally, if not more, from the political consequences of economic reform. The decay of Party cadre domination in local and grassroots politics might create a power vacuum but also meant the rise of a more autonomous society. These tangible benefits of reform for citizens made likely an alignment with the central elite to smash bureaucratic opposition to reform. This alignment was, of course, not without a price for citizens. One may interpret the seeming lack of political opposition arising from representative activities during reform years in any number of ways. But evidence suggests a tacit social contract in which citizens did not make political trouble for the regime in exchange for the leadership's continuous commitment to economic reform as well as to a heightened citizen participation and representation in the governmental process.

The Central Leadership

With Party cadres and citizens standing at the two ends of the political spectrum, the central leadership developed its own bureaucratic interests distinct from those of either cadres or citizens—though one must be careful not to consider the leadership monolithic in terms of its orientation toward reform.[48] Throughout their careers, Deng and other influential Party elders had never accepted the basic principles of Western democracy. Their ultimate goal and primary concern was nothing less than to maintain the communist rule.[49] But over time the communist leaders had to satisfy two conditions, as they seemingly did in the 1950s—a period they cherished as the good old days. One was the faithful adherence of Party cadres at all levels to the regime, as they would be entrusted to carry out Party policies, control the society on the Party's behalf, and crack down on dissidents and other anti-Party elements. To retain Party cadres' political devotion and make them effective ruling instruments, the leadership conferred on them various privileges and powers. Another condition that was equally important if governance was to be sustainable in the long run was to consolidate the social base of support for the regime without the inefficient resort to overt terror or coercion. To meet this condition, the leadership had to be responsive to some of the expectations of the citizens—insofar as they did not cause damage to Party hegemony.

In the post-Mao era, however, the trade-offs between the two conditions—that is, their mutual exclusion—became increasingly apparent to Party leaders. Economic reform could be seen primarily as a means to regain public support by improving the standard of living, considering that the Chinese economy was on the brink of bankruptcy and popular resentment was reaching a dangerous point. But this reform could not yield the desired effects unless Party leaders divested cadres of considerable power. Furthermore, the central decisionmakers found themselves in an embarrassing situation in which, with no alternative institutional forces, they had to depend upon antireform cadres to implement reform. Deng attempted to circumvent Party cadres by making use of the conflict in fundamental interests between cadres and citizens. More specifically, Deng took advantage of the mass enthusiasm for reform to exert pressure upon Party cadres. This strategy was surprisingly similar to that adopted by Mao in the Cultural Revolution. Mao used the masses' fanatical worship of him to mobilize them against his rivals within the Party and their local followers whom he could not remove through normal procedures. But Deng differed from Mao in some major ways. Since Deng gave top priority to the maintenance of the normative order of Party rule, he did not intend to remove immediately (even if it was technically possible) most of Party cadres from their offices. Instead, he allowed ordinary citizens to participate in the reform process through institutionalized channels and supervise the implementation of the reform policies formulated by the Party center. In order to make this supervision effective against powerful cadres, citizens had to be granted a degree of genuine authority.

The second stage of political reform resulted in a new institutional arrangement with some democratic elements (Figure 1.1). In this political power game, Deng divided the traditional, monolithically structured Party-state bureaucracy into three parts. He extracted administrative power from the local Party apparatus and transferred it to the government, which was to be structured as an executive organ with some autonomy. The major function left for the Party apparatus was to maintain the so-called political and ideological leadership and guarantee that local policymaking adhered to the general guidelines set by the Party center. At the same time, he shifted some local decisionmaking power to a reconstructed people's congress. In the resulting configuration, the Party committee and the people's congress coexisted as decisionmaking organs and exercised double oversight over the government's performance. Meanwhile, Deng skillfully played two cards against each other. According to the central spirit as embodied in various Party and legal documents, the people's congress must accept the "political leadership" of the Party committee, which is defined as the "leading force," and the Party committee must respect the status of the people's congress as the "highest organ of state power." This new, seemingly paradoxical institutional arrangement was deliberately set up to create a situation in which the Party committee and the people's congress contended for power, with the higher level of authorities as arbitrator and the Party center dominated by Deng as supreme judge. Whoever was going to get the upper hand had to demonstrate that he was more faithful to Dengism and the central line than were his rivals. In order to avoid direct collision between the Party committee and the people's congress and defend the Party's hegemonic appearance, the government essentially functioned as a buffer zone.[50]

If mechanisms of checks and balances were established only within the Party-state bureaucracy, China would not have made much progress toward

Figure 1.1   China's Restructuring of Institutional Powers Since 1987

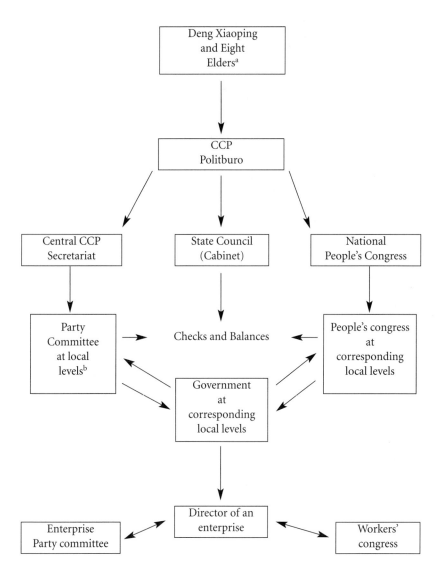

a. Deng Xiaoping died in 1997 at the age of ninety-three; the Eight Elders were (in order of personal power and influence) Chen Yun (d. 1995; 90); Li Xiannian (d. 1992; 83); Peng Zhen (d. 1997, 95); Yang Shangkun (d. 1998, 90); Wang Zhen (d. 1993; 85); Bo Yibo (89); Deng Yingchao (d. 1992; 88); Song Renqiong (88).

b. These checks and balances occur at the levels of province, city, county (urban district), and township.

democracy. In the triangular power relations between the Party committee, the government, and the people's congress, however, the latter developed a capacity as a representative institution that went beyond what was typical for just another Party-state organ. Certainly, the elections of people's deputies were far from democratic in any period of the reform era. The system of indirect elections above the county level ensured Party cadres some levers to remove from the list of final candidates anyone who was politically dubious and untrustworthy. In other words, one could hardly expect political opposition—let alone organized opposition—to elbow its way into the congress. But because of the need to bring real people's voices into the congress and have the legislature serve its function, central authorities denied Party cadres an explicitly dominant role in elections of congressional deputies and government officials by allowing limited competition among candidates with censored but not necessarily the same reform programs and welfare promises, as well as by strengthening the legislative procedures in which the majority of deputies had a final say. Thus, when the people's congress imposed structural constraints upon the Party apparatus, it assumed a potentially political nature that transcended that of a confrontation between two Party organs or two groups of Party cadres. China's legislative representativeness and its institutional capacity to articulate and defend the interests of constituencies seem to have considerably exceeded those of a typical communist legislature.[51] It contributed to the decline of the Party cadre hegemony in almost all aspects of China's social, economic, and political life.

In the entire reform process, Deng never hinted that he was interested in a Western-type democracy. Instead, he just attempted to repair some structurally "weak" aspects of the one-party system in order to perpetuate it. Or as some scholars suggest, reform was designed as "a substitute for liberalization, not a sign of it."[52] Yet the bolstered status and enlarged powers of the people's congress as the major institutionalized channel for citizen participation and representation had nothing to do with democratization in any real sense. It was merely part of Deng's strategy by which "people power" should be expanded just enough to deter Party cadres' moral and political (measured by loyalty to the central line) misconduct, but it must be so carefully restrained that it could never ascend to a position to challenge the "party leadership," which was defined first and foremost as the supreme authority of the Party center.

It is against this background that we may better understand the nature of China's political reform. In what was basically a contention for power and a conflict of bureaucratic interests between local Party committees and people's congresses—the latter partially representing the people—the leaders in Beijing played with the tactics of alignment, dealignment, and realignment. When a reform was frustrated by Party cadres, when their political corruption rose to an intolerable level, or when gestures of democratization were necessary under pressure from below or outside, the central leadership tended to align with citizens through the legislature and stressed "democratic participation" against the "overconcentration of power" in Party apparatus. They would accordingly tip the balance of power between the Party committee and the people's congress toward the latter's side. But when regime legitimacy increased as "diffuse support" accumulated (mainly arising from the success of economic reform and improvement of popular livelihood),[53] when Party cadres' grievances and alienation increased, when the pressure for democratization was relaxed and hence the need for democratic symbolism was reduced, and particularly when perceived social chaos and political opposition (such as Tiananmen) loomed large, central leaders would switch their alliance to Party cadres and emphasize the party leadership principle against what they called the "bourgeois liberalization." Nevertheless, although this political game in the guise of democratic reform had been sponsored and to a large extent manipulated by Deng, he could hardly play it over time without paying a price.

In recent years, along with the further decay of Party influence in the workplace as the culture of the market economy has gradually permeated Chinese society, the Party has had increasing difficulty in keeping the legislature under its control. Except for a few isolated cases, political opposition was nowhere to be found in congresses throughout the reform years. The preferences and demands of Chinese constituents—insofar as they were strong enough to be publicly voiced at a risk—were not immediately threatening to the regime. Macropolitics, such as the multiparty system and claims for political freedoms, appeared more or less irrelevant to many policy issues, especially those concerning citizens' welfare and other private matters. Largely as a consequence, legislative and deputy activities remained highly depoliticized. But behind this apparent depoliticization hides an enormous potential political crisis for the communist regime. As the legislature continues to sharpen its teeth in the policymaking process, and as the legislative authority is widely recognized and accepted in Chinese society, the people's congress is becoming a likelier hotbed for political opposition. This tendency will greatly narrow the policy options for the Party center when it faces politically dissenting opinions arising from the legislature. For all its limitations, then, Deng's political reform since the 1970s has paved a smoother road for incremental and constitutional evolution toward a Western-type democracy than have the Eastern bloc countries. Of course democratic opposition in China has yet to establish a solid social base upon which to take root, grow, and triumph.

Methodology and Organization of This Book

This book is based on field research I did in China in June 1989–January 1990, May–July 1996, and November–December 1997[54] and a critical reading of a variety of Chinese sources and policy documents; it also draws extensively on the research of Western China specialists.

Much of my fieldwork was in the cities of Wuxi and Xishan and their adjacent counties and townships in Jiangsu Province, where I interviewed a large number of scholars, government officials, congress deputies, enterprise managers, Party cadres, and ordinary citizens. I also conducted a number of interviews in the United States and Singapore. My questions focused on the interviewees' personal experiences in political reforms as well as their attitudes and viewpoints. I also gained access to some meeting minutes and proceedings. For understandable reasons, the information gathered through the fieldwork was not entirely reliable and needs careful scrutiny, but the interviews did provide me with much firsthand information not otherwise available. To guarantee anonymity and confidentiality, I have not named my sources but simply labeled the information acquired from interviews as "author's interviews," or "(au. int.)." Where it is meaningful, I note the year of the interview.

I collected a large amount of material from Chinese scholarly works, reports, and news stories but used only a small proportion. These Chinese references can be divided into two kinds: journals and newspapers published in China and Chinese publications based in Hong Kong and Taiwan. Interpreting both officially censored and highly commercialized publications such as these poses a challenge to a China specialist. My judgment regarding their reliability and accuracy is partly based on my personal experience as a research fellow at the Chinese Academy of Social Sciences (1983–1986). I also attempted, where possible, to use the results of my fieldwork to verify the authenticity of some reports. In any case, I have tried to adopt the standards most commonly applied in U.S. scholarship on Chinese studies and to use material from these publications on a conditional and selective basis. I hope the reader will understand the methodological limitations inherent in empirical research on China, a country whose political system in many ways remains obscured.

Western scholars differ in applying functionalism or structuralism or something else to the study of the role of the legislature in communist states.[55] Some stress that the legislature may be very "functional" to the rule of a single dominant party.[56] Others argue that no communist legislature can be approached from a purely structural-functional standpoint since "'system maintenance' . . . is not at issue regardless of the activity of a legislature."[57] In the Chinese case, Kevin O'Brien suggests an "integrated historical-structural approach" that "investigates all functions associated with legislatures and all structures associated with legislative activities."[58] For all the apparent strengths of these approaches, they fail to note that the discussion of the "functions" of a legislature in communist states makes little sense unless one uses these functions to measure the status of a legislature in the hierarchical power structure and its changes over time. As William Welsh puts it, we can tell what these (representative) institutions are doing, "but we cannot really tell how much difference they make."[59]

Although I start with a functionalist analysis, I go far beyond that to adopt an approach I would call political organism.[60] Although I do discuss the evolution of some functions of each of the three major institutions, I focus on the organic changes of the institutional power relationships and their democratic implications. I present a macrodiscussion of the shifting coalitions and alignments among the central leadership, the local and grassroots Party cadres, and the subordinate population on the one hand and a microanalysis of the structure of power involving the Party committee, government, and people's congress at the central, subnational, and grassroots levels on the other. To gauge the democratic significance of China's political reform, I concentrate on the extent to which the people's congress represents ordinary citizens and whether and how it makes a real difference vis-à-vis the Party committee in the governmental process.[61] I use the three models of the legislature Michael Mezey formulated as an analytic tool and, where relevant, place China's people's congress in a comparative framework.[62]

This book is divided into eight chapters. Following this introduction, Chapter 2 presents an analysis of the changes in power structure of China's industrial enterprises brought about by a combination of economic and political reform. I discuss the origins, accomplishments, limitations, and consequences of the efforts at democratizing enterprise management and examine the alliances and opposition among the central leadership, enterprise cadres, and ordinary workers as well as the three-cornered power struggle among the workers' congress, the enterprise Party committee, and the director.

Chapter 3 is devoted to an analysis of direct and indirect elections of deputies to people's congresses at various governmental levels. By presenting a negative correlation between the extent of openness and the level of the election, I show how the leaders in Beijing discouraged local cadres from rigging direct elections so as to guarantee a degree of citizen representation in the legislature, and I examine why they refused to extend the principle of direct election to levels higher than the county and urban district. Chapter 4 deals with the reforms regarding the elections and appointments of government officials. It further highlights the ambivalence Party leaders displayed toward the election of congress deputies. They demanded that government officials be competent and faithful in the implementation of reform. For this purpose, they had to prevent Party cadres from rigging elections in order to offer profitable government posts to their protégés. But the central elite did not trust people's deputies either. So they tried to maintain a balance between cadre control and deputy initiative. But this strategy did not always work well, as both the cadres and deputies attempted to overextend their prescribed functions.

Chapters 2, 3, and 4 cover the whole process of political reform; Chapter 5, in contrast, probes into Deng's motivation for the second-stage political reform. Through an analysis of a large number of Party-state documents and leadership speeches, I try to explain how this phase was driven by the political structural bottleneck of economic reform as well as tension within the Party. I scrutinize Deng's strategy, which aimed to create checks and balances that would lead to the execution of reform programs. I emphasize those elements that shaped the thinking on the separation of the Party from government. Chapter 6 describes how this new institutional arrangement started from the central level, at which the unique structure of authority and sources of power made the reform less successful or meaningful. I examine the conflicts between the central Party Secretariat and the State Council over government affairs and the expanded authority of the National People's Congress (NPC) and its Standing Committee, as well as the NPC's potential antagonism with the Party center (the Politburo and Secretariat) over control of the State Council.

Chapter 7 provides a microanalysis of the changes in the relations of authority in the local governmental process. I look at the main measures taken in local political reform and assess their political meanings and structural consequences. The separation of the Party from government at local levels was carried out more forcibly and effectively than at the central level. It broke up the traditional power monopoly of Party committees by depriving them of executive power and reducing their influence over local legislation and policymaking. At the same time, the local congresses carved out an increasingly important institutional role in both legislation and supervision of the government. In many locations they rose as one of the three major powerful actors—along with Party committees and governments—in the policymaking process, contributing substantially to the decline of the Party cadre hegemony in local politics. But as a top-down process sponsored by the Party center, local power restructuring has been placed under considerable central manipulation and has proceeded largely according to the central blueprint. More than in the political reform at the central or grassroots levels, the Party center had to make deliberate efforts to strike a balance of power between local Party committees and people's congresses to prevent either side from slipping out of control.

In Chapter 8 I summarize the effects of increasing institutionalized citizen participation and representation and the overall decay of Party influence in the policy process. Concluding that the Chinese reform has not yet disentangled politics from economics, I attempt to analyze the fundamental limits and inherent flaws of the reform strategy. I argue that substantial power resources left in the hands of Party cadres make political corruption the Achilles' heel of China's one-party system, denying the possibility of any partial solution. It may easily turn into a highly explosive political issue and generate social pressure for political change. Finally, I suggest some approaches to further research on China's democratic prospects.

Notes

1. For instance, the democratization of many Catholic nations and Confucian East Asia (South Korea and Taiwan) has, if not buried, greatly weakened the cultural determinism of democracy. See Wiegel, "Catholicism"; Moody, *Political Opposition*; Friedman, *Politics*; Mernissi, *Islam and Democracy*. The research on the democratic transition of Latin America and southern Europe led to the discovery of a new, so-called pact-based mode of democratization. The relevant theory downplays the socioeconomic preconditions of democratic transition and the role of mass mobilization and instead stresses the significance of the personal calculation of autocrats and their strategic interaction—that is, bargaining and cooperation—with opposition leaders. This theory is built mainly on the following works, among others: O'Donnell and Schmitter, *Transitions from Authoritarian Rule*; Di Palma, *To Craft Democracies*. It has developed into two "embryonic subdisciplines": transitology and consolidology. See Schmitter with Karl, "The Conceptual Travels."

2. In 1984 Huntington predicted: "The likelihood of democratic development in Eastern Europe is virtually nil." See Huntington, "Will More Countries Become Democratic?" In a study of comparative democratization published in 1989, the authors made a "basic" decision not to include any communist countries on the grounds that there was "little prospect among them of a transition to democracy." See Diamond, Linz, and Lipset, *Democracy in Developing Countries: Asia,* preface. This sort of dim view among political comparativists was evidently influenced by the scholars in the field of communist studies. Even Skilling, who with his "group theory" found in the Soviet system something similar to the Western pluralist pattern of diffusion of power, saw little hope "for an early advance to a more pluralistic society in the Soviet Union or elsewhere in Eastern Europe." Skilling, "Interest Groups."

3. Friedrich, *Totalitarianism*; Friedrich and Brzezinski, *Totalitarian Dictatorship*; Linz, "Totalitarian and Authoritarian Regimes."

4. That communist studies failed to benefit from developments in social science concepts, theory, and methodology was observed and pointed out many years ago. See Fleron, *Communist Studies*. After the mid-1960s, the totalitarian model was increasingly challenged or revised. But neither Rigby's conception of the Soviet Union as an "organizational society" nor Skilling and Griffiths's "group theory" nor Hough's "institutional pluralism" successfully shook the dominance of that model. For all these "revisionist" arguments, see Rigby, "Traditional"; Skilling and Griffiths, *Interest Groups*; Hough, "The Soviet System."

5. I borrow this term and its definition from Nodia, though I disagree with his application of it. See Nodia, "How Different?"

6. Karl and Schmitter, "From an Iron Curtain."

7. Jowitt, "The Leninist Extinction."

8. Rowen claims that China will become a democracy around the year 2015. This claim is based on the alleged expansion of grassroots democracy, the move toward a "rule of law," and the "media self-liberalization." Even if the empirical evidence provided is reliable, it is still unclear in what specific way the current trends would lead to institutional democratization. See Rowen, "The Short March."

9. Diamond, "Is the Third Wave Over?" This view is also shared by many China specialists. See Baum, "China After Deng."

10. Przeworski and Teune, *The Logic,* p. 19.

11. Townsend and Womack, *Politics,* pp. 22–26.

12. Weber, *Economy and Society,* section on the "sociology of law."

13. It resulted to a large extent from the emergence of a rough balance between the crown and the nobility, in which, according to Moore, "the royal power predominated but left a substantial degree of independence to the nobility." Moore, *Social Origins,* ch. 7.

14. For historical comparisons, I have dropped the American case here. If the differences between China and Western Europe far outweigh their similarities and considerably reduce the value of a comparative study, then American democracy is even more incomparable. This is largely due to what Alexis de Tocqueville referred to in his *Democracy in America* (1835) as "the great advantage of the Americans": They are born equal instead of becoming so. This observation deserves our attention because many people tend to explore the issue of China's democratization based on the American democratic experience.

15. But the pattern of democracy imposed from the outside is still applicable today to a small country, as manifested by the U.S. role in some regime changes in Central America. See Di Palma, *To Craft Democracies,* p. 188.

16. Karl, "Dilemmas of Democratization." As Bova suggests, in order to assure members of the old elite that their vital interests will not be threatened, democratization requires some initial institutional compromises, often taking the form of explicitly negotiated pacts that contain one or more of such obviously undemocratic components as restrictions on participation, a limited policy agenda, or limited contestation. This pattern of democratization is of wide applicability. See Bova, "Political Dynamics."

17. The negative correlations between democracy and Asia's traditional power structures and political cultures are examined by Pye in his *Asian Power.*

18. Friedman offers a strong counterargument in favor of the possible role of the Chinese traditional value system. According to Friedman, the mainstream Mencian tradition of Confucianism is premised on popular support as the basis of legitimate rulership, and China's religious heritage tends to be pantheistic, pluralistic, and inclusive, which is "in contrast to the monistic West that has a history of far more intolerance." See his chapter "Democratization: Generalizing the East Asian Experiences," in Friedman, *Politics.* Although he nicely indicates that all cultures are rich in conflicting political potentialities, he may have overemphasized the significance of a few isolated prodemocratic phrases in classic Confucian works. His view is, to a lesser extent, also shared by Moody. When explaining why democracy developed in Europe and America but not in East Asia, Moody argued that the problem is not social values in isolation but rather values as they interact with a particular social pattern or structures in particular historical situations. See Moody, *Political Opposition,* ch. 1.

19. Scalapino, *Politics,* pp. 71–131.

20. Of course, the attitude of the contemporary middle class toward democratization is not always positive or the same as its role in European history, described by Lindblom in his *Politics and Markets,* pp. 161–169. It is contingent upon various situational factors such as class structure, socioeconomic equality, and the likelihood of extremist politics. In addition, the middle class itself needs to be disaggregated in the analysis of its political role. A more complete discussion on this subject is found in Rueschemeyer, Stephens, and Stephens, *Capitalist Development.* In Spain, Brazil, and some other countries, the business community was actually not unified in democratic transitions. See O'Donnell and Schmitter, *Transitions from Authoritarian Rule,* p. 20.

21. Kim, "Marx, Schumpeter."

22. South Korea was about 75 percent rural and 25 percent urban in 1961. By the late 1980s, the figures had been reversed. More than 75 percent of the population identified themselves as the members of the middle class; the World Bank calculated that percentage as 55. Steinberg, "The Republic of Korea." The same trend was also found in Taiwan, though the reported percentage of the middle class was a little lower than in South Korea. Tien, "Transformation."

23. For a long list of these variables, see Huntington, *The Third Wave*, pp. 37–38.

24. Bunce, "Comparing East and South."

25. In his comments on an earlier version of this chapter, Barrett L. McCormick cautioned me to avoid overdrawing the contrast between democratization as national liberation in Eastern Europe and something else in China. I found his argument quite persuasive that in terms of the "invention" of civil society and culture, China and Eastern Europe were not starkly different. I do not fully agree with him, though, on the role of nationalism in China's democratic development. See McCormick and Kelly, "The Limits."

26. This characterization of the Soviet case is not without controversy. Some scholars identified signs of a liberal democratic development and even a certain degree of Western-style participation in the Soviet Union after the 1960s. See Hough and Fainsod, *How the Soviet Union Is Governed*; Lewin, *The Gorbachev Phenomenon*. If these observations were accurate, they might help explain the quick collapse of communist power in the Soviet Union, which would perhaps be much less likely in China even if Deng adopted Gorbachev's strategy.

27. At the end of the 1970s when economic reform was initiated, most of the key Party-state positions at the highest level were gradually seized by either Deng's protégés or the veteran leaders who were purged in the Cultural Revolution and owed their rehabilitation to Deng. By contrast, when Gorbachev entered the Politburo in 1980, he was twenty-four years younger than the average of the other members. He was elected general secretary by a narrow margin in 1985 and faced challenges from powerful Brezhnevite hard-liners.

28. See Roeder, *Red Sunset*, ch. 9.

29. For a more detailed discussion of the Soviet legislative restructuring in the Gorbachev era, see S. Goldman, "The New Soviet Legislative Branch."

30. Bialer, *Stalin's Successors*, ch. 1; Nolan, *State and Market,* p. 218.

31. Young, "The Strategy of Political Liberalization." According to Young, in the critical period of the transfer of institutional powers, Gorbachev sought to maintain a balance between the Right and the Left. But an abortive coup made his centrist position no longer possible.

32. Bova, "Political Dynamics."

33. Shirk argues that given the relationship of "reciprocal accountability" among Party elite, China's economic reform was arranged to allow regional and local bureaucrats to benefit from it through preferential policies. In addition, reform decisions were made by consensus to ensure that the losers did not lose too much. See Shirk, *The Political Logic*. The explanation offered by Goldstein revolves around the alleged pre-reform differences between China and other socialist systems in terms of central-local institutional relationships. He suggests that during the Maoist years the control and management of enterprises was transferred to the localities. The empowered local regimes were adept at turning economic reform to their advantage to promote local growth. See Goldstein, "China in Transition." Some economists stress the Chinese success in creating a newly emerging private sector outside and in parallel with the state planning system. Even though this private sector brought about dynamic market

forces that had an increasing impact upon the state sector, the basic structure of the command economy remained unchanged. See Brus, "Marketisation and Democratisation"; McMillan and Naughton, "How to Reform a Planned Economy." In Solinger's view, China's economic reform had little effect in redistributing power because it was not intended to transform Chinese economy in a real market direction; see Solinger, *China's Transition.*

34. Otherwise it would be hard to understand why in 1986 political reform was reactivated by reformist leaders who were persuaded by liberal intellectuals and local reformers that economic reform was reaching its political structural limit and could not be deepened without further political reform.

35. Shirk makes the point straightforwardly: "Under communism, ordinary citizens are excluded from the political game . . . because the rules of communist political competition prohibit party politicians from mobilizing social support. The political playing field is restricted to the party and government officialdom." See Shirk, *The Political Logic,* p. 82. Although this observation seems to be true in former communist states in Eastern Europe and the Soviet Union, it does not apply exactly to Chinese communist politics. Its inadequacy may be seen from the role of Red Guards and mass mobilization for power struggle within the Party in the Cultural Revolution.

36. Some Western scholars note that Gorbachev was never a democrat in the Western sense. His goal was just a kind of enlightened authoritarian rule. See Hough, *Russia and the West,* pp. 209–212.

37. The aspects of marketization in Gorbachev's economic reform before he turned to political reform were not clear. On the one hand, he proposed to decentralize enterprises; on the other, some of his initial economic measures—such as the intensification program and state certification for quality control—took on obvious features of recentralization. See Hewett and Winston, *Milestones,* part 1. Gorbachev's economic reform was milder and more limited in nature than Deng's but met with stronger resistance from the bureaucracy. His strategy of political liberalization can be better understood within this context.

38. So, as he argues, Mao's state was "not so autonomous as to be able to defend itself against society's attacks upon it." See Blecher, "The Contradictions."

39. The efforts for the revitalization of the Party-state bureaucracies started right after the initial period of the Cultural Revolution characterized by violence and social disorder. But until Mao's death, these efforts failed to produce stable political institutions because of a variety of problems different from those faced by Deng at the end of the 1970s. See Harding, *Organizing China,* chs. 9, 10.

40. The "mass dictatorship" was a major Maoist ruling mechanism. It meant terrorist political control maintained through a tight social network composed of mass organizations in residential areas and work units that were under the direct and absolute control of Party branches at the primary level.

41. A good example was the campaign against "spiritual pollution" in 1983 that was launched by conservative Party leaders in an effort to reassert the orthodoxy of Marxism-Leninism and Mao Zedong Thought. It met with widespread resistance and lasted only twenty-eight days.

42. Tang Tsou, *The Cultural Revolution,* p. xx.

43. From a theoretical perspective, the loosening of the control over the economy would inevitably give rise to a more autonomous society. As classic European examples show, the separation of economy from politics weakened the functions of the state and made it less involved in social life. The inherent logic is clearly explicated by Dahl, who argues that for a highly centralized economy to exist, "there would have to be a completely centralized social order with access to social, economic, and physical

sanctions concentrated in the hands of central authorities." See Dahl, *Polyarchy,* ch. 4. Also see Lindblom, *Politics and Markets,* part 5.

44. The concept of Party cadres in Chinese politics has changed over time. In the Maoist system, Party cadres or Party organizations *were* the Chinese bureaucracy, with the "government" and the "people's congress" nothing more than a facade. Since the early 1980s, as the government gradually acquired its distinct functions and some administrative autonomy, the term "Party cadres" has become ambiguous. For my analytic purposes, "Party cadres" should be differentiated during the reform years. In this book, I use the term to mean professional Party cadres who do not concurrently hold any posts in the government or any administrative posts in industrial enterprises. So this category does not include the government officials, congress leaders, or enterprise managers who simultaneously serve in the Party committee of the equivalent administrative level. Also, I have tried to minimize the use of the word "cadres," which in many works on Chinese politics under Mao ambiguously refers to all (Party-state) bureaucrats with fixed state salaries. See Kraus, "The Chinese State."

45. The intensity of the opposition to reform from Party cadres depended largely on the extent to which their vital interest was affected by reform. Since the cadres at a given administrative level were to be institutionally separated, their personal stakes in the reform were different. Without question, Party cadres—if seen as a political elitist stratum—suffered from reform. As some chapters in this book suggest, however, those who managed to transfer in time to top government posts lost less in terms of power and privileges and were even able to profit a bit in some respects. Not surprisingly, it was professional Party cadres who were victimized most by reform.

46. In analyzing the conflict of interests between Party leaders and cadres, we run into the problem of differentiating local cadres vertically. Party cadres at different levels of government were hurt by reform to different degrees. Regional leaders, typically those at the provincial level, were more highly located within the Party-state power hierarchy than local and grassroots cadres. Many of them maintained a long-standing client-patron relationship with and were deliberately protected by central leaders. Nathan's factionalism model indicates that such a clientelist political structure, called a faction, consists of only one or a few layers. See Nathan, *China's Crisis,* ch. 2. In the Chinese context, this structure usually covered the provincial level but could reach even to the municipal level in some areas. I found that the lower the administrative level is, the more Party cadres suffered from reform or the less their interests were cared for by the leadership in Beijing, and hence the more vehemently they tended to resent the Party center. This phenomenon could be most clearly seen from the system of election of people's deputies, which I discuss in Chapter 3. It also closely related to what Shirk calls the "reciprocal political accountability." That is, the more highly positioned cadres were, the more likely they would be the constituents of central leaders and play a role in the choice of the latter. See Shirk, *The Political Logic,* part 2.

47. The attitudes toward reform of various social strata and groups have been popularly formulated in Chinese society as "warm at both ends and cold in the middle *(liangtou ri, zhongjian leng)*, meaning that the central leadership and ordinary citizens are enthusiastic about reform but the bureaucracy is cold. We cannot, however, treat ordinary citizens as an undifferentiated aggregate when we discuss their role in the reform process. It is less debatable that the overwhelming majority of Chinese peasants won more than they lost in rural reform. In urban areas the consequences of economic reform and social responses were more mixed. Zhu Guanglei divides the attitudes of workers—which were quite similar to those of many other urban social groups, such as teachers, employees in shops, and hospitals—into four periods. In the first period (1980–1984), economic reform achieved remarkable success in the countryside but proceeded at a

slow pace in cities. Impressed by the speed with which peasants got rich, workers had great passion for and high expectations about reform. In the second period (1985–1986), the everyday life of workers came to be affected by reform both positively and negatively. Although they complained about inflation, they were by and large satisfied with the obvious improvement in their livelihoods. In the third period (1987–1989), workers' support for reform declined as a result of reform-related political corruption, higher inflation, job insecurity, and emerging socioeconomic polarization. But even so, their general attitude toward reform still remained positive, as they hoped that the reform would be brought onto the "right" track. My own interviews suggested that in this period workers developed a stronger consciousness of political reform. They believed, or were led to believe by liberal intellectuals and students, that most of the negative results of reform could not be eliminated unless the political system were transformed. In the fourth period (after 1989), workers held a more realistic view of reform, better understanding its mixed outcomes. To use Zhu's words, they became "more mature." See Zhu Guanglei, *Dafenhua Xinzuhe,* ch. 1. After the fifteenth Party congress of October 1997 passed a resolution to privatize most of China's state-owned enterprises, the sense of insecurity and frustration among workers certainly grew stronger.

48. One can identify three groups in the reform process among Party leaders. The first group, with Deng at its core, advocated radical market reform but refused any move toward political liberalization and pluralization. The second group, headed by the top conservative leader, Chen Yun, was opposed to the capitalist orientation of reform. It favored reforming the economy within the framework of the socialist planning system. The third group comprised the leaders of the younger generation, such as Hu Yaobang and Zhao Ziyang. They faithfully implemented Deng's economic reform programs but showed more sympathy and tolerance for political liberalization than did Deng. See Harding, *China's Second Revolution,* chs. 4, 5, and 7; Fewsmith, *Dilemma of Reform,* chs. 5–7; Dittmer, *China Under Reform,* ch. 3. Throughout the reform era, the first two groups somewhat alternatively prevailed in the central policy agenda that was characterized by a style of compromise or, as Lieberthal indicates, the shift between the two very different policy packages. See Lieberthal, *Governing China,* ch. 5. Generally speaking, Deng remained dominant partly because of his relatively "central" position on reform. Intentionally or not, Deng maintained a sort of balance between radical reformers and conservatives and usually managed to let his ideas determine the reform agenda. Since the divergences on reform at the Party center did not evolve into an intense struggle, there were no clear signs of a Soviet-style political alliance—that is, conservative leaders at the center aligning with local cadres against the central reform policies. I do not elaborate on the conflicts of opinions at the highest level during the Deng period; rather, I treat the Party center as a basically monolithic actor. This is not because I believe the cleavages among central leaders were insignificant but that they were not relevant enough to political reform, especially at local and grassroots levels. Because the decisionmaking of the Politburo under Deng was characterized by a process of compromise and consensus, central leaders as a rule managed to solve their differences first at Politburo meetings before speaking to both Party cadres and the people with one voice.

49. Particularly repulsive to Deng, it seemed, was the American-style separation of powers. According to the private interviews (made in 1995–1997) with former CCP general secretary Zhao Ziyang, in early 1989, before Tiananmen, when Zhao asked Deng about the bottom line of his political reform, Deng mentioned three principles: (1) Factions were allowed within the Party, (2) the ban on unofficial newspapers and public criticisms of leaders could be lifted (but the criticisms must conform to consti-

tutional regulations), and (3) Western-style separation of powers must be absolutely prohibited. See Zhang Fen, "History Will Do Justice."

50. As I show in Chapters 3, 4, and 7, avoiding direct confrontation with the Party committee was important to people's deputies since they did not want to be suspected of being anti-Party. Also, if any decision made by the Party committee were vetoed by the congress, it would not damage the Party's hegemonic appearance.

51. It seems that China's legislature has acquired a role in power relations more prominent than any of the legislatures in communist Eastern Europe and the USSR. In Western literature, communist legislatures are typically portrayed as carrying out two major largely symbolic functions: communication (contact or linkage between rulers and ruled) and mobilization (to generate public "support" and enhance system legitimacy). In predemocratized Eastern Europe and even in the USSR, the function of communication could sometimes go beyond symbolism and benefit citizens in a concrete way. Deputies communicated the needs and wishes of citizens to the government and helped remedy citizen grievances. See Loewenberg and Patterson, *Comparing Legislatures;* Nelson, *Local Politics*; Vanneman, *The Supreme Soviet*. In some countries, such as Yugoslavia and Poland, the legislatures did exhibit some law-affecting, if not lawmaking, activities. But although all these functions and activities might have led the government to be more responsive to popular concerns, they did not seem to have produced an impact upon the communist monopoly of power even at local levels. Yet some scholars have held that the legislatures in communist states were used as a means of Party control over the bureaucracy or as a means for the Party to check up on the performance of the government and its conformity to Party policy. See White, "Some Conclusions"; Welsh, "The Status of Research." To the extent that this function was genuine and operative, it bore some similarities to the Chinese case. But since the relationships among the legislature, the Party apparatus, and the bureaucracy in these countries were not precisely defined, it was not clear to what extent and how this function actually affected the reallocation of power resources.

52. See O'Brien, *Reform Without Liberalization,* p. 178.

53. I borrow this concept from Wahlke and Easton. Diffuse support "consists of a reserve of support that enables a system to weather the many storms when outputs cannot be balanced off against inputs of demands." See Easton, *A System Analysis,* p. 273. Also see Wahlke, "Policy Demands." This concept is useful here as it helps explain the phenomenon of negative correlation between the Party-sponsored economic and political reforms. In other words, in China the attempt to democratize normally suffered as economic reform achieved successes. Deng and his colleagues believed the improvement in the living standards of the masses made it less necessary or urgent to increase regime legitimacy and maintain social stability by means of political reform. It would also lighten the pressure from below for political changes.

54. The 1997 fieldwork for this study was conducted by my wife, Xu Shuhong, in Xiamen, Fujian Province.

55. A comparison of the two approaches may be found in Polsby, "Legislature."

56. White, "Some Conclusions."

57. Nelson, "Editor's Introduction."

58. O'Brien, *Reform Without Liberalization,* ch. 1.

59. Welsh, "The Status of Research."

60. The functional approach is justified to argue that the legislature is functionally adaptable and has never been limited to the function of lawmaking. See Wheare, *Legislatures;* Riggs, "Legislative Structures." The recognition of this fact is particularly important when one studies a communist legislature in transition. Although the

"functions" in a communist context can be deceptive, it would be helpful to take them as the starting point of the analysis.

61. It seems that the people's congress in China has never become a hot topic for academic research among Western China scholars. But a number of academic works on or related to this topic have been produced, including O'Brien, *Reform Without Liberalization;* O'Brien and Li, "Chinese Political Reform"; O'Brien, "Chinese People's Congresses"; O'Brien, "Agents and Remonstrators"; O'Brien and Luehrmann, "Institutionalizing Chinese Legislatures"; McCormick, *Political Reform,* chs. 3 and 4; McCormick and Kelly, "The Limits"; McCormick, "China's Leninist Parliament"; Tanner, "Organizations and Politics"; Tanner, "How a Bill Becomes a Law"; Nathan, *Chinese Democracy,* ch. 10; Shi, *Political Participation;* Benewick, "Political Institutionalisation." These works offer excellent analyses of the changing functions and roles of the people's congress in China's political life, particularly in the making of laws and the election of people's deputies. But my book differs substantially from those works in three ways. First, I focus exclusively upon the role of the people's congress in the reallocation of powers, or the conflicts, competition, and cooperation between the Party committee and the people's congress. Second, whereas most of the works concentrate largely upon the people's congress at the national level, the NPC, the emphasis of this work is on representative institutions at subnational levels. Third, the discussions concerning elections thus far deal mainly with direct elections of congressional deputies at the level of the county, urban district, and township, whereas I emphasize indirect elections of congressional deputies and government officials.

62. Mezey identifies three models of the legislature: the policymaking model, representational model, and system-maintenance model. "These models," he argued, "represent constructs in the minds of people that specify what a legislature should be and the activities with which it should be concerned." See Mezey, *Comparative Legislatures,* p. 13.

2

The First Step: The Reform of Power Relations in Industrial Enterprises

The democratic reform of management structures in industrial enterprises was an important component of China's political and economic reforms after 1978. It meant the workers' spontaneous and direct participation in elections and the administration of the enterprise. This new style of participation contrasted with the Maoist mass line and mobilizational politics in major ways. As long as they did not challenge "party leadership," ordinary workers and staff members in many enterprises could share some power in the management of their enterprises—especially on issues relating to their welfare—through institutionalized channels. In addition, the enterprise director, rather than the Party committee, became dominant in enterprise affairs, and Party cadres were dispossessed of administrative power and were marginalized in the decisionmaking process.[1]

The restructuring of power in industrial enterprises differed from that at government levels. Although economic reform theoretically involved all levels, it failed to have an immediate impact upon the Party cadres' monopoly of government power until the mid-1980s, when political structural reforms became necessary to remove obstacles to further economic reform. By contrast, largely because power, production, and individual welfare are so closely intertwined in enterprises, any reform aimed at increasing economic efficiency and profits could not be separated—even in its early stage—from a substantial overhaul of the management structure. As far as its political aspects were concerned, enterprise reform started with the modest and limited goal of partially satisfying workers' demands for democratic participation and was soon accelerated because of its perceived positive role in improving the quality of economic decisions. But workers' participation, combined with industrial reforms, caused a chain reaction and yielded unexpected political results, leading to a broader structural transformation of China's enterprises. For all its fundamental ideological limitations and apparent lack of political challenges, this systemic change (in addition to similar reform measures enforced in other kinds of urban work units) produced a massive impact upon China's political development after the late 1970s. It significantly undermined the power position of Party apparatus in industrial enterprises and eroded the foundation of the Party's organizational control over workers. The loosened Party control at the bottom of Chinese society contributed much to China's transition from a totalitarian state to what some scholars defined as a form of authoritarianism.[2]

This chapter presents a microanalysis of the backgrounds, accomplishments, limitations, and consequences of the Chinese efforts at "democratizing" enterprise management. It explores how the alliances and opposition among the central leadership, enterprise cadres, and ordinary workers evolved over time and discusses the three-cornered power struggles among the workers' congress, the enterprise Party committee, and the enterprise director.

Elections of Enterprise Leaders

After the communist takeover in 1949, democratic management of enterprises was emphasized as the embodiment of "people's democracy." But until the end of the 1970s, the direct election of enterprise directors or managers was never attempted.[3] Party organizations controlled the selection of the cadres at all levels, including enterprise leaders. In contrast with government officials, whose selection went through ritualistic electoral procedures during certain periods, enterprise leaders were as a rule simply appointed by the higher authorities with little or no consultation with the workers.

Experiments with Enterprise Elections

The first nod toward democratization of enterprise management came from Deng Xiaoping in October 1978.[4] Tentative direct elections in enterprises started in early 1979. By the end of 1982, 15,320 factory directors, 23,505 workshop heads, and 52,337 group leaders had been elected democratically.[5] The electoral process was usually divided into four stages.[6] The first was the so-called mobilization stage at which the central decision for enterprise elections was proclaimed. At the second stage, a committee on democratic elections was formed; it consisted of representatives of the enterprise Party committee, trade union, and the workers' congress (if it had been established) and was presided over by the Party secretary. The committee collected the names of the candidates. After what was called a period of consultation and discussion, a list of formal candidates was determined and presented to the workers on the election day.[7] To avoid the appearance of manipulation, the higher authorities usually discouraged the Party committee from proposing the candidates in its own name, but Party cadres were still in a position to remove those they disliked from the final list.

At the third stage, an assembly of the workers (or deputies of the workers' congress, if the enterprise was large) was convened to elect the director. (For the election of workshop and group heads, only the workers of that workshop or group needed to be called together.) At the assembly the candidates delivered campaign speeches typically promising improvements in production and welfare. Then the workers were allowed to ask them questions, after which they voted by secret ballot. If the voters did not like the candidates on the ticket, they were free to fill in the names of people they preferred. Finally, the outcome was announced. The elected director was authorized to form a "cabinet" (something like a management committee), which was to be presented to the higher authorities for approval.

These elections did result in a change of leadership in some enterprises, based more or less on the preferences of the employees. In Beijing, workers cast votes to choose their directors at 560 enterprises. In 240 of them, the incumbents were defeated and replaced. Among the enterprises controlled by a local government department of Beijing, only 130 of 1,200 directors or section heads retained their posts after elections.[8] In Wuhan the directors of twenty-four large and medium-size state enterprises were elected democratically in 1984, and just four of the incumbents retained their posts. Of the new directors, six were former deputy directors and fourteen were former workshop heads.[9]

Presumably because the initial effects of democratic elections were encouraging to Party leaders, a Party-state document stipulated, for the first time, that the workers' congress in state enterprises was authorized "to elect leading administrative personnel of the enterprise in accordance with the arrangements (i.e., directives) of the higher organ."[10] In collective enterprises democratic elections of officials were mandated legislatively In the revised constitution adopted in December 1982, a new article (article 17) explicitly provided that "collective economic organizations practice democratic management in accordance with the law, with the entire body of their workers electing or removing their managerial personnel and deciding on major issues concerning operations and management."[11]

Reactions from Cadres and Workers

Not surprisingly, enterprise Party committees usually preferred the incumbents, most of whom were Party members and previously appointed by them. Like elected politicians, the incumbents should possess some natural advantages in the election. That so many were voted out of office seemed to underscore both their unpopularity and the credibility of democratic elections. But questions concerning the political implications of the elections remained. How serious a challenge to the Party committee did the elections pose? Since Party cadres were authorized to organize the elections and were thus supposed to influence their results, how could they allow their favorite candidates to be defeated?

To be sure, the publicized directives from the highest leadership that prohibited any manipulation of enterprise elections played a deterrent role. The cadres would lose if they were informed against for undermining elections at a time when Party elites were sensitive to disloyalty to their new reformist policy. Later I analyze the reasons Party elites did not want to see enterprise elections turned into nothing more than "false democracy." Here, to see why the elections could yield some meaningful results, we need examine workers' attitudes and understand the rationale for a certain degree of tolerance on the part of Party cadres.

Although no competitions with politically or ideologically pluralistic platforms were allowed, workers appeared to show great enthusiasm for choosing their bosses; this suggested the usefulness of the elections in meeting workers' demands for democratic participation. After the directors of some enterprises in Wuhan were elected in 1984, the workers set off firecrackers to celebrate.[12] In the Wuhan printing and dyeing mill, when the municipal Party secretary announced that the workers' congress had the right to elect the director, he received prolonged applause and cheers.[13] In another factory, a number of workers volunteered to offer rewards to the candidates to encourage more people to run for office.[14]

Several factors seemed to contribute to the workers' interest in the elections. First, the elections resulted in the quick and evident improvement in the personal relations between directors and workers. In Mao's China, enterprise cadres were designated by the higher authorities; they were accountable not to their subordinates but to their superiors. This placed the cadres in a position to behave unscrupulously and to ignore workers' concerns. The elections made directors more responsive to workers. Within a short period after the director was elected in a Shanghai factory, he allegedly solved fifteen long-standing problems involving workers' welfare.[15] A worker described it this way: "In the past the enterprise administrator just tried every possible means to curry favor with the Party secretary and the higher authorities because his post and power were virtually decided by them. Now, although the elected director still would not dare to offend the Party secretary, he has to please the workers as well" (au. int.).

Workers were enthusiastic about elections as well because of the increased power the elected director wielded over enterprise affairs to which the workers' material interests, such as income and bonus, were directly linked. As discussed in detail later in this chapter, after the system of "factory director responsibility under Party committee leadership" was restored in 1978, the director's executive power began to expand while the Party committee was discouraged from interfering in enterprise administration.[16] In May 1984 the director's authority was further strengthened when Premier Zhao announced the gradual establishment of the factory director responsibility system (FDRS; since the late 1980s it has also been called the enterprise manager responsibility system). The director was authorized to assume full responsibility for the factory and took on major control of its affairs.[17] In fact, the establishment of FDRS constituted just a component of the reform of industrial administration at the macrolevel. At the core of this reform was the expansion of autonomy of the industrial enterprise and a gradual but significant change in the relations between state and enterprises, especially on financial issues, which made enterprise elections more economically meaningful to the workers.[18]

In the pre-reform, mandatory-planning economy, nearly all activities in an enterprise—such as those regarding employment, properties, raw materials, production, supply, and marketing—were under the complete control of the state. The profits were partly turned over to the state and partly retained for reinvestment in the enterprise. Losses were absorbed by the state.

The first step in allowing enterprises greater independence from the state was the introduction of a system of profit retention in early 1979. Under this system an enterprise could retain a certain proportion of its profits for discretionary spending. But state quotas for profit delivery would increase as profits increased. In April 1983 the profit retention system was replaced by "tax for profit" (*ligaishui*). It was stipulated that after a short transitional period, enterprises would be allowed to retain all their after-tax profits and become fully responsible for their own profit and loss. In late 1986, tax for profit came to a premature end and was replaced by programs that were to organize financial relations between state and enterprises according to a general "contractual responsibility system." As William Byrd suggested, despite considerable variation, these reform programs "involved a contract-based relationship" that "required the factory directors to be in positions of authority, and hence they often led to a substantial increase in their *de facto* powers."[19]

This series of industrial reforms made a big difference in workers' welfare and bonuses because they gave the enterprise discretionary power over a large portion of its profit. Workers became more concerned about the economic efficiency and profitability of their enterprises. Given the newly established authority of the director, his or her capability and qualifications to a great extent determined the enterprise's quality of management and hence its efficiency. In some poorly run enterprises, democratic elections were understood by the workers in terms of what became a popular slogan: "Select competent people for running the factory!" (au. int.). In other words, the workers elected their director not just for the sake of democracy or self-respect but also for their own material interests. Elections tended to expand the resources available for welfare and also resulted in a more responsive welfare policy.[20]

No doubt democratic elections undermined the power base of the enterprise Party committee. In the past the director was usually appointed on the basis of consultation between the Party committee and the higher authorities. In some cases the director's post was concurrently held by the Party secretary. Now elections were organized by the Party committee and supervised by the next higher authorities, usually a relevant government bureau (*ju*). This supervision was more than a mere formality, as the two institutions often had different interests in the elections. Since bureau officials were usually held responsible by their own superiors for the economic efficiency of the enterprises under their jurisdiction, they would be better served if more capable directors were elected (au. int.).

The elections changed the status of the director, who had been an appendage of the Party committee by the early 1980s. It threatened the almighty status of the latter, particularly during those years when the Party committee was increasingly discouraged from interfering in the concrete administrative work that was now defined as within the director's authority. Such elections also tended to affect the image and prestige of the Party committee among the workers. Many Party cadres have kept up a constant criticism of elections, calling them competitions of eloquence and the ability to canvass votes that resulted in the election of two kinds of people: those who never offended anybody but were mediocre or incapable and those who were competent but lacked moral integrity.[21]

Although there were complaints about fraudulent practices from time to time (au. int.), it appeared that the strategy more commonly used by Party cadres in the elections was to play the card of "political and ideological criteria" against the candidates they perceived as possible troublemakers. The Party committee was not necessarily able to make sure its favorite candidates were elected, but it could exert considerable influence to prevent those it disliked from winning; however, this influence decreased after its power was gradually but substantially reduced during the late 1980s. The key method by which the Party committee could manipulate the elections was in drawing up the final list of formal candidates. Although workers were theoretically free to vote for anybody, it was very difficult for those not on the list to be elected, no matter how popular they might be among the workers. During the early 1980s, the pressure of the "party leadership," although it had relaxed a bit, was still heavy. It was risky for workers to canvass votes for candidates not officially endorsed because such an action would be interpreted as confronting the Party committee (au. int.).

As already mentioned, despite extensive "consultation and discussion," the final list of candidates was decided by the committee on democratic elections. The members of this committee were not elected but appointed, by top Party cadres in the enterprise until the mid-1980s, thereafter by the management committee. Most if not all committee members were Party cadres, trade union officials, workshop or section heads, and model workers. Party cadres could easily reject candidates on the grounds that they did not respect party leadership and were therefore politically unqualified. After the mid-1980s, the decisionmaking function of the Party committee was further limited following its loss of executive power, but it usually took charge of examining the backgrounds and qualifications of the candidates, and its recommendation still had some weight (au. int.).

The electoral results might have disappointed some workers who had expected a bigger change in power relations. Nevertheless, perhaps contrary to what many people would imagine, voters did not show a strong anti–Party committee inclination. In fact, the candidates most likely to be elected were those who were both popular among the workers and maintained amicable relations with the Party boss. To be endorsed by the Party committee did not necessarily mean rejection by the voters. Some workers still habitually held the Party committee in awe; some did not want to provoke the anger of Party cadres; still others thought an elected director friendly to the Party committee would be conducive to economic efficiency (au. int.). This phenomenon seemed to be more common in small enterprises in which workers and cadres were familiar with one another and shared certain interests. The people there did not have a strong sense of the difference made by Party identification, and they tended to avoid confrontation (au. int.).

Discriminatory Regulations

The legal stipulations about director elections varied with the ownership of the enterprise. Throughout the 1980s, the democratic election of directors or managers was legally required and enforced only in "collective economic organizations." In state-owned enterprises, it depended on the extent to which local government officials thought it necessary. To understand the significance of this distinction, some knowledge about China's economic structure is needed. Except for a small number of privately owned enterprises emerging in the economic reforms, China's industrial enterprises were divided into two large ownership categories: state ownership and collective ownership.[22] State-owned enterprises were defined as the main body and leading force in the national economy. These enterprises were usually characterized by the strategic importance of products, large scale of production, and large number of employees. They were directly controlled by different levels of government.[23]

Collectively owned enterprises played a subsidiary role even though their number exceeded that of state enterprises. Although they theoretically enjoyed more freedom in their operations, collective enterprises were not autonomous as this notion is understood in the West, but were controlled by local state agencies to varying degrees. In 1979, China's enterprises totaled 350,000. Among them, 80,380 were state owned (24 percent) and 270,120 were collective (76 percent). In 1988 the number of enterprises increased to 500,000. The state-owned total reached 90,910 (20 percent), whereas the collective total reached 390,540 (79 percent). But there were far more employees in state enterprises than there were in collective ones. The employees in the former came to 32.08 million (71 percent of all employees) in 1979 and 42.29 million (69 percent of all employees) in 1988. In collective enterprises, there were 13.28 million employees in 1979 and 18.50 million in 1988, who made up 29 and 30 percent of the totals, respectively.[24]

Although elections in collective enterprises were institutionalized, it was never definitely stipulated in the constitution or in any Party-state document that the same electoral system must also be established in state enterprises. Democratic management was stressed equally within both kinds of enterprises, but in state enterprises the priority obviously was given to worker participation in the decisionmaking process rather than to their direct election of leaders. In the "Provisional Regulations" of 1981, a vital qualification was added to the function of the workers' congress to elect the director and was later incorporated almost intact into a law.[25] Despite increasingly strong demands for greater workplace democracy, the law states equivocally that the workers' congress of a state enterprise has the right to elect its director or manager in accordance with government arrangement. As the authorities interpreted it, this "arrangement" has two meanings. First, under the existing system, directors of *some* enterprises must be appointed and removed by the state "in order that state ownership can be made palpable"; second, if an election were needed, the concrete procedures for it must be determined by the government.[26]

The Party leadership's refusal to abandon the power to appoint and remove officials in state enterprises brought to light Party leaders' distrust of workers' choices and their attempt to retain a certain degree of organizational control. In the era of reform, what dominated Deng's thinking was the maintenance of social stability under the existing political system in which the working class was expected to play a decisive role.[27] But the ambiguous legal provisions did not seem to suggest that the directors of state enterprises should be designated by the higher authorities. They probably just implied room for maneuver. In most areas, indeed, local authorities preferred to designate directors of state enterprises, especially the large-scale ones. They themselves benefited enormously from their power to assign these profitable posts. But in some provinces or cities where the leaders were relatively reform minded or the workers showed a strong desire to elect their bosses, directors were chosen through democratic election in state enterprises. The city of Wuhan was frequently cited as a model in that regard: It had 1,951 enterprises whose directors were popularly elected in 1984. Among them, 1,077 were state enterprises and 874 were collective ones.[28]

The practice of electing directors in state enterprises was, although not legally prescribed, often publicly commended. This sort of compromise or balance, which we may call "fuzzy politics," is characteristic of China's political reforms. On the one hand, Party leaders were reluctant legally to require democratic elections in all enterprises; on the other, they encouraged such elections in public. Such encouragement was perhaps important to Party leaders for its symbolic significance. It enabled them to shift the responsibility to local cadres if the masses complained of a lack of democratic reform. The leaders seemed to be aware that without legal enforcement, it was very difficult to introduce free elections into an enterprise because of the resistance of Party bureaucrats. The relatively small number of state enterprises that held elections showed that when government officials were placed in a position to decide for themselves whether the directors of the enterprises under their jurisdiction should be appointed or elected, they generally chose the former. But this preference did not always conform to the principle of flexibility the leaders sought to establish. Under certain circumstances, it hurt the Party's image as a serious democratic reformer. A Party-state leader suggested that whether the directors of state enterprises were appointed or elected must be determined according to the specific needs and concrete conditions of each enterprise: "We should not have an undifferentiated pattern."[29]

Workplace elections with really democratic elements would erode Party authority in grassroots politics and alter the state-society relationships. In a totalitarian state—which, according to Sartori, is "the imprisonment of the whole of society within the state, an all-pervasive political domination over the extra-political life of man"—this trend would contribute in the long run to the decline of Party hegemony and the emergence of a more autonomous civil society.[30] Unlike rural economic reforms that were spontaneously started by the Chinese peasants in 1978, the urban political reform involving the restructuring of power—even at the basic level—was tightly and consistently controlled by the Party leadership.[31] Democratic election of enterprise directors was by and large a product of the Party-state's policy. But why did Party elites have to adopt such a policy? The answer should be based on an analysis of both political consequences and economic effects of the elections.

Without question, Party elites initiated enterprise elections primarily as a response to the pressure from below to change some of the political rules. After a period of experiments, they had reason to feel relieved that the elections did not pose obvious political threats or challenges. Despite the variety of forms the elections took, rarely were macropolitics involved in the debate. In most cases the election proceeded in an environment where wider political issues, such as political pluralism or multiparty competition, appeared to be almost entirely irrelevant. Some reports concerning details of the electoral process highlighted how pressure was exerted upon the candidates in the elections for a reform orientation and better management.[32]

To illustrate the neutral if not positive political effects of the elections to the Party, we may also examine the political identity of elected directors. According to a study of the democratic elections of directors in twenty-four large and medium-sized state enterprises, more than 95 percent of the workers participated in the recommendation of candidates. Engineers and technicians, who were relatively apolitical, constituted more than 80 percent of the candidates. Among the twenty-four elected directors, eighteen were Party members. The other six, after being elected, hastily submitted their applications for Party membership.[33]

Party leaders' attitudes toward enterprise directors' elections appeared to be guided as well by economic considerations. From their perspective, as markets played an increasingly important role, industrial enterprises were no longer required to be subordinate administrative units of the government. Gordon White's study shows that in industrial reforms of the 1980s, great efforts were made to base the relationship between state and enterprises on a share of profits. The changes from the system of profit retention to tax for profit and then to the contractual responsibility system in fact revolved around the revision of the rules for such a share.[34] In the beginning the official policy was to let the state take a larger share of the profits of more efficient enterprises. Later this policy of "whipping the fast ox" was found to have dampened the incentives of enterprises to increase their profits. The new reform measure was to maintain or increase the size of the state's slice of the pie by making the pie larger. Increasing the economic efficiency of enterprises and hence their profits therefore became the top priority of industrial reform.

Some official sources indicated that since the candidates usually won over the voters by promising reform, elected directors tended to adopt bold innovations to improve enterprise performance and often made big differences.[35] Ironically, the original democratic significance of elections tended to be obscured by their "conspicuous" economic effects. Even Deng Xiaoping praised elections for their role in selecting more competent enterprise leaders. "In some enterprises and other units," he said, "cadres who volunteered for leading posts or were elected to them by the masses have achieved much in little time and proved more capable than cadres appointed from above."[36]

Public-Opinion-Based Appointments

Perhaps because of these perceived merits of employees' participation in the choice of directors, measures were taken to base appointments as well on popular preference. A study in the provinces of Hunan, Hubei, and Anhui in June 1985 showed that the directors in more and more state enterprises were determined by a combination of appointment and public opinion poll. There were three patterns:

1.   The director was appointed by the higher authorities. After a certain period, say, one year, a "democratic appraisal" and vote of confi-

dence were held. If the director failed to win the confidence of the majority of the employees, they might demand his removal and a new appointment.

2. On the basis of a democratic appraisal of the qualifications, the employees recommended by vote their preferred candidates for appointment.
3. The employees recommended the candidates, but the qualifications of these candidates were strictly examined and screened by the higher authorities. Only those considered eligible were presented to the voters for election.[37]

These patterns of appointment persisted into the early 1990s and were not limited to the three named provinces.[38]

After political reform appeared to be suspended following the 1989 Tiananmen massacre, enterprise elections drew more criticism from Party cadres.[39] But the way the director was chosen in state enterprises did not seem to change. The appointment of state enterprise directors by the government still needed to be more or less endorsed by the employees to be effective. Election was still one of the three major ways the director was selected in state enterprises, but it was acknowledged that such elections had not been widely practiced.[40] By contrast, the election of lower officials such as workshop heads appeared to be more common.[41] A notable case of elections of top officials in state enterprises was that of the Capital Steel and Iron Company (CSIC), which had more than 200,000 employees and was ranked first in taxes paid for profits among China's 500 largest companies. After 1986 the chairman and deputy chairman of the "factory committee" (i.e., board of directors) and the general manager of CSIC were reportedly directly elected by the employees and appointed by the government. Until Zhou Guanwu, the Party secretary and chairman of the factory committee, stepped down because of a corruption scandal in 1995, the so-called CSIC experience was highly publicized and touted by the authorities.[42] As a model of enterprise elections, it also had a positive social impact.[43]

In late 1992 a major reform concerning "managing mechanisms" in state enterprises was introduced.[44] This reform was actually a restoration of the part of the tax for profit plan that had been canceled in 1986. Because it demanded that state enterprises be fully responsible for their own profits and losses, this reform led to further emphasis on the capability of the directors and opened the way for competition in the appointment process. In 1994 the Henan provincial government decided to establish a "system of open and democratic elections" in all state enterprises that had failed to show profits. By late 1995, nearly 200 state enterprises in Henan were managed by democratically elected directors who reportedly brought the dying enterprises back to life.[45]

The Three-Way Struggle for Management Power

Although ordinary workers enthusiastically embraced the democratic election of their bosses, they did not seem to regard it as vital to their interests—and so did not desperately demand it. During the 1980s, spontaneous mass demonstrations were not rare, but it was never reported that people went into the streets to protest the lack of democratic elections in their workplace. Why did the Party leaders' insistence on retaining their power to designate directors to state enterprises apparently not infuriate the workers? As I have just mentioned, compared to past practices official appointments became less arbitrary and were to some extent based on consultation with the employees. In addition, we need to consider an equally important aspect of "democratization" of the enterprise: the changed role of the workers' congress in the decisionmaking process.

As soon as they began to democratize enterprises, it was evident that central Party elites placed greater emphasis on the participation of employees in decisionmaking than on the elections of officials. In contrast to the elections, which were defined by ambiguous and discriminatory regulations, the workers' role in and right to administration of their enterprise, whether state or collectively owned, were firmly established by law.

The workers' congress (an abbreviation of "the congress of workers and staff members") was formed in 1957 and existed as an ornament until 1966. During that period, it was even less than a rubber stamp, since no major decisions required its formal approval. After 1978 the workers' congress was gradually restored and endowed with real functions. In the 1981 "Provisional Regulations," the congress was proposed as a major institution through which to run the enterprise "democratically." By the end of that year, the workers' congress had been set up in almost every major industrial enterprise in the cities of Beijing, Shanghai, Nanjing, Tianjin, Ha'erbin, and Guangzhou,[46] and the reform was rapidly extended to the rest of the country. In Jilin Province the workers' congress system was introduced into more than 7,000 of 7,945 enterprises of various types and sizes by the mid-1980s.[47] In March 1988 those provisional regulations became, without significant alteration, the "Law of the State-owned Industrial Enterprises of the PRC." But statistics show that more than 10 percent of state enterprises still had no workers' congress by 1992.[48]

The workers' congress was composed of representatives directly elected for a term of two years by workers and staff members, with work groups, work sections, workshops, or offices as the electoral units. The law conferred on the workers' congress five functions and powers. The first was to examine and make suggestions on the plans drawn up by the directors concerning major issues of the enterprise. The second was to approve or veto these plans, in particular those that directly involved employees' welfare, such as wage adjustments, bonus distributions, housing allocations, labor safety devices, and rewards and penalties. The third was to make decisions independently regarding the workers' welfare. The fourth was to appraise and supervise cadres at all levels of the enterprise and recommend their reward, punishment, or dismissal. The fifth was to elect directors if need be.[49]

In its structural aspects, the reform of enterprise management was similar to the reform of government. Central to this reform was reorganization of the triangular power relations among the three major actors: the workers' congress, Party committee, and director. Since the workers' congress was in a position either to elect or to exert an influence on the appointment of the director, there could be a positive-sum relationship between them. By contrast, there was a fundamental conflict of interests between the workers' congress and the Party committee. The exercise of power by the former required the latter to give up its dominance.

Initially, Beijing used much caution in reducing the power of the enterprise Party committee. All directors, whether popularly elected or appointed from above, and workers' congresses were required in principle to accept directions from the Party committees, at least on major issues. This arrangement was officially called the "FDRS and the workers' congress system," both under the leadership of the Party committee. In fact, these two systems existed before the Cultural Revolution and were restored to "normal" as part of the post-Mao setting-wrongs-right policy. But the restoration of the pre-1966 systems failed to produce any effects that workers perceived as reform. Moreover, the workers' violent rebellion against the authorities in the early Cultural Revolution suggested that these systems did not function successfully or to the workers' satisfaction even before 1966.

The failure of the initial reform measures to meet workers' expectations can be seen plainly from official sources.[50] Added to this was the post-Mao leaders' worry that Party bureaucrats exasperated the workers by suppressing their desire for democratic participation and continuing their own monopoly of power in the Party's name. The Party journal *Hongqi* (*HQ*) acknowledged that only a few workers' congresses worked well: "Most workers' congresses were treated more or less as mere formalities. The workers complain bitterly about it." To make things worse, many of these cadres were corrupt and pursued their personal interests by hook or by crook. *HQ* blamed Party cadres for the strained relations between them and the workers.[51]

Reinterpretation of "Party Leadership"

The awareness that cadres had often transformed the principle of party leadership into despotism within the workplace led to an official reinterpretation of "party leadership." A *Gongren Ribao* (*GRRB*) editorial defined "party leadership" as "educating Party members and cadres so that they know how to respect the workers' status as masters and revise all behavior infringing upon the workers' democratic rights."[52] Soon thereafter, its special commentator demanded that the Party committee withdraw from production and welfare affairs.[53] Xiong Fu, a senior propaganda official, argued that "party leadership" must be used to strengthen "democratic management."[54]

Of course, to define the Party committee leadership as mainly advising and helping the workers to practice democracy had double implications. Given their traditional distrust of spontaneity in the people's behavior and Deng's repeated insistence on party dictatorship as unchallengeable, Party elites were concerned that mass participation might get out of hand. They needed Party organizations to caution workers about the limitations they had to accept to make their participation "democratic," not "anarchic." A *Renmin Ribao* (*RMRB*) commentator warned that there were a number of wrong views on the issue of democracy, the most striking of which was "to think that we can have democracy without party leadership."[55]

These somewhat abstract and general affirmations of party leadership did not give Party cadres much comfort. In a May 1984 report, Premier Zhao Ziyang formally removed the phrase "under the leadership of the Party committee" from the original formulations concerning the FDRS and the workers' congress system.[56] In October 1984 a Party conference passed a decision that reconfirmed the commitment to the separation of the Party committee from concrete enterprise management and demanded a greater role for the workers' congress in decisionmaking and in the supervision of the administrative leadership.[57] The tendency to reduce the functions and influence of the Party committee developed further and was extended to many institutions during the late 1980s. In line with the new thinking embodied in Zhao's report to the thirteenth Party congress, the Party groups (*dang zu*) in many government departments were to be gradually abolished.[58]

Party Leaders' Distrust of Cadres

Party leaders' rhetoric and the measures taken for demoting Party cadres were obviously more than pure propaganda. They were evidence of sharp conflicts between Party bureaucrats triggered by the market-oriented economic reforms and the predicament these conflicts caused the Party in its exercise of dictatorial power.

The decrease in the power of Party organizations was incremental. It was initially driven by the leadership's worry about popular resentment against corrupt, authoritarian Party cadres, particularly those in the workplace, where personal welfare and career were involved. In November 1980 Chen Yun, the number-two figure in the Politburo, cautioned that the cadres' conduct would decide the Party's life or death. At a Party conference held in October 1983, he once again focused on the problem of the cadres' abuse of power for private gain. "Many criminals guilty of corruption," he charged, "were Party members or, if not, were protected by them. If we do not take severe measures against them, the Party will lose its popularity."[59] At this conference, the Central Committee decided to launch a nationwide movement to correct the "unhealthy tendency" within the Party.

A detailed discussion of corruption related to the economic reforms is not necessary for our purposes. Suffice it to indicate that all the efforts to eliminate political corruption proved to be fruitless. Summing up the effects of two years of intense "rectification," Chen Yun expressed his deep disappointment. "With respect to the conduct within the Party and in society," he admitted, "there still exist serious problems. Fundamental improvement remains very difficult to achieve."[60] Bo Yibo, who took charge of the rectification movement, complained that in some work units defiance of the Party's discipline among Party members had developed to a grave extent.[61] As another Party leader said, bureaucratism, exploitation of power for private interests, patron-client relationships, and money worship had become epidemic within the Party.[62]

As economic reform deepened, it soon became apparent that problems with Party cadres went beyond just corruption. In fact, the positive role of many cadres in enterprises in defending party leadership was canceled out by their negative attitude and damage to the reforms. They produced more problems for party leadership than they solved.

It was no secret that a large portion of basic-level professional Party cadres resisted economic reform for fear of losing power and privileges. Many of them (40 percent in 1983) joined the Party and were placed in leading positions during the Cultural Revolution by exhibiting loyalty to the Gang of Four and by attacking the "capitalist-roaders," represented by Deng, who were restored to power after Mao's death.[63] The decision to undertake the rectification movement implied that many Party members and cadres had not rid themselves of the shackles of ultraleftist thinking. "They take a hostile attitude toward the basic policies [of reform] adopted [since 1978]. Some comply in public but oppose in private. Some even defy them undisguisedly."[64]

On the issue of economic reform, to be sure, Party cadres should not be treated as an undifferentiated aggregate. The increasingly complex economic environment and changing relationships between state and enterprise required those with professional knowledge to achieve leadership positions in industrial enterprises. In fact, many well-educated cadres managed to shift to administrative posts to avoid loss of power in the shake-up of management structures. But the majority of cadres, who owed their Party position to their "revolutionary qualifications" and political loyalty, were left with no proper role to play in the new situation in which traditional political work was either abolished or greatly diminished.

The leadership's increasing disgust with basic-level cadres was reflected in the efforts to discredit them publicly. *HQ* took the unusual step of publishing an investigation about the character of Party members in both urban and rural areas. In this report only 30 percent of the basic-level Party branches and Party members were ranked as "good."[65] A propaganda pamphlet compiled by the municipal Party committee of Beijing sneered at the poor education of Party members. It disclosed a 1984 statistic claiming that almost 80 percent of Party members were illiterate or had attended only primary or junior high school.[66]

The mutual political distrust and conflicting interests on reform between Party elites and cadres became a major motive in political reform. As discussed in Chapters 6 and 7, Party cadres at different levels and in different areas suffered to different degrees. Local and regional cadres were higher up in the Party's hierarchy of power and could even play a role in the choice of central leaders, whereas cadres at the basic level were too distant from the center to have any bearing on policy- or decisionmaking. They were unlikely to establish personal relations with the leaders, and so the leaders had fewer scruples in enforcing reforms at their expense. But the leaders discriminated between urban enterprise cadres and rural cadres. Even though they might have a lower opinion of rural cadres than of urban ones, as Jean Oi's study of rural reforms found, the leaders had to continue to rely on rural cadres to maintain the state's control mechanisms.[67] On the one hand, the huge number of peasants and their dispersion over vast areas made the Party's organizational control more necessary in the countryside; on the other, peasants and rural cadres shared interests in thwarting certain state policy goals, such as in grain procurements. As a result, the leaders found it difficult to use peasants to check cadres' power. Moreover, the leaders distrusted peasants even more than they did rural cadres. By contrast, in urban enterprises reform sharpened the conflicts between workers and cadres, and the leaders found in workers a reliable force to circumvent cadres' attempt to block reform. This shift of reliance for ensuring reform success was made quite clear by *HQ,* which urged the workers' congress to use its power to accelerate enterprise reform.[68]

Party Committee Versus Director

During the early 1980s, Party leaders' caution against possible harmful consequences of democratic reform and their ambivalence toward basic-level cadres caused much hesitation and confusion in the new interpretation of "party leadership" in the enterprise. Party cadres exploited this confusion to enter into rivalry not only with the workers' congress over decisionmaking power but also with the director, elected or appointed, over administrative power. In his study of Party-management relations of this period, Heath Chamberlain shows how the ambiguities in the principle of "divided responsibility" between directors (for administration) and Party cadres (for leadership) led to the violation of this principle in practice, with the latter attempting to maintain their grip on management and factory affairs.[69]

As stated earlier, the FDRS under Party committee leadership was a matter of restoration, not reform.[70] Before the Cultural Revolution, however, Party committee leadership was stressed. When the system was restored at the end of the 1970s, official emphasis shifted to the director's assuming full responsibility. But there were no explicit and mandatory stipulations for that. What made things more complicated was that many directors were now elected democratically and were not necessarily Party committee members. Some were not even Party members. For those appointed directors, their appointment and authority no longer derived mainly from their position in the Party. This situation immediately raised a question: Who played the lead role and occupied the central position in an industrial enterprise? In reality, the fight for executive power between the Party secretary and the director caused chaos in the management of many enterprises for a time.[71]

In 1982 the Shanghai Towel and Sheet Company investigated the relationship between the Party secretary and the director in the forty-six factories under its jurisdiction. In its report the company classified three types of relationships. The first type was alternation: The Party secretary and director thought that both of them were Party cadres and worked for the Party, and so there was no division of labor between them. In this case the two men were usually equally competent and experienced and also had good personal relations. The second type was interference: There did exist a division of labor, although not always strictly in accordance with official stipulations. The secretary and director could cooperate well in ordinary circumstances, but if problems occurred, then the secretary, rather than help the director, overstepped his authority and directly interfered in the administration. The third type was classified as supersession: In this instance the division of labor was ambiguous. The director was relatively weak in character or capability, and the secretary pushed aside the director and actually took over the administrative power. The report concluded that all three types violated the Party's reformist policy.[72] During this period the principle for divided responsibility remained unclear, and the relationship between the Party secretary and the director could be harmonious only if one of them tended to shun confrontation (au. int.).

By 1984 more and more signs suggested that the restored FDRS under Party committee leadership did not function as expected in most of the enterprises. A researcher attributed the failure to the Party committee efforts to maintain control, which impeded the director's assumption of full responsibility on the one hand and made democratic management difficult on the other.[73] An authoritative working manual for enterprise Party secretaries argued that adding the leadership of the Party committee to the FDRS equation caused confusion of duties and responsibilities. "It results in slow decisionmaking and inefficient production management."[74]

The New Role of the Party Committee

After the Party committee lost its leadership role within FDRS, it was endowed with three new major functions: (1) to support the director's authority, (2) to guarantee and oversee the implementation of the Party-state's principles and policies, and (3) to strengthen the Party's ideological and organizational work.[75] Although these functions allegedly best embodied party leadership, it was a simple fact that none of them involved concrete affairs of the enterprise—such as production, promotion, and welfare—and hence actual power. To prevent Party cadres from retaining power by various excuses, an *HQ* article declared void the notion that the Party committee was the core of leadership in the enterprise: "It must not be mentioned again."[76]

In the new system, therefore, the Party committee was theoretically degraded to something like a consultant body. Indeed, as several scholars suggested, such an arrangement met desperate resistance from well-entrenched cadres. Andrew Walder's study indicates that Party secretaries still had at their disposal (and exploited) some means of power, such as the right to be consulted on appointments of officials and to have the ear of the director's Party and government superiors.[77] Yves Chevrier also argues that the overall formal organizational superiority of the Party, its moral and political rights, and its ideological and propaganda roles enabled Party committees in each enterprise to maintain a convenient beachhead for protecting their influence over enterprise management.[78] But generally speaking, although "party leadership" in enterprises was still mentioned from time to time, it became a so-called ideological and political leadership that had no substantive content.[79] Although the new tasks assigned to Party cadres still left them room to maneuver, they were placed in an increasingly disadvantageous position in the power struggle.[80]

After the thirteenth Party congress of 1987, this model began to be applied to the government level and made it even more unjustifiable for the Party secretary to compete for power with the director. Once conflicts occurred, the Party secretary was no longer easily able to secure favor from his superiors in the Party. In one sharp personal collision in an enterprise, the Party secretary announced the director's expulsion from the Party organization. In response, the director ordered that the Party secretary be fired from the enterprise.[81] The Party committee was essentially left with little to do.[82] Many Party cadres grumbled that under the circumstances it was better to dismiss the Party committee.[83] Even Hu Yaobang, the Party general secretary, had little inkling of the Party committee's new duties. "After FDRS was instituted," he suggested, "new experiences have to be accumulated and new stipulations made concerning how the Party committee should work."[84]

The plight in which Party cadres found themselves could be seen through their own complaints that erupted in the media following the 1989 events. They quoted slogans common in enterprises, such as "Follow the workshop head, you get a monthly bonus; follow the Party committee, you just do your duty" or "It is preferable to run errands for the director until your legs are broken than to pour a cup of tea for the Party secretary."[85] They described the reforms as "spring for the director and autumn for the Party secretary" and said cadres were "politically dejected and financially in abject poverty."[86] They hoped that reports such as those claiming "if the number of professional Party cadres was cut by half, production would double" and the accusation that the Party secretary must be an opponent of reform would never appear again.[87]

The substantially reduced power of Party organizations led to a drastic reduction in the number of (professional) Party cadres. Among 414 state enterprises in Zhuzhou in Hunan Province, the number of Party cadres was cut by 65 percent within several years after 1984. Their representation in the total number of the employees decreased from 1.58 to 0.49 percent. At the same time, 65.6 percent of the apparatuses specifically for political education in enterprises were dissolved. Party members had to pursue political activities in their spare time.[88] During the late 1980s, more and more Party secretaries began to hold the post of deputy director of their enterprises. A researcher suggested that to deprofessionalize the post of the Party secretary in this way could sidestep potential conflicts between the secretary and the director.[89]

Workers' Congress Versus Director

In the three-cornered power game, the director did not just assume supreme executive power. The rapid expansion of his authority also tended to infringe upon the functions of the workers' congress. In the enterprises in which the directors were elected, democratic management would suffer less because the workers' congress, after all, controlled the choice of the director and could consequently influence his decisionmaking to some extent. By contrast, in a state enterprise whose director was appointed from above, his dominant position was a double-edged sword. It both constrained the Party committee and tended to squeeze out the workers' congress. The mid-1980s presumably witnessed the high point of democratic management. Thereafter, the workers' congress tended to decay as an organ of power, this time not because Party cadres attempted to come back in command but because the director tried to assume dictatorial power.

Basically, the weight of democratic participation would vary with the specific conditions of each enterprise. Its effectiveness in balancing the director's power could reportedly be found in some state enterprises in Liaoning Province. When antagonism existed between the workers and the administration, the workers' congress refused to pass the proposals made by the director and brought him into a stalemate.[90]

After the mid-1980s, democratic management tended to be eroded by the director's increased authority. A 1989 survey concluded that the workers' congress could exert significant influence over the decisionmaking in only 15 percent of the enterprises. In 30 percent of them, democratic management was "very weak."[91] In not a few cases, the director replaced the Party secretary as the new despot. In a factory of Changsha, the director used an electric club to threaten workers. A factory director in Tangshan carried handcuffs with him when he inspected the workshops.[92] The director's attempt to monopolize power so as to muzzle the workers' congress evoked strong complaints among the workers: How could you challenge the director when he was authorized to fire you or deduct a part of your wage or bonus (au. int.)? A researcher charged that the more developed the "contract management responsibility system," the more the status of the workers declined. Employees became little more than tools of production; they were "masters without power."[93] Many workers defined their situation in the enterprise as five nos: no position, no office, no power, no merits (merits, if any, were attributed to the director), and no benefits.[94]

During 1989–1990 I did fieldwork on workplace democracy at a radio factory, a state enterprise, in Wuxi. Before 1984 the factory had the FDRS under Party committee leadership. Major decisions were made at the meetings of the Party committee, which were dominated by the secretary. The director was at most responsible for concrete implementation of these decisions. It was therefore understandable that the Party secretary was regarded as the boss who had the final say on factory affairs. Then in 1984 the director assumed sole responsibility for all the factory affairs without, at least theoretically, the Party committee's leadership. In 1986 this factory began to try the contract management responsibility system, which further strengthened the director's authority. Representing the factory, he signed a profit contract with the state each year that set a target for either profits or losses.

After 1984 the functions of the Party committee gradually changed. It was forced to withdraw from factory administration and play a subsidiary role in the decisionmaking process. The new major role assigned to the Party committee and its secretary was to take care of the so-called ideological problems among Party members. The decisionmaking power was transferred to the workers' congress and the director.

In this factory the director was not elected democratically but was appointed by the municipal government. Perhaps to embody party leadership, the director's position within the Party committee did not change throughout the 1980s. After 1984, when he was appointed director by the government, he was simultaneously appointed by the municipal Party committee as deputy Party secretary of this factory. However, the director's authority derived not from his Party post but from his government appointment. In other words, he was no longer a tool of the Party committee or an assistant to the Party secretary but a director in the real sense of the term.

The most important power the director acquired was to appoint officials. Indeed, the relevant Party-state documents suggested that the director should consult the Party secretary and the masses on major issues, appointment of officials in particular. At least according to the Party secretary of this factory, the director rarely consulted him and never took his lead on appointments. As a result, the leading executive posts at all levels in the factory were occupied by the director's trusted followers.

Until 1984 almost all issues in this factory—ranging from production to the employees' welfare—were decided behind closed doors by the four to five people who formed the Party committee. As the committee tended to be marginalized, the decisionmaking mechanisms became a little more complicated and from time to time confused. Theoretically, the workers' congress replaced the Party committee as a decisionmaking organ. Major decisions were to be deliberated and approved by the workers' congress. But because of its size, the workers' congress proved to be unwieldy and inefficient in policymaking. In reality, the factory director, with the help of his followers, manipulated the policy process.

In late 1987, perhaps to avoid the concentration of power in the hands of the director, the factory was instructed to establish the Committee of Factory Management as the de facto decisionmaking organ. One-third of the members of this committee were representatives of the workers' congress. It was stipulated in this factory that on major issues concerning management, production, and sale of products, the director must call committee members together for discussion and consult them sufficiently. However, final decisions were not made by the one-member-one-vote principle but rather by the director himself according to his own understanding of what represented the opinion of the majority and the best interests of the factory. What made the director more powerful was that he was theoretically authorized to fire workers, although he rarely did so.

The employees' welfare belonged within the power sphere of the Trade Union Committee, whose leaders were directly elected by the workers through the workers' congress. This committee held two meetings per year to discuss all the major issues of the factory. But its power to make decisions was limited to welfare issues such as wage increases, bonus distributions, and housing allocation. On other issues it could only make recommendations to the director. In fact, the Trade Union Committee rarely bothered to address these matters and just left them to the Committee of Factory Management and the director.

I interviewed three people in this factory: a top Party cadre, a leader of the Trade Union Committee, and an ordinary worker. All of them agreed that the director was the most powerful person in this factory. But their attitudes toward this state of affairs were quite different.

As expected, the cadre bitterly resented the "unrestricted" expansion of the director's power. He argued that party leadership could hardly be reflected in the factory management. "Since the director's power was neither controlled by the Party committee nor by the workers' congress, the masses were discontented." Making use of his superior position in the Party, he attempted to compel the director to submit at intra-Party meetings. He found that without control over factory affairs, he could hardly establish authority even among Party members. He had complained to his superiors several times but was ignored.

According to the worker, the employees were pleased to see the professional Party cadres lose their power and privileges. The workers often mentioned them with biting sarcasm: The only work these cadres now did was "to drink tea, read newspapers, and complain" all day. As regards democratic participation, the worker suggested that ordinary workers were concerned about their welfare. Except for a few "ambitious" activists, they did not have much interest in discussing issues irrelevant to their welfare. Many of them seemed to be satisfied with their right to elect those who decided on their welfare. To be elected or reelected, the members of the Trade Union Committee did try their best to defend the workers' interests. Perhaps for this reason ordinary workers, unlike Party cadres, had no strong feeling against the director's assumption of power.

The trade union leader basically agreed with the worker. He asserted that he understood why the director had to hold supreme power: The director was appointed by and must be responsible to the government. For one thing, the director was, on behalf of the factory, obliged to pay a certain amount of tax to the state per year; this was required by the contract between the director and the government. But on issues like this, there was actually a conflict of interest between the director and the workers. The workers were not familiar with or did not care enough about the factory's legal obligations to the state, and the workers preferred, if possible, to increase their own bonuses by paying less enterprise tax. He also mentioned a major factor in the weakness of the workers' congress's policymaking function. As the horizontal and vertical relations of the enterprise changed significantly, the laws and regulations concerning its operation became increasingly detail oriented and sophisticated. Ordinary workers did not have enough professional knowledge to make rational decisions.

The results of my fieldwork and other relevant documents suggest that the decay of the workers' congress seemed to have less to do with political or ideological factors than with structural problems with democratic management that emerged as Chinese enterprises accelerated their pace toward capitalist-style administration.

Ironically, efforts at democratic management might be impeded in the long run by capitalism-oriented reforms. The change in the relations between state and enterprise intensified a process that was bringing the latter closer to the Western model. Because of the director's personal responsibility for the performance of the enterprise, his relations with employees had to be increasingly based on contract of service and wage labor. The director's authority over employment would inevitably destroy the foundation of workplace democracy.

The tendency to undermine democratic management may be seen from labor-capital relations in China's more capitalist, foreign-invested enterprises, whose number rose rapidly since the late 1980s (most of them funded by Taiwanese and overseas Chinese).[95] In most of these enterprises, no Party organizations or cadres existed; to be hired or avoid being fired, in fact, many Party members had to hide their Party identity.[96] There were no channels such as the workers' congress for democratic participation. Some reports said that it was even difficult to establish trade unions to protect the legitimate rights of the employees. In early 1993 the twelfth congress of the National Trade Union passed a new regulation that stipulated that in foreign-invested enterprises, trade unions represent and defend the interests of the employees in their consultation and negotiation with management. But managers resisted official efforts to establish trade unions. By September 1993, of more than 50,000 foreign-funded enterprises only 4,272 had trade unions. To encourage more foreign investment, the Chinese government turned a blind eye to this lack of compliance.[97]

Leaders' Efforts to Balance Power

More profound economic reform perhaps called for the director's almost dictatorial power, but if the authorities acquiesced, Party elites were obviously reluctant to see the workers' congress and the Party committee reduced to complete powerlessness. In early 1985, presumably because the government did not want the director's assumption of full responsibility to be obstructed, the workers' congress was ambiguously defined as neither the supreme power organ nor a consultative body.[98] But an *HQ* commentator warned that the expansion of the director's power must be accompanied by greater supervision from the workers; for that purpose, "a series of effective measures must be taken."[99] In some enterprises a committee to check on the director was formed as a branch of the workers' congress. Its task was to examine the performance of managers, including the director, every six months and suggest reward, criticism, punishment, or dismissal.[100] In some others, committees were created for specific issues such as production, safety measures, technical training, and welfare. These committees included both officials and workers' deputies. They took charge of overseeing and reporting on the director's implementation of the resolutions passed by the workers' congress.[101]

During the early 1990s, several models for democratic management were recommended. These models evaded a crucial question concerning the power relations between the workers' congress and the director but aimed to strengthen the channels through which employees' opinions and suggestions reached the director.[102] When a senior official commended the CSIC, he argued that the important basis of its success was "the employees' direct participation in and supervision of the decisionmaking process of this enterprise."[103]

An analysis of the delicate modification of the forms and priority of democratic management suggests that although the significance of democratic management was never played down publicly, it now contained more elements of propaganda. If the workers' congress was intended to act as an institutionalized channel to balance the power of first the Party secretary and then the director, then this function was obviously deemphasized and seemed to have decayed. These recommended models reminded people of Mao's "mass line," which encouraged Party cadres to listen to the opinions of the masses but never gave the masses veto power in the policy process. In any case the institutions for democratic management and the legal provisions that authorized the workers' congress to approve or reject major decisions made by the director still existed. At the press conference held after his election as premier in March 1998, Zhu Rongji promised that the "ongoing democratic elections, appraisal, and supervision of enterprise directors or managers" would continue,[104] in effect providing the employees with the means to seize power from the director and/or Party secretary.[105] Presumably to discourage employees from doing so, the function of the trade union in serving the employees' welfare was officially emphasized.[106] This might be understood as an effort to win employees' support for the director's assumption of supreme power by satisfying their demands regarding their welfare.

By contrast, the relationship between Party leaders and cadres became more ambiguous. That a large number of workers took to the streets in 1989 in support of the students and in defiance of cadres' warnings obviously aroused vigilance on the part of Party elites.[107] Soon after the June 4 massacre, Jiang Zemin, the new Party general secretary, demanded that enterprise Party committees take measures to strengthen political and ideological work.[108] The fourteenth Party congress in late 1992 passed a new Party constitution requiring the Party's grassroots organizations in enterprises to "participate in decisionmaking on major issues" (article 32).[109] A *Qiushi* (*QS*) article argued that the correctness of decisions and party leadership could not be guaranteed unless Party organizations participated in the decisionmaking process.[110] A Party document of 1994 warned that the organizations of the Chinese Communist Party at the basic level were the weakest since 1927 and that the Party had to place top priority on rebuilding them.[111]

However, room to retreat from the management structures of enterprises established in the 1980s was limited. Although Party cadres attempted to grasp the postmassacre opportunity to make a comeback, no institutional measures were reportedly taken to restore them to power. The confusing signals from Beijing suggested that the central leaders had no intention of allowing them to return, especially after the tense political atmosphere following Tiananmen relaxed.[112] The emphasis, if any, on the status of Party organizations in power structures of enterprises proved to be basically symbolic rather than substantial.[113] The significant changes that have taken place in China's economic and administrative structures seem to have caused irreversible decay of Party cadres' influence in industrial enterprises.

Conclusion

The process of the "democratization" of enterprise management in China reveals some of the logic behind the Party-sponsored reform. As we have seen, Party leaders and basic-level cadres were involved in a fundamental conflict of interests on the issue of reform, explaining why it was possible for workers to share some real power over enterprise affairs in a communist one-party context. Party leaders and workers stood at the top and bottom, respectively, of the administrative power hierarchy. Thanks to the considerable vertical distance between them, the policymakers in Beijing did not have to fear that the "negative" impact on Party power of limited participatory democracy in industrial enterprises would reach to the highest level. Instead, their primary concern was how to satisfy workers' expectations of reform and democratic participation and hence prevent them from taking to the streets. Limited democratization of enterprise management, free of any political threats, was not only helpful in attaining this objective but also checked any enterprise cadres who tended toward corruption and antireform actions.

Democratic management thus posed a direct and immediate threat to enterprise cadres. Although these cadres surely shared the fate of Party leaders in defending the one-party system, they were obviously reluctant to place their personal gains in jeopardy for the Party's long-term goal. What mattered to them was only the actual power in their hands. In the Chinese context, Party power used to penetrate almost every corner of the country and all aspects of social life. Cadres who lost power would accordingly lose authority, respect, social status, and all the accompanying privileges. Democratic participation by definition enabled employees to share and restrain—if not take away—cadres' power, and cadres understandably resisted it.

From a broader perspective, my analysis of the conflicting interests of Party leaders and cadres involved in enterprise reform suggests that during the post-Mao period, to talk abstractly or generally about the Party-people relationship in the workplace is no longer appropriate. In the restructuring of power in enterprises, the relationship between ordinary workers and central leaders was quite different from that between workers and enterprise cadres. The former could be more positive-sum than zero-sum under certain circumstances, whereas the latter had to be zero-sum. The leadership's readiness—even though conditional and to a certain extent symbolic—to support employees against enterprise cadre opposition to their democratic participation complicated workers' attitudes toward the Party's role in China's sociopolitical life.

Nevertheless, Party leaders' ambivalence toward worker clout was evident. It was essentially a reflection of the enormous dilemma inherent in the Party-sponsored political reform. Party leaders' distrust in the spontaneity of workers was spotlighted by two facts: (1) In state-owned enterprises the democratic election of directors—albeit a reality in many areas—was never officially institutionalized or legally enforced, and (2) in spite of the measures taken against enterprise Party committees, the leadership still needed them to play a policing role (i.e., as the so-called supervisor and guarantor) in an effort to prevent the emergence of political opposition and to retain at least some organizational control over workers. Since Party leaders, Deng in particular, always treated workplace democracy not as an ultimate value but as an expedient, it was unavoidably affected by their changing economic and political considerations. The reassertion of Party power following Tiananmen, though largely symbolic, best illustrated the fundamental limitations of China's "democratization" of enterprise management.

Yet the power of the workers' congress tended to decay as China's industrial enterprises accelerated their movement toward capitalist-style management after the late 1980s. In many enterprises the director was authorized supreme power to handle the relationship between state and enterprise and to deal with the increasingly complex economic environment. It is ironic indeed that as manifested in the management structure of China's foreign-funded enterprises in recent years, the development of capitalism in China would not only undermine the foundation of Party hegemony but also make workplace democracy suffer.

It seems, however, that as long as the one-party system endures, the central leadership still needs "democratic management" as, among other things, a propaganda subject and a strategy to neutralize social opposition to the political system. Although the focus of official propaganda shifted to "party leadership" after 1989 and Party cadres' informal power and influence subsequently increased more or less, no institutional measures were taken to bring them back to power. Once legislatively mandated and institutionally guaranteed, workers' right to democratic participation can hardly be repealed without evoking strong protests or producing grave consequences. In any case the Chinese-style democratic management of enterprises appears to be a phenomenon peculiar to China's transitional period. It will perhaps continue to exist to varying degrees and in different forms until it is replaced by a new and more stable management pattern.

Notes

I am thankful to Sage Publications for permission to base Chapter 2 on my article "Democratic Reform of Management Structures in China's Industrial Enterprises," published in *Politics and Society* 23, 3 (September 1995): 369–410.

1. Enterprise Party cadres are basic-level cadres who, in the analysis of the Chinese political reform, differ from those I refer to as "local cadres" at government levels.

2. Harding calls it "consultative authoritarianism." See Harding, "Political Development." Other scholars apply the "fragmented authoritarianism" model to the analysis of China's post-Mao governmental process. See Lieberthal, "Introduction," in Lieberthal and Lampton, eds., *Bureaucracy,* pp. 1–30.

3. In the drafts of the "Regulations Concerning State-Owned Industrial Enterprises" proclaimed by the CCP Central Committee in 1961 and 1965, the workers' congress was conditionally empowered to elect enterprise officials. But no evidence could be found that elections—even ceremonial ones—were ever held. See Yu Chunsheng, "Comparative Study."

4. "Workshop directors, section chiefs and group heads in every enterprise," he demanded in a speech, "must in the future be elected by the workers in the unit. Major issues in an enterprise should be discussed by workers' congresses or general membership meetings." Deng Xiaoping, "Greeting the Great Task." Also see Kang Yonghe, "Democratically Elect Heads."

5. Yu Chunsheng, "Comparative Study."

6. The description of the electoral process was based both on the experiences recommended in Du Yuelin et al., *Zenyang Xuanju Chejian Zhuren,* and on my interviews.

7. In some enterprises, such as the Shanghai number 12 Cotton Mill, a list of candidates was presented based on the results of an opinion poll. See Zhou Ping, "An Important Step."

8. QZZY, *Qiye Minzhu Guanli,* p. 416.

9. Ibid., pp. 258–262. My interviews showed that it was not uncommon for candidates who were not Party members to get elected, especially after the mid-1980s. But it was also fairly typical for these candidates, once elected, to apply for Party membership. Many of them felt that without Party identification they would have no prestige or authority, particularly in an enterprise where Party members constituted a relatively high percentage among the personnel.

10. See the "Provisional Regulations."

11. See *Beijing Review,* no. 52 (December 27, 1982), pp. 10–29. For the definition of collective economic organizations, see note 22.

12. Zheng Haihang, "On the Unity."

13. QZZY, *Qiye Minzhu Guanli,* p. 250.

14. Ibid.

15. Zhuang Zhenhua and Zhou Jiquan, "Democratic Management."

16. In a 1980 speech, Deng demanded that the Party committee not only exercise "collective leadership" but also withdraw from concrete management under a division of labor. Deng Xiaoping, *Selected Works,* pp. 302–325.

17. See Zhao Ziyang, "Report on the Work of the Government," May 15, 1984.

18. For a detailed discussion of the central government's considerations in expanding enterprise authority, see Fewsmith, *Dilemmas of Reform,* ch. 2.

19. Byrd, "Chinese Industrial Reform, 1979–89."

20. As Chen Yizi, former director of the influential China Research Institute for Economic Reform, suggested, Chinese citizens treasured their right to elect their bosses more than they did their right to elect deputies to the people's congress and government officials. The percentage of turnout for elections of the former was higher than for elections of the latter. He explained this phenomenon in terms of the effects of the elections on individual livelihood. "Work-unit ownership in China," he argued, "keeps all the basic necessities of the people's life under the control of the work unit. Their interests are concentrated in the work unit . . . so the citizens would not be satisfied unless their workplace was democratized." See Chen Yizi, *Zhongguo,* p. 117.

21. Chen Xiaochun and Zhang Qinglin, "An Investigation."

22. According to official theory, state ownership was also called ownership by all of the people. It was a form of public ownership in which all of the people (the state) possessed the means of production. By contrast, collective ownership—though a form of public ownership as well—meant that the means of production in the collective economic organization were owned and operated only by its employees. Wang Zhengxiang and Zhang Jinhai, eds., *Zhongguo Jingji,* ch. 4.

23. A study by Christine Wong indicates that in 1983, 25,000 large enterprises nationwide were controlled by the central government; 30,000–40,000 medium-sized to small enterprises were controlled by provincial and city governments; and 40,000–50,000 enterprises were run by prefectural or county governments. See Wong, "Between Plan and Market."

24. Guojia Tongjiju, ed., *Zhongguo Gongye.*

25. It was the "Law of State-Owned Enterprises in the PRC," passed by the first session of the Seventh NPC in early 1988.

26. Wang Jinzhong, "The Workers."

27. From the democracy movement of 1978–1980, the campaign against spiritual pollution of 1983, and the campaign against bourgeois liberalization of 1987 to the 1989 massacre, Deng and other Party elders were constantly haunted by the thought of workers' joining the intractable intellectuals and the restless students against the regime. Their vigilance was intensified by the Solidarity movement in Poland during the early 1980s, as reflected in a dramatic change in the government's attitude toward Solidarity. Initially, the official mass media were sympathetic to the workers in their reports on the events in Poland. Before long, the tone changed, Party leaders becoming concerned that a similar uprising of workers might also take place in China (au. int.).

28. QZZY, *Qiye Minzhu Guanli,* p. 258.

29. See Chen Junsheng, "Study New Conditions." Chen was deputy secretary-general of the State Council.

30. Sartori, *The Theory of Democracy Revisited,* p. 198.

31. The origins of China's rural reform, characterized by decollectivization, were quite unusual in a totalitarian context. It was a peasant innovation that, as Kelliher argues, "reveals peasant power at its height under a strong state. . . . It flourished with at least the tolerance of somewhat more distant officials. But as national policy after 1982, family farming was implemented with the government's habitual insensitivity to local concerns." See Kelliher, *Peasant Power,* pp. 105–107. This case, however, should not lead us to conclude that Chinese citizens could have considerable freedom of action in changing the existing power structure even at the grassroots level or during a relatively "liberal" period. Some scholars indicate that even in the case of family farm-

ing, peasant power was quite limited and the Party-state had strong enough organizational control over its process. See Unger, "The Decollectivization."

32. QZZY, *Qiye Minzhu Guanli,* p. 250.

33. Ibid., pp. 258–262.

34. See White, *Riding the Tiger,* ch. 4.

35. Zheng Haihang, "On the Unity."

36. Deng Xiaoping, *Selected Works,* p. 308.

37. QZHHAD, "A Preliminary Study."

38. Dai Huaying, "Only If the Status of the Workers."

39. The merits of this method were also questioned from a nonpolitical perspective. "At present," a *QS* article indicated, "the directors or managers in state enterprises are mainly appointed by high authorities with the approval of the employees." But the author found fault in this method, saying these authorities often appointed directors with an eye toward easier vertical management and ignored the requirements of the production and business of the enterprises themselves. By contrast, the employees based their approval on their own interests and lacked a long-term vision. See Wu Jian, "Arouse the Initiative."

40. The other two ways were direct appointment by the higher authorities and engagement by a contract. Cui Lan, "No. 32 Lecture."

41. For example, in a major factory in Beijing, 60 percent of the workshop or section heads were elected by the employees. See Sun Zhenyuan, "Place Focal Point."

42. Wang Hongchang, "Economic Democracy." Also see the reports in *ZLB,* May 19, 1992.

43. For example, following the CSIC model, the president of Tongji University, one of China's major universities, was elected democratically in December 1994. "The First Democratically Elected University President."

44. In 1992 the "Regulations Concerning the Change" were proclaimed.

45. Gu Wenhong and Shan Guoxing, "An Investigation."

46. Yu Yannan, "Seriously Implement."

47. *GRRB,* June 12, 1985.

48. Cui Lan, "No. 32 Lecture."

49. Wang Jinzhong, "The Workers."

50. Beijing Tezhonggang Chang, "Support the Workers."

51. "Some leading cadres," it criticized, "use improper means to benefit themselves, their children, and relatives in matters of vital interest to the masses, such as promotions, wage increases, and housing." See Yu Yannan, "Seriously Implement."

52. *GRRB,* June 10, 1981.

53. *GRRB,* July 25, 1981.

54. According to Xiong, the democratic consciousness of the working class can never arise spontaneously or naturally. It results only from the Party's propaganda, education, and guidance. Xiong Fu, "On Democratic Management."

55. *RMRB,* December 29, 1986.

56. Zhao Ziyang, "Report on the Work of the Government," May 15, 1984.

57. See "Decision of the Central Committee."

58. For more details, see Chapter 5, notes 72 and 77. The practice of abolishing Party groups following the thirteenth Party congress was reported in Meng Xiangxi, "The Thinking."

59. *GMRB,* June 16, 1986.

60. Chen Yun, "Speech at the Sixth Session."

61. *RMRB,* June 30, 1985.

62. Zhang Yun, "The Improvement."

63. See Hongqi Zazhi Bianjibu Zhengzhishi, ed., *Xinshiqi Dangde Jianshe.*

64. The whole text of the decision can be found in *HQ,* no. 20 (October 16, 1983), pp. 3–11. A good illustration of the opposition to the economic reforms among Party cadres was the campaign against "bourgeois liberalization" launched at the end of 1986 when student demonstrations forced Party General Secretary Hu Yaobang to step down. Originally, the leadership agreed that this campaign should aim to correct the tendency of liberalization in the political domain and must not touch the economic reforms. However, many cadres viewed this as a golden opportunity to reverse the reforms on ideological grounds. Zhao Ziyang, who succeeded Hu, listed the following as the prevailing "wrong views" on the reforms: Some people regarded enterprise contracting as "privatization"; some criticized FDRS in enterprises as "abolishing party leadership"; some thought the household contract system in the countryside a "sabotage of the basis of collective economy"; and some simply equated commodity economy with capitalism. See Zhao Ziyang, "Speech at the Conference of Propaganda." Even *JFJB,* a usually conservative newspaper, expressed worry. "Some people," its commentator charged, "exploit the campaign against bourgeois liberalization to defame or oppose the reforms" (cited in Dong Hu, "Chinese Politics"). Given the widely reported actions taken by Party cadres against the economic reforms, Dong Hu quoted Deng Xiaoping as pledging, "China's policy of reform and openness can neither be changed nor slowed down."

65. Zhang Yun, "The Improvement."

66. Beijing Shiwei Lilunbu, ed., *Xinshiqi Dangde Jianshe,* p. 103. The leadership was eager to change the composition of the Party. Given the perceived enthusiasm of the educated elites toward the reforms, the Central Committee transmitted a report drafted by the Party's Organization Department to the whole Party in early 1985, claiming that it was of "extremely great significance" for brilliant intellectuals to join the Party: "It is absolutely not allowed that the qualified intellectuals continue to be excluded from the Party." *RMRB,* March 15, 1985. According to Lee, 45.5 percent of Party members were peasants and only 7.8 percent were specialists in 1981. Party members constituted only 13 percent of all specialists. Lee, *From Revolutionary Cadres,* ch. 12.

67. Oi, *State and Peasant.*

68. Chen Bingquan, "A Great Reform."

69. Chamberlain, "Party-Management Relations."

70. After the communist takeover in 1949, the enterprise management structures in China changed several times. During the early 1950s, they copied the Soviet model and established the director-in-command system (*yizhangzhi*). Under this system the director held supreme power in an enterprise, with the Party committee being relegated to the sidelines. In 1956, as the Party strengthened its control over Chinese society, the director-in-command system was replaced by the FDRS under the leadership of the Party committee. The director was demoted to a concrete executor of the Party committee's instructions. Andors, *China's Industrial Revolution;* also see Brugger, *Democracy and Organisation.* During the Cultural Revolution, the position of director was canceled.

71. According to Chamberlain's research, conducted during the mid-1980s, when it came to the question of "Who's in charge of the enterprise?" the Party committee and its secretary still prevailed. They had three levers at their disposal: their power to "supervise" enterprise operations, their continuing role in personnel management, and their disciplinary authority over all members of the Party organization. See Chamberlain, "Party-Management Relations."

72. SMBG, "How to Handle the Relationship."

73. Xu Bing, "A Study."

74. Zhang Gongchang et al., *Zenyang Danghao Qiye Dangwei Shuji,* p. 11.

75. See "Decision of the Central Committee."

76. Cao Zhi, "Improve and Strengthen." That Party document was the "Provisional Regulations Concerning the CPC Organizations in Industrial Enterprises," promulgated in 1982.

77. Walder, "Factory and Manager."

78. Chevrier, "Micropolitics."

79. With respect to how to exercise ideological and political leadership in practice, the experience of the Beijing Knitting Wool Factory was recommended. The Party committee in this factory reportedly fulfilled its obligation by doing the following: propagating Marxism and the Party's current policies; telling every employee to comply with the factory's rules and regulations; solving "problems" according to suggestions by employees; cultivating morale; promoting economic performance; urging Party members to play the vanguard's exemplary role; and helping the director and defending his authority when he was in trouble. See "How Does the Party Committee?" Yet the director was asked to pay due respect to the Party committee so that the latter could function as a guarantor and supervisor. In that regard, the director in a Shanghai plant did "quite well." He "seriously consulted" the Party committee on every major issue. *GRRB,* June 17, 1985. But he did not have to worry much about opposition from the Party committee. Just to make a gesture of respect was enough on his part.

80. The articles of Chamberlain, Chevrier, and Walder are quite insightful in their analysis of how Party secretaries exploited sources of informal power at their disposal to attempt to continue their domination of enterprise affairs. I found that Party secretaries' use of their power sources became less and less effective after 1986. Perhaps two factors contributed to this trend. One was the acceleration of political reform at the government level during the late 1980s, which aimed at restricting the power of professional Party cadres in government departments. The other involved the change in the relationships between state and enterprises that placed the director in a central position.

81. Hou Dinghe, "On the Scientific Separation."

82. An interesting question here is: "To what extent could the Party secretary use intra-Party levers to constrain the director?" Chevrier stresses the effectiveness of these levers: "The fact that enterprise managers are overwhelmingly party members and formally bound by party discipline and loyalty limits their power as managers" (Chevrier, "Micropolitics," p. 115). The problem with this argument is that during the 1980s Party discipline and loyalty were increasingly judged not by cadres' Party position but by their performance in implementing the (reform) policy formulated by the highest leadership.

83. Cao Zhi, "Improve and Strengthen."

84. Ibid.

85. Liu Liantie, "Stabilize the Ranks."

86. Li Shen, "Adjust the Mentality."

87. Ibid.

88. Hunan Shengwei Yanjiushi, "To Promote Reforms."

89. Hu Guozhang, "The Tendency."

90. The speech made by Zhu Jiazhen, vice governor of Liaoning Province, published in *QYGL,* no. 5 (May 1990), pp. 6–7.

91. Xiao Huazhang, "Fully Arouse."

92. Ibid.

93. Ruan Jianming, "The Suggestions."

94. Hu Zuogen, Zhang Shusheng, Chen Guangping, and Ding Zhenxiang, "The Self-Perception."

95. This tendency also existed in joint-stock enterprises without foreign investment. Since this kind of enterprise is still in the experimental stage and not widespread, I do not include it in my discussion.

96. China's official statistics indicate that up to early 1993 there were no Party members in 30 percent of the foreign-invested enterprises. Party organizations existed in less than 50 percent of them. Yu Yunyao, "Thought on Strengthening." One reason there were so few Party members might be the smaller likelihood of their employment by these sorts of enterprises, most of which were administrated by managers from overseas.

97. For more detailed reports on labor-capital relations in China's foreign-invested enterprises during the early 1990s, see "Labor-Capital Relations."

98. Chen Bingquan, "A Great Reform."

99. Xu Bing, "The Workers' Status."

100. Zhang Wenqi and Fang Xiangming, "The FDRS Must Be Based."

101. Chi Huiling and Jia Weizhuan, "Democratic Management."

102. SDMG, "Accelerate Development"; Guan Zaiyuan and Zhang Jianguo, "Let the Workers"; Feng Bowei, "Seriously Carry Out the Enterprise Law"; Wang Liujie, "Some Suggestions," and Ji Li, "The Important Channels," in QZGY, ed., *Minzhu Duihua,* pp. 71–76 and pp. 77–83.

103. Yuan Baohua, "State Enterprises."

104. *MB,* March 20, 1998.

105. By using the legitimate power of the workers' congress, employees also could stand up to the attempts by higher authorities to infringe upon "enterprise autonomy." Examples are found in Shen Jiali, "When Will the Controversy?"

106. Zhao Ziyang, "Report on the Work of the Government," March 25, 1987. In communist China the trade union in industrial enterprises has always existed. But it traditionally played a trivial role, its task little more than distributing movie tickets and organizing parties or tours. At the radio factory where I did fieldwork, the power of the trade union was expanded to cover issues such as housing allocation and even wage increases. But it was never made clear and concrete in Party-state documents what exactly belonged to the "welfare issues" that the trade union could decide independently.

107. Though the workers, as Walder observes, did not participate in the 1989 demonstrations in a highly organized way. Walder, "Urban Industrial Workers."

108. "CPC to Boost Ideological Work."

109. Such a provision did send an encouraging signal to resentful Party cadres. But it did not seem to have much significance because the final authority over decisionmaking was still in the hands of the director or the workers' congress. Perhaps to prevent Party cadres from taking advantage of this provision to seize power, a central Party journal recommended an example to enterprise Party committees concerning how to participate in decisionmaking and to be the "political core" of the enterprise: "The Party committee [in the Wafang Bearing Factory] participates . . . in order that the decisions made conform to the Party-state's policy and the employees' interests. But it must not dominate or take over the administrative affairs of the enterprise, and it should support the director's independent exercise of his power." See Wafang Zhouchengchang Dangwei, "Increase the Vigor."

110. The author explicitly criticized previous relevant provisions in Party-state documents that defined the role of the Party committee as that of "supervision" and "guarantee." "If Party organizations do not participate in decisionmaking," he asserted, "and if they just supervise and guarantee after the decisions are made, 'party leader-

ship' is just an empty word, because such supervision does not mean power to correct wrong decisions." He also charged that in some enterprises the director held the Party committee in contempt and never gave it a chance to participate in the policy process even if it had a strong desire to participate. See Tao Jiuyuan, "The Thinking." Given the timing of publication of this article, such a charge was suggestive. It implied that Party cadres' comeback efforts were not fruitful. One could get a strong impression that even Party leaders themselves hesitated about how to redefine the role of the Party committee in state-owned enterprises. A notice sent by the Central Committee to regional Party committees in early 1997 again underscored the "political leadership" of the Party committee in state-owned enterprises and the importance of its participation in the making of major decisions. See "The CCP Central Committee's Notice." But seven months later, at the fifteenth Party congress, it was decided that most of state-owned enterprises would be privatized.

111. See the report from Beijing, published in *SJRB*, September 24, 1994. In September 1994 a plenary session of the Central Committee passed a decision on strengthening Party-building. For the whole text, see *RMRB* (overseas edition), October 7, 1994.

112. While stressing party leadership, the Party's propaganda machine also demanded that Party cadres be satisfied with their no-power status. A *QS* article criticized those professional Party cadres who "are still obsessed with power": "They always have a sense of loss and complain that without power in hand, their opinions have no weight." See Maoming Shiyou Gongsi, "The Conception."

113. According to a survey officially conducted among leading Party cadres in state-owned enterprises and institutions at the turn of 1991, only 17 percent of Party cadres showed high morale. One of the three alleged reasons for low morale was the feeling of a large number of Party cadres that they were badly hurt or unjustly treated by the democratic enterprise reform. *SJRB*, January 31, 1992.

3

Two Systems for Electing
People's Deputies

In communist politics, elections never play as central and spectacular a role as they do in Western democratic politics. Until the late 1970s, when the CCP leaders talked about the "people's democracy" in China, they basically meant the "mass line" and mass mobilization rather than any kind of elections. In their works and speeches, voting and its association with democracy were rarely mentioned. Obviously, the CCP leaders, Mao in particular, did not intend elections to be the channels through which the people participated in the "democratic" administration of the state. During the pre-reform years, elections in China were little more than a ritual or public show, highlighting the nature of the people's congress as a rubber stamp. Elections played such a negligible part in China's political life that when the electoral system was simply abolished after 1963, not many citizens seemed to have noticed.[1]

After the electoral system was restored at the end of the 1970s, its nature and functions underwent some important changes. A couple of variables may explain these changes. As self-proclaimed Marxists, the CCP leaders placed great rhetorical emphasis upon the participation of the people in government, aiming to show the "superiority" of the communist regime to the pre-1949 Kuomintang regime and the "feudal" dynasties. To base regime legitimacy upon such propaganda claims could, under certain circumstances, embarrass the leadership. After the Cultural Revolution destroyed the credibility of Mao's "mass line," post-Mao leaders were compelled to seek a different form of "people's democracy." They found in elections—even if still ritualistic to a high degree—a new source for the legitimacy of not just the communist regime but also the new leadership.

Second, Party leaders over time seemed to believe that some popular influence on government might be helpful to the rationalization of policymaking mechanisms. Taking into consideration the past disasters of both bureaucratism and Mao's political radicalism, post-Mao leaders intended the electoral reform, as part of the broader efforts to strengthen the legal system, to bring Chinese citizens into the policymaking process through institutionalized channels. Third and most important, as economic reform introduced more market mechanisms and weakened the central planning system, it threatened the power and privileges of the entrenched Party-state bureaucracy and met with their increasing opposition. Central leaders attempted to subdue and control the bureaucracy by dividing it into three parts that would check and balance one another. A key measure of the strategy was to strengthen the people's congress and use it as a countervailing force against antireform Party cadres. To ensure successful implementation of reform policies and balance the Party committee authority, the congress must avoid functioning as merely another Party-state organ or falling entirely into the hands of Party cadres. Harnessing citizens' enthusiasm for reform, central decisionmakers tried to bring real popular voices into the legislature through more open elections of people's deputies.

This chapter is devoted to an analysis of direct and indirect elections of deputies to people's congresses at various levels. I discuss the negative correlation between the degree of openness or citizen influence and the level of election. Under the new (1979) electoral law, the principle of direct election of people's deputies applied only at the county and urban district level. Above that level, deputies were elected by those of next lower-level congresses. As with the election of chiefs in the workplace, Party leaders usually discouraged local cadres from rigging direct elections, unless challenges to party leadership occurred, so as to guarantee a certain degree of spontaneous citizen participation and representation in the people's congress, as well as impress ordinary voters with the seriousness of democratic reform. As the level of election rose, however, it became further away from the masses and closer to the central power in the Party-state hierarchy. On the one hand, "democratic symbolism" was less necessary; on the other, central leaders' concern with the political loyalty of deputies increased. It was just this concern that underlay the center's refusal to extend the principle of direct election to levels higher than the county and district. It also explains why central leaders tended to grant tacit permission to local cadres to intervene in indirect elections. The different methods and double standards the central leadership adopted in the election of people's deputies can best be explained by their awkward predicament in the political reform. They expected that deputies could bring some of the politically "harmless" people's preferences into the policy process but took every precaution against the deputies' becoming independent enough to challenge the Party center on major political and economic issues. So the center still needed Party cadres to maintain considerable control over the election of deputies, particularly those at the provincial level.

Increasing Citizen Influence over Direct Elections

The first electoral law of communist China was issued in March 1953. But from 1953 to 1979, direct elections were held only three times, in 1954, 1956, and 1963. As highly symbolic gestures, these elections were essentially part of the communist mobilizational politics. Democratic symbolism per se, though, made sense in China's historical and cultural context in which common people had no living memory of ever having been granted such a chance to "participate" in government. In these elections ordinary citizens were excluded from the nomination process, which was under the Party apparatus's complete control. All the candidates for congressional seats, like those for government offices, were designated by the Party committees of the corresponding level, based on the candidates' political loyalty, revolutionary qualifications, and patron-client ties. Any form of electoral competition was neither available nor conceivable. Since the number of candidates was exactly the same as that of positions, no choices were left for the voters. Furthermore, citizens could not refuse to go to the polls because it would be interpreted as a bad attitude toward the regime and invite political discrimination. As James Townsend observes, the election principles of the CCP in the 1950s and early 1960s aimed at "maximizing the extent of popular participation in the electoral process and minimizing the opportunity for election of candidates unacceptable to the CCP."[2]

The 1979 Electoral Law

The second electoral law was enacted on July 1, 1979. After being suspended for sixteen years, popular elections were restored. Compared with the 1953 law, the new one embodied some important innovations. First, although direct election of people's deputies in cities remained at the level of the municipal administrative district, it was extended from the township to county level in the countryside.[3] This expansion was touted to the general public as major democratic progress.[4]

Second, the procedures for nominating candidates were improved and concretized in a way that encouraged spontaneous citizen participation. The 1979 law stipulates that nomination of candidates can be made by the CCP, various democratic parties, mass organizations, or any voter seconded by no less than three others. The final list of candidates must be worked out through "discussion and consultation" among the voters or by a primary vote. Moreover, ordinary voters—like the parties and organizations—were equally entitled to use various forms of publicity to support their candidates. In the 1953 law, the right of voters to nominate candidates was stated in an ambiguous and abstract way. In fact, there were no feasible means available for such nomination.

Third, under the new law the number of candidates in direct elections should be 50 to 100 percent larger than the actual number to be elected, offering voters some limited choices. (This new system, established to create a modest amount of competition among candidates, is called *cha'e xuanju* in Chinese, which means "difference election." For ease of understanding, I refer to it as "competitive election.") The new law also provided that all voting must be conducted by secret ballot rather than a show of hands.[5] In addition, constituents were theoretically conferred discretionary power to supervise and recall their representatives. Since July 1979, direct elections have been held six times, in 1979–1981, 1983–1984, 1986–1987, 1989–1990, 1992–1993, and 1997–1998.[6]

After two tentative elections in some areas in late 1979 and early 1980, nationwide direct elections began in late 1980 and were completed by the end of 1981. Meanwhile, the Central Committee urged local Party committees to guarantee the "unobstructed" exercise of voters' democratic rights and not to make elections deceptive or pure ceremony.[7] In contrast with the practice in Mao's China, the authorities did not caution the electorate to show support for Party candidates but instead appealed to them not just to participate in electoral activities but also to vote for their favorite candidates, defying any possible manipulation or interference from cadres. Denouncing Party cadres' autocratic style as the "biggest obstacle" to democratic elections, a *Renmin Ribao* (*RMRB*) editorial demanded waging a "resolute struggle against any violation of the legal stipulations" regarding direct elections.[8]

"Antisystem" Election Campaigns

Like the budding economic reforms and open-door policy, the restoration of parliamentary elections was taken by the mass public as the sign of a promising new era. But the degree of enthusiasm for elections varied among social strata. The crackdown on the democracy movement in late 1979 forced liberal reformers to turn to legal channels to participate in and influence Chinese politics. Electoral reform seemed to provide them with an opportunity.[9] Since such reformers concentrated in universities and colleges, spontaneous election campaigns first started there.

Direct elections tended to be more competitive and politically irritating in university campuses than elsewhere. The most radical electoral activities occurred in Peking University (Beida). Under the protection of some open-minded university officials, the election evolved into a somewhat Western-style campaign. More than ten students with different political viewpoints and backgrounds ran in 1980 for deputy of the Haidian District (an administrative district of Beijing). Most of the candidates had their own electoral programs and campaign teams, and they engaged in debates that challenged orthodox ideology and political taboo. The antisystem campaigning escalated in the later stages of the campaign, some students publicly questioning the leading role of the CCP. One poster, for example, argued that the CCP was not qualified to lead the Chinese revolution and reforms. Speeches went far beyond the ideological limits set by the authorities but received cheers from the audience.[10]

In other universities in Beijing, competition among the candidates was equally intense, but the campaign style and speeches were less politicized. Most candidates adopted the strategy of making promises on concrete issues. Generally, the first direct elections in these campuses unfolded in a politically tolerant context and did look like an embryonic form of free elections.[11]

The unprecedented election campaigns in Peking University drew much attention, particularly from Western media. Some reports tended to treat Peking University as a typical rather than a unique case and led Western audiences to overestimate the democratic initiative of Chinese voters. Reporters expected the people's grievances to translate into anti-Party or antisystem voting behavior.[12] Although political debate could also be heard occasionally in the elections at a few other universities, such as Fudan University in Shanghai, Heilongjiang University in Ha'erbin and Hunan Normal College in Changsha, macropolitics was far from becoming a hot theme (au. int.). The spontaneous race seen in most of Beijing's universities could rarely be found beyond the capital city.

Party Cadres' Obstruction of Elections

Despite warnings from Beijing, local cadres' violation of the electoral law was reportedly widespread. Some cases were spotlighted because the illegal behavior aroused strong protest among the voters. A peasant with Party membership wrote an anonymous letter to a law journal and complained about the cadres' "undisguised" manipulation of elections in his region. According to him, the Party secretary demanded that every Party member, Communist League member, and cadre pledge to vote for the candidates he designated or it would be regarded as a violation of Party discipline.[13] *Shanxi Ribao* (*SXRB*) reported several cases of rural cadres' employing trickery to infringe upon the voters' legitimate rights in elections. In one electoral district, the cadres watched as voters filled out their ballots and "advised" them to vote for their nominees. In another district the election committee added a cadre to the list of congressional deputies by forging ballots. When the authorities sent an investigation team there, the local cadres "took advantage of their power and positions to seek revenge against those who exposed their mistakes."[14] All these reports concerning cadres' attempts to circumvent electoral law or intimidate voters seemed to upset central leaders and frustrated their intentions for elections. In a public warning to local authorities, they condemned some "leading" local cadres for being "deeply infused with feudalistic autocratic thought."[15] In a summarizing report, the top central election official, Cheng Zihua, pledged to fight some "grave" problems with local election cadres.[16]

First Revision of the 1979 Law

The first nationwide direct election held during 1979–1981 was by nature experimental. The leadership saw it as a test of societal responses by which they could determine how far they needed to go with electoral reforms in meeting popular expectations. Liberal reformers saw it as a test of the ideological and political limits. Ultimately, however, both tests failed to yield definite results because local Party cadres, as the executors of the electoral reform, were in a position to make a big difference in the degree of electoral openness and freedom. Unlike the elections of workplace chiefs or government officials, direct elections of people's deputies did not immediately threaten these cadres' authority, at least during the initial years, when the congress still had no teeth. Tolerance toward politically "improper" campaign speeches varied greatly with local cadres' personal inclinations. Hu Ping won the most votes in the Peking University district through his advocacy of freedom of expression. Even though he spoke like a dissident, the authorities acknowledged his election and qualifications as a congressional deputy.[17] In the graduate school of the Chinese Academy of Sciences, Chen Ziming, a liberal scholar, made critical speeches and was elected as well. As he recalled, he did not get into trouble for political deviation because he enjoyed the protection of the Party committee in his school.[18] Cao Changqing was not so lucky: He won a high percentage of the votes in the Heilongjiang University district of Ha'erbin, but the local authorities refused to confirm his election because of his "extremist views and wrong ideological orientation."[19]

Signs of "bourgeois liberalization" in the direct elections of some universities apparently upset a number of Party leaders. Both the Party Ministry of Propaganda and the Ministry of Higher Learning urged the leading cadres in Peking University to stop the Western-style competitions and penalize those students involved. But encouraged by the ambiguous attitude of some top-level leaders who managed to keep their promise not to interfere, the university cadres refused to yield to the pressure from above.[20] Later, in a gesture that was quite unusual, Party general secretary Hu Yaobang met with the election activists of some of Beijing's universities. Using obscure language, Hu gave what seemed to be his approval of their campaigns: "I do not think campaigning is wrong," he was quoted as saying, "but even if what you do is right, it does not necessarily mean that you are wise. It is a wise man who does right things at a right place and at a right time."[21]

But the situation was soon clarified. Even Hu could not resist heavy pressure from within the central leadership to prohibit campaigning against the system. In his report to a session of the National People's Congress summarizing the first direct elections, Cheng Zihua bitterly denounced the Western-style electoral activities.[22] Unlike the rhetorical or symbolic reprimands of local cadres who broke electoral law, the condemnation of the antisystem campaigners did not just look harsh on paper but translated into revenge once the opportunity arose. One or two years after the 1980 elections in Peking University, graduating students who had challenged party leadership and questioned the political system faced unemployment and other struggles. Hu Ping could not find a job for three years. Some of his fellow students were sent to poor and remote areas; others saw their applications for graduate studies blocked (au. int.).

The discriminatory actions taken by the leadership against antireform cadres and antisystem candidates reflected a basic contradiction in the electoral reform. As they made tentative efforts to transform elections from sheer symbolism into more substance, the leaders were extremely fearful that political opposition might emerge through legalized channels to threaten the regime.[23] As Brantly Womack observes in his study of the 1980 county-level elections in China, since the election reform is a creature of established political power, "its threat to the establishment makes it vulnerable to a policy reversal."[24] In 1982 the electoral law was revised. Article 30 in the 1979 version provided that political parties, mass organizations, and voters were entitled to use "various forms of publicity" to support their candidates. In 1982 this article was amended to read: "The election committees should introduce the candidates to the voters; the political parties, mass organizations, and voters who recommend the candidates can introduce them at group meetings of the voters." According to an official interpreter, the original stipulation was revised because it was not strictly defined and too easily misunderstood and misused. "For example, in some places," he claimed, "a few candidates imitated bourgeois campaigning. They delivered campaign speeches that produced politically harmful effects and also put up confusing posters irrelevant to the elections."[25] But the alteration—aimed at eliminating the possibility of appealing directly to voters with antiregime messages—raised much controversy among legal scholars. Some openly questioned its justifications.[26]

In the second (1983–1984) and third (1986–1987) direct elections, much less discussion on political issues among the candidates was reported. This trend toward electoral "depoliticization" might reasonably be attributed to the revision of the electoral law. And it also indicated the effectiveness of the authorities' strategy of "killing the chicken to frighten the monkeys." On the one hand, to leave the democratic image of the election unstained, the authorities tried to play down or cover up the penalties for the antisystem candidates. On the other, they sent a clear message to intimidate potential political troublemakers, and deterred them from deviating into bourgeois liberalism. But the "various forms of publicity," though deleted from the law, were not explicitly prohibited, thanks to the pressure mainly from the intellectual community as

well as the divergence of opinions in leadership circles (au. int.). Thus, courageous dissidents could still voice their political views openly and be elected.
For example, in 1987 Li Shuxian, wife of famous dissident Fang Lizhi, demanded the removal of the ban on free thinking and called upon her audience
to rise up for democratization. She won 89 percent of the vote and was overwhelmingly elected.[27] As a U.S.-based journal of Chinese dissidents commented, it showed that Chinese citizens should and could "exploit every opportunity available to strive for more political rights."[28]

In the conflict of opinions discernible from the confused and changing
signals coming out of Beijing, the hard-liners obviously got the upper hand
over the reformers regarding the handling of the antisystem campaigns. Since
Deng set forth party leadership as the highest principle, any politically
provocative election campaigns would place the more liberal leaders in such
an embarrassing position that they could hardly voice any support for these
campaigns. Nevertheless, the compromise and consensus-building between
reformers and hard-liners that characterized "Politburo politics" under Deng
softened the latter's stand and allowed elected deputies like Li to get away
with anti-Party speeches. As Li's election and her performance as a deputy
manifested, even some Party elders widely seen as political hard-liners took
care to avoid an antireform image and showed a willingness to respect electoral law and election outcomes (au. int.).

Second Revision of the 1979 Law

Despite some seemingly isolated campaigns against the system, Party leaders
appeared impressed with the positive results of citizens' "depoliticized" participation in elections. They openly expressed sympathy for voters who foiled
local cadres' attempts to rig elections and acknowledged their "wisdom" in
electing good candidates.[29] Aside from the apparent purpose of creating democratic credibility for the regime, this well-publicized endorsement of citizen
initiative also seemed to reflect a consensus within the central leadership to
make direct elections as "free and fair" as possible, provided that the one-
party system was not touched. Even so, Party leaders' rhetoric against local
election officials' abuse of power did not turn into disciplinary action. The
1982 revision of the electoral law involved no notable alterations to prevent
local cadres from obstructing the implementation of the law or effectively
guarantee the fairness of the election process. On the contrary, as mentioned,
the revision discouraged campaigning and was virtually a retreat from the
1979 law. Unless local cadres were deadly serious about reform and politically courageous as well, candidates would not be offered the chance to make
public speeches or advertise their viewpoints. This was particularly to the dis-
advantage of the obscure candidates without any organizational backing, who
badly needed such opportunities to make themselves known to the voters and

hence compete with the Party cadres and professionals who easily garnered publicity. In the 1983–1984 nationwide elections, the 1982 revision proved a disaster in terms of social reaction. A survey conducted by a group of scholars in March 1985 showed that 42.8 percent of the citizens said they had little or no interest in elections of people's deputies; only 25.6 percent gave serious thought to their votes. Just 19.7 percent of the surveyed voters thought the elected deputies were qualified, whereas 58.5 percent did not even know who the elected deputies were or what they had done for the constituents.[30]

The failure of the electoral reform to meet the electorate's expectation—one of the main purposes of the reform for regime legitimation—was certainly among the considerations that compelled a second revision of the electoral law in 1986. But the crucial factor might be found in the perceived pressing need for real and substantial institutional reform at this point. As discussed in Chapter 5, in a new wave of political reform the people's congress was expected to play a balancing role vis-à-vis Party cadres and government officials to ensure the smooth execution of economic reform programs. But it was becoming quite clear that the potential enthusiasm for reform on the part of people's congresses could not be converted into an institutional capacity, or a certain degree of legislative autonomy, required for effective balancing, could not be achieved unless vigorous actions were taken to weaken Party cadres' control over the nomination and election of people's deputies and hence over congresses.

Arising from these considerations, the article concerning nomination of candidates was modified once again in 1986: Nomination of candidates was to be made by the various political parties, mass organizations, or any voter who obtained the endorsement of no less than nine others. The meaning of the new regulation has to be analyzed in its specific context. Given the de facto exclusion of ordinary citizens from the nominating process in many areas, this revision in effect favored the increase of popular influence in a couple of ways. First, it stripped away the special privileges of the CCP in nominating candidates and at least nominally placed it on a level with the "democratic parties" (*minzhu dangpai*). Although these parties theoretically had to accept the CCP leadership and were essentially no different from satellite parties, some of their members—particularly the young and newly recruited—were trying to develop a fresh sense of party identity and to seek more organizational independence from the CCP (au. int.). With legal status equal to that of the CCP in recommending candidates for people's deputies, these parties gained influence. Second, raising (from four to ten) the number of voters it took to nominate candidates perhaps should not be seen as deliberate discouragement of voter initiative. As official judgment later showed, it instead served to "make the [free] nominations more thoughtful and the candidates more electable."[31] Probably under instructions from the Party center, supplementary administrative regulations were announced in some regions to ensure that Party cadres would not rig the nomination process. In Beijing, candidates nominated by political parties and mass organizations could not exceed 20 percent of the total number.[32] In Shanghai and Guangzhou, they could not exceed 15 percent.[33]

An increase in the number of spontaneously nominated and elected congressional deputies was evident in the 1986–1987 direct elections in some areas. Two legal scholars in Nanjing found that in Baixia District and Liuhe County, 75 and 88 percent of the voters participated in the nomination of candidates, respectively. The first-round nominations produced 1,992 and 2,824 candidates. Among them, 98 and 99 percent were nominated by the masses. A total of 68 and 86 percent of the voters took part in the second-round nominations, called "democratic consultation." At the final stage, the number of the candidates on the formal list was reduced to 338 and 492, from whom 197 and 279 deputies were to be elected. Among these candidates, 307 and 459 were originally recommended by the masses, whereas only 31 and 33 were chosen by the parties and organizations.[34] Although these data might be inaccurate, the basic conclusion did not deviate far from the results of both my own interviews and other unofficial sources.[35] An NPC report claimed that more citizen participation in the election process improved the quality of the deputies. Of 0.57 million deputies at the county level, those who had received higher education increased from 11.2 percent (1983–1984) to 14.8 percent (1986–1987) and 16.6 percent (1989–1990); the illiterate deputies decreased from 2.7 percent to 0.9 percent (1986–1987).[36]

As a county congress official who well knew the "secrecy" of the Chinese elections explained, the critical source of citizen influence is the "right to *nominate* the candidates for deputies."[37] In that regard the "people power" seemed to rise to new heights in the 1992–1993 elections, contrary to what one might imagine after Tiananmen. In some areas, such as the districts of Wuxi, the percentage of the candidates nominated by the citizens reached a record high, ranging from 40 to 70 by a conservative estimate (au. int.). In the process of "consultation," aimed to cut the number of candidates to that stipulated for the final competitive election, the constituents took a tougher stand against Party cadres and pressed election officials to put more citizen-nominated candidates on the formal list. In two counties of Jiangsu, some township congressional deputies organized the voters in a boycott. They took joint actions to reject all the candidates recommended by the cadres who failed to respond to the demands of the masses.[38] In the 1997–1998 direct elections, more than 60 percent of the candidates were selected by the citizens in some counties.[39] An official source claimed that in "many" areas, citizen nominees constituted 50 to 90 percent of the (final) candidates.[40] But Party leaders' discouragement of using various forms of publicity to support candidates led to an underrepresentation of ordinary citizens among deputies.[41] A study of two district congresses of Shanghai found that Party cadres and factory managers were overrepresented, resulting partly from their famous names as well as established social networks. In these two districts, 59 percent and 69 percent of the deputies were Party members. Most were cadres.[42]

Electoral campaigning may become the cause of confrontation between Party leaders and citizens. A survey found that 47.2 percent of the voters (75.7 percent among those with higher education) were displeased with the simplistic way the authorities stipulated they get to know the candidates. As many as 67.5 percent of the voters generally favored the introduction of campaigning into the electoral system.[43] In the late 1980s, some liberal scholars appealed for the reappraisal of the 1980 election campaigns in Beijing's universities. One defended campaigning for its positive effects in acquainting the constituency with the candidates and in producing a more responsive government.[44] Another argued that election campaigns embodied the principle of equal opportunity and fair competition.[45] This debate lasted into the 1990s. A legal scholar blamed the lack of campaigns in elections—which caused many to be elected against their own will—for the deputies' indifference to their duties.[46]

An analysis of voting behavior may suggest that it is inappropriate to interpret citizen support for election campaigning as an intention to turn campaigns into a form of political opposition. But some social groups, such as the intelligentsia and students—upon whom Western values of democracy had produced a greater impact—did make every effort to expand political freedoms through election campaigns (au. int.). In any case, despite the appeal and pressure mainly from the intellectual community, when the electoral law was revised for the third time in 1995, still no mention was made about the "forms of publicity" or campaigning.[47] The leadership's refusal to yield, to be sure, reminded people of the limits of the reform: Institutionalized popular participation in the governmental process had to be rendered completely risk-free to Deng's regime. And the chance that dissidents would get into congresses by taking advantage of electoral procedures had to be minimized.[48] But since campaigning as an electoral form was not illegal, the political tolerance of local cadres and the courage of the candidates could make a difference.

Indirect Elections: How Popular Will Is Deflected

For Party leaders, direct elections performed two major functions whose priority shifted back and forth. The first function was its democratic symbolism; that was the main objective of the political reform of the early 1980s. As economic reform turned around in the mid-1980s, the election gradually acquired a substantial content and was aimed more toward making the legislature a balancing actor in the policy process. But how could direct elections at the county level affect the power structure of government above that level? Or to what extent could the "people power"—which Deng came to find instrumental to his purposes—be brought by direct elections into China's political structure at large? The role of people's deputies over government versus Party cadres at the same administrative level is discussed in Chapter 7. Here I explore how direct elections influenced elections of people's deputies at higher levels and what political implications it had.

What Is the Meaning of the Indirect Election?

We might begin by analyzing how the leadership explained the role of direct elections in the "democratization" of the governmental process. In 1980 Peng Zhen, a senior Party and legislative leader, painted a rosy picture of Chinese democracy arising from direct elections. He argued:

> Direct elections at the county level were the foundation for the elections of organs of state power at all levels throughout the country. Holding direct elections at the county level enables the people to exercise direct control over the county people's congress. The county people's congress will elect its standing committee, the county people's government and deputies to the people's congress at the provincial level. The provincial people's congress will elect its standing committee, the provincial people's government and deputies to the NPC. Thus, through people's deputies, people's congresses and their standing committees, and people's governments, the people of the whole country can manage state affairs and master their own destiny as well as the destiny of the nation and the state.[49]

This statement was partially correct in that if direct elections were made really free and fair, citizens would be able to have some say in local government—perhaps some control over part of "their own destiny." But in China's electoral system, the direct election of county-level congressional deputies hardly meant citizens' practical management of government affairs. The actual power, if any, directly elected deputies were granted constitutionally was limited to only the lowest levels (county, township, and urban district) of government. Under the system of indirect election of congressional deputies above the county level, the popular will embodied in direct elections was increasingly weakened as the level of election rose. It essentially evaporated once elections reached to the top leadership. The direct election was therefore too negligible to have any substantial impact on the issues of national politics or on the decisionmaking process at the highest level. To understand the power-related differences between direct and indirect elections, some knowledge about China's hierarchical structure of government and its electoral system is helpful (see Figure 3.1).

Figure 3.1   China's Electoral System Since 1979

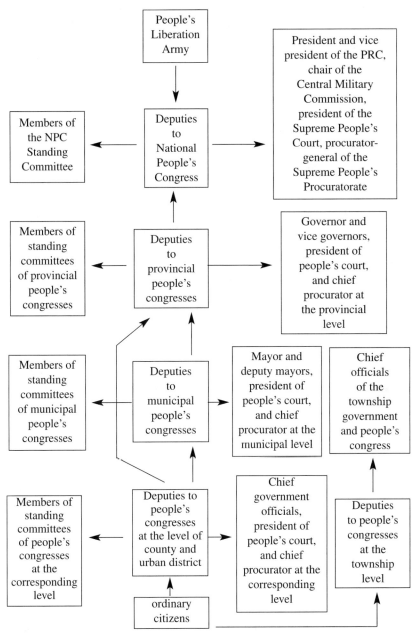

Note: Arrows indicate who elects whom. See note 49. At the central level, the premier and cabinet members, nominated by the PRC president and premier respectively, must be approved by NPC deputies by vote.

The administrative hierarchy in China is divided into five levels: township; county and municipal district (this level also includes small cities without administrative districts); city; province (including "autonomous regions" such as Tibet and Xinjiang and municipalities directly under the central government such as Beijing, Shanghai, Tianjin, and Chongqing); and the central government in Beijing. A people's congress exists at each level. An outstanding feature of China's 1979 electoral reform was to enhance direct elections from the township to the county level. Deputies to the people's congress above the county or municipal district level were elected by the deputies at the next lower level. For example, only the deputies of a provincial congress were qualified to elect the deputies to the NPC. They themselves were elected by municipal and county congress deputies. In principle, government officials were elected by the people's deputies of the same administrative level.

Thus the higher the level of congress, the more distant the election of its deputies from the ordinary people. As the congress gained some institutional muscle, especially after the mid-1980s, in relation to the Party committee and government of the corresponding level, indirect elections—the election of NPC deputies in particular—became increasingly critical to the central efforts to restructure power above the county level. Peng Zhen's bewitching description of the democratizing role of the legislature would perhaps be more realistic if indirect elections were held in at least as "free and fair" a way as were direct elections and if elected deputies at all levels performed as trustworthy representatives of their constituents. But as the level of elections went up, the cadre control tightened and popular influence weakened. If dissidents like Li Shuxian could still manage to get into county-level congresses through direct elections, it was extremely unlikely in indirect elections. In many areas, local cadres' manipulation of the procedures of indirect elections was effective enough to prevent those whom the cadres considered to be politically dangerous from being elected or even making the roster of candidates.

Article 28 of the electoral law provides that when deputies of a regional people's congress elect deputies of the higher-level congress, the presidium of the regional congress collects the names of the candidates nominated by various political parties, mass organizations, and deputies and submits them to all the deputies for deliberation, discussion, and consultation. The final candidates are determined on the basis of the preferences of the majority of the deputies.

A careful reading of the article suggests that except for the "deliberation, discussion, and consultation"—ambiguous terms typical of communist propaganda—there are no institutional guarantees of a democratic process. There are no specific procedures for the expression and serious consideration of deputies' preferences. Xie Qichen, a legal expert and close observer of elections, describes the typical process of indirect elections this way: The most powerful actor was the organizational department of the Party committee at the corresponding level. Before a people's congress convened, the cadres of this department would submit to the Party secretary a tentative list of candidates for the next-higher congressional seats. After consulting with the heads of relevant Party and government departments, the Party committee presented this list in its name to the congressional presidium. The presidium circulated the roster among the deputies for "discussion" and additions. The presidium collected comments and suggestions from the deputies and determined the final list of candidates for competitive election. Xie observes that in the whole process the masses were complete outsiders. Even ordinary deputies had few or no chances to inquire about the candidates.[50]

Party Cadres' Role in Indirect Elections

Indirect elections, then, were mainly deputies' business and on the whole closed to the public. Compared with direct elections, they appeared to be less exciting. In fact, very few public reports on details of indirect elections ever appeared. Party leaders also rarely referred in public to violations of legal provisions relating to indirect elections. The noticeable silence on this matter seemed to result from certain political considerations. First, Party cadres in charge of indirect elections ranked higher than those involved in direct elections. Some of them, especially those at the provincial level, could even reach central leaders' personal clientele networks or become their constituents in the Central Committee. So central leaders had to be careful not to offend them. To be sure, no evidence was available that the central authorities issued any definite directives to limit public reports, good or bad, on indirect elections (au. int.). But if they had wanted to see more reports, they could have conveniently done so through the propaganda machine in their hands. Second, the obvious reluctance of central leaders to bring indirect elections into the open exposed the electoral reform as in part propaganda strategy. Ordinary citizens' expectations of democracy were supposed to have been met by direct elections. Since the masses were neither involved in nor had much knowledge about indirect elections, they would take it for granted that indirect elections were at least as democratic as direct elections (au. int.). Negative reports about them would only disillusion citizens and dampen their enthusiasm for direct elections.[51]

The mass media under a communist system usually keep bad news under wraps. Since publications provided little information, my field research during 1989–1990 focused on indirect elections. I tested the relevant data once again in my second round of fieldwork in 1996.[52] My findings offer a glimpse of how indirect elections were actually conducted at the municipal level. China's electoral reform during most of the 1990s—in terms of legal procedures and degree of openness or fairness—was largely frozen at the 1988 level.

My interviews with election officials and congressional deputies produced slightly different versions. According to a senior official of the Wuxi municipal congress, the candidates for the municipal congressional seats were nominated in two ways. First, Party cadres of various administrative districts and government bureaus recommended candidates on the basis of the "mass opinions," as the quota and proportion of representation required. These candidates were then introduced to the deputies of each district congress. Thereafter, these district deputies collected comments from the masses and, after consultation among themselves, determined the final list of candidates. This way more or less conformed to what Xie describes as the typical process, from the initial submission of the names of candidates to the making of the final list. There was also a second method for nomination that Xie fails to mention. A small number (10–30 percent) of the candidates were handpicked by the municipal Party committee. Through the "consultation with various democratic parties and mass organizations," the municipal Party committee directly added to the final list some candidates who did not have an identifiable constituency.[53] Without question, the Party cadres placed special significance on the election of these candidates.[54]

For their part, the deputies told somewhat different, more detailed inside stories about their elections. One, a well-known local physician, was a deputy of the Wuxi municipal congress and a member in its standing committee. He was not a CCP member but a member of a satellite party. Before his election in 1987, he was not a deputy of any district congress, though he was a member of the Chongan District branch of the Chinese People's Political Consultative Conference (CPPCC).[55] Since he took an active part in the discussion on government affairs at CPPCC meetings, he felt that he had made a good impression on the Party cadres. A cadre from the election office of Chongan District visited his hospital and found out what his colleagues thought of him—the only link in the election process that involved the masses. After consulting the hospital's Party committee, this cadre talked with the physician and asked his views on some issues. The physician then attended a meeting of the ten candidates for the municipal congress from Chongan. The topic of the meeting was: "If you are elected, what role will you play?" No sensitive political questions were raised. The physician spoke about how to improve health care and environmental sanitation. The cadres presiding over the meeting noticed his "excellent" speech and immediately decided to add him to the final candidates. For a period after that, he was, it seemed, forgotten. Then one day he was suddenly informed that he had been elected to the tenth municipal congress by the deputies of his district's congress.

As he recalled, at no point in the whole process was he asked if he himself wished to be a people's deputy. He was totally ignorant of the information about him that was circulated among the district's deputies, that is, his constituents. In fact, as he frankly admitted, he had neither enthusiasm nor time for the job as deputy. "But if the cadres settled on you and the deputies elected you even against your own wishes, you have to accept it anyway. Otherwise you run counter to the expectation of the Party and the people." Indeed, he considered his election a reflection of the Party's trust in him. In his view it was improbable that someone like him would be directly elected by the masses because "the masses usually voted for CCP members and model workers."

The physician's account of his election was confirmed by two other deputies: a famous model worker of a large grocery and a CCP member and an automobile mechanic in a factory who was not a Party member. Despite the differences in profession, party affiliation, sex, and age among the three, their elections shared certain key features: First, they were nominated directly by the cadres in their district or work unit, not by district congressional deputies. In fact, this practice should not be considered a violation of electoral law, which provided that parties, organizations, and deputies are equally qualified to nominate candidates. If the deputies abandoned their right to do so, the cadres theoretically were not to blame. A crucial difference between direct and indirect elections was that in the former case nomination of candidates by parties and organizations was officially dissuaded or even strictly limited to a certain percentage in some areas, and it was therefore more likely for many, if not most, of the candidates on the final list to be nominated by the masses.

Second, the three deputies never expressed any interest in the seat. And their own opinions were not solicited beforehand. They had no idea who nominated them until after being elected. As the mechanic recalled, a quota of municipal people's deputies was allocated to his factory. To keep an "appropriate" mix among the deputies, it was demanded that this quota be filled by an ordinary worker with no party affiliation. The mechanic speculated that he was selected because he worked diligently and was on friendly terms with both the cadres and his colleagues. In addition, none of the three deputies ever campaigned to win votes among the district deputies. As the grocery worker observed, there were occasional attempts to canvass votes. But these activities were organized not by the candidates themselves but by the cadres of their work units or districts, in the hope that the election of one or more deputies from their jurisdiction might bring tangible benefits, such as a certain amount of influence over government policy.

Third, they were totally ignorant of the election process. They were not asked to prepare a résumé and knew nothing about the materials by which the deputies got to know them or how many deputies actually voted for them. The mechanic was quite surprised when he first learned of his election from the newspaper.

As the law required, the three municipal deputies participated in the election of deputies to the Jiangsu provincial congress. The candidates for the provincial congress were of two kinds: those—most of whom were celebrities—put forward by the provincial Party committee whom the cadres in charge explicitly warned were must-elect candidates and those who were usually recommended by municipal Party and government departments. For each candidate, a résumé (generally not prepared by the nominee) was distributed among the deputies, and basically ceremonial discussions were held before the election began. Most candidates for the provincial congress were not selected from among the municipal deputies.

An empirical study by Xu Zhifu found that although over 85 percent of the (final) candidates were chosen by the masses in direct elections in Jiangsu, most candidates in indirect elections were selected by the Party and "mass" organizations. He gave an example to illustrate how far cadres' selections might deviate from popular preferences. After a leading cadre of a university lost the (direct) election for a district congressional seat, the Party department nominated him for the provincial congress (two levels higher than the district congress), and he was elected. The residents in his district complained that it was unbelievable that a person who failed to win enough votes to be even a district deputy could be elected to the provincial congress.[56] Another study found that when the authorities announced that some people were candidates, their closest colleagues were taken aback, a clear indication that such candidacy had no popular base at all.[57] In the 1992–1993 elections in a county of Jiangsu, all candidates for the next higher-level congress were "suggested" by the Party committee. Many deputies simply boycotted the election.[58] In a closed-door meeting, Hu Jingtao, a member of the Politburo standing committee, mentioned a number of "scandals" in the 1992–1993 indirect elections of municipal and provincial deputies. He charged that in some cities and provinces the elections were organized in an extremely irresponsible way. The election officials did not prepare even the simplest résumés for candidates, and some "local leading cadres" privately determined the final list of candidates and issued "internal directives" regarding which candidates the deputies must vote for or against.[59]

The strong tendency of Party cadres to control indirect elections arose perhaps partially from the expansion of legislative power, which made cadres want to land their own people in congresses. Also, the critical remarks from the Party center were neither publicized nor followed by firm action to eliminate election scandals. Contrasting sharply with that in direct elections, just 10 to 20 percent of candidates were on the final list in indirect elections nominated by deputies.[60] Among them the percentage of those elected was even lower. The official statistics concerning the 1987–1988 indirect elections in twenty-seven provinces revealed that of the 646 final candidates on average for each provincial congress, only 105 (16 percent) were nominated by municipal or county-level deputies; a mere twelve of them (2.5 percent) got elected.[61]

As Party cadre influence accrued layer by layer in indirect elections—especially when the NPC deputies were elected at the provincial level—one could hardly expect any significant initiatives from the constituents (i.e., next lower-level deputies). A 1991 NPC brochure disclosed the following data: In 1988, 2,970 deputies to the NPC were elected from among 3,872 candidates by provincial congressional deputies. Of these candidates, 84.9 percent (3,286) were nominated by the political parties (mainly the CCP); 14.9 percent (586) were jointly nominated by the deputies. After the "democratic consultation," 3,549 remained on the final list. And 93.7 percent of them (3,327) were those originally nominated by the parties, and only 6.3 percent (222) by the deputies. Among the candidates picked by deputies, twenty-eight were elected—that is, only 0.94 percent of the NPC deputies were originally recommended by provincial deputies.[62]

Problems with Deputy Initiative

Yet it was not entirely unlikely for popular will to play a part in indirect elections. People's deputies had three levers to affect elections. The first was the right to nominate candidates. Any deputy seconded by no less than nine others could put forward a candidate. The second was at the stage of "consultation and discussion." No matter which level of cadres or leaders had nominated the candidates, deputies could still have the names removed from the final list. Since cadres were usually cautioned to "respect" the opinions of deputies—and doing so demonstrated that the cadres were genuine reformers—a candidate rejected by a large number of deputies had much difficulty getting onto the final roster (au. int.). Third, even if candidates managed to get on, the deputies could vote them out in competitive election.

It could be assumed that Party cadres always tried to maximize their authority and expand their personal influence by discouraging any deputy initiative. But did people's deputies think that the process of indirect election—whose outcome they themselves were supposed to determine—was democratic? If not, why didn't they protest against it? What were the main obstacles to their exercise of constitutionally conferred powers?

Indeed, not every deputy was happy with the Party role in indirect elections or chose to keep silent about it. Zhang Songquan, a municipal deputy in Jiangxi, denounced the organization department of the provincial Party committee for its attempt to have the election of deputies to the provincial congress proceed exactly in line with its arrangement.[63] In the 1992–1993 elections of NPC deputies, more than 1,500 provincial deputies reportedly abstained or spoiled their ballots.[64] In Hebei Province some deputies wrote "protest" and "predetermined" (*nei ding*) on their ballots. In fifteen provinces formal elections did not start until one or more "rehearsals" were held and the cadres rested assured that their favorite nominees would not be voted out.[65]

Nevertheless, it seems that the deputies so critical of the cadres' manipulation of indirect elections were few. And most of their grievances did not escalate to outright rebellion. Most of the congressional deputies I spoke to in 1989 and 1996 did not bother to conceal their dissatisfaction with the "weak function" of the congress in contrast to that of the municipal Party committee. But they voiced no vehement complaints about the process of indirect elections either. Neither did they mention resentment in that regard among their congressional colleagues. Although this apparent apathy or tolerance might seem to suggest that deputies lack a certain democratic ardor or sense of accountability to their constituents, several structural factors practically obstructed deputy initiative and assertiveness.

First, the discouragement of campaigning made it technically difficult for people's deputies to nominate candidates. In direct elections many candidates were nominated by citizens because there was daily personal contact between them; citizens knew these candidates quite well. As a rule, people's deputies at all levels in China were not professional.[66] They had to perform their duties as deputies in their spare time and got together only when the congress was in session (once a year for only three to four weeks). Therefore, deputies had few opportunities to get to know one another. And there was no satisfactory basis for them to assess who among their colleagues was better qualified for a seat in the next higher level of congress (au. int.). Moreover, deputies directly elected by the masses at the county or district level tended to be popular cadres, model workers, brilliant professionals, or people who stood out in other ways. It was difficult for such deputies to find similarly qualified people for even higher positions. They had no alternative but to choose, through competitive elections, from among the candidates settled on by Party cadres (au. int.). Second, because popular cadres, singers, athletes, and other celebrities were most electable, Party cadres fixed upon them as potential candidates for direct elections.[67] Many were not political activists and had no interest whatsoever in being elected.[68]

A vicious circle was evident in indirect elections. In the nomination and (indirect) election of people's deputies at one level higher than the county or urban district (that is, the municipal or provincial level), Party cadres usually wielded more discretion than in direct elections. As the level of election rose, so did the level of cadre influence. To be elected (read "appointed") a congressional deputy was generally regarded as an honor and a sign of high social status.[69] To the extent elections were rigged by cadres, deputies owed their seats primarily to the Party. As a Chinese observer mocked, in sessions of congress many deputies did nothing but keep saying, "Thank the Party. Thank the leaders."[70] Since their own seats were essentially granted by the cadres, they tended passively to accept the lists of candidates cadres supplied for the next higher congress. To some extent, it was a return of favor (au. int.).

Meanings of the Double Standard

In the Party-sponsored electoral reform, the central leadership apparently applied a double standard to congressional elections to serve their political purposes. By limiting the number of Party nominees in direct elections, among other things, the leadership did make some sincere attempts to protect citizens against local (low-ranking) cadres' interference and manipulation.[71] But they never made equally serious efforts to dissuade Party cadres from attempting to monopolize nominations in indirect elections. An NPC document acknowledged the different approaches toward the nominations jointly made by deputies and admitted that some cadres did not respect the deputies' right to nominate. "They always hope that congressional deputies will not exercise that right spontaneously. In some areas they tried to persuade deputies' nominees not to accept nomination or requested the deputies to withdraw it." With profound implications, the document departed from its usually harsh comments on this kind of overbearing cadre. It fell short of denouncing this behavior as undemocratic or law breach, but just explained it away as a "divergence in understanding (of the electoral law)."[72]

The Party center of course acted deliberately when it turned a blind eye to local cadres' attempts to control indirect elections or gave them a simple slap on the wrist. Yet there is no evidence that the leaders in Beijing explicitly instructed or encouraged local cadres to rig indirect elections to guarantee the election of their favorite people.[73] Then again, as any local cadre knows, the absence of criticism from above implies tacit consent or approval in Chinese politics (au. int.). It is therefore reasonable to suspect that cadres kept a hand in indirect elections not just to maximize power but to comply with the hidden agenda of the Party center. Conflicts still existed, though, between Party leaders and local cadres over the degree of control.

Corresponding perfectly with its varying attitudes toward cadre domination in direct and indirect elections, the Party propaganda machine applied quite different criteria to measure the extent of electoral "democratization." The democratic nature of direct elections was allegedly embodied in the increasing number of candidates nominated by the masses. By contrast, the assertion about the popular base of indirect elections was founded, quite paradoxically, upon the improvement in elected deputies' cultural quality, their younger age, and the reduced proportion of CCP members, as well as avoiding the over- or underrepresentation of a particular social group or class in congresses. Considerable progress was made in these respects. According to

Table 3.1   Contrasts in Deputies to the Ninth and Tenth Municipal People's Congresses of Wuxi, Jiangsu, March 1983 and January 1988

	Deputies to the Ninth Congress	Deputies to the Tenth Congress
Number	814	586
Male	615 (75.55%)	451 (77%)
Female	199 (24.45%)	135 (23%)
Under the age of 35	126 (15.5%)	93 (15.9%)
Between 36 and 55	504 (61.9%)	412 (70.3%)
Between 56 and 65	148 (18.2%)	66 (11.3%)
Above 65	36 (4.4%)	15 (2.5%)
CCP members	523 (64.25%)	363 (61.9%)
Members of the "democratic parties"	62 (7.62%)	57 (9.7%)
No party affiliation	40 (4.91%)	21 (3.6%)
The masses[a]	189 (23.22%)	142 (24.3%)
Han nationality	806 (99.02%)	581 (99.1%)
Minority nationalities	8 (0.98%)	5 (0.9%)
With higher education	242 (29.7%)	247 (42.2%)
With middle-level professional education[b]	58 (7.1%)	57 (9.7%)
With high school education	389 (47.8%)	257 (43.8%)
With elementary school education	125 (15.4%)	25 (4.3%)
Workers	237 (29.11%)	156 (26.6%)
Peasants	62 (7.62%)	46 (7.9%)
Military	13 (1.60%)	9 (1.5%)
Cadres	209 (25.68%)	153 (26.1%)
Intelligentsia	191 (23.46%)	144 (24.6%)
Returned overseas Chinese	7 (0.86%)	5 (0.9%)
Others	95 (11.67%)	73 (12.4%)
Deputies to the previous congress	246 (30.2%)	200 (34.1%)

Source: Based on materials provided by the Wuxi municipal SCPC.
Notes: a. "Masses" denotes those without party affiliation or government position.
   b. In China's educational system, middle-level professional education (*zhong zhuan*) is equivalent to senior high school.

the statistical data provided by the Wuxi municipal congress, from 1983 to 1987 the percentage of deputies with higher education increased from 29.7 to 42.2; those who only attended elementary schools decreased from 15.4 to 4.3 percent. At the same time, the percentage of deputies with CCP membership decreased from 64.2 to 61.9; the deputies over the age of fifty-six decreased from 22.6 to 13.8 percent (Table 3.1). Such changes seemed to represent a nationwide tendency, particularly at and above the municipal level. Among the 2,980 deputies of the ninth NPC (1998), 81.2 percent had received higher education, compared to 44.5 percent in the sixth NPC (1983) (see Table 3.2).

The double standard in the election of congressional deputies and the deliberate limitation of citizen influence in indirect elections may be explained by the overall strategy of Deng's political reform. As the Party committee at each level was pressured to withdraw from government and the policy func-

Table 3.2   Contrasts in NPC Deputies from 1978 to 1998 (in percent)

	Fifth NPC (1978)	Sixth NPC (1983)	Seventh NPC (1988)	Eighth NPC (1993)	Ninth NPC (1998)
Workers	26.7	14.9	[a]	11.15	[a]
Peasants	20.6	11.7	[a]	9.4	[a]
Military	14.4	9	9	8.96	8.99
Cadres	13.4	21.4	24.7	28.27	33.16
Intelligentsia	15	23.5	23.4	21.8	21.7
Returned overseas Chinese	1	1.3	1.6	1.21	1.24
CCP members	72.2	62.5	66.8	68.4	66[b]
Members of satellite parties and no party affiliation	8.9	18.2	18.2	19.21	15.44
With higher education	–	44.5	56	68.74	81.20
Total number	3,497	2,978	2,970	2,978	2,980

Sources: MB, March 4, 1998; *WHB*, March 3, 1998, p. A6; *RMRB*, March 11, 1988; *XHYB*, no. 580, 2 (March 30, 1993), pp. 8–9; Ren Yan, "On the Superiority of the People's Congress System in Our Country," in QRCBY, ed., *Lun Woguo*, pp. 232–254; Liao Gailong, Zhao Baoxu, and Du Qinglin, eds., *Dangdai Zhongguo*, pp. 192–193; Pu Xingzu et al., *Zhonghua*, pp. 30–31.

Notes: a. The combined percentage of workers and peasants was 23 in 1988 and 18.89 in 1998.
b. This 1998 figure is an estimate provided by Chen Zhinong in "The CCP Strengthens Its Control."

tion of the people's congress as a countervailing institutional force was strengthened, indirect elections assumed increasing importance in the political structure that far exceeded that of direct elections. In China's administrative hierarchy, the county was the lowest rank (except for the township) in the countryside, whereas the urban district was the basic administrative unit in cities. Even if direct election at this level were entirely open to free competition, "people power" could hardly reach the central level. It was diluted again and again in the scrutiny and screening that led up to the center through the municipal and provincial levels. The location of the county and urban district at the bottom of the national administrative ladder also explains why electoral activities at this level could be and even had to be depoliticized. Citizens were aware that the deputies they chose lacked the capacity to move the Party center and the political system in a particular direction. People therefore tended to be realistic and just expected the deputies to do something to improve the quality of life. For their part, deputies were aware that playing with sensitive macropolitical topics in elections, if not simply a waste of time, might very likely backfire, voters considering it impracticable (*bu qie shiji*) or even a desire to "curry favor by claptrap" (*hua zhong qu chong*) (au. int.). The Party center's pragmatic need for popular influence over government through legislative channels on the one hand and the tendency of depoliticization of candidates and constituents—easing the leadership's worry about potential political dangers inherent in elections—on the other were mutually reinforced to allow a certain degree of democracy in direct elections.

But indirect elections differed in two main respects. First, they occurred at higher administrative levels, closer to the national center of power. If the people's congress were granted real authority, the deputies, especially at the provincial level, could participate institutionally in making government policy that would affect a large population and a vast territory. Moreover, these deputies could wield legal weapons, such as elections of NPC deputies and vetoes of instructions from Beijing, to pose a formidable threat to the dominance of the Party center. Their political loyalty to the regime was therefore especially critical.[74] Except for specifying who could not vote or stand for election, the electoral law did not require that people's deputies demonstrate particular political attitudes. But after the mid-1980s, more and more congresses at all levels made a supplementary stipulation that those nominated as candidates must stick to the "four cardinal principles" and support the policies formulated by the Central Committee.[75] Although there were no definite legal provisions concerning the cultural qualifications of congressional deputies, the NPC established a bottom line: the ability to examine legislative documents.[76]

Indirect elections further differed from direct ones in that (mostly at the provincial level) many Party cadres and government officials were involved in Party leaders' personal clientelist networks and placed under the direct and tight organizational control of the central Party apparatus. In other words, it was less necessary at this level for the Party center to use democratic indirect elections and a powerful people's congress to check the power of the Party committee.

Tighter Party control over indirect elections signified the readiness on the part of the center to let people's congresses and deputies play a greater role in policymaking. Perhaps it was just this readiness that underlay the double standard, by which not democratic procedures but the education of deputies and their ability to make constructive suggestions on government affairs received special emphasis in indirect elections. In 1986, before a new round of nationwide elections, the Central Committee issued three documents that highlighted the educational attainments and younger age of deputies, who thus were able to make significant contributions to government work and engage in politically productive social activities. Nomination should not be merely an honor.[77] Most regional congresses passed similar regulations. For example, in Chengdu and Chongqing, candidates for people's deputies had to be able to read.[78] Central directives prior to the 1992–1993 and 1997–1998 nationwide elections also demanded the firmer establishment and wider application of the principle of competitiveness in indirect elections.[79]

Conclusion

Throughout the reform of the electoral system, the CCP leaders showed considerable respect for democratic procedures—so long as they did not impinge on Party supremacy and domination. If the election of people's deputies showed any sign of democratic progress, it was first and foremost because of its depoliticized nature. Party leaders' discouragement of campaigning and prohibition of political opposition in elections disclosed their real intention of making the participation of Chinese citizens in government, as in the workplace, basically apolitical. Macropolitical issues were kept out of the reach of the masses.

For all their efforts to strengthen the citizen's part in direct elections, Party leaders' ambiguous attitudes or feigned ignorance toward cadre manipulation of indirect elections, often a typical tactic in political reform, indicated their ambivalence toward the role of congressional deputies. They hoped that deputies would have day-to-day contact with the masses to make their preferences heard in legislation, be smart enough to contribute to government work, and, most important, effectively supervise the formulation and implementation of reform programs. But deputies must not be so assertive or so independent as to stray from the Party center on major political and economic issues.

If this is indeed what Deng and his colleagues had in mind, then the results of the electoral reform should not disappoint them. As the relevant data suggest, a large proportion of the population seemed to appreciate the leadership's efforts to expand freedom of choice in direct elections at the expense of local cadre influence. Except on some university campuses, political challenges to Party hegemony in elections were rare, even in an environment where mild or implicit criticism appeared to be tolerated. Most of the people's deputies directly elected by the masses were CCP members, cadres, and professionals loyal to the establishment. In short, with just a few exceptions, the deputies' loyalty to the regime remained reliable.

Popular political participation cannot be equated with democracy unless, to say the least, political opposition and competition are allowed. The weak political opposition in Chinese society, as manifested in the voting behavior of citizens, made the "democratization" of the electoral system particularly deceptive and misleading not only to outside observers but also to the voters themselves. Although some criticized the regime's discouragement of election campaigns, the vast majority of the Chinese population, it seemed, paid little attention to this and other political and ideological limits on elections. In other words, citizens, the masses and deputies alike, "cooperated" with the central leadership to make elections apolitical and "democratic."

A couple of reasons may explain the seeming lack of interest in using elections to showcase larger political issues. First, the political atrocities under Mao remained fresh in popular memory. Even in the era of reform, political terror still hung over electoral activities. Although both direct and indirect elections provided voters with an opportunity to express their preferences and vote for whomever they liked, few were inclined to speak out or vote against the Party. This was especially the case for deputies whose election of the next higher level of congress was under closer supervision of Party cadres.

Second, one needs to examine how direct elections related to citizens' main concerns. As shown in the previous chapter, the welfare of Chinese citizens was for the most part managed by work units. Government policy usually had no immediate consequences for their daily lives, so governmental elections could hardly arouse citizen enthusiasm in the first place. In this respect, Chinese citizens were not very different from American citizens as Dahl describes them or from the Schumpeterian notion of "the typical citizen."[80] As Chinese citizens tended not to link their welfare with macropolitics, many of them cast their ballots for those with CCP membership when they acquired a certain degree of freedom of choice among the candidates. They did so not necessarily out of either love or fear of Party cadres but simply because deputies with Party membership—with all its accompanying political influence and privileges—were better positioned to serve constituents (au. int.). The voting behavior of citizens displayed an obvious pragmatic and materialistic tendency.

Finally, as the people perceived it, the importance of elections was decided mostly by the actual power of the people's congress. Even though the central leadership attempted to establish the authority of the people's congress, the fundamental limits remained unchanged. For all the rhetoric about legislative supremacy, the congress never truly dominated local law- and policymaking, nor did it maintain an ultimate control over the government (as in Western parliamentary democracies). As we see in the next few chapters, even during China's most "democratic" period after the late 1970s, both direct and indirect elections of people's deputies decided only who would share power with Party cadres in selecting government officials and formulating government policies. It should be noted, though, that both legislative authority and popular perception of it continued to improve slowly and steadily during the 1990s.

Notes

1. Elections were publicly denounced during the Cultural Revolution. "Blind worship for elections is . . . a conservative thought," an *HQ* editorial charged. "The revolutionary committees have been the most revolutionary representative organs of power of the dictatorship of the proletariat. They are not produced by elections but by the actions of the broad masses of the revolutionary people. . . . Such a way conforms to the proletarian democracy more than elections do." *HQ,* no. 4 (April 1968), pp. 5–12.

2. Townsend, *Political Participation*, ch. 5. Also see O'Brien, *Reform Without Liberalization*, ch. 4. The Maoist pattern of election bore a strong resemblance to that of other communist states. See *Pravda*, "Elections."

3. Cities in China are divided into three categories according to size, population, and strategic importance. In the first category are supercities that are at the same administrative level as provinces, and come under the direct jurisdiction of the central government; they are Beijing, Shanghai, Tianjin, and Chongqing (since 1997). In the second category are large and medium-sized cities. The cities belonging to these two categories are divided into several administrative districts. Small cities fall into the third category, which is not further divided. They are at the same level as districts of the cities of the first two categories in China's administrative hierarchy. People's deputies in these small cities are directly elected to the municipal congresses. In the countryside, there are two administrative levels: county and township. (The village should theoretically or legally be treated as an autonomous workplace, but in many areas local authorities tend to regard it as the lowest level of the government.) In 1989 the county of Wuxi had jurisdiction over thirty-five townships.

4. Cheng Zihua, minister of civil affairs and director of the nationwide direct election, praised it as "a major revolution" in China's electoral system. *RMRB,* August 4, 1980.

5. The 1953 law provided that voting could be conducted either way. In the 1954 elections, the method of raising hands was generally used, allegedly due to widespread illiteracy. In the 1956 and 1963 elections, the secret ballot was introduced in most areas.

6. According to the 1982 constitution, a term in the county-level congress consisted of three years, so direct elections were held every three years. (Terms in congresses above the county level lasted five years.) But in an amendment passed in 1993, the three-year term was changed to a five-year term for the county-level congress. Guowuyuan Fazhiju, ed., *Zhonghua Renmin Gongheguo Xinfagui Huibian,* vol. 1, 1993, pp. 3–5.

7. See "No. 7 Document of the CCP Central Committee, [*zhong fa*] 1980," in QXZXB, ed., *Diyijie Quanguo,* pp. 25–34.

8. *RMRB,* August 10, 1980.

9. As Nathan indicates in his discussion of the 1980 elections, the restoration of elections greatly encouraged many Chinese democrats who believed that elections represented "not just a chance to speak out but a chance to alter the structure of state power through the congresses." See Nathan, *Chinese Democracy,* p. 209.

10. Much of my discussion here on the 1980 direct election in Peking University is based on my interviews with Hu Ping and Fang Zhiyuan, two of the leading candidates in that election who are now in exile in the United States.

11. A detailed and uncensored account of the 1980 direct elections in the universities of Beijing is found in Huang Ho et al., eds., *Kai Tuo.*

12. For instance, a headline in the *New York Times* of November 29, 1980, read, "In Peking Election, Ballot Is Secret, Campaign Is Hot." The article's author, Fox Butterfield, writes, "In Peking's universities the elections have turned into intently fought contests and have produced sharp debate over the most pressing political and economic issues." Strictly speaking, this situation occurred in Peking University alone.

13. Yi Ming, "Is It Legitimate?"

14. *SXRB,* November 1, 1980. Also in *FBIS Daily Report: China,* November 12, 1980, p. T2.

15. Lu Cheng and Zhu Gu, "Earnestly Guarantee."

16. Although he lashed out at anti-Party campaigning, in his report of September 3, 1981, Cheng also mentioned the following problems relating to local cadres' breach of the electoral law: (1) They arbitrarily increased or decreased the number of candidates; (2) among the elected deputies there were too many Party members, too many men, and too many cadres; and (3) in order for more cadres to be elected as deputies, the constituency in the areas where Party-government organs concentrated was made much smaller than in other areas, so that even a few dozen voters could elect a deputy. (The legal provision was that an electoral district have 2,000 to 6,000 voters and produce one to three people's deputies. On average, every 2,000 voters were to elect a deputy.) Cheng stressed that nomination of candidates and competitive election were two key links in "electoral democratization." *RMRB,* September 3, 1981.

17. As Hu Ping told me in telephone interviews, during his three-year term (1980–1983) as a deputy, he performed his duties normally. No one ever questioned his qualifications. But he found it quite difficult to discuss political issues at the sessions of the district congress (as he had in his election campaign). One reason was that the topics assigned to the deputies for discussion rarely touched on ideology. Also, most of his congressional colleagues showed little interest in political affairs.

18. Chen Ziming, "Who Is the Person?"

19. He Ping, "Writing the History."

20. As Fang Zhiyuan recalled in our interviews, right from the beginning the attitude of the Party committee of Peking University toward the election campaigns of 1980 was: no support, no opposition, and no recommendation. When the election was over, the hard-liners in the Ministry of Higher Education suggested that some candidates—Fang was one of them—should be dismissed for their "wrong" speeches and activities. But the university Party committee refused to do so and explained perfunctorily that they could persuade these students to correct their "mistakes."

21. Jian Jun, "The 1980 Elections."

22. "In this election," he charged, "some people exploited the opportunities of electing people's deputies to launch the so-called campaigns. They failed to comply with socialist laws and exercised anarchism and extreme individualism. They colluded secretly, made demagogic speeches, and openly opposed the four cardinal principles. We must resolutely oppose those kinds of activities." *RMRB,* September 12, 1981.

23. The results of the first free election in many authoritarian states made this fear quite understandable. In many cases authoritarian rulers and groups sponsored elections and lost or did much more poorly than they had anticipated. As Huntington explained it, the "false confidence" of the dictators played a part: "Authoritarian regimes normally provide few feedback mechanisms, and dictators naturally tended to believe that they had sufficient rapport with their publics to win their endorsement." See Huntington, *The Third Wave,* ch. 4.

24. See Womack, "The 1980 County-level Elections."

25. Xu Chongde, "How Many New Developments?"

26. Wang Xinxue, "Comments"; Sun Liming, "On Socialist Competition."

27. Dong Taifang, "The Significance of Li Shuxian."

28. Dong Xusheng, "Li Shuxian."

29. In his report to the NPCSC in February 1980, Cheng Zihua claimed that the candidates recommended by citizens proved to be much better qualified than those selected by Party cadres. See QXZXB, ed., *Diyijie Quanguo,* pp. 88–97.

30. Yan Xiansheng, "The Investigation."

31. Wang Chongming and Yuan Ruiliang, *Zhonghua Renmin Gongheguo Xuanju Zhidu,* p. 77.

32. Pan Bo'wen, "The Direct Election."

33. Ibid. Liu Chong, "The Electoral System." This limitation was applied to the percentage of the candidates selected for the final list. It was a crucial link in the entire nomination process. As McCormick's research shows, the final list of candidates was in practice usually established by the election committee dominated by Party cadres. McCormick, *Political Reform*, pp. 139–143.

34. Kong Lingwen and Yuan Xiangmei, "The Investigation on the Direct Election of Deputies," in Zhao Baoxu, ed., *Minzhu Zhengzhi*, pp. 259–271.

35. An unofficial nationwide survey disclosed a voter turnout of 72.7 percent, 61.8 percent of whom went to the polls allegedly because of their trust in the "democratic" nature of the elections. See Min Qi, *Zhongguo Zhengzhi Wenhua*, p. 229. Although we should not take at face value the opinions Chinese citizens express in public surveys, these surveys might provide some useful clues. A poll conducted by researchers in Jilin Province found that 52.3 percent of the voters thought that the election embodied the people's will. A total of 66.1 percent believed that the final list of candidates was drawn up in a democratic way, whereas 28.3 percent charged that it was decided by Party cadres. And 66.2 percent said that they were satisfied or relatively satisfied with the elected deputies. See Wang Huiyan et al., "An Investigation Report on Citizens' Sense of Election," in Zhao Baoxu, ed., *Minzhu Zhengzhi*, pp. 285–309.

36. QRCBL, "On the Conditions for Direct Election in 1987," in QRCBL, ed., *Xuanju Wenjian Huibian*; *RMRB*, March 22, 1991.

37. *MB*, November 25, 1997.

38. Tian Zhen, "People's Deputies."

39. *MB*, November 25, 1997.

40. Hou Zhaoxun, "The Elections." The author claimed that the procedures for this direct election were simplified to guarantee the voters' right to "equal participation."

41. The difficulty with which the candidates without office got elected seemed to be a widespread problem, not necessarily caused by individual cadres. In Dongshan District (Guangzhou), one constituency had a high proportion of people in education. At the first stage, the citizens and the Party-government organs nominated 117 primary candidates. Only four candidates were left on the final list after screening at two meetings of voters. Among them only one was a CCP member, but all were local celebrities: Three were school principals or deputy principals. Many candidates attributed their removal from the final list to the lack of their own publicity. Ruan Jihong, "Some Aspects."

42. Mei De'ying, "On the Direct Election." Even some cadres had no interest in being nominated. As Shi argues, winning elections usually did these cadres no good but losing could be a disaster. See Shi, *Political Participation*, pp. 34–39.

43. Wang Huiyan et al., "An Investigation Report."

44. He Shilu, "Some Problems with the Elections of Basic-level People's Deputies," in ZDZTGYX, ed., *Guanyu Zhengzhi Tizhi Gaige*, pp. 182–191.

45. Xu Yaotong, "A Socialist Electoral System."

46. See Guo Guangdong, "Voters' Mentalities."

47. The 1995 revision included three changes that deserve attention. In the previous versions of the law, the size of population represented by each provincial deputy and NPC deputy in urban areas had to be five and eight times larger, respectively, than in rural areas. These were reduced to four times larger, which meant that the number of peasant deputies would increase in each provincial congress and in the NPC. Second, in the past the office of direct election at the township level had to accept the leadership of the election committee at the next higher level. The revision called for

accepting the leadership of the standing committee of the next higher level congress. Considering Party cadres' heavy participation in the election committee (au. int.), this revision should weaken Party cadres' influence over the township-level direct elections. Third, the preliminary election was restored in indirect elections. This should reduce cadres' control over the final list of candidates. Guowuyuan Fazhiju, ed., *Zhonghua,* vol. 1, 1995, pp. 1–8.

48. As mentioned before, the extent of political control over direct elections varied across the country, depending on local authorities. Two recent cases, both in Shaaxi Province, showed that it was very difficult for the candidates who were clearly identified as dissidents to make the final list: The candidates were endorsed by enough voters, but the election officials dropped their names from the list on the grounds that they did not meet the requirements. One was even placed under house arrest on election day. *MB,* January 18, 1998, p. A8; *ZGSB,* December 21, 1997.

49. *FBIS Daily Report: China,* September 4, 1980, pp. L12–L13. Peng Zhen's statement was not entirely accurate. In China the counties were divided into two categories in terms of their administrative status. Those in the first came under the direct jurisdiction of the provincial government, and those in the second—many of which were adjacent to major cities—under the municipal government. The deputies in counties of the second category were qualified to elect deputies only to municipal congresses.

50. Xie Qichen, "A Second Comment."

51. But keeping indirect elections behind closed doors had a major downside. As one scholar argued, the failure of elections to attract voters' attention was caused by the lack of public and objective reports through which voters could get to know the performance of their representatives, including how the latter elected higher-level deputies. Guan Xing, "On Citizens' Right Not to Vote," in Zi Mu, ed., *Minzhu de Gousi,* pp. 167–177.

52. Much of my fieldwork on this issue was done in Wuxi, Jiangsu Province. Wuxi, located between Shanghai and Nanjing, was a medium-sized industrial city with a population of over 1 million. It was divided into four administrative districts (Nanchang, Beitang, Chongan, and suburbs). I interviewed the senior officials of the municipal congress and several people's deputies. These deputies, elected by the deputies of a district congress, in turn elected deputies to the provincial congress of Jiangsu.

53. This was perhaps the basis of Burns's argument that China's nomenklatura system also covered some delegates to people's congresses. Burns, ed., *The Chinese Communist Party's Nomenklatura System,* p. xxiii. Congressional approval was, though, less secure for Party-appointed candidates for congressional seats than for government offices.

54. These two methods of nominating candidates were introduced in a report dated November 12, 1982, submitted by the municipal congress of Wuxi to the Jiangsu provincial congress. As one of my interviewees alleged, they were used in the two indirect elections held in 1983 and 1987.

55. For a discussion of the CPPCC, see Chapter 7, note 16.

56. Xu Zhifu, "On the Role of People's Deputies in Political Democratization," in Zhao Baoxu, ed., *Minzhu Zhengzhi,* pp. 185–196.

57. SSKZ, "Improve the System." The logic of this electoral system was that the higher the administrative level was, the more common this phenomenon. Although little about the process of electing deputies to the NPC was publicly exposed, it was still possible to get a glimpse of it from a few reported interviews with NPC deputies. Duan Fakui, elected to the NPC in 1987, had undertaken a big public-contract project

to plant trees in a mountainous region in Yunan Province. He had worked hard, succeeded, and become well known in just a few years. One day when he was planting trees in the mountains, someone drove up and told him that he had been elected as the deputy to go to Beijing. Long after his election, he learned how it came about. Initially, he was not on the list of candidates, but an election official whose name he did not know suggested at a meeting that it would be appropriate to have a contractor among the peasant candidates. Most of the participants agreed. Since Duan was famous for his achievements among the contractors, he was selected. Yang Minqing, *Zhongguo Da Xuanju,* pp. 83–84.

58. Tian Zhen, "People's Deputies."

59. Luo Bing and Li Zijing, "Spectacles." In contrast with scandals in direct elections, those in indirect elections were rarely made public.

60. The percentage of candidates initially nominated by deputies should be much higher. For instance, in the 1992–1993 election of NPC deputies in Shanghai, of the total 127 initial candidates, seventy were recommended by the Party committee and fifty-seven (44 percent) by the deputies. See Pu Xingzu et al., *Zhonghua,* p. 139.

61. Hao Weilian, "The Progress."

62. QRCBY, ed., *Renmin Daibiao Dahui Zhidu Jianshe Sishinian,* pp. 200–201.

63. In this election, according to the head of the department, the quota assigned to the city was eleven. One had to be recommended by the provincial Party committee; two by the prefectural Party committee, one for city leaders, two for intellectuals, one for returned overseas Chinese, one for workers, and one for peasants. The next day the deputies discussed the résumés of the eleven candidates. Immediately after the discussion, the cadres distributed the ballots on which the eleven names were printed in advance and asked the deputies to vote for them. Zhang and some other deputies protested that this did not conform to normal electoral procedures, but they were ignored. Zhang had to abstain from voting. "This was a no-difference election without a primary selection," he complained. "It evidently violated the electoral law." Zhang Songquan, "The Election."

64 . Luo Bing and Li Zijing, "Spectacles."

65. Ibid.

66. Some of the members of the standing committee of the people's congress (SCPC) at each level were professional and full time. The documents issued by the Central Committee in 1986 demanded that the number of professional SCPC members be increased. There was much debate among scholars and deputies about whether or not people's deputies should be professionalized. As Sun argued, deprofessionalization of people's deputies had two merits: (1) They would not divorce themselves from the masses or work practice, and (2) they were in a position to apply Party policy and congressional resolutions directly to the basic-level work units. But it had disadvantages, too, such as the lack of time for deputies to perform their duty and limited chances to establish connections with more voters and find out their opinions and demands in time. See Sun Bingzhu, "Formulate Legal Provisions Concerning the Duties of People's Deputies and Bring Their Role into Full Play," in ZFXYW, ed., *Xianfa yu Gaige,* pp. 507–519.

67. A major criterion used by Party cadres to nominate candidates in indirect elections was professional achievement, or, to use official parlance, their "contributions to the motherland and people." For instance, of the municipal deputies of Hangzhou, 55.7 percent were model workers. Zhao Chenggen, "A Survey and Analysis of the Deputies of the Municipal People's Congress of Hangzhou," in Zhao Baoxu, ed., *Minzhu Zhengzhi,* pp. 228–241. For a long time, Party leaders did not see anything wrong with this criterion. Liao Hansheng, vice chairman of the NPC Standing Com-

mittee, spoke proudly of the qualifications of the deputies to the seventh NPC. "Among the NPC deputies," he claimed, "there are a number of advanced workers who have made outstanding contributions to the reforms and four modernizations. Among them are model workers, shock workers of the New Long March, March 8 standard-bearers, entrepreneurs proficient in management, leading cadres of enterprises, scientists and technicians who have made important inventions, model educators faithful to the educational cause, scholars and athletes who have won honors for the country, Lei Feng–style advanced individuals, and the heroes who have defended our motherland or helped people to tide over after natural disasters or maintained public order and safeguard the construction of modernization." See *Bulletin of the NPC Standing Committee* (1988). "Shock workers of the New Long March" and "March 8 standard-bearers" were honorary titles for young and female model workers, respectively.

68. Even some highest-ranking NPC deputies expressed no interest in this kind of "honor" or no time for its responsibilities. A reporter interviewed Yang Xilan, a seventh NPC deputy. Yang was a famous volleyball player and, with her teammates, had won a number of medals in international competitions. Her election was quite typical among the NPC deputies. The reporter asked her, "Does your election mean honor or responsibilities?" She replied, "Honor. I regard it as a reward. For such an important conference, I can only manage to attend its opening ceremony. It is hard for me to carry out the responsibilities of a people's deputy, such as going among the masses to collect their opinions. As such, I prefer not to be elected." See Yang Minqing, *Zhongguo Da Xuanju,* pp. 82–83.

69. As Yang Li observed, the people's congress was little more than an honorary institution in the perception of many citizens. Yang Li, "A Study." A number of scholars were openly critical of conferring "people's deputy" as an honorary title. As one charged, this "badly undermines the role of people's deputies and degrades the status of the congress as the highest organ of power . . . because the congress is neither an association of elders nor a representative conference of heroes and model workers." Liu Xia, "Reform of the Political Structure." Duan, an experienced deputy, described the congress as almost a "gathering of heroes" (*qun ying hui*). He gave three examples. One deputy was a scientist. When the congress was in session, he attended merely the opening and closing ceremonies because, for the purpose of checking the number of attendants and votes, the deputies had to register at the opening ceremony and to vote on the resolutions at the closing ceremony. For the rest of the time, he could be found only in his laboratory. Another deputy, a model worker, never spoke at congressional sessions during her five years in office. Another, when asked to comment on government work, always "smiled without saying a word." Duan Muzheng, "On the Improvement."

70. See Chen Mo, "Further Improve the System of Electing People's Deputies," in Zi Mu, ed., *Minzhu de Gousi,* pp. 158–167.

71. This observation is supported by the empirical study Shi did in Beijing. The changes in the system of (direct) elections enabled voters to get rid of or humiliate the officials they disliked. Shi's findings suggest that the mobilization model could no longer be applied to electoral activities. Shi, *Political Participation,* chs. 4, 5.

72. QRFW, "The Conditions."

73. But at the provincial level the leadership did care about the election of some "rising political stars" as NPC deputies, as they did in the provincial intra-Party elections of deputies to the national Party congress. These stars were typically relatively young regional leaders who performed to the satisfaction of the Party center and were internally selected by the central leaders as their successors. If they failed in any elections, it would damage their careers and the center's promotion plan (au. int.).

74. The leadership's—mainly Deng's—emphasis on the political loyalty of people's deputies or their intolerance of any political challenges from them was best illustrated by the case of Hu Jiwei. Born in 1916, Hu was a veteran communist and a famous journalist. After the Cultural Revolution, he was appointed as editor in chief of *RMRB*. In 1989 he was an NPC deputy and an NPCSC member. In the prodemocracy movement in Tiananmen, he appealed to the leadership to accept the demands of the demonstrators. After martial law was proclaimed, he took the lead in signing an open letter that demanded an emergency NPCSC session to discuss the situation. Although he did nothing beyond his duty, he was severely reprimanded after the massacre for his "disagreement with the Central Committee." Under pressure from above, the Sichuan provincial congress, by which Hu was elected to the NPC, in March 1990 "unanimously" passed a resolution and expelled Hu from the NPC. See Wang Kejia, "Hu Jiwei."

75. See Ye Lingling, "On the Requirements for Elected People's Deputies," in HZXK, ed., *Faxue Lunwenji*, pp. 96–107.

76. Ye Lingling, "On the Requirements."

77. QRCBY, ed., *Renmin Daibiao Dahui Zhidu Jianshe Sishinian*, pp. 195–196.

78. Ibid.

79. Chen Hongyi, "1993: A New Term." The methods for competitive election differed in direct and indirect elections. In indirect elections the number of candidates had to be 20 to 50 percent larger than the number to be elected, in direct elections, 50 to 100 percent. For example, in the 1992–1993 election of NPC deputies in Guangdong Province, 116 deputies were elected from 151 candidates, and the difference was 33.1 percent. See Pu Xingzu, et al., *Zhonghua*, p. 139. An *FZRB* commentary complained that despite the central efforts (to make elections more competitive), many deputies were still not competent. "Their sense of responsibility is weak. And some do not even have basic knowledge about China's constitution and laws." See Yang Changjun, "Look for Higher-quality Deputies."

80. Dahl, *Who Governs?* "The typical citizen," according to Schumpeter, "drops down to a lower level of mental performance as soon as he enters the political field." Schumpeter, *Capitalism*, pp. 250–268. Brittan argues that politics does not and cannot provide rewards and incentives for everybody, as economics does. Quoted in Sartori, *The Theory of Democracy Revisited*, p. 107.

4

Elections and Appointments of Government Officials

The reform of elections of people's deputies did not proceed in isolation. It was part of China's political institutional reform, which was sponsored by post-Mao leaders not just to enhance regime legitimacy but also to render public policies more rational and responsive to citizen needs as long as doing so did not compromise the communist one-party system. As economic reforms proceeded, policy rationalization and responsiveness acquired a new and broader meaning. It went beyond everyday welfare of citizens and touched the basics of the economic planning system. But the problems inherent in reforming a Leninist system soon surfaced: Neither policy rationalization nor a profound economic restructuring could succeed unless the long-established political structure was overhauled. This structure was characterized by Party cadres' complete control of both policymaking and executive powers at all administrative levels, without even a minimum of institutional checks and balances. For the economic transformation to be accomplished, changing the overconcentration of power in the hands of Party cadres was necessary.

Nevertheless, to effect this change would pose an enormous dilemma for the central leadership because, as nondemocratic reformers, they would not abandon the cadres or look for an alternative force to execute reforms. Instead, they decided to undo the complete overlap of functions of the Party committee and government. In separating the two, some Party cadres would be turned into professional cadres in the sense that they held no other positions than intra-Party posts and were institutionally represented by the Party committee. Some cadres would become government officials who—even though they were Party members or retained positions within the Party—would have incentives to look after and develop their own bureaucratic interests, differing from or even contradicting those of the Party apparatus. At the same time, some other cadres were to transfer to revived and strengthened people's congresses that were supposed to provide citizens with an institutionalized channel to participate in the policymaking process. This political restructuring was designed to transform the government from nothing more than an appendage of the Party committee, as it was during Mao's regime, into an executive branch bearing some resemblance to the cabinet in a Western parliamentary system. It was to be placed under the double control of the Party committee and the people's congress of the same administrative level.

The Party-government separation (discussed in greater length in Chapter 5) was a critical link in China's political reform process. Only in this changing structural context can we really comprehend the significance of the elections of government officials. Since this institutional rearrangement—which went far beyond typical communist formalism and symbolism—was intended to create some mechanisms of checks and balances among the three institutional actors, government officials could not continue to be entirely controlled by Party cadres and serve as their agents. Thus, the traditional way in which the Party committee appointed government officials on a largely arbitrary basis had to be abandoned.

This chapter discusses the reforms regarding the election and appointment of government officials, as well as members of the standing committee of the people's congress (who were elected in the same way as government officials).[1] Compared with people's deputies, whose extended role gave them only a share of power with Party cadres in policymaking and matters of administrative personnel, government officials, as supposedly autonomous policy executors, were certainly more important in the Party-state hierarchy. The reform highlighted the same ambivalence Party leaders displayed toward people's deputies. They demanded that government officials be competent and faithful in implementing the Party's reformist policies. For this purpose, they had to prevent Party cadres from rigging elections in favor of their protégés. But Deng and his colleagues did not trust people's deputies either, even if the latter's loyalty to the regime seemed to be unquestionable. So the Party center tried to walk a tightrope, maintaining a balance between cadre control and deputy initiative. But this strategy did not always work, as cadres and deputies alike often overextended their authority.

1979–1986: Tentative Reform

According to the local organic law adopted by the fifth NPC on July 1, 1979, elections of government officials followed principles and procedures similar to those for indirect elections of people's deputies.[2] There were only two major literal differences between the 1979 law and the 1954 law: (1) In the earlier law candidates for government offices were nominated by people's deputies jointly or individually. In 1979 the relevant provision was modified to read "nominated by the presidium of the people's congress or jointly by [at least ten] people's deputies' (article 20); and (2) the previous "exact-number" method, that is, nominating as many candidates as positions, was revised to "competitive election": nominating more candidates than positions (article 20). As far as the procedures were concerned, the "competitive election" was the sole meaningful legal innovation. A fundamental provision remained unchanged: Government officials at all levels were not directly elected by ordinary citizens.

Changes in the election of officials should be assessed not just by the revisions that appeared on paper but also by the extent to which these legal provisions were abided by in practice. During the ten years following the adoption of the 1954 law, because people's deputies were designated by the authorities, that the deputies elected government officials only served to give the latter a spurious constitutional legitimacy. Under the no-choice electoral system, dissent regarding Party nominations was almost never heard.[3] During the Cultural Revolution, even this ritual election was abolished. To make elections of officials appear more of a reform than simply a return to the past, the Party propaganda machine urged Party committees at all levels to respect the initiatives of deputies.

To the disappointment of the leaders, however, the tentative elections of officials during 1979–1981 were far from impressive examples of reform. The law provided that major officials be elected by the congress of the corresponding level. The mechanisms of indirect elections, as we saw in Chapter 3, provided Party cadres with opportunities to manipulate the nomination process and at each government level distort the preferences directly expressed by ordinary citizens. In fact, Party cadres' violations of the law was more widespread and undisguised in elections of officials than in indirect elections of congressional deputies. In some counties in Liaoning and Yunnan Provinces, the candidates for county heads officially announced as winners did not, as legally required, get more than half the votes.[4] Cheng Zihua acknowledged that the implementation of the competitive election policy "met with strong resistance." "In some localities," he charged, "at the time of electing county heads the method of nominating as many candidates as the positions was used. Some candidates were nominated just for the sake of 'accompanying the chief candidate.'"[5] In Xishan, Jiangsu Province, Party cadres had trouble finding candidates willing to play such an "accompanying" role, because defeat, even though it was known to be internally arranged beforehand, would still damage their public images (au. int., 1989).

Despite their harsh criticism of cadres who refused to allow genuine competition in the first nationwide elections, the leaders in Beijing succumbed to pressure from local authorities to cancel this policy in the election of officials. The 1982 version of the local organic law stipulated that elections of government officials could involve either a "different number" or an "exact number" as long as the final list of candidates was decided on by a preliminary vote. Since there were no concrete and explicit legal procedures concerning the so-called preliminary vote, it often turned out in practice to be "democratic discussion and consultation" among the voters—usually Party cadres' favorite "democratic" measure. It meant that they acquired largely discretionary powers to decide which candidates were "preferred" by the majority of voters and hence suitable for exact-number elections. This revision, however, proved short-lived and was revised again four years later.

As the Party center's fluctuation suggests, the competitive election of officials was more problematic than it had expected. Unlike indirect elections of people's deputies, elections of officials involved the allocation of more power and hence greater personal stakes. Cadres' influence over the electoral process determined the extent to which they were able to control the elected officials. By the same token, people's deputies seemed to have more enthusiasm for nominating candidates for government office—regardless or in defiance of cadre instructions—than for the next higher congress (au. int.). For example, in Fanyu County of Guangdong, Party cadres nominated the incumbent deputy Party secretary as the sole candidate for the county's top government post (i.e., the county head). But the county congressional deputies jointly nominated the Party secretary of an enterprise, who was also a member of the standing committee of the county Party committee, to run against the cadres' pick. To the cadres' surprise, the deputies' candidate was elected.[6]

Fanyu was not alone. A report of the Ministry of Civil Administration (August 1981) indicated that in some areas the lists of candidates for government posts drawn up by Party committees differed widely from those proposed by people's deputies. Unwilling either to "discourage deputy initiative" or risk nominating potential dissidents, the ministry suggested a compromise: In elections of officials, the lists of candidates needed to be approved—rather than drawn up—by Party committees in advance; if any of these candidates was defeated in competitive elections, the election outcome must be respected.[7]

This compromise seemed to favor deputy initiative. It did not stress that the Party committee had to nominate candidates but simply allowed the committee to reject any candidate it disliked. The veto power granted to the Party committee was not surprising given the political situation. At the onset of the reform, Deng proposed the division of powers, demanding that the Party chief not simultaneously take the top government post. This division—which developed into a significant reform policy of Party-government separation in 1986—was based on the assumption that at a given administrative level the government must accept the leadership of the Party committee. It would be less problematic if the Party chief could arrange the election of the government chief. But if the government chief owed his election more to the people's deputies than to the Party committee, then he would have to keep the committee at a distance. One should note that at the twelfth Party congress of

1982 Hu Yaobang appealed to let the government "work independently," and this demand was incorporated into the new Party constitution. During this period (1982–1986), though, Party leaders were not yet prepared to limit the Party committee influence over government affairs to any significant degree.

But the suggested compromise should not lead one to overestimate the power of deputy initiative. In fact, the Fanyu case by no means represented a prevailing pattern. The freedom local authorities had to choose between the two electoral methods according to the 1982 local organic law was tantamount to the cancellation of competitive elections. This was made evident by a legal reversal in 1986 that categorically prohibited the preliminary vote. As an official source disclosed, the reason for its prohibition was that cadres used the preliminary vote as a pretext for exact-number elections.[8] An investigation found that once the method of competitive election was not legally enforced but merely recommended as an alternative, none of China's provincial congresses adopted it in the nationwide elections.[9] In other words, all major provincial government heads were elected without competition or choice and were to a large extent designated by the provincial Party committees (more precisely, by the Politburo, which usually decided top provincial posts behind the scenes but might offer more candidates for the provincial leadership and congressional deputies to choose from). Moreover, local cadres took the 1982 revision as a signal of the reassertion of Party domination over government appointments. It was reported that the county (government) heads were arbitrarily dismissed by the county Party committees without the approval of the county congresses.[10] Government officials at the levels of county and township were legally elected for a term of three years (five years after 1993). In many areas they were transferred in midterm to other posts by the Party committees without consultation with the congresses. One local voice complained, "One thousand votes cannot compete with a [Party] transfer order."[11]

1986: The Principle of Multiple-Candidate Elections

In 1986 the local organic law was revised again. In stronger language, competitive election was stipulated as the *sole* principle for elections of government officials. The revision of 1982 essentially restored Party cadre control over the elections of government officials. Since officials held more substantial power and received closer public scrutiny than deputies, this backdown tarnished the democratic credibility of the electoral reform. In single-candidate elections, the citizens failed to find what role their "representatives" played (au. int.). Moreover, government officials owed their positions entirely to and thus were only responsible to the cadres. This, too, caused discontent among people's deputies. According to Wang Hanbin, secretary-general of the NPC Standing Committee, a major purpose of competitive elections of officials was to enable deputies to "supervise officials."[12]

The primary cause of the revision, of course, was that the economic reforms had reached a critical phase that forced the Party center to put the principle of Party-government separation—which up to then still remained mere rhetoric—into serious practice. To overcome cadre opposition to reform, Beijing warned local Party committees not to interfere "too much" in government affairs; Party committee bosses were no longer to allocate government offices.[13]

Although central leaders always upheld the Party committees' right to recommend cadres for "key" government posts, which was supposed to provide the organizational guarantee for top-down control from Beijing, they considered an alteration of election procedures to give congressional deputies a chance to balance the institutional leverage of local Party committees.[14] Since congresses and deputies were usually beneficiaries of and zealous about the reforms, competitive election would enable them to pick out from among the Party committee nominees those who were similarly reform-minded. Increasing deputy influence over the election of officials would also lead to more effective legislative oversight of the government's implementation of reform programs and neutralize the antireform tendency of the powerful Party apparatus. In short, competitive election looked like a good solution to the dilemma by which the Party center could trust neither local cadres nor congressional deputies exclusively to proceed with reform.

Thus, the 1986 local organic law provided that for the offices of the administrative chief (such as governor, mayor, and county head) and also for the posts of SCPC chair and secretary-general, president of the court, and chief procurator, the number of candidates should exceed the number of positions by at least one. If just one candidate was nominated (assuming that the Party or deputies failed to find more than one qualified person to nominate), the election might be conducted in an exact-number way. For the offices of deputies to the chief (e.g., vice governor and deputy mayor), the number of candidates should exceed the number of positions by one to three.[15]

The second simultaneous revision of the local organic law and the electoral law in late 1986—combined with the Party-government separation—yielded what was often referred to as a "democratic climax" in a new round of nationwide elections that unfolded from December 1986 to June 1988. The significance of the change in the elections of officials lay in the nomination of candidates and the competitiveness of elections.

More Deputies' Nominees Elected

The revised law stipulated three channels to nominate candidates. The first was the recommendation of the Party committee; the second was through deputies. Any deputy seconded by no less than nine others or any SCPC member seconded by no less than four others at the municipal and provincial levels and no less than two others at the county level was qualified to make nominations.[16] The third channel, involving the presidium of the people's congress, was quite deceptive because nearly all candidates the presidium nominated came from the list of those recommended by the Party committee.[17] An official source suggested that the number of deputies' nominees in the 1986–1988 elections increased. In twenty-seven of China's thirty-one provinces, there were 646 formal (final) candidates for the provincial-level offices, mainly governors, vice governors, and SCPC chairs and vice chairs. Eighty-four percent of them (541) were nominated by the presidia of provincial congresses, without question, on instruction from provincial Party committees; 16 percent (105) were spontaneously nominated by provincial people's deputies.[18] This percentage, albeit relatively small, represented a remarkable rise in deputy initiative: Up to that time deputies had never freely selected the formal candidates for such senior government posts. "For the first time in our country," a central Party journal declared, "the deputies of provincial congresses exercise their right to nominate and choose supreme regional leaders."[19] As it turned out, some of the deputies' nominees got elected. The official data collected from twenty provinces indicate that eight of the total sixty-seven were elected to top provincial offices—among them three vice governors, three SCPC chairs, and one president of the court.[20]

Below the provincial level, more candidates nominated by deputies were elected to government offices. [21] For example, in Guizhou Province those nominated and elected by congressional deputies in 1987–1988 included seven county heads, thirty-four deputy county heads, six chairs and thirteen vice chairs of county-level SCPCs, and 829 heads and deputy heads of townships.[22] In Hunan they included seven mayors, county heads, and urban district heads; thirty-seven deputy mayors, deputy county heads, and deputy district heads; eight chairs and thirty-one vice chairs of county-level SCPCs; six presidents of the court; and three chief procurators.[23]

More Competition Among Candidates

Several reports suggested that the principle of competitive election was generally adhered to. In twenty provinces, 471 formal candidates competed for 349 positions of provincial governments and SCPCs; that is to say, on average one of every three candidates had to lose.[24] Competitive elections produced governors of eight provinces, nearly all vice governors, presidents of fifteen provincial-level courts, eleven chief procurators, and chairs of twelve provincial SCPCs.[25] In Beijing and Shanghai, there were ten formal candidates for seven offices of deputy mayors.[26] The election of top government officials was most spectacular in Shanghai. Although political opposition was completely absent, the election did have a certain Western twist. As a Chinese reporter who had never seen such a scene exclaimed, "Eloquence, skills for touching the audience, and even appearance make a difference!"[27] The 1987–1988 elections seemed to have won the approval of the general public and were applauded by a proliberal magazine as the "most gratifying event in 1987."[28] Other observers, though, noticed that in administrative levels lower than the province, elections became less competitive.[29]

If macropolitics hardly entered into the elections of people's deputies, it was even more taboo in the elections of officials, even though these were multiple-candidate races. Despite its sometime political tolerance in direct elections of deputies, the Party categorically prohibited any advocacy of different ideologies or political platforms by candidates. Nonetheless, because of the highly dependent role of local officials in China's hierarchical administration, this fundamental political limitation—as many voters perceived it—did not seem to matter a great deal in local elections.[30] Unless candidates pointed to political corruption, an issue that could stir up strong emotions among the masses, attacks on the political system at large and appeals for, say, a multiparty system might appear entirely irrelevant to the local issues the citizens, deputies, and officials were primarily concerned about (au. int., 1989, 1996). Given deputies' political orientations and their generally risk-averse behavior, candidates for government offices would most likely ruin their chances to get elected if they were to criticize the regime. Moreover, ordinary citizens could consider challenges to party leadership less meaningful in an era when the central leaders appeared to be carrying out reforms in the people's favor. In any case, competitive elections raised the possibility of defeat, which strengthened government officials' accountability to deputies as well as the effects of legislative oversight (au. int.).

With local elections of officials made competitive, elections of state leaders were still practically based on the old exact-number method. NPC deputies were both qualified and authorized to nominate more candidates and hence make the elections competitive. Even if they failed to do so for clear reasons, it was entirely at their discretion to vote for or against the candidates. As required by law, any candidate had to win an absolute majority of the votes to be elected. In a single-candidate election, therefore, there was still a likelihood of defeat, which would be widely seen as a humiliating loss of face within China's social and cultural context and could effectively destroy a candidate's political career. Presumably partly for this reason, as the elections were under way in the first session of the seventh NPC March–April 1988, all reporters were asked to leave. "All of a sudden," as one described it, "the atmosphere became tense." Some reporters expected shocking news.[31]

The "shocking news" soon came. For the first time in PRC history, the ballots (numerous by Chinese standards) cast against the candidates for the state leadership were announced.[32] Four factors, singly or combined, might have invited negative votes: the candidates' senility, their conservative image, the perceived lack of experience for the posts concerned, and the lack of visible accomplishments in government. The votes against Wang Zhen aroused special interest because he was a well-known hard-liner who allegedly played a key role in deposing Hu Yaobang and criticizing the "bourgeois liberalization."[33] Eight deputies wrote Hu's name on the ballot for the PRC presidency, an obvious protest against his dismissal.[34]

1990s: More Rebellions of People's Deputies

After Deng's south China trip of February 1992, during which he implied the coming acceleration of market reforms, the short "glacial epoch" of reform following Tiananmen ended.[35] Although the ice first melted only in economic reform, the effects were soon felt in the political arena. Along with the revival of market reforms, congressional deputies began to stand up to Party cadres' attempts to restore control. Many local congresses tried to flex their institutional muscles in the 1992–1993 elections and indeed had a greater impact than during any period of the 1980s. But this time the legislative "independence" was not the work of the central leaders but a product of deputies' spontaneous defiance. For this reason, the Party center did not give its usual blessing to the deputies' initiative but instead warned against it.

Perhaps what aroused the central leaders' vigilance was not just the increasing number of instances in which people's deputies refused to accept the candidates for government offices recommended by Party organizations and cadres. More surprising to them was that the spontaneity occurred rather frequently at the provincial level and exhibited a momentum that, if not contained, might threaten the rules of the political game as formulated by Beijing. At such a high administrative level, most personnel—that is, candidates for top government posts—were only nominally proposed by provincial Party committees. It was an open secret to the deputies that these people were actually designated by the Politburo or even personally by Deng or the Party general secretary. To see just what threat was embodied in the veto of these candidates, let's look at some concrete cases.

In January 1993 the provincial congress of Zhejiang set out to elect a new governor. Based on the recommendation of the provincial Party committee, the congressional presidium nominated the incumbent governor, Ge Hongsheng, as a candidate. Ge had been promoted from an alternate member of the Central Committee to a full member at the fourteenth Party congress just three months before. His rise within the Party hierarchy was seen as a special favor from the center and portended a possibility of entering the central leadership circle in Beijing. Initially, a single-candidate election was prepared to guarantee his reelection, but at the protest of the deputies it was changed to a multiple-candidate contest. The deputies obviously ignored the signal from above and spontaneously nominated two candidates for governor as Ge's rivals. One of them quit on the grounds that he did not want to compete with Ge, a Party nominee. Although the Party committee lobbied the deputies hard to ensure Ge's victory, Ge garnered only 326 votes from a total 759. Wan Xueyuan, an incumbent who ranked lowest among the vice governors, was elected by an absolute majority to be governor of one of China's most prosperous provinces.[36] In the competitive election for vice governors of the province, most Party nominees were defeated, whereas six of the nine candidates nominated by deputies got elected.[37]

The election of governor in Guizhou Province in January 1993 was more politically provocative. The provincial Party committee recommended Wang Chaowen, the incumbent governor. Chen Shineng, an incumbent vice governor, was nominated by the deputies to compete with Wang and eventually won the election. Before 1989 Chen had been deputy minister of light industry. He openly supported the students in the prodemocracy movement and after the Tiananmen massacre was demoted to the poor and remote Guizhou as punishment.[38] Some reports revealed that after the Party-nominated candidates for governorship lost the election, the results were not immediately announced but were submitted to the Politburo for its "ruling." It was allegedly Jiang Zemin who instructed the authorities in charge to make the results public and accept the deputies' choices.[39]

But Jiang's action in this case should not be construed as an appreciation of congressional initiative. In fact, the central leadership was quite upset, even shocked at their loss of control of elections at the provincial level. Their worry related to a major decision passed by the fourteenth Party congress. Since Mao's death in 1976, it has become a convention to hold the national Party congress (which occurs every five years) five to seven months earlier than each NPC. For instance, the eleventh Party congress of August 1977 was followed in March by the fifth NPC.[40] This pattern, replicated by regional Party congresses and legislatures above the county level, has special meaning, highlighting as it does Party dominance over the congress: Once the fundamental policy guidelines and changes of personnel were determined at the Party congress, it was the responsibility of the people's congress to legitimate them and work out detailed, concrete policy measures. After the mid-1980s, when the Party congress made important decisions it usually allowed some limited flexibility for people's deputies to display their initiative and demonstrate that the congress no longer played a rubber-stamp role but was capable of forcing some changes in Party decisions. But if this "constructive" function of the congress exceeded the prescribed limits, it would disturb the "strategic deployment" (*zhanlüe bushu*) designed by the Party center and compel it to make adjustments that might bring about new conflict.

After the mid-1980s, as a result of Party-government separation, the secretaries of Party committees at all levels—including the center—usually did not hold government posts, whereas top government officials still concurrently held key positions in the Party committee. On the eve of the fourteenth Party congress, Deng instructed the Politburo to restore the previous practice of the Party secretary's concurrently holding the leading government post. Deng's change of mind allegedly originated from the "lessons" learned from the collapse of communism in Eastern Europe and the Soviet Union. He understood the collapse mainly as a warning that the Communist Party could not delink itself from concrete economic affairs and administration. He also believed that the next generation of Party leaders must have administrative experience to survive socioeconomic modernization. Otherwise, Party power would have no solid foundation and would eventually be marginalized.[41]

Although it was not clear what role Jiang played in shaping Deng's idea, this reversal gave a boost to his ambitions. Jiang felt it quite inconvenient to travel abroad without a head-of-state title and was happy to take on the offices of both Party general secretary and PRC presidency. Moreover, preparing for the post-Deng era, Jiang did not want to lose contact with economic matters that theoretically were the exclusive domain of the premier and his cabinet, the State Council (au. int., 1996). Out of these considerations, the fourteenth Party congress passed a secret decision that virtually abolished the separation of Party and government established at the previous congress in 1987.[42]

In line with this new thinking, the first secretary of the provincial Party committee should or might (as this was not rigidly stipulated) concurrently hold the SCPC chair in each province, with the aim to strengthen party leadership (read "control") over the legislature.[43] Since SCPC chairs were elected in the same way as governors, the Party center's aim would be defeated if the Party secretary lost in the election of the SCPC chairperson. It was against this background that the central leadership, while accepting the fait accompli of elections in some provinces, sent urgent directives to provinces in which the elections had not yet been completed and instructed the provincial Party committees to adopt the single-candidate principle in the elections of governors and SCPC chairpersons. Multiple-candidate elections were to be used only for vice governors and vice SCPC chairpersons.[44] But as mentioned, even a single-candidate race was no guarantee of election. So during this period, rather than siding with deputies in a conflict between Party committee and legislature, the central propaganda organs appealed to the whole party to defend the authority of the Central Committee and demanded tighter Party discipline in elections.[45] It seems that the rebellions in some provincial elections in 1992–1993 directly caused the expansion of Party committee influence—without question, according to the central instructions—over personnel issues in the 1997–1998 elections.[46]

The heavy pressure from above worked in Sichuan Province. In the 1992–1993 election of the governor, Xiao Yang—unpopular among many local cadres and deputies but a must-elect candidate—won by an overwhelming majority.[47] But in Anhui Province the deputies showed less respect for the central authority. Fu Xishou, the single candidate for governorship designated by the Politburo, failed to garner an absolute majority of votes, and the congress was kept in session until Fu got elected.[48] In Guangxi Province the Party's candidates for governorship and SCPC chairmanship were elected only after four "preliminary" elections. Deputies threw out 40 percent of the Party nominees for other government offices.[49]

Similar electoral outcomes were seen at subprovincial levels. In Bajiao Township of Deyang, Sichuan, the deputies rejected the candidate nominated by the authorities and elected Wang Zhoulong, a peasant entrepreneur, as head of the township. Presumably because this defiance obviously targeted local cadres and had no implications for the Party center anyway, and because it took place at a very low administrative level and generated no political dangers, it was officially cited as evidence that whoever sticks to the Party's reformist line and has an outstanding work record would win the people's support.[50] Since such reports about deputy initiative, or "rebellion," in elections of government officials were rather sporadic, it is not unreasonable to speculate that many similar cases went unreported. In some areas the Party committee's nominees might not have been challenged by candidates nominated by deputies but had to take up the deputies' gauntlet, the latter having learned where their legitimate power lay and how to take advantage of election procedures to secure government officials' deference to legislative authority.[51]

In 1992–1993, despite growing signs that the authority of the Party center was shaken among provincial deputies, not many deputy rebellions were documented in the NPC elections. But the lack of turmoil did not last long. At an NPC session in 1995, two must-elect candidates for vice premiership got record low votes, to the astonishment of the Politburo.[52] This evident contempt for the Politburo's "supreme" authority may be analyzed from four angles. First, the rebellions of provincial deputies, who were the constituents of NPC deputies, in turn affected the NPC vote. Second, the authority of the Politburo headed by Jiang Zemin declined as the health of Deng, Jiang's patron, deteriorated.[53] Third, Tian Jiyun, the second highest leader of the NPC and a Politburo member, expressed open sympathy with NPC deputies who demanded multiple-candidate elections for the vice premiership and that campaign speeches be made to the deputies.[54] Support from within the top leadership circle perhaps prompted more votes against the two candidates for vice premier. This apparent cleavage among the central elites might be seen as another sign that as Deng's influence decayed, some NPC leaders tried to make greater use of the NPC's proclaimed status as the highest organ of state power to contend with the Central Committee or the Politburo.[55] Fourth, as some observers argued, the negative votes served as a protest from the regions whose representatives complained about the Party center's discrimination in aiding regional socioeconomic development as well as promoting regional leaders to the central institutions.[56]

To fully understand the significance of negative votes in the elections of state leaders, one must consider China's specific context. The Politburo still maintained a rather secure position to ensure that no candidate would be vetoed (i.e., the negative votes would not exceed 50 percent). But the negative votes, though not necessarily numerous, represented an implicit protest from NPC deputies that the Party center could never afford to ignore. Furthermore, candidates who failed to get elected by a comparatively high percentage suffered a blow to their prestige, which was extremely important if they aspired to establish their personal authority among both Party-state bureaucrats and citizens. Perhaps recognizing the importance of winning more votes, top Party leaders personally lobbied many provincial delegations of NPC deputies on the eve of the election of state leaders by the ninth NPC in March 1998, and requested them to guarantee that the candidates for the PRC presidency (Jiang Zemin), NPCSC chair (Li Peng), and premiership (Zhu Rongji) be elected with no less than 92 percent of the vote, and others, such as vice premiers and vice chairs of the NPCSC, no less than 86 percent.[57] Although the election of Zhu, widely seen as a radical and competent reformer, was a certainty, many deputies and officials worried about the percentage of votes he would win.[58]

In this election the competitive principle was only applied to the race for NPCSC seats (134 were chosen from 141 candidates).[59] And the Party center found that its lobbying efforts did not pay off among a relatively large proportion of the NPC deputies. Li Peng got only 80.9 percent of the votes, in contrast with his predecessors Wan Li (97 percent in 1988) and Qiao Shi (97.6 percent in 1993),[60] Han Shubin, the candidate for the office of procurator general, was elected with a record low 65 percent of the votes, which was perhaps particularly discouraging to Jiang Zemin, as Han was known to be Jiang's protégé and Jiang had reportedly proposed his candidacy.[61]

Obstacles for Deputies' Nominees

Since competitive elections provided congressional deputies with the chance to reject the candidates who were supposed to be designated arbitrarily by Party cadres, one might expect that more of the deputies' nominees were elected. Certainly the opposition of cadres to competitive elections during the early 1980s was well known, and it would seem that deputies would take advantage of the competitive principle—which had been firmly established at subnational levels as a result of their pressure—and vote for non-Party nominees after so many years of Party committee domination. Nevertheless, a quantitative analysis of the general results of competitive elections does not lend strong support to this assumption, though in recent years the percentage of deputies' nominees who got elected has indeed increased.

Let us take a look at the percentages of the Party's and deputies' nominees and their elections. In the twenty provinces for which relevant information was available, there were 471 candidates altogether for provincial government offices in the 1987–1988 elections. Among them 404 (86 percent) were Party nominees (nominated in the name of the presidia of provincial congresses) and sixty-seven (14 percent) recommended by deputies. Ultimately, 349 were elected. Of them, 341 (97.7 percent) were Party nominees and only eight (2.3 percent) were originally nominated by deputies. In other words, 84 percent of Party nominees were elected, whereas only 12 percent of the deputies' nominees were elected.[62] Below the provincial level, it seems, deputies' nominees were even less electable. In Chongqing the municipal Party committee recommended fifty-seven candidates for municipal government offices. At the same time, the deputies nominated as many as eighty-eight candidates, a clear indication of their enthusiasm and initiative in the matter. But only four (4.5 percent) of the deputies' nominees got elected, whereas forty-eight (84 percent) of the Party nominees were voted into office.[63]

That very few of the deputies' nominees could really compete with Party nominees and prevail in a competitive election—in which deputies themselves were the constituents with a fiarly high degree of voting freedom—was quite similar to the phenomenon of indirect elections of congressional deputies (discussed in Chapter 3). Since elected offices of government were located in the administrative structure in such a way that they would interact with the Party apparatus much more closely and directly than did deputies, an outside observer may speculate that Party bosses' pressure upon deputies with Party membership to vote for Party nominees might have played a decisive role, as Party members constituted the majority of deputies.

Such pressure surely existed to varying degrees, as evidenced both by my interviews and official sources.[64] Party cadres usually had enormous personal stakes in landing their own people in government offices or making government officials feel that they owed their election primarily to the Party (committee). A central Party journal discussed the question: If the Party (cadres and apparatus) and the people differ on a candidate, with whom should a congressional deputy with CCP membership side? While claiming that the deputy should first of all perform as the people's representative and vote as they mandate, the author mentioned several cases in which local leading Party bodies—without "democratic consultation" in advance even within the Party—often forced deputies with Party membership to vote for Party nominees and proposals.[65]

But pressure from Party cadres probably does not offer an exclusive explanation. An examination of the propaganda materials and Party-state documents would suggest that by the 1992–1993 elections the central leadership did not explicitly or implicitly encourage Party committees at subprovincial levels to impose their preferences upon deputies or rig their voting.[66] According to one of my interviewees, the day before the congress opened, the deputies with Party membership were usually called together to study the Central Committee documents, an effort to inform them of the center's latest thinking as well as impress upon them their political superiority, as non-Party deputies were not eligible for this "privilege."[67] But the municipal Party committee did not instruct them or hint which specific candidates they should vote for, so their voting decisions were based mainly on their own assessment of the candidates' credentials. Moreover, all voting in elections was conducted by secret ballot, allowing the deputies to vote freely without being identified (au. int.).

Therefore, one has to turn to the deputies themselves for part of the explanation of their voting behavior. Deputies may have been reluctant to endorse their colleagues' nominees because of their relative obscurity and regional limitations. The legal requirement for nominating candidates to government office was not stringent: Any deputy could easily put forward a name when seconded by no less than nine others. But conventional wisdom holds that easy nomination may not result in easy election, but rather the opposite. As one can see from the elections of people's deputies, raising the threshold of nominations would in effect make deputies' nominees more electable. Yet effortless nomination and less than sophisticated procedures led many deputies to nominate candidates either out of parochial interests or without a broad base of deputy support.

In the twenty provinces for which data are available, only three vice governors nominated by deputies were elected. Certain fundamental disadvantages of deputy nominations were evident. Liu Yuan was jointly selected as a candidate for Henan's vice governorship by more than one hundred deputies who came from Zhengzhou, the provincial capital city where Liu was a deputy mayor; Xinxiang; and the Henan provincial government apparatus. The large number of deputies who spontaneously nominated one candidate was unusual, suggesting that this candidate must be someone special. Liu's popularity and high profile actually resulted more from the fact that he is Liu Shaoqi's son than from his administrative achievements as a deputy mayor. Liu Shaoqi was president of the PRC and was tortured to death in the Cultural Revolution. His popular policies during the early 1960s and his tragic end won him profound sympathy among Chinese citizens. By contrast, Zhang Runxia, an elected vice governor of Anhui, was selected as a candidate by fewer than forty deputies; they came from the Anqing region and the city of Tongling, where she was mayor.[68]

Before the nomination process began, then, these two candidates were local leaders and well known only to the deputies from the regions where the candidates worked. As mayor or deputy mayor, each had probably done an excellent job and achieved a great deal, as their spontaneous nomination reflected. But one could reasonably suppose that in any province there were many local leaders with equal qualifications and work records. Several provincial congresses had more than 1,000 deputies who came from every corner of the province.[69] It would be difficult for the deputies from a city to persuade their colleagues from other areas that their own mayor was best qualified for the provincial leadership—all the more so because, as indicated earlier, people's deputies in China were not professional and met only once a year. Consequently, they hardly knew and trusted one another. They might even be afraid, for good reason, that if local leaders got elected, they would take special care of their parochial interests. The worry was particularly justified in the provinces where the quarrels over the reallocation of resources and the granting of socioeconomic prerogatives among areas intensified local efforts to lobby provincial authorities (au. int., 1996). Liu's election was not surprising, given his family background. Zhang's election was reportedly attributed mainly to the skillful lobbying efforts of her nominators.[70]

Another problem with deputies' nominations was allegedly their unfamiliarity with specific legal provisions concerning the separation of the Party from government, as well as the lack of knowledge about China's administrative structure (au. int., 1996). These provided justifiable grounds for election officials simply to exclude many deputies' nominees from the final list.[71]

In contrast, the inherent strengths of Party nominees—aside from the tangible Party influence over the voting process—were virtually unrivaled. Deputies' enthusiasm for nominating their own candidates did not necessarily arise from their distrust of Party nominations. In fact, deputy initiative might not represent anti-Party inclination at all. This was, of course, not surprising if one considered how people's deputies themselves were elected. Still, if most deputies believed, as their voting pattern might suggest, that Party nominees were more electable, one should not make the simpleminded assumption that deputies voted for Party nominees because they owed the Party a favor. There were other sources of this pro-Party candidate belief. One was that compared with a number of nominations "casually and rashly" made by deputies, Party nominations seemed more thoughtful, built on a careful and complete scrutiny of the candidates' records, and hence were more credible. In that regard, both as an institutional tradition and as a one-party system required, Party apparatus alone possessed the necessary facilities and the personal files (much of their contents confidential) to select candidates.[72]

If the attitudes of candidates toward reform constituted the basis of deputy choices, as some people would logically imagine, then the criteria used for Party nominations were not necessarily unfavorable to reform, particularly after the late 1980s. The seeming paradox was that Party nominees, once elected, tended to follow the Party apparatus more closely, but they did not have to be less reform-oriented than deputies' candidates. Despite interference from conservative Party elders, until 1989 the policy agenda at the highest level had been largely dominated by relatively young, open-minded Party leaders such as Hu and Zhao, who were backed by Deng most of the time, depending on policy issues. In 1980 Deng proposed political integrity, youth, better education, and professionalization as the four criteria for promotion of cadres.[73] The establishment of the new criteria compelled a partial reshuffle of local Party committees during the early 1980s.[74] A large number of reformers—or more exactly, those who appeared sympathetic to reform or for whatever reasons were more likely to be its promoters—had been appointed to key local Party posts.[75] As market reforms gave a new momentum to political reform in 1986, the emphasis in the selection of Party cadres shifted from devotion to the Party, Marxism, and the regime to support of Deng's reform programs, as well as to the ability to execute reform policies to initiate a new developmental phase. In February 1986 the head of the CCP Ministry of Organization, which usually appointed and removed Party cadres, told reporters that the selection of cadres must be based on their achievements in promoting reforms and economic modernization.[76] In late 1986 the ministry announced that all those who proved incompetent to carry through reforms must be dismissed.[77]

Consequently, in the 1987–1988 elections the professional Party cadres who searched for candidates for government offices differed considerably in political and ideological orientation from those of the early 1980s, who were either veteran cadres with traditional thinking or the beneficiaries of the Cultural Revolution disgusted with the new leadership. Even though many old-style cadres survived the reshuffle, they felt heavy pressure to exhibit reform enthusiasm to remain in office. The "democratic" quality of Party cadres was also to be improved through limited intra-Party "democratization." For example, in Shaanxi the secretary of the provincial Party committee was appointed allegedly following recommendations by the citizens.[78] It seemed that Party nomination was no longer monopolized by a single person or small circle or determined entirely by patron-client relations (au. int.). In January 1986 the Central Committee issued a notice stipulating a stringent procedure for the selection of Party cadres to guarantee the quality and commitment required for reform.[79]

Indeed, the multiple-candidate election offered an opportunity for people's deputies to choose. But the competitiveness and freedom of choice was quite limited, and deputies did not exactly leap at the chance: There was no significant increase in the number of government officials nominated by deputies. If Party nominees were not more electable, at least they were not less so because they were the Party's picks. Whether a candidate was nominated by the Party apparatus or by the deputies did not seem to make a substantial difference in political terms to a considerable proportion of deputies (au. int., 1996). Although deputies were more or less the citizen's representatives and had a popular base, they refrained from contending with the Party apparatus. Thus, if the competitive election of government officials was politically meaningful, it was not in the higher likelihood of electing dissidents but that it added some uncertainties to elections that served to break up the complete Party cadre monopoly of influence over elections and elected officials. Deputies were provided with a screening process to exclude Party nominees whose moral behavior, integrity, or attitudes toward reforms were doubtful. Only when congressional deputies demonstrated a real capability and willingness to destroy the prospects of an official's political career did the threat produce a massive impact upon legislature-government relations.

Appointments of Nonelected Government Officials

The congressional role was not limited to the election of chief executives but extended to the selection of cabinet members. Deputies seemed to be more assertive in this latter role, as suggested by their more frequent rejections of candidates. After the Party-government separation, local Party committees were left with five functions. The most meaningful was to recommend cadres for key posts in local governments. Although major government offices such as governor and vice governor were ultimately determined by competitive election, Party committees' recommendations carried heavy weight. After being elected, government chiefs formed their cabinets. The law provided that candidates for cabinet posts be approved (by secret ballot) and officially appointed by the SCPC. Party committees were authorized to recommend cabinet members, which they did by two slightly different methods, depending on the relationship between the committee and the congress. One was that the Party committee sent a list of exact-number candidates not directly to the SCPC but to the government chiefs. This list was then submitted to the SCPC in the government's name (au. int.). Another method was simpler: The Party committee, bypassing the government chiefs or in most cases preparing the list jointly with them, sent it directly to the Party group (*dang zu*) of the SCPC.[80] Either way, it was clear to all SCPC members that these candidates were basically the nominees of the Party committee.

After receiving the list, the SCPC Party group and the "chair's meeting" met separately to discuss it.[81] If a majority of the participants for each meeting disagreed, the list was returned to the Party committee for reconsideration. If the Party committee insisted there would be no changes, then the Party group and the chair's meeting had to accept it and submit it to the SCPC for a vote.[82] As with the congressional presidium in the elections of government chiefs,[83] it was quite difficult and unusual for the leading organs of the congress to reject Party committee nominees. To comprehend why, one must turn (in addition to the interlocking system analyzed in Chapter 7) to a basic contradiction inherent in political reform from the outset.

It was a CCP tradition established from the time of the communist takeover in 1949 that the Party must maintain its organizational control over the state and society through its monopolistic power to appoint Party cadres, government officials, and all kinds of power-holders from top to bottom within China's bureaucratic hierarchy. This principle was known as "Party control of cadres" (*dang guan gan bu*). Throughout the reform period, although Deng and other leaders recognized the need to make changes in the traditional forms of appointments, they never completely gave up the principle of cadre control. Deng's political reform relating to that matter amounted to little more than the introduction of a balancing influence; specifically, it allowed citizens and their representatives, whose political attachment to the regime should be unquestionable in the first place, to participate in the selection of government officials to constrain potential cronyism. This popular role was to add one more assurance that in addition to their political loyalty, made largely certain by cadres, officials would be reform-minded, honest, and competent. As such, when the Party center was keen to deny Party apparatus an arbitrary power over appointments of officials, it never encouraged the congress to perform a more than complementary balancing function. Concern with the possible undermining of organizational control accounted for the leadership's lack of enthusiasm for, if not anxiety about or aversion toward, the local congressional rejection of Party (committee) nominees and deputy initiative in nominations of candidates for either elected offices or cabinet posts, particularly at and above the municipal level.

Even if the SCPC leadership unconditionally accepted the Party's list of candidates, there was no guarantee of final approval of a majority of SCPC members. The election of government chiefs and appointment (approval) of cabinet members differed in the depth of the involvement of the congress (articles 8 and 44 of the local organic law). The former was an open event and required a plenary congressional session; its outcome was therefore more unpredictable. By contrast, the latter was the closed-door business of the SCPC, and its small size made it relatively easy for Party authorities to manage and lobby (au. int.).[84] When a Party nominee for major government office lost election, it certainly threw the predetermined personnel deployment into disarray. But the election results could hardly be overridden because of both the publicity surrounding the election and the unwieldy scale of the plenary session. The Party recommendation of candidates for cabinet posts, unlike its suggestions for elected offices, usually followed the exact-number principle. No alternative candidates were ready if anyone on the Party list failed to win SCPC endorsement. Since cabinet posts were hierarchically lower than elected offices, the selection of candidates tended to be more personalized. For all these reasons, the SCPC veto was more provocative to the Party committee than defeat in elections and yielded more serious consequences to the future working relationship between Party committee and legislature (au. int.).

Whereas legislative approval in the early 1980s was still a sheer formality, the SCPCs actually turned down candidates for cabinet posts during the 1987–1988 elections. Official statistics revealed that of 1,144 candidates in twenty-nine provinces recommended for provincial cabinet posts, forty-nine (4.28 percent) were rejected.[85] Albeit small, this percentage marked a notable increase. From 1983 to March 1987, in twenty-two provinces only 1.4 percent of the Party nominees for offices of this rank were vetoed.[86] The voting behavior of SCPC members seemed to vary widely across the country. In Hubei as many as seven of the total thirty-seven candidates (18.9 percent) were rejected by the provincial SCPC in late 1987.[87] In March 1990 a county SCPC voted out four of the forty-four Party committee nominees. Standing up to the resentful cadres, the SCPC cautioned them that approval or rejection all depended on the results of the (secret) balloting that could neither be controlled nor negotiated.[88] In a county adjacent to Beijing (Changping) in 1988–1994, the county SCPC demanded that all candidates for county cabinet posts must pass an examination on legal knowledge (the constitution, laws, and government regulations).[89]

The SCPCs rejected Party nominees either because they disagreed with the Party committees over the candidates' qualifications or because the committees did not provide information regarding the candidates that was detailed or clear enough for SCPC members to make a satisfactory decision.[90] Still, in some areas the SCPC deliberately made trouble for candidates before it accepted them in order to show its legislative teeth and let the candidates know that they owed their positions to the SCPC.[91] As expected, the disapproval of candidates brought the SCPCs into sharp collision with the Party committees in some provinces. Some Party cadres contended that since the SCPC members were well aware of who determined the list of candidates, their disapproval stood for intentional antagonism with the Party committees. It seemed, however, that Party cadres' resentment failed to win public sympathy from Party superiors or Party leaders, who needed to set themselves up as examples in complying with legal procedures and deferring to the "popular" will. Some reports suggest that at the municipal and county levels, the SCPC's rejection of Party nominees for cabinet posts had a contagious effect and became more common and widespread after the mid-1980s.[92]

Conclusion

The election of government officials bears a strong resemblance to the indirect elections of people's deputies. Since government offices and congressional seats differed in importance, the dilemma of the Party-sponsored political reform was more clearly exposed in that the central leadership found it even more necessary and difficult to achieve a balance between Party apparatus control and legislative autonomy.

Throughout the reform process, in sharp contrast with their public attitudes toward direct elections of people's deputies, Party leaders never showed much zeal for deputy initiative in the nomination of candidates for government offices. Instead, after the mid-1980s, when a substantial political restructuring was required to circumvent the increasing opposition to economic reform from the entrenched Party-state bureaucracy, the leadership in Beijing made serious efforts to establish the multiple-candidate principle for the election of government officials. The significance of this measure could be gauged more accurately from the overall political reform strategy. The new institutional arrangement partly characterized by the separation of the Party from government aimed to create workable mechanisms of checks and balances within the Party-state power hierarchy. But this separation would lose much of its intended utility if Party cadres were allowed to place the elections and appointments of government officials under their complete control. So while it did not encourage deputy initiative in nominations, the Party center attempted to enable congressional deputies to make a choice, based logically or supposedly on pro-reform criteria, among the Party (committee) nominees through multiple-candidate elections.

As I show in later chapters, this strategy worked well in that government officials now owed their seats and hence were responsible not only to the Party committee but to the people's congress as well. As a consequence, they were somewhat effectively brought under the double supervision of the two institutions. In that process, then, the central authorities admirably performed their balancing act: When congressional deputies had to be assertive or courageous enough to make an "appropriate" impact upon the elections, the Party center tried to expand deputies' freedom by legally establishing the competitive election principle. But when (as the 1992–1993, 1995, and 1997–1998 elections showed) the deputies attempted to strive for more autonomy in determining regional leaders, particularly at the provincial level, and so disturbed the Politburo's planned personnel changes, Beijing demanded more unconditional obedience to the central authority and strengthened Party discipline.

In the elections of officials, the people's deputies had yet to develop a real sense of representativeness as defined in Western democracies. Even if in some areas it appeared there was no lack of deputy initiative, most deputies did not seem to appreciate it and tended to vote against the candidates nominated by their colleagues. For a variety of reasons, many deputies, especially those with Party membership, still deferred to pressure from the Party committee. But the deeper sources of this phenomenon should perhaps be sought in certain structural variables in China's political system and social context. The prohibition of political competition and campaigning in the Western sense, deeply rooted parochialism and regionalism among a large number of deputies, and lack of legal professionalism were among the elements that prevented election of a higher percentage of deputies' nominees to government office.

But if the deputies' political loyalty to the regime seemed to remain reliable, they had gradually developed their own bureaucratic interests. As the paramount leader, Deng, was approaching the end of his life, the Politburo, headed by Jiang Zemin, was increasingly losing its authority over regional leaders and congresses as well as over NPC deputies who were elected by provincial congresses. Since the 1990s the deputies and local congresses have taken greater advantage of the situation created by the accelerated market reform to wield their power in the election of officials, with an obvious aim, as the analysis in Chapter 7 suggests, to achieve and maintain greater control over the government as against the influence of the Party committee. This tendency will make it even harder for central leaders to restrain deputy initiative within the limits they wish for without impeding market reform or tarnishing their reform image.

Notes

1. For a detailed discussion of the functions of SCPCs, see Chapter 7.
2. The whole name of the law is the "Organic Law of the Local People's Congresses and Local People's Governments."
3. As Burns shows, under the nomenklatura system established by 1955, Party nominations were made not by Party cadres of the same administrative level but by higher Party authorities. Party committees exercised formal authority over senior personnel appointments two levels down the administrative hierarchy. Burns, ed., *The Chinese Communist Party's Nomenklatura System,* p. xvi. This would make it riskier for deputies to disagree.
4. QXZXB, ed., *Diyijie Quanguo,* p. 149. This was a violation of the 1979 organic law, which provided that to be elected a candidate must win more than half the votes of the total number of the people's deputies.
5. For Cheng Zihua's speech of August 3, 1980, see *FBIS Daily Report: China,* August 4, 1980, p. L9.
6. QXZXB, ed., *Diyijie Quanguo,* p. 33.
7. Ibid., pp. 45–46. Burns, ed., *The Chinese Communist Party's Nomenklatura System,* pp. xxx–xxxi.
8. QRCBY, ed., *Renmin Daibiao Dahui Zhidu Jianshe Sishinian,* pp. 191, 194.
9. Luo Shugang and Liu Jinxiu, "The Shock."
10. Liao Guanxian, "Can the County Head Be Appointed?"
11. Wang Shuhua, "Don't Substitute Transfer Orders."
12. *Bulletin of the NPC Standing Committee,* 1986, p. 89.
13. As several studies show, in the early 1980s the electoral reform failed to change patronage politics in the selection of officials. The single-candidate election

made the nomination process especially important. Lee, *From Revolutionary Cadres,* pp. 280–282; McCormick, *Political Reform,* ch. 4.

14. In public the leadership more often than not tipped the scale in favor of congressional deputies—not necessarily as a propaganda tactic. Party leaders might have recognized that under the strong tradition of Party hegemony, particularly with their special emphasis on the "organizational guarantee," deputies were in an inherently weak position to challenge Party committee nominees for government offices. In April 1995 *RMRB* sent a stern warning to the Party committees "in some areas" that "gravely violated the Party's democratic principle" by allowing the Party secretary to form the cabinet (meaning that all the candidates for top government posts were predetermined by the Party secretary). *RMRB* charged that the Party secretary who did so "virtually aimed to create his own faction and did not differ from the warlords during the early Republican period." *RMRB* Pinglunyuan, "The Party Secretary."

15. The full text of the 1986 local organic law is found in *Bulletin of the NPC Standing Committee,* 1986, pp. 72–85. Note the provision that the election of administrative chiefs could be conducted by the exact-number method if only one candidate were nominated. According to the letter of the law, there was nothing wrong with this. It was quite possible that just one candidate was nominated either by the Party apparatus or the congressional deputies. Since no similar provision was made for the election of less important officials (such as deputies to the chiefs), it could be taken as a hint that competitive election might not necessarily be extended to top government posts.

16. One may find that this requirement made deputy nomination of officials more difficult at and above the municipal level than at the county level.

17. Wu Changqi and Chen Jiyu, eds., *Difang Renda Zhidu,* ch. 4; also au. int.

18. QRCBY, ed., *Renmin Daibiao Dahui Zhidu Jianshe Sishinian,* p. 200.

19. Luo Shugang and Liu Jinxiu, "The Shock."

20. Ibid. Another source indicates that five candidates nominated by deputies were elected vice governors, for Shanghai, Tianjin (provincial equivalents), Henan, Anhui, and Zhejiang. Cai Dingjian et al., "A Study of How to Elect Vice Chiefs of Local Governments," in QRCBY, ed., *Renmin Daibiao Dahui Zhidu Luncong,* pp. 201–205.

21. Lu Yun, "China Speeds Up Democratization."

22. QRCBY, ed., *Renmin Daibiao Dahui Zhidu Jianshe Sishinian,* pp. 198–199.

23. Ibid.

24. Luo Shugang and Liu Jinxiu, "The Shock."

25. QRCBY, ed., *Renmin Daibiao Dahui Zhidu Jianshe Sishinian,* p. 200.

26. Hu Guohua, "The New Milestone"; Mao Yongxiong, "A New Beginning."

27. Mao Yongxiong, "A New Beginning."

28. Shu Zhan, "Competitive Election."

29. According to calculations by some of China's legal scholars, in the 1987–1988 elections at the provincial level the percentage of chief executives (governors) elected through competitive elections was 26.6, while it was just below 10 at and under the municipal level in some provinces. Cai Dingjian et al., "A Study."

30. Many local government affairs do not seem to be decisively affected by the dominant national ideology either in China in its era of reform or in many Western democracies. Thus, campaign speeches of candidates for government office do not have to be political declarations. In Italy, while the central government was dominated by the center-right Christian Democrats during the late 1980s, more than 1,200 mayors were communists in whose elections the Italian Communist Party's ideological outlook actually had neither much relevance nor strong appeal. See LaPalombara, *Democracy,* ch. 9; Hine, *Governing Italy,* ch. 3. This raises a question: Even though

political pluralism obtains in China, how will opposition politicians win local government office with a reliance upon an alternative ideology?

31. Yang Minqing, *Zhongguo Da Xuanju,* pp. 114–132. Before the election was held, the NPC deputies spent two days discussing the candidates for state leadership. As Yang observed, reporters were not allowed to listen to the discussions. Closed-door voting seems to have become a convention; it was also adopted in the recent election of the state leadership by the ninth NPC in March 1998. People generally believed that the authorities did not want a possibly embarrassing situation—that is, if some top leaders got "too many" negative votes—to be immediately made public. *MB,* March 16, 1998, p. A10.

32. The elections yielded the following results: Yang Shangkun, candidate for the PRC presidency: 2,725 pros, 124 cons, and 34 abstentions; Wang Zhen, candidate for the PRC vice presidency: 2,594 pros, 212 cons, and 37 abstentions; Deng Xiaoping, candidate for the chair of the Central Military Commission: 2,850 pros, 25 cons, and 37 abstentions; Wan Li, candidate for the NPCSC chair: 2,808 pros, 64 cons, and 8 abstentions; Li Peng, candidate for the premiership: 2,854 pros, 18 cons, and 5 abstentions. Never before had China's mass media publicly reported how many ballots were cast against the candidates. The sources for these data and also for the information about votes for minor state leaders are Yang Minqing, *Zhongguo Da Xuanju,* p. 124; Mu Qing, "What Does It Mean?"

33. Mu Qing, "What Does It Mean?" Ge Fengchen, "Deng Xiaoping." A few deputies, almost all of whom were from Taiwan, Hong Kong, or overseas, voted against some candidates on the grounds that they could not get enough information about the candidates and therefore had no idea whether they were qualified. See Jiang Yaochun and Ma Yijun, "Reports."

34. Yang Minqing, *Zhongguo Da Xuanju,* p. 124.

35. In some areas people's deputies reportedly revived even before Deng's 1992 trip. In a by-election of two vice governors in Hunan in April 1991, the deputies' nominee defeated a Party nominee, perhaps for the first time at the provincial level after Tiananmen. See QRCBY, ed., *Difang Renda shi Zenyang Xingshi Zhiquande?* pp. 266–268.

36. *SJRB,* February, 1, 1993; Lu Ren, "The Merger."

37. Luo Bing and Li Zijing, "Spectacles."

38. *SJRB,* February, 1, 1993; Chen Hongyi, "1993: A New Term."

39. The report appeared in *WHB,* China's official newspaper in Hong Kong, which usually represents the opinions of Beijing. Quoted in *SJRB,* February 8, 1993.

40. The twelfth Party congress convened in September 1982. Since then, it has been regularly held in October (of 1987, 1992, and 1997). See table 3.2 in Lieberthal, *Governing China,* pp. 80–81.

41. The discussion here is based on the materials published in *JBYK,* a pro-Beijing journal in Hong Kong: Zhang Mo, "Two Conferences"; Liu Jiang, "The 8th NPC Has New Features." *JBYK* publisher Xu Simin held a senior position in the CPPCC and was an "old friend" of Deng and some other Party leaders. The reports on high-level politics in Beijing in his journal appear true. Since it exposed an important decision that was not reported elsewhere, I made some inquiries about it in Beijing in 1996, which largely confirmed the *JBYK* reports. The alleged reason for not announcing this decision even to local Party cadres was the unwillingness of Jiang and the new Politburo to tarnish their image as reformers or to cause an impression of a political regression. Also, the priority of the decision was placed only on the provincial level.

42. Zhang Mo, "Two Conferences"; Liu Jiang, "The 8th NPC."

43. Liu Jiang, "The 8th NPC."

44. My interviews in 1996, as well as Lu Ren, "The Merger."

45. *RMRB,* February 4, 1993. At a deeper level of analysis, the provincial legislative veto of the candidates nominated by the Politburo for top provincial government posts reflected intensified central-local conflicts. Jiang Zeming managed to land his people in key regional positions to strengthen the central authority. But his efforts were resisted by native regional leaders who attempted to protect local interest against the impingement of the central government. The conflicts were particularly intense in the provinces of northeast and south China. *ZYRB,* January 28, 1995. The veto of the Politburo's nominees essentially represented a concerted opposition in some areas backed by regional Party apparatus. *RMRB* appealed to local Party committees to keep in line with the center "ideologically, politically, practically, and organizationally." See *RMRB* Pinglunyuan, "Local Party Committees." When Jiang Zemin attended an NPC group discussion in March 1995, he complained about the lack of strong local support for the central decisions. *SJRB,* March 17, 1995, p. A20.

46. In a commentary published by its journal *Dangjian Yanjiu* (Research on party building), the CCP Department of Organization demanded that in the 1997–1998 elections, any major issues regarding personnel changes must be internally and collectively discussed within the Party committee. Each Party committee member must resolutely carry out its decisions. Quoted in *MB,* January 5, 1998, p. A9.

47. Li Yu, "The People's Congress." The Xiao Yang case was quite interesting. He was perceived as having close personal relationships with influential central leaders but was not welcomed within the circles of Sichuan Party cadres. So in the fourteenth Party congress, the Sichuan delegation defied the instructions from the Politburo and managed to let Xiao lose in the elections of Central Committee members.

48. Liu Jiang, "The 8th NPC"; Li Yu, "The People's Congress."

49. Chang Qing, "The Percentage."

50. Chen Hongyi, "1993: A New Term."

51. An example was Bo Xilai, whose father was the influential Party elder Bo Yibo. He ran for reelection as mayor of Dalian (Liaoning). Although he was the sole nominee for the position and was proposed by the authorities, he felt quite nervous about his election because many deputies criticized him sharply at the congressional session. He visited each group meeting of deputies to explain, apologize, and seek support. He "burst into tears" when he learned the news of his election. "Bo Xilai Was Reelected."

52. At a Party session in 1994, Wu Bangguo and Jiang Chunyun were promoted to the central Party Secretariat from Shanghai and Shandong Province, respectively, and were scheduled to be elected vice premiers by the NPC the next March. Before the election, central leaders made massive efforts to persuade NPC deputies to vote for them. According to predictions, the two candidates would get more than 90 percent of the votes. But the percentage of support turned out to be 86 for Wu and 63 for Jiang. Until then, the percentage of votes for candidates for state leadership had never been lower than 95. See Ao Feng, "NPC Deputies."

53. Ibid. Jiang Zemin, a regional leader (Shanghai Party secretary) and a technocrat, was handpicked by Deng to fill the position of Party general secretary in June 1989. Although he brought with him to Beijing some of his followers from Shanghai, he had yet to consolidate his power base at the Party center as well as his personal authority.

54. Luo Bing, "Tian Jiyun's Speeches"; also *SJRB,* March 17, 1995, p. A20.

55. This issue is analyzed in detail in Chapter 6.

56. Wang Yuyan, "Local Forces." This judgment seems to be confirmed by the dismissal of Jiang Chunyun, who had just served half of his term, by the ninth NPC.

According to a Hong Kong reporter who interviewed several NPC deputies, Jiang's vice premiership failed to convince many other regional leaders. Lang Fang, "Why Was Jiang Chunyun Deposed Halfway?"

57. Li Zijing, "Jiang Zemin." Strictly speaking, the premier and vice premiers were not elected but approved by vote.

58. *MB*, March 17, 1998, p. A12.

59. Peng Weixiang, "A Witness."

60. Jin Ziyan, "Why the Percentage of Votes?"

61. *MB,* March 18, 1998, p. A15.

62. Yan Jiaqi, a deputy of the municipal congress of Beijing, indicated that 99 percent of candidates on approved nomination lists were elected, whereas only 1 percent of the candidates nominated by ten or more deputies were elected. Cited in O'Brien, *Reform Without Liberalization,* p. 214. Although it was not clear whether Yan's data refer to the nationwide election of officials or just the elections in Beijing's municipal congress, these data verify the small percentage of deputies' nominees who got elected.

63. Yuan Guanghou, "Democratic Whirlwind." Of course not all of these candidates could be placed on the final list for competitive election, because its numbers far exceeded the required difference between the number of candidates and the number of seats. For example, there were forty-four candidates, most of whom were nominated by deputies, for the seven offices of mayor and deputy mayor in Chongqing; this number had to be cut to only ten. It was implied in the report that the formal candidates were determined by a preliminary vote among the deputies.

64. For instance, prior to the election of governor in Shandong in March 1995, the organization department of the provincial Party committee sent people to persuade deputies to vote for Li Chunting, a Politburo nominee and an incumbent vice governor. Li got elected, although many deputies initially preferred a more liberal candidate. *SJRB,* March 14, 1995, p. A14.

65. Wan Sha, "To Whom Should the People's Deputy?"

66. But the provincial level was an exception, as mentioned in the previous section. Since the candidates for the top provincial government leadership were usually selected by the Politburo, any veto would be seen as a challenge to—or at least disrespect for—the central authority. Also, provincial leaderships were too important for the Party center to allow congressional deputies to have a decisive influence in their selection.

67. My other interviews found that despite the absence of a written rule, this was a prevailing pattern in many areas. But there is as yet no hard evidence that this kind of Party member meeting prior to congressional sessions has had a visible effect on the voting results.

68. *LWZK* Jizhe, "Observe."

69. In 1988 there were six provincial congresses with more than 1,100 deputies. The provincial congress of Sichuan had the largest number of deputies: 1,475. See Chen Mo, "Further Improve the System of Electing People's Deputies," in Zi Mu, ed., *Minzhu de Gousi,* p. 161.

70. *LWZK* Jizhe, "Observe."

71. Here is a typical case: In Chongqing the congressional presidium nominated Sun Tongchuan, an incumbent deputy mayor, for the office of mayor. The deputies nominated four candidates against him: Xiao Yang, the incumbent mayor; Yu Hanqing, the incumbent deputy secretary of the municipal Party committee; Jin Lie, the incumbent chairman of the municipal commission of economic planning; and Guo Daiyi, the manager of the Chongqing Iron and Steel Company. Among the four candi-

dates, three were not eligible for quite simple reasons. Xiao had been elected municipal Party secretary in the local Party congress just one month before. According to the principle of the Party-government separation, he could not hold the mayorship concurrently. Yu had been officially nominated as a candidate for the municipal SCPC chair. It was obviously inappropriate and also very rare to have one person assume the two offices. Guo's candidacy should have had no problems from a Western perspective. But in China's traditional administrative hierarchy and also according to the rules for promotion to which many Chinese citizens and deputies were mentally accustomed, Guo's incumbent position was simply too low for the mayorship. The formal candidates for mayorship must be just two. Since Xiao enjoyed high popularity in his term as mayor, a preliminary vote among the deputies selected him, over his own opposition, as the only alternative candidate to compete with the Party-nominated Sun. Before the election started, Xiao tried hard to persuade the deputies to comply with the Party-government separation principle and to vote against him. But many deputies ignored his request. It turned out to be a close race. Sun won by a narrow margin (385 vs. 324 votes). Yuan Guanghou, "Democratic Whirlwind."

72. The examination of candidates' records and qualifications was usually conducted by the organization departments of Party committees at various levels. During the late 1980s, SCPCs began to join Party committees in doing this work or did it independently in some areas. This made official nomination of candidates look more "thoughtful." See Huang Liqun and Jiang Guofang, "The Standing Committees."

73. These four criteria were first proposed by Chen Yun and strongly endorsed by Deng. See Deng Xiaoping, *Selected Works,* p. 308.

74. A case study is found in Forster, "The Reform."

75. The official statistics disclosed that 1.27 million veteran cadres who joined the communist revolution before 1949 had retired by the end of 1985, and 469,000 young and middle-aged cadres were promoted to the leading positions above the county level. As a result, the average age of cadres at the provincial, municipal and county levels decreased from sixty-two, fifty-six, and forty-nine in 1982 to fifty-three, forty-nine, and forty-four, respectively. The proportion of the cadres who received higher education increased by 45 percent. These new cadres, as a *RMRB* commentator claimed, "have become the backbone in carrying forward reforms and the four modernizations." *RMRB,* June 26, 1986.

76. Ibid., February 11, 1986.

77. Ibid., January 5, 1987.

78. Ibid., February 11, 1986. This kind of report by a Party propaganda machine should not be taken just literally. For political purposes, it might not be important whether the report was true to the facts. By commending a specific case in *RMRB*, the Party center might simply aim to set an example for the whole country or Party to follow.

79. The procedure emphasized two crucial links: democratic recommendation by the masses and a collective decision by the Party committee according to the majority principle. *RMRB*, February 2, 1986.

80. QRCBY, ed., *Difang Renda shi Zenyang Xingshi Zhiquande?* pp. 282–283.

81. The people's congress at each level had a diarchial structure. The Party group, usually comprising four to five members, was theoretically the Party representative in the congress, and its principal function was the handling of the relationship between the congress and the Party committee at the same level. The "chair's meeting," which was usually attended by chair and vice chairs of the SCPC, was to be the supreme organ within the congress to decide upon day-to-day legislative matters and agenda. Unlike a Party or a government department, the chair's meeting had no legal authority

over the deputies. But in reality, since the congress theoretically had to accept the "political leadership" of the same-level Party committee, the Party group often overrode the chair's meeting if a conflict of opinion occurred. Au. int., 1989, 1996.

82. QRCBY, ed., *Difang Renda shi Zenyang Xingshi Zhiquande?* pp. 282–283.

83. The congressional presidium was not a standing organ. It was typically formed during the elections and took care of election affairs.

84. This difference did not apply to the township level, as the township congress has no standing committee. According to the 1995 amendment of the local organic law, the township congress should set up (elect) one chair and one or two vice chairs as a partial substitute for the standing committee.

85. QRCBL, "The Reasons."

86. Ke Qi, "Thinking over the Power of Appointment and Removal," in Zi Mu, ed., *Minzhu de Gousi,* pp. 135–146.

87. QRCBL, "The Reasons."

88. QRCBY, ed., *Difang Renda Xingshi Zhiquan Shili Xuanbian,* pp. 285–286.

89. Ibid., pp. 290–291.

90. QRCBL, "The Reasons."

91. Au. int., 1996; QRCBY, ed., *Difang Renda Xingshi Zhiquan Shili Xuanbian,* pp. 285–286. Any perceived "disrespect" might provoke the legislature. A most recent case was found in Fengtai District, Beijing. In February 1998 the district Party committee and government jointly appointed the head of the (government's) planning committee without going through the legislative procedures. The district congress voted to oust him after he had been in office a month and a half. *MB,* March 29, 1998, p. A11.

92. Zhao Baoxu, ed., *Minzhu Zhengzhi,* pp. 96–97, 128–129, 143. In Nanjing and Wuhan, the candidates for municipal government offices had to pass examinations on legal knowledge organized by the municipal SCPC.

5

The Strategy
for Restructuring
Power Relationships

From a broader perspective, elections of both people's deputies and government officials were not isolated reform measures. Since China's political restructuring was sponsored by the central elite out of pragmatic considerations and consistently manipulated by them for situational needs, the extent to which the electoral reform was seriously carried out and what impact it was intended to produce upon the power structure hinged upon the overall reform strategy. After it started around the turn of the 1970s, China's political reform was propelled by a combination of factors that kept changing. The most basic of them, to use Deng's words, was a necessity to solve the problems in the "leadership and organizational systems," or, more specifically, to alter the "overconcentration" of power in the hands of Party cadres. If this requirement was not so urgent during the early 1980s, it would soon become so as economic reforms met with the restraints of the political structure that were, first and foremost, embodied in the opposition of powerful Party apparatus.

The different motivations and goals of the two stages of political reform accounted for the repeated legal electoral revisions from 1979 to 1986 and the subsequent increase of citizen influence. Based on an analytical reading of wide-ranging policy documents, the leadership speeches, and all kinds of official propaganda materials, this chapter attempts to explore the strategy of political reform as the leaders in Beijing designed and modified it and to provide some insight into their considerations, apprehensions, and realistic policy options. It places considerable emphasis upon the separation of the Party from government, which has been a key step in restructuring the triangular relationships of power at all of China's administrative levels.

The Political Reform on Paper, 1978–1985

To understand the separation of the Party from government in the Chinese context, one must distinguish first between totalitarian and authoritarian single-party systems and then between single-party and multiparty systems. In most political systems, political parties play an important role in the governmental process, perhaps because the government is not and can never be in itself a coherent, independent political force. So it has to be a government-by-party. As Myron Weiner and Joseph LaPalombara suggest, in nontotalitarian single-party systems in African and Asian countries, the government and party also tend to become indistinguishable.[1] With a few exceptions, such as the United States, political power is heavily concentrated in the hands of political parties in Western democracies, particularly in many Western European parliamentary systems.[2] But the nature of government-by-party is substantially different in single-party and multiparty systems. In the former, some conditions necessary for democratic party government do not exist.[3] In addition, among all types of single-party systems, perhaps none goes further than the communist system in fusing party and government.

During the 1960s several academic works on China's government structure and policy process described the changes effected by the Chinese structural reforms during the post-Mao period.[4] Western China specialists seemed to have a broad consensus that by the mid-1960s Party organizations and state institutions in China overlapped to such a great extent that to distinguish them was either impossible or meaningless.[5] According to A. Doak Barnett, the Party organizations penetrated and dominated the state apparatus in a variety of ways, two of which were most important. One was a kind of "shadow government" formed by the Party committee at all levels whose functions replicated and overpowered those of the real government.[6] Another was the monopolization of key leadership posts of government bodies by Party members, who were directly subject to Party instructions from above.[7] The Party and state were made even less distinguishable by the role of the Party chief (the secretary of the Party committee), who as the indisputable supreme leader at any given administrative level concurrently held the chief government post in most areas. In other areas the Party chief appointed and directed the government chief, who usually occupied the second place in the Party committee. Under the Mao regime, Party policies, without being formally converted into state laws, were codes of conduct that dominated China's social, political, and economic life.[8]

When the Cultural Revolution with all its upheavals was brought to an end, post-Mao leaders recognized the flaws in the traditional Party-state structure and the governmental process in which the Party, or rather its local organizations and cadres, performed the functions that should have been performed by the government. This impingement upon the authority of the government concentrated all powers—from the formulation and implementation of public policies to the day-to-day management of citizen welfare—into the hands of the Party committee (or more accurately, the Party chief) at each level, without any institutional checks and balances to prevent abuse or misuse of power. But to overhaul this well-established structure of authority would not be an easy undertaking, as it would have to touch on the most sensitive political issue, that is, the Party's leadership position. The dilemma involved was quite obvious: The Party center, out of the changing considerations at different stages of economic reform, needed to destroy the monopolistic power position of Party organizations and cadres and allow their authority to be balanced against. But at the same time the leadership had no alternative but to continue to rely upon them to maintain Party control of the populace and defend the regime against any potential threats arising from the people. This problem was both practical and theoretical. Any measure to weaken Party organizations and cadres must be implemented and explained in a way that would not encourage social disobedience. The Party's lofty status as the "leading force" and its hegemonic appearance must be left intact. The idea of letting Party organizations retreat from center stage to backstage—which later evolved into a major reform strategy known as the "separation of the Party from government" (*dang zheng fen kai*)—initially emerged as a tentative effort to solve this dilemma.

How the Idea of Party-Government Separation Was Shaped

This idea, along with the general conception of political reform, was gradually shaped at the start of the post-Mao years. Just as Lowell Dittmer suggests, China's reform in the early stage "is more clearly defined by the recent historical errors that it is trying to escape from than by any self-conscious vision of the future."[9] What Deng first identified as a source of past errors was Mao's patriarchy, which allegedly caused the disasters of the Cultural Revolution. In the landmark communiqué of the Third Plenum (December 1978), it was implicitly acknowledged that because of Mao's "leftist" mistakes, for a period in the past "democratic centralism" in the true sense had not been carried out, "centralism being divorced from democracy and there being too little democracy."[10] Not surprisingly, from the very beginning of his return to power, Deng was the main force behind what was known in the West as "de-Maoization." But Deng's denouncement of the Cultural Revolution did not stop at Mao. He also blamed the system of party leadership for the lack of democracy. In a 1978 speech to the senior Party cadres, he criticized the "rigid" thinking and acting "according to fixed notions": "Strengthening Party leadership is interpreted as the Party's monopolizing and interfering in everything; exercising centralized leadership is interpreted as erasing distinctions between the Party and the government, so that the former replaces the latter."[11] This speech already disclosed some basic elements of Deng's thinking about changing the role of Party apparatus. After Deng had established and consolidated his dominance at the Party center around the turn of the 1970s, he went further with his critique of the "faulty" system.[12]

With the "reform" under way in the countryside, essentially a restoration of family farming through decollectivization, Deng sent a clear signal of political reform, setting its sights on the monopoly of power by Party organizations at all levels. In an August 1980 speech to the Politburo, Deng attacked the "inappropriate and indiscriminate concentration of all power in Party committees in the name of strengthening centralized Party leadership." In this speech, the first programmatic document for China's political reform, Deng raised the possibility of redefining and virtually diminishing Party functions. "We have tried several times to divide power between the central and local authorities," he claimed, "but we never defined the scope of the functions and powers of the Party organizations as distinct from those of the government and of economic and mass organizations."[13] Three days later, when an Italian journalist asked him about how to avoid another Cultural Revolution, Deng stressed the necessity of tackling the "problems in our institutions" and announced that the Party center was "preparing to start with the restructuring of our institutions."[14]

If Deng's speeches were still quite general and at first circulated only among senior cadres, the Party journal *HQ* soon converted them into specific proposals and made them known across the country. Its commentary "The Party Cannot Substitute for the Government" was important in the history of the post-Mao reform not just because it demanded in definite terms that Party committees get rid of administrative work and instead concentrate on the "issues concerning basic policies and political orientations" but also because it attempted to reinterpret "party leadership" and enshrine this reinterpretation in the orthodox ideology. The author suggested new ways to think about "strengthening" party leadership. He saw no problems whatsoever with the principle of Party domination over everything, given the Party's status as the leading force. But this principle never meant that the Party should take care of everything.[15] This article, which unmistakably represented the opinions of the Politburo, laid the theoretical foundation of the political reform that followed. But as we will see, how to construe the central "spirit" still caused much controversy in the local restructuring of power.

If these theoretical formulations merely proposed changes to the Party apparatus's "functions" without an explicit intention to limit its power, then the twelfth Party congress (September 1982) presented a more mature and straightforward scheme. In his report to the congress, Party general secretary Hu Yaobang defined the Party as neither an organ of power nor an administrative organization. He asserted that an appropriate division of labor between the Party and the government was required to make sure that the government would work independently and efficiently. At the same time, Hu was careful not to allow his speech to be mistaken as downgrading the Party's status. He stressed that the decisions on major governmental and economic issues must still be taken by the Party. All the Party members in government, institutions, and enterprises must be resolutely obedient to the Party leadership in Beijing and execute Party policies.[16] Some of Hu's main points were incorporated into the new Party constitution, which provided that "Party leadership consists mainly in *political, ideological, and organizational leadership. . . .* The Party must conduct its activities within the limits permitted by the constitution and laws of the state. It must see to it that the legislative, judicial, and administrative organs of the state and the economic, cultural, and people's organizations work actively and with initiative, independently, responsibly, and in harmony."[17] No matter how much propaganda was inherent in these claims and whether or not Party cadres would comply with the provision, its explicit inclusion in the Party constitution was unprecedented in CCP history.[18] Deng and his colleagues attempted to present themselves as serious "democratic" reformers and to derive the "legitimacy" of the reforms from the transformation of, to use James Scott's term, the discourse of the public transcript, which was to prove a costly political liability.[19] In the reforms to follow, this change of the discourse was taken as a high-powered weapon by the people's deputies and government officials who strived for greater autonomy and tried to resist interference from Party cadres.

Why the Separation Failed in the Early 1980s

Until the mid-1980s, however, all the announcements made by the Central Committee, Party-state documents, and legal provisions regarding the change of Party functions largely remained on paper. They failed to produce any notable impact upon the old Party-state structure of authority. Following Deng's speech, some tangible changes did take place. Several Party elders took the lead to quit the State Council (cabinet). In an NPC session of September 1980, Party chairman Hua Guofeng was forced to resign from the post of premier. Some of the most senior Politburo members, such as Deng Xiaoping, Chen Yun, Li Xiannian, Xu Xiangqian, and Wang Zhen, ceased to serve concurrently as vice premiers.[20] During this period, many Party committee secretaries at the provincial, municipal, and county levels were relieved of their government posts. These steps were intended to turn the government into more than a Party appendage, at least formally, and enable it to perform as an executive organ with administrative autonomy.

Nonetheless, as far as actual exercise of power was concerned, these measures did not seem to solve any problems. A central issue to be addressed was how Party committees and cadres at each level should work if they did not perform government functions. Or to put the question another way, how

could the Party's "political and ideological leadership" be translated into concrete functions and responsibilities of Party committees? For one thing, if a
Party secretary quit the chief government office but as secretary was still empowered to keep that office under his complete control, it made no difference
whether he held the two posts concurrently. Some reformers, who were later
authorized to work out more effective reform strategies, tried to find out why
the earlier measures for the Party-government separation failed to take effect.
"One of the main reasons," they found, "was that these measures were only
limited to a formalistic division of the administrative realm between the Party
apparatus and the government. They did not result from a recognition of the
essential distinctions and connections between the two."[21]

Delving deeper, we find that the failure of the experimental efforts to separate the functions of the Party and government—along with the ups and
downs of electoral reforms during the same period (1979–1985)—was caused
mostly by the central leadership's own hesitation and apparent ambivalence
toward the limitation of Party (apparatus) power, which was crucial to any
meaningful political reform. In the early 1980s, the reforms in the countryside
rapidly developed to precipitate the collapse of the commune system. And the
newly established production responsibility system made remarkable
progress. In urban areas workers' participation in the management of enterprises not only served a propaganda purpose but seemed to give an immediate
boost to productivity as well. In general, this was a phase of rapid overall economic growth and improvement in people's livelihood.[22] In a situation full of
hope, an all-round economic reform that aimed to shake the foundation of the
command economy was proclaimed in 1984 and foretold greater prosperity to
come. As the primary sponsor of these changes, Deng saw his personal prestige rise to new heights.

But paradoxically, regime legitimacy, bolstered by earlier reforms, did
not extend to further political reform. Instead, as some scholars observed,
these economic and social changes did not "convince most Chinese leaders of
the need for democratization; if anything, they became more firmly convinced
of the opposite: the need for enhanced political stability."[23] In late 1983, in a
reversal of his typical pro-reform rhetoric, Deng turned against what he called
the "spiritual pollution" and blamed Party organizations and cadres for their
"weakness" in combating the tendency of "bourgeois liberalization."[24] In
early 1985 Deng once again denounced the "worship of Western democracy
and liberty" and threatened to punish the liberal reformers.[25] Although Deng
did not publicly retreat from his previous stand on political reform, he obviously suspended it by keeping silent about it.[26] As societal expectations
climbed, Deng balked at taking any substantial and forceful steps toward political reform, worried that economic restructuring and the social mobilization
that accompanied it could create chaos.

A Change in the Situation, 1985–1986

But this muddy situation and Deng's equivocal stand did not last long. In the summer of 1986, political reform seemed to regain momentum all of a sudden and was greatly accelerated. This time the proposed reform policies went further in their most sensitive aspects than those of the early 1980s. They revolved no more around a theoretical exploration of the "appropriate" functions of Party organizations and cadres but went straight to the point of taking away their executive power. Since central leaders once again confirmed their commitment to building up a powerful people's congress that thus far still swayed between its traditional rubber-stamp status and its cautious quest for genuine authority, Party organizations and cadres also faced the potential threat that congresses would share policymaking power and weaken the Party (apparatus) control over the government.

This abrupt and dramatic change in the course of reform in 1986 invited a great deal of speculation. Some Western scholars viewed it as a move toward political liberalization aimed at paving the way ideologically for further market reforms. More specifically, they believed, political reform was being used to counter the conservative Party leaders' opposition to market reforms on ideological grounds because more significant issues, such as those relating to the ownership of production, had been proposed as the next reform targets.[27] This perspective is appropriate in that it sought the causes of the revived political reform in the problems with economic reform and highlighted the ideological conflicts involved in economic reform. Indeed, the reactivation of political reform at this critical moment of economic reform was partially intended to remove ideological objections that came from leadership circles and local cadres alike. But by overemphasizing the divergence of opinions on economic reform among top leaders, such a view may have missed a more important dynamic.[28]

As mentioned earlier, the Politburo's decisionmaking during the Deng regime was characterized by compromise and consensus, and the Party center was keen to maintain a public image of unity and harmony.[29] So when the Politburo adopted a reform measure, it should have absorbed some of the ideas of conservative Party leaders such as Chen Yun, whose opinions had nearly the same weight as Deng's (au. int.). Moreover, even if certain market elements might not conform perfectly to some of the Party elders' ideological convictions, their personal positions, influence, and privileges were not supposed to be affected. So there were no persuasive reasons to believe that they would desperately oppose the adopted reforms, such that Deng and other reformist leaders would have to launch a political war against them (as Gorbachev did in the Soviet Union in 1989). More important, in assessing the nature of proposed policies and their effects, Party elders would surely see that this political reform was intended to go far beyond the ideological level and to bring about massive institutional changes in which principally Party apparatus and cadres at subnational levels would be victimized. In other words, the main target of this second wave of political reform was not conservative Party elders in Beijing but local Party apparatus and cadres.

The next question should be, Why did Deng and his cohorts resort to a serious restructuring of political power at this moment and appear determined to victimize Party organizations and cadres who, right after the communist takeover in 1949, had been the basic support of the regime? To answer this, one has to take into account the formidable obstacles the economic reform had encountered and analyze how China's political and economic structures, as in other communist systems, were fused into a whole that made any partial solution difficult. Thus far, there have been numerous works on China's economic reform in the West. Some of them analyze, from both macro- and microeconomic perspectives, the impact upon the framework of China's command economy as market forces were introduced.[30] Some explore the sociopolitical consequences of the economic reform.[31] Still others examine how industrial reforms were shaped by a variety of political factors, including political institutions, and how a communist bureaucracy managed to circumvent reform measures to its advantage.[32] But it seems that few have discussed at length how economic reform was bottlenecked by the existing political power structure (not just institutions per se) and could progress only if political reform cleared the way. Many studies indicate the flow of power effected by economic reform among traditional political institutions, but few scholars explore the extent to which the power drained from these institutions, creating a kind of power vacuum to be filled by market forces and, to a certain degree, citizens and their representatives in congresses.

Prior to its officially announced start in 1984, urban economic reform was already cautiously and tentatively moving forward. As indicated in Chapter 2, during this period the changes took place mainly in the tax system and the status of industrial enterprises within the administrative structure. In early 1979 a system of profit retention was established to alter industrial enterprises' entire dependence on the state. In 1983 this was replaced by the tax for profit that would allow enterprises to retain all their after-tax profits and become fully responsible for their own profit and loss. Relating closely to the changes in the state-enterprise financial relationships, enterprises acquired greater autonomy. To prepare for the removal of state protection, the system of factory director responsibility under Party committee leadership was restored in 1978, aiming to improve economic efficiency and productivity of enterprises and meet the target set by the new tax system.

But up to 1984 these measures failed to produce a tangible impact upon the internal management structure of enterprises or the traditional vertical relations of authority. On the one hand, factory directors had been authorized to assume full responsibility for their enterprises, but they had to accept the leadership of enterprise Party committees who were "dissuaded" from interfering in directors' work. Since Party committees actually could not exercise their leadership without bothering about enterprise administration, this restored system yielded little effect in diminishing the power of Party committees (au. int.). On the other hand, if this system was expected to increase enterprise autonomy as against the state (Party-government), it would be doomed to failure as long as Party committees still maintained complete control in enterprises. Enterprise Party committees were never supposed to have any "autonomy," and they were required by Party discipline to be obedient vertically to next higher-level Party organizations, which should be at the government level and also control the government. Therefore, despite the changes on paper, the vertical power relations—-the control over enterprises by the Party-government—-remained intact and the expansion of enterprise autonomy soon arrived at its structural limitations (au. int.).

During the early 1980s, the logic of China's Stalinist system as the "fusion of politics and economics" was displayed clearly enough.[33] The lack of substantial progress in urban reform was caused by both the lack of determination on the part of the Party center to loosen the grip of the Party-state bureaucracy on enterprises and the success of Party cadres in thwarting any such attempt. Arising from this predicament, also thanks to the relatively stabilized situation of reform in the countryside, was the central decision to shift the priority of economic reform to cities. And this time, as more market mechanisms would be adopted, the whole structure of the command economy was to be overhauled.

In October 1984 the Central Committee passed a decision to launch a total economic restructuring. Acknowledging the ineffectiveness of urban reforms thus far, the decision proposed several major economic innovations whose implementation required a significant restructuring of power relations, including the removal of much of the power over economic matters traditionally wielded by the Party apparatus at all levels. The first measure involved the enterprise-government relationship and deprived the government of its "administrative means" to dictate to the enterprise.[34] The second was to alter the predominance of mandatory planning and would considerably weaken some of the major traditional functions of the government.[35] The third was even more immediately threatening, as it called for eliminating "such bureaucratic maladies" as organizational overlapping and overstaffing and promoting a new generation of cadres who were "knowledgeable in modern economics and technology and imbued with a creative innovative spirit" (section 9).

Despite a massive propaganda campaign to advertise the decision, it seems that no action followed. Nearly two years after this decision, except for the continuous controversy about the tax system and a modest industrial price reform,[36] there was little evidence that this major Party initiative had "been faithfully carried out and . . . achieved great successes."[37] Instead, all signs suggested that this decision simply failed to move the bureaucracy to action.

It would of course be inappropriate to attribute the failure of the new reform programs entirely to the opposition from the bureaucracy.[38] But it was quite evident that the old economic planning system created a Party-state bureaucracy that depended upon it to survive. The symbiotic relationship between the two had to be destroyed for economic reform to make progress. When a senior reform adviser recalled why the reforms outlined in the 1984 decision were blocked, he indicated their potential impact upon the established political power as a primary factor.[39] Many local leaders even publicly defied the Party center and refused to implement some reform policies on the grounds that China should not take the "capitalist road."[40] When Zhao Ziyang visited Wuhan in April 1985 to find out how the 1984 decision was carried out, he found that nothing had happened. Local governments resorted to all sorts of schemes and intrigues to fool the Party center and did nothing to loosen its grip on power.[41] For one thing, many enterprises met with great difficulty in getting rid of control from above. On a later occasion, Zhao stressed that the key precondition for the success of economic reform was the streamlining of the Party-government and its devolution of power (*jian zheng fang quan*). In early 1986 Zhao already realized that to rescue economic reform, political structural reform was not only unavoidable but had become very urgent.[42]

As the top executor of Deng's reformist thinking, Zhao would have easy access to and heavy influence over Deng. In June 1986 Deng broke his six years of silence on political reform and placed it squarely on the agenda. In a speech to the leading members of the Central Committee, Deng launched a vehement attack upon the Party-state bureaucracy for keeping a "tight grip on power, making it impossible for the lower levels to act on their own." He claimed:

> We have to make a careful analysis to find out how to go about political reform. Early in 1980 it was suggested that we reform the political structure, but no concrete measures to do so were worked out. Now it is time for us to place political reform on the agenda. Otherwise, *organizational overlapping, overstaffing, bureaucratism, sluggishness, unreliability and the taking back of powers granted to lower levels* will weigh us down and retard the progress of our economic reform.[43]

A few weeks later, Deng once again cautioned senior Politburo members that "many institutions are resisting" the Party policy of devolving powers. "The reform of the political structure and the reform of the economic structure are interdependent," he asserted. "Without political reform, economic reform cannot succeed, because the first obstacle to be overcome is [some] people's resistance."[44] In September Deng further stressed the necessity of political reform for economic reform.[45]

A careful reading of the senior Party leaders' speeches and Party documents during this period suggest that economic reform was the major but not sole motivation for the revival of political reform. In fact, as the widespread resistance among Party-state cadres against economic reform seemed to reach a climax following the 1984 decision, it intensified the potential antagonism between the central leaders headed by Deng and local cadres, especially relatively low-ranking ones. This conflict had been latent since Deng's assumption of supreme power, and at the initial stage of reform Deng raised the issue of the disloyalty of a considerable number of Party cadres to the new Party leadership and its reform programs.[46] Following two previous screenings to purge the Gang of Four's followers, an even larger scale "Party rectification campaign" was launched during 1983–1985. But the number who were eventually removed from office turned out to be very small. Except for senior regional leaders such as those at the provincial level, disloyal cadres were extremely difficult to weed out.[47] The 1984 nomenklatura reform that decentralized control of personnel management perhaps compounded the difficulty. As a result of that reform, much more nomenklatura authority was transferred to provincial, municipal and county Party committees.[48]

In addition to the political and ideological problems, corruption or abuse of power for private gains among cadres had risen to a level unacceptable to the central leadership in the mid-1980s. In September 1985 Chen Yun publicly condemned a "significant proportion of Party committees and cadres" for taking advantage of the open-door policy and colluding with foreign businesspeople in all kinds of unlawful activities. He threatened that if this happened again, it would not be enough to punish the individuals involved; the Party committees concerned would also bear the responsibility.[49] This bitter sentiment against local Party cadres seemed to prevail among top leaders and contribute to a consensus for the need to take action.[50]

Furthermore, even if cadres were neither disloyal nor corrupt, their competence in executing reform policies was seriously questioned. Among more than 20 million Party cadres in 1983, only 19 percent had received higher education. By the end of 1982, China had more than 4,000 county Party secretaries and heads; only 4 percent of them had a university diploma, and 69 percent had no more than junior high education. Cadres trained in modern economic management, urban construction, foreign trade, and so on were rare.[51]

Reallocation of Institutional Powers

The stagnation of economic reform during 1985–1986 sent a warning to Deng and his colleagues that they might ultimately be unable to escape from the problems generated by the inherent connections between the economic and political systems. Local cadres refused to cooperate in the execution of reform programs, further eroding the weak base of mutual trust between them and Party leaders. Although the Party center made great efforts to improve the cadre quality through a new recruitment drive,[52] it could not get rid of the old cadres immediately or find reliable alternative institutional forces to maintain Party rule and implement Party policy. By comparison, Deng had more profound distrust of the masses, whose spontaneous participation, as he saw it, had caused the chaos of the Cultural Revolution.[53] For all their problems, cadres would never turn into a subversive force against the communist regime, which was not only the basis of all their powers and privileges but also Deng's own primary concern. Party leaders and cadres at least shared one fundamental objective: the stability and consolidation of the one-party system.

But this common goal did not prevent the escalation in tensions between the two sides. As the leadership saw it, economic reform could not be stopped just because local cadres did not accept it. A successful economic restructuring, too, was important to the perpetuation of the regime, as it would—by meeting the people's desire for a better material life—preempt any political opposition arising from economic discontent.[54] The popular enthusiasm for reforms and the strong likelihood that the successes of reform would develop social support for the regime constituted a basis for a likely alliance between the central elite and the masses against reform obstructers. In any case, the political loyalty of Party cadres and the support of citizens for the regime were of equal weight in maintaining the sociopolitical order. If the central leadership attempted to continue utterly to rely on Party cadres and for that purpose to leave the old economic and political structures intact, it would undermine the social foundation of the regime and hence make it more vulnerable and precarious. But if the leadership abandoned cadres and reverted entirely to citizen support through economic reform, the Party would lose effective control mechanisms if social rebellions occurred.

And so there were contradictions, twists, and turns as Deng tried to maintain Party hegemony in the reform process. As the dismissal of Hu and Zhao among other things demonstrated,[55] not only did Deng have strong opinions about the orientation and extent of reforms, but as the CCP's patriarchal leader, his ideas and whims could largely dominate the agenda of China's political reform.[56] An analytical reading of Deng's speeches during 1986–1987 suggests two things. First, although he recognized the need to make changes in the political structure, he was still very cautious not to give any signals that would encourage making party leadership an issue. He repeatedly emphasized that his bottom line was "being firm about leadership by the Party"[57] and insisting upon the four cardinal principles to provide a "fundamental guarantee of our basic socialist system" in an era of reform and openness.[58] Second, as regards specific measures, Deng appeared irresolute and confused. He admitted that the question concerning the content of political reform was "very complex." "Since every reform measure will involve a wide range of people. . . , and affect the interests of countless individuals," Deng argued, "it is therefore especially important for us to proceed with caution."[59]

But some general principles and specific objectives could be identified from Deng's speeches.[60] On a theoretical level, he believed that the Party must maintain its leadership but better exercise it. This could be done only by altering the power monopoly of Party apparatus and cadres. For the urgent purpose of pushing forward economic reform, the Party-government separation had to be enforced. It no longer involved just the deprivation of executive powers of Party apparatus and professional Party cadres. To make the separation more practicable and compulsory, citizen influence should be brought in to restrain the remaining policymaking power of Party apparatus. In two speeches in late 1986, Deng modified his typical condescending attitude and rhetoric about how "to educate the masses" and instead emphasized the importance of making use of the people's enthusiasm for reform.[61]

Here is a puzzle to be solved: Since Deng expected the masses to play a role, how did he relate it to democratization? Where should the masses be located in the power restructuring? It seemed that Deng did not like to refer to political reform as "democratization." Obviously, this kind of conceptualization was essentially Western and would shake the people's confidence in the "superiority" of China's socialist democracy, which only required some repair through reform. For all Deng's hesitation, equivocation, or confusion, one thing was certain: Deng never allowed political reform to evolve into Western-type liberalization and democratization.[62] He apparently had a special distaste for the U.S. style of separation of powers simply because such a system had "no efficiency."[63] But Deng did not categorically equate the American system with a system of checks and balances. In fact, he exhibited some flexibility toward the latter.[64] Even if Deng himself was not enthusiastic about it, there was evidence that other leaders were, and they tried to exert influence over Deng. Zhao Ziyang argued that a system of checks and balances was indispensable for curbing political corruption.[65] In an internal discussion of political reform that aimed to prepare documents for the thirteenth Party congress scheduled for October 1987, a major topic was how to handle the triangular power relations among the Party (organizations), the government, and the people's congress, particularly making the congress a highly authoritative legislative and supervisory institution.[66] Peng Zhen was clearly the most active advocate of expanding congressional authority.[67] When Deng rattled on about political reform in 1986 and showed uncertainty about how to carry it out, Peng went straight to the heart of the restructuring of the Party committee–congress power relations. He claimed that party leadership did not mean that the opinions of the Party committee must be taken as "supreme instructions." "The Party can issue orders to its members," Peng asserted.

"But it cannot issue orders directly to the people's congress and government. All the fundamental, long-term, and important issues must finally be decided by the congress," which had a mandate from the people to exercise the supreme power.[68]

The scheme of political reform passed by the thirteenth Party congress did not originate solely from Deng but rather was a result of consultation, deliberation, and compromise among the top-level leaders.[69] Deng's speeches suggest that since there were no successful examples to follow, he took a tolerant attitude and allowed these measures to be implemented on an experimental basis. It should not be surprising, then, if Deng later withdrew his endorsement and modified his stand when he perceived the "threats" inherent in the structural consequences. In any case, this Party congress ultimately established political reform as the Party's new orthodoxy. For cadres, officials, and citizens, political loyalty now had a new meaning and a new target. All players in this restructuring game were compelled to seek theoretical justifications for their scramble for power from the Party congress documents and demonstrate their devotion to the new Central Committee and its reform agenda. Presumably considering the unpredictable consequences, political reform was specified in a general and somewhat ambiguous way in Zhao's report, leaving room for flexible interpretation or correction. But if one screens out the clichés and propaganda, much of substance could be recognized.

Zhao's report set a bottom line for political reform: never to "introduce a Western system of separation of the three powers and of different [political] parties ruling the country in turn." But the specific measures proposed would give observers a strong sense of separation and balancing of powers, though practicable mainly at subnational levels.[70] At the core of the whole reform package was a reinterpretation of the functions and responsibilities of Party apparatus, which was to take away considerable power from local Party committees and professional Party cadres without altering their lofty political status. Zhao once again revised the definition of "party leadership" formulated at the twelfth Party congress and simplified it to "political leadership," meaning that the Party should determine political principles, point the political direction, make or propose policy decisions, and recommend cadres for key posts in organs of state power (section 5).[71]

As the changed Party role required, the power previously possessed by Party committees would virtually be dismantled into three parts. Local Party committees and cadres should play a role like that of traffic police and ensure that all governmental and legislative activities proceed in line with provided regulations and within the limitations set by the Party center. The execution of policies and administrative affairs fell to the government, which was responsible to both the Party committee and the people's congress of the same administrative level. To keep "inappropriate" Party interference in government work to a minimum, Zhao demanded a gradual abolition of the Party group (i.e., the so-called leading Party members' group) in each government department.[72] In addition to its supervision of the government through the rights to approve government work and elect and recall officials, the people's congress was granted far-reaching legislative power.[73] Although even the formalities of this new institutional arrangement had little in common with the American-style separation of powers, it bore some structural resemblance to Western European parliamentary systems.[74] A fundamental difference was, of course, that no organized political opposition or competition was allowed to enter the governmental process in China.

Presumably in order not to give an impression of Party domination over the highest organ of state power, the Party congress documents did not elaborate in detail on the role of the people's congress, except for endorsing the revisions of the electoral law made ten months before that aimed to bring more citizen initiative into elections of people's deputies and government officials. But soon after the Party congress, senior Party leaders with offices in the NPC demanded great enhancement of congressional authority. Peng Chong, a Politburo member and vice NPCSC chairman, urged local congresses to strengthen their "supervisory" role and told them that it would be "normal" for them to reject the Party committee nominees for government offices.[75] Chen Pixian, another Party and NPCSC leader, advised congresses to "respect and obey" party leadership but stressed that the relationships between the Party committee and the congress "are not like those between superiors and subordinates." He reassured local congresses not to be afraid of "confronting the Party committee" (*chang dui tai xi*).[76]

Ample evidence proved that the reform was no longer simply empty talk. In July 1988 the Central Committee announced its decision gradually to dismiss the Party groups (*dang zu*) and the Party commissions for inspecting discipline within various departments of the State Council.[77] Prior to the start of a new round of nationwide elections of people's deputies in 1987–1988, the Central Committee sent provincial Party committees a directive stipulating the elimination of the posts of deputy secretary and standing committee members in local Party committees who did not hold positions in the government but were charged with directing government. The number of the standing committee members was also to be cut.[78]

According to Zhao's report, the "political leadership" exercised by the Central Committee and local Party committees differed. The Central Committee should formulate political principles; point the political direction; make major policy decisions on internal and foreign affairs, economy, and national defense;[79] and recommend persons for leading posts in the supreme state organs. The "political leadership" of the Party committees at the provincial, municipal, and county levels was limited to five functions: (1) to carry out directives from higher Party organizations and from the Central Committee; (2) to ensure the implementation in their local areas of directives from governments of higher levels and from the State Council; (3) to propose policy decisions on important local issues; (4) to recommend cadres for key posts in local state organs; and (5) to coordinate activities of the various local organizations.[80] Among these functions, the second and fifth were largely meaningless. The first was tricky. If the Central Committee had really been separated from the State Council, the directives from the former and higher-level Party organs should only deal with intra-Party affairs, such as rectification of the conduct of Party members, which did not involve any administrative power. The other two functions (the proposal of policy and recommendation of cadres) were important but ambiguously defined. For example, what was an "important" issue for which Party committees should propose a policy decision? And who could serve as the judge or arbiter? What sort of post in local governments should be reasonably defined as "key"? What if Party committee decisions and recommendations were rejected by people's congresses?

The Party center never offered definite solution to these problems. Perhaps the leaders themselves were unsure of the feasibility and consequences of their innovations. Zhao's report suggested that the relations between local Party committees and state organs at the same administrative level "should be worked out through practice and gradually become standardized and institutionalized." More likely, the leadership deliberately left these issues unresolved because, as later practice showed, the power struggle in local politics based on different understandings of Party guidelines put Beijing in a position to arbitrate according to its own opportunistic preferences and requirements. It was in this context that the three-way contest for power and influence among Party committees, governments, and people's congresses unfolded.

No matter how the new Party line was construed, one thing should not be mistaken: Power was to be redistributed, with Party apparatus and cadres receiving far less than they once had. And the vacuum would be filled by congresses, which provided ordinary citizens with chances to participate in the policy process. An *RMRB* commentary warned against the rising discrimination of the general public against cadres. In the process of Party-government separation, it charged, "some people use offensive language to denounce Party cadres and see them as useless. Cadres felt very dejected and depressed. . . . The separation does not mean casting off Party cadres as a burden." Yet the author also cautioned cadres to accept the changes and to "adapt themselves to their new tasks."[81]

Although the dilemma of reform required the sacrifice of Party organizations and cadres, it would be wrong to think that central leaders were ready to go far in that direction to ensure market reform success or intended to seek an alternative base of support both for the regime and for reform. If for a time the Party center seemed to favor a more autonomous government and a more powerful congress, it should be comprehended mostly as a pragmatic situational tactic. When cadre influence decayed and the relations of authority gradually tipped in favor of congresses, the real objective of political reform as intended by the leadership was exposed more clearly. During the early 1980s, Party apparatus successfully blocked urban economic reforms, and it proved extremely difficult for the feeble legislatures to shake their firmly established authority. The Party center needed to jump-start the process of rearranging power relations. For that purpose, all kinds of central directives and mandatory provisions were announced and enforced to bolster the status of the government and congress versus the Party committee. In Tiananmen in 1989, Deng and other conservative elders were alarmed by the signs that political reform had undermined party leadership and local and grassroots Party committees had lost their authority to such an extent that they failed to deter their subordinates from publicly defying the regime. Then the political pendulum swung back.

Deng's balancing skills were evidently inherited by Jiang Zemin when he claimed that the CCP was the governing party and must have a stronger sense as such. In that internal speech, his definition of "party leadership" virtually returned to that of the twelfth Party congress of 1982, with special emphasis on the importance of the Party's "organizational leadership." He changed the third function of local Party committees from proposing policy decisions to discussing and deciding on all important policies, which all organs of power would then implement.[82]

It is an intriguing question whether or how the leaders could reverse political reform when they had already effected structural changes. To what extent could they toy with the balance of power without paying a heavy price? The economic dynamics of political reform never really faded away during the post-Tiananmen period, particularly after Deng called for accelerated market reform in early 1992. Presumably for this reason, much rhetoric about "strengthening party leadership" and combating the "bourgeois liberalization" following Tiananmen did not translate into an overall institutional restoration. The Party center was still very prudent when it came to the highly sensitive power relations between Party committees and people's congresses. In fact, with the exception of Jiang's speech as part of the Tiananmen crackdown, one could hardly find evidence from Party documents or leaders' speeches that Beijing strongly encouraged a Party committee comeback at the expense of congresses or attempted to abolish the mechanisms of checks and balances already established between the two. As some other chapters show, during the 1990s people's deputies and congresses in many areas tended to perform their functions in a more assertive and defiant way. They had consciously developed a bureaucratic interest that was hard to suppress. When the political pendulum swung back, the range was small and the policy options for the leadership were few.[83]

Conclusion

A basic conclusion may be drawn from the discussions in this chapter: The major dynamics of the second stage of political reform differed from those of the first. They were generated by the necessity of breaking through the political structural bottleneck when the economic reform reached a critical threshold. More specifically, the Party cadre opposition to economic reform intensified the vertical intra-Party conflicts that forced the leadership to choose between two difficult options: either to abandon economic reform or to sacrifice Party cadres.

The vertical cleavages within the CCP—or rather the antagonism between the Party's ruling group headed by Deng and a significant proportion of local and grassroots cadres—were not merely caused by the conflict of interests involved in economic restructuring. As a historical legacy of the Cultural Revolution, they actually existed on the first day of Deng's return to the Politburo in 1977. These cleavages, initially of a more sentimental and ideological nature, were widened by the leadership's programs of economic reform, which posed a formidable and immediate threat to local cadres' powers and privileges. Although opposition from these cadres thwarted the implementation of economic reform, the leadership encountered enormous difficulty purging them. This predicament strengthened the determination of the Party center to destroy the long-standing monopoly of power (to use Deng's more delicate term, the overconcentration of power) in the hands of Party organizations and cadres and to invite a greater extent of institutionalized citizen participation and representation through people's congresses.

The leadership's efforts against local cadres appeared serious, but their hesitation and ambivalence were also quite evident. Making use of the mass enthusiasm for reform to circumvent cadres' refusal to cooperate, the Party center managed to divide the old unified power structure into three parts and to create some mechanisms of checks and balances among Party committees, governments, and congresses. But the leadership provided only vague descriptions of the powers and functions of the three institutions, particularly those of Party committees and people's congresses. One may reasonably speculate that uncertain of the consequences of reform, the Party center wanted to keep for itself maximum flexibility in interpretation and room for maneuver and to secure its own position to arbitrate and control in institutional power struggles, especially at local administrative levels.

This would explain why the leadership in Beijing kept changing its attitude toward political reform. During a certain period when market reform was blocked, it cautioned Party committees to respect the status of congresses as the highest organ of state power and not to interfere in government work. When Party authority declined, as during the Tiananmen incident, and when threats to Party domination seemed to arise from the populace, the leadership reverted to the emphasis of the necessity of people's congresses to accept the "political leadership" of Party committees. Only by taking Deng's balancing strategy into account can one understand the nature of the restructuring of power relationships and the three-cornered contest for power at all administrative levels. But as the next two chapters show, since the 1990s the Party center has met with increasing structural difficulties in manipulating the reform process.

Notes

1. See Weiner and LaPalombara, "The Impact of Parties."

2. It is just what "partyocracy" means. Herman Finer goes so far as to allege that in the representational process the party becomes "king." Cited in Beer, *British Politics*, p. 88.

3. LaPalombara uses some criteria to distinguish Western party government from party dictatorship under authoritarian regimes. In a study of Italy, a typical partyocracy, he argues that party government presupposes the existence of a pluralistic democracy and polyarchy and must meet four specific conditions. See LaPalombara, *Democracy*, pp. 210–212.

4 . For a brief analysis of these works, see Lieberthal and Oksenberg, *Policy Making in China*, ch. 1.

5. This "party-state" conception is challenged by Zheng, who argues that the different organizational rationale and logic followed by the CCP and the state institutions caused conflicts between the Party and the state, and it is therefore "not only conceptually constructive but analytically imperative to distinguish the state from the Party." But Zheng also highlights the dependence upon the CCP of the Chinese state and its lack of autonomy. See Shiping Zheng, *Party vs. State.*

6. According to Harding, this power flow from the government to the party began with the San-fan campaign of 1951–1952 and was completed by the early 1960s when the entire state apparatus became largely redundant. See Harding, *Organizing China*, p. 284.

7. Barnett, *Cadres,* ch. 3.

8. Some comparative studies are available for this subject. Schurmann's study shows that the Communist Party, as an organization, played a far more important role in China than in the Soviet Union under Stalin. For one thing, "though party membership was universal among Soviet leaders of the Stalin period," he argues, "there was no administration by Party committees, such as has been the case in Communist China." See Schurmann, *Ideology and Organization,* p. 174.

9. Dittmer, "The Origins."

10. *Beijing Review,* no. 52 (December 29, 1978), pp. 6–16.

11. Deng Xiaoping, *Selected Works,* pp. 151–165.

12. In a speech in August 1980, Deng pointed out: "It is true that the errors we made in the past were partly attributable to the way of thinking and style of work of some leaders. But they were even more attributable to the problems in our organizational and working systems. . . . If even now we still don't improve the way our socialist system functions, people will ask why it cannot solve some problems which the capitalist system can. . . . I do not mean that the individuals concerned should not bear their share of responsibility, but rather that *the problems in the leadership and organi-*

zational systems are more fundamental, widespread, and long-lasting, and that they have a greater effect on the overall interests of our country." Deng Xiaoping, *Selected Works,* pp. 302–325; italics mine. When mentioning the necessity of reforms, Deng was careful to use the terms "leadership and organizational systems" and "working system" instead of "political system." On another occasion, Deng once again attributed Mao's mistakes to the "system." "Comrade Mao made many correct statements, but the faulty systems and institutions of the past pushed him in the opposite direction." *Selected Works,* p. 283.

13. Ibid., pp. 302–325.

14. Ibid., pp. 326–334.

15. "As much evidence has demonstrated," the author argued, "party leadership will be weakened rather than strengthened if Party committees handle those affairs which should have been handled by administrative organs. This is because Party committees, if bogged down in miscellaneous governmental business, will have no time to deal with the problems within the Party itself." Jing Dong, "The Party."

16. *HQ,* no. 18 (September 16, 1982), pp. 6–30.

17. *Beijing Review,* vol. 25, no. 38 (September 20, 1982), pp. 8–21; italics mine. The so-called organizational leadership meant that Party organizations and cadres at all administrative levels should hold the power to nominate candidates for government posts.

18. In 1954 in his report to the first NPC, Liu Shaoqi, NPCSC chairman, said: "The CCP members must play an exemplary role in complying with the constitution and all other laws." In 1956, when Deng Xiaoping, the Party general secretary, addressed the eighth Party congress, he pointed out that every Party member must obey the Party constitution and state laws strictly. But never before had it been definitely stipulated that the Party as an organization must also act in accordance with state laws. For this reason, *MYF* commended the relevant revisions in the 1982 Party constitution as "an innovation and a major characteristic of the new Party constitution." *MYF* Pinglunyuan, "The Party."

19. "The public transcript is," Scott argues, "to put it crudely, the *self*-portrait of dominant elites as they would have themselves seen." The power-holders must maintain the appearance represented by the public transcript that constitutes the legitimacy of their domination. Scott, *Domination,* p. 18.

20. "Reshuffle of State Leading Personnel."

21. Chen Yizi and Chen Jinfu (Bianxiezu), eds., *Zhengzhi,* p. 27.

22. The first half of the 1980s saw the most rapid growth of China's national economy. Various economic data and comparisons can be found in Zhao Ziyang, "Report (1987)." According to official statistics, people's living conditions improved more during 1979–1985 than during any period of the PRC history. See Yuan Mu, "Some Comments."

23. Halpern, "Economic Reform."

24. Deng Xiaoping, *Fundamental Issues,* pp. 24–40.

25. Ibid., pp. 113–115.

26. A careful examination of Deng's speeches quoted by the Party propaganda machine shows that during the period between 1980—when he promised to reform the "leadership and organizational systems"—and 1986, he made little mention of political reform.

27. See Fewsmith, *Dilemmas of Reform,* ch. 6. From Harding's point of view, there were three reasons Chinese "radical" leaders reinserted the question of political reform in mid-1986. First, they wanted to sustain the momentum when economic reform seemed to be faltering. Second, there would need to be widespread agreement to

reduce the ideological constraints for more far-reaching economic reforms. Third, the leaders believed that further political liberalization would be needed to prevent abuses of power, create greater stability, and make government more responsive to the people. See Harding, *China's Second Revolution,* pp. 191–192.

28. By comparison, the difference of opinions among the central leaders appeared to be greater on the extent of political liberalization. On this issue Deng sided with other conservative elders against younger reformers such as Hu and Zhao throughout the 1980s. Deng made a clear-cut distinction between economic and political liberalizations. In 1987, when political reform was rising to new heights, Deng launched the campaign against "bourgeois liberalization." Goldman, *Sowing the Seeds;* Baum, *Burying Mao.*

29. This seems to be a major feature of politics in other communist states, too, such as the Brezhnev period of the Soviet Union. See Hough and Fainsod, *How the Soviet Union Is Governed.*

30. See Reynolds, ed., *Chinese Economic Reform;* Byrd, *The Market Mechanism.*

31. Watson*, Economic Reform;* Perry and Wong, eds., *The Political Economy;* Wasserstrom and Perry, *Popular Protest.*

32. A major work is Shirk, *The Political Logic.* Shirk does discuss the conflicts among political institutions emerging from industrial reforms, as well as the mechanisms of consensus and compromise that defused the potential antagonism. But she seems to emphasize the redistributional politics of economic interests rather than power reallocation.

33. Bialer, *Stalin's Successors,* ch. 1; Nolan, *State and Market,* p. 218.

34. The decision (section 6) charged that for a long time enterprises were "appendages of administrative organs." "From now on," it demanded, "government departments at various levels will, in principle, not manage or operate enterprises directly." It particularly cautioned city governments "not to repeat the past practice of mainly depending on administrative means to control enterprises." This change would drastically diminish the authority of the governments at all levels. See Chapter 2, note 23.

35. The objective was to reduce the scope of mandatory planning and extend guidance planning that was to be "fulfilled mainly by use of economic levers." The decision (section 4) specifically provided that except for "major products" and "major economic activities," "other products and economic activities that are far more numerous should either come under guidance planning or be left entirely to the operation of the market."

36. Byrd, "The Impact."

37. The only exception was that at the end of 1984 the Party center decided to open fourteen coastal cities to foreign investment and expand their commercial links with the outside world. It was reported that this decision—obviously with no consequences whatsoever to power structure—was effectively carried out by local governments concerned. See Gu Mu's speech (December 24, 1986), in *JJRB,* December 25, 1986.

38. During the late 1980s, the issues hotly debated among reformers revolved around price reform and ownership reform. The former would inevitably cause inflation, whereas the latter affected employment. Even some reformers believed that these were too sensitive to be attempted in Chinese society then. In fact, ownership reform had to wait until the leaders made up their minds to enforce it in the fifteenth Party congress of October 1997. Yet it was true that policymakers in Beijing did not enshrine the reforms in the orthodox Marxist ideology and therefore made them ideologically unacceptable to many veteran cadres. See Chen Yizi, *Zhongguo,* ch. 4; Fewsmith, *Dilemmas of Reform.*

39. "A fundamental reason why China's economic reform could not continue after 1984," Chen Yizi argues, "was the inadequacy of the preparation for political reform" to reallocate political interests (power). The transformation of the command economy did affect the political power of a significant proportion of the Party-state bureaucracy. Chen Yizi, *Zhongguo,* chs. 3, 4. Until he became an exile in the United States after the Tiananmen crackdown of 1989, Chen was one of Zhao Ziyang's policy advisers.

40. Ibid.

41. Li Yongchun, "The Party's Thinking of Political Reform Was Shaped and Deepened in the Two Historic Transformations," in Li Yongchun and Luo Jian, eds., *Shiyijie Sanzhong Quanhui yilai,* pp. 30–41.

42. Ibid.

43. Deng Xiaoping, *Fundamental Issues,* pp. 141–144; italics mine.

44. Ibid., pp. 145–148.

45. "Whenever we move a step forward in economic reform," he told a Japanese delegation, "we are made keenly aware of the need to change the political structure." Ibid., pp. 149–151.

46. In a speech on July 29, 1979, Deng manifested the virtually irreparable rifts within the Party and suggested the deepest source of the mutual distrust and hostility between Party leaders and cadres: "We must take note of the fact that a fair number of people are still opposed to the Party's current political and ideological lines. The system of ideas they cling to is, generally speaking, that of Lin Biao and the Gang of Four, according to which the present policies of the Central Committee are retrograde and Right opportunist. On the pretext of supporting Comrade Mao Zedong, they are following the principle of the 'two whatevers.' In fact, they are merely peddling the old stock in trade of Lin Biao and the Gang of Four in new guise. *Most of them were promoted during the Cultural Revolution and they have their own vested interests.* They yearn for the past, because *the present policies do not yield much advantage to them.* Through effort on our part, some of them may change their attitude, but perhaps not all can do so. *If we entrust power to those who have not changed, how can we expect them to listen to the Party?* They'll stir up trouble whenever there's a chance." See Deng Xiaoping, *Selected Works,* pp. 196–199; italics mine.

47. See Lee, *From Revolutionary Cadres,* chs. 7, 10. Lee's study shows that Party committees at the various levels exercised enormous discretionary power in deciding who should be purged. But many Party committees (mainly their secretaries) simply had no taste for it. It was technically difficult to conduct the investigation that was the basis of purges, and the complicated network of patron-client relations in Chinese officialdom and society hampered efforts.

48. For more information on this subject, see Burns, ed., *The Chinese Communist Party's Nomenklatura System,* introduction.

49. *Chen Yun Wenxuan, 1956–1985,* pp. 309–311.

50. In a speech on January 17, 1986, Deng also complained that some Party cadres' style of work and behavior "are shockingly bad," and he threatened to "expel some of them" from the Party. See Deng Xiaoping, *Fundamental Issues,* pp. 136–140. In a conversation with his advisers, Zhao Ziyang expressed his deep concern about the "darkness" of the grassroots Party rule. See Jin Zhong, "Zhao Ziyang."

51. Luo Haigang, "Promote a New Generation," in Li Yongchun and Luo Jian, eds., *Shiyijie Sanzhong Quanhui yilai,* pp. 99–118.

52. Ch'i, *Politics,* chs. 5, 6; Lee, *From Revolutionary Cadres,* ch. 10.

53. This has to be considered a major reason Deng refused any move toward Western-type democracy. In meeting with U.S. president George Bush in February

1989, Deng claimed that a multiparty election would throw China into a terrible social disorder like the Cultural Revolution. "Given China's huge population," he asserted, "there would be demonstrations on the streets everyday, and then economic construction would be doomed to failure." *Deng Xiaoping Wenxuan, Disanjuan,* pp. 284–285.

54. Deng's logic held that reforms would accelerate economic growth and increase economic efficiency and therefore "demonstrate that the socialist system is superior to the capitalist system." Deng Xiaoping, *Selected Works,* pp. 224–258.

55. As Party general secretaries, Hu and Zhao were easily deposed by Deng in 1987 and 1989, respectively, mainly because they disagreed with Deng on how to handle the "bourgeois liberalization."

56. Of course this statement does not imply that Deng wielded absolute power as Mao used to. Actually, both conservative elders and younger reform-minded leaders were in a position to exert influence over Deng, and very often compromises had to be worked out. But in any case Deng always had the final say, whether as a paramount arbitrator or balancing effect.

57. Deng Xiaoping, *Fundamental Issues,* pp. 149–151.

58. The "four cardinal principles" were to (1) keep to the socialist road, (2) uphold the dictatorship of the proletariat, (3) uphold the leadership of the Communist Party, and (4) uphold Marxism-Leninism and Mao Zedong Thought (Deng's speech on March 30, 1979). Two years later, Deng stressed that the "essence" of the four principles was the third. See Deng Xiaoping, *Selected Works,* pp. 166–191, 367–371; Deng Xiaoping, *Fundamental Issues,* pp. 171–173.

59. Deng Xiaoping, *Fundamental Issues,* pp. 149–151. In a later speech (June 12, 1987), Deng clarified what he meant by "a wide range of people" and "countless individuals." It was "mainly cadres, including the veterans." Deng Xiaoping, *Fundamental Issues,* pp. 186–196.

60. From June 1986 to June 1987, Deng delivered more than ten speeches on political reform that were used as the blueprint for the reform to follow.

61. In a speech to some central leaders in September 1986, Deng claimed that in his opinion the purposes of political reform "are to bring the initiative of the masses into play, to increase efficiency and to overcome bureaucratism." In a later speech (November 9, 1986), Deng emphasized the need to "release the people's initiative by delegating powers to lower levels" and "to motivate workers and intellectuals, democratizing management by letting them participate in it. The same [principle] applies to every other field of endeavour." Deng Xiaoping, *Fundamental Issues,* pp. 152–153, 158–160.

62. It is interesting to note that during the reform period Deng no longer used the classic Marxist perspective, which stresses the class nature of Western "bourgeois democracy," to reject it. Instead, he opposed Western-style democracy on the grounds that it did not suit China's social conditions. "Democracy can develop only gradually, and we cannot copy Western systems," Deng argued in December 1986. "If we did, that would only make a mess of everything." Deng Xiaoping, *Fundamental Issues,* pp. 161–166. In a speech to a Hong Kong delegation, Deng claimed that he was not against the parliamentary elections held in Western states, but China could not adopt them. ZZWY, ed., *Shi'erda Yilai Zhongyao Wenxian Xuanbian,* p. 1365.

63. "We cannot . . . introduce the system of a balance of three powers," Deng claimed. "I have often criticized people in power in the United States, saying that actually they have three governments. . . . The three branches often pull in different directions, and that makes trouble. We cannot adopt such a system." Deng Xiaoping, *Fundamental Issues,* pp. 161–166.

64. In what might be a response to a question, Deng said in September 1986 that problems *might* arise "if we place *too much* emphasis on a need for checks and balances." See Deng Xiaoping, *Fundamental Issues,* pp. 152–153; italics mine.

65. As a former adviser to Zhao recalled, in 1987 the advisers submitted to Zhao some proposals that suggested expanding the power of the people's congress, mutual checks between the Party (committees) and the governments, and independence of the judiciary. When Zhao sent these proposals to Deng, Deng asked him if they would lead to the American-style separation of powers. Zhao replied that he did not mean that, but "we cannot have no checks and balances"; otherwise corruption would be generated. See Jin Zhong, "Zhao Ziyang."

66. Chen Yizi, *Zhongguo,* ch. 5.

67. It was well known in Beijing's political circles that for expanding his own influence, NPCSC chairman Peng Zhen (1983–1988) made aggressive efforts to boost the authority of the people's congress in the name of defending reform. But even so, there is no reason to believe that his public speeches in favor of the legislature represented only his personal views. According to both Party discipline and the Politburo norms under Deng, any speech made by a senior leader like Peng must be approved by the Politburo in advance and hence represent the opinions of the Party center (au. int.). It should be reasonable to assume that given Peng's role and assigned (NPCSC) job, the opinions of the Politburo concerning the people's congress were mostly left to Peng to make public.

68. Peng Zhen, *Lun Xinshiqi,* pp. 324–331. In a speech on September 6, 1986, Peng cautioned that the government at all levels must accept the legislative oversight. "If not, it is against law." Ibid., pp. 332–343.

69. The most important document of this Party congress was the political report delivered by Zhao Ziyang. *Beijing Review,* vol. 30, no. 45 (November 9–15, 1987), documents section.

70. This was one of the main paradoxes in Deng's concept of political reform. Deng might have wanted to seal the lips of conservative Party people who kept making trouble for his reforms in saying they amounted to "taking the capitalist road" or "Westernization." This was Deng's typical tactic. It was out of just this consideration that he defined China's market reform as building "*socialism* with Chinese characteristics." But a stronger likelihood was that by denying any resemblance between China's Party-government separation and the American-style separation of powers, Deng was warning against political opposition.

71. In that regard there was a significant difference between the central and local levels. Only at the central level could the Party committee (the Central Committee) "*make* policy decisions." Local Party committees were only authorized to "*propose* policy decisions" (section 5). (Italics mine.)

72. According to the 1982 Party constitution (chapter 9, articles 46–48), a Party group must be formed in the leading body of a central or local state organ, people's organization, economic or cultural institution, or other nonparty unit. The Party group must subject itself to the leadership of the Party committee that approves its establishment. This stipulation was apparently aimed to maintain Party control over the state and society. In line with Zhao's speech, the 1987 version of the Party constitution modified the relevant clause to provide that a Party group "*may* be formed" in the central- and local-level people's congresses, CPPCC, people's organization, or other nonparty unit whose leadership is produced by elections (italics mine). The 1992 and 1997 versions restore the 1982 stipulation in that regard with the only exception that the establishment of a Party group is not compulsory ("must") but optional ("may"). For an

English text of the 1992 Party constitution, see Lieberthal, *Governing China,* pp. 383–402. Also see note 77.

73. For the entire package of the political reform and its objectives, in addition to his report at the thirteenth Party congress, see Zhao Ziyang, "On the Separation."

74. In European parliamentary states, the system of checks and balances is weak and limited. As Smith argues, as the need to organize the popular vote gave rise to national and mass parties, assembly members were no longer able to act as individuals. "Party government and party discipline meant that the legislature lost its substantial power over government." See Smith, *Politics,* pp. 189–192. In the Chinese case, with the communist one-party system in place, checks and balances had to be very feeble, and where they did seem to exist they were essentially not exercised in the Western sense for lack of political pluralism.

75. Peng Chong, "The Main Points of the Speech to Heads of Local SCPCs (November 17, 1987)," in QRCBY, ed., *Zhonghua Renmin Gongheguo,* pp. 610–612.

76. Chen Pixian, "On the Supervisory Power of the People's Congress and Its Standing Committee (November 30, 1987)," in QRCBY, ed., *Zhonghua Renmin Gongheguo,* pp. 612–614.

77. *RMRB,* August 1, 1988. In each department and institution of the central government, two Party organizations existed by then: *dang zu* (Party groups) and *dang zhi bu* (Party branch) or *dang zong zhi* (general Party branch) if the number of Party members was large. *Dang zu* was a supreme decisionmaking group and usually had three to five members, whereas *dang zhi bu* or *dang zong zhi* only took care of routine intra-Party affairs, such as admitting new Party members and organizing political study among Party members. Many local governments and institutions had a similar arrangement. The measure to abolish the Party group was never enforced at the central level and seemed to have been entirely forsaken after Tiananmen. My field research suggests some variations at local administrative levels. During the 1990s only local people's congresses retained Party groups and most government departments and institutions had only one Party organization, that is, the Party committee (*dang wei*), which took charge of both decisionmaking and all kinds of intra-Party affairs. A local government department with a Party committee should be less subjected to the control of Party authorities at the next higher level than one with a Party group, because Party group members must be appointed by Party authorities and hence cannot be elected or effectively influenced by ordinary Party members. Also see note 72.

78. *RMRB,* January 21, 1988.

79. Interpretation of the phrase "make major policy decisions" is a crucial matter. It was perhaps made intentionally ambiguous. Theoretically, the decisions taken by the Central Committee should not be final until approved by the NPC. But the NPC was constitutionally authorized to reject any Party decision. And this rejection, as the NPC "rebellion" during Tiananmen manifested, was no longer just a theoretical likelihood as a sense of autonomy and power developed among NPC deputies, whose votes could not be controlled. This potential threat may account for the leadership's double standard, by which it encouraged local congresses to challenge Party committees but never encouraged the NPC to do the same, obviously because the Central Committee was beyond challenge.

80. Zhao Ziyang, "On the Separation."

81. *RMRB'* Pinglunyuan, "Defending." Party cadre opposition to these reform measures was also recorded in Chen Yizi, *Zhongguo,* p. 119.

82. This speech, made in December 1989, was not made public until half a year later. See Jiang Zemin, "Strive to Build the Party." But no specific actions were report-

edly taken. As Chapter 7 suggests, this change in the central attitude—which proved temporary—seemed to have no impact on the Party-legislature relations in local politics. Around the mid-1990s China's legal scholars set off a discussion about whether the legislature should supervise Party apparatus. Some scholars argued that since the CCP's status as the governing party was "decided" by the people through the legislature, the legislature naturally had a legal right to supervise Party apparatus and cadres. Tie Li, "The Party." A senior NPC research official openly defended the role of the legislature as a counterweight against the Party, maintaining that the nature of legislative supervision was nothing less than checks and balances of power. Cheng Xiangqing, "The Supervision."

83. The development of political reform after Tiananmen was not all negative, and it had to keep pace with the ongoing market reform in some aspects. One indication of its progress was the continuous diminution of the Party-state bureaucracy. The March 1993 Party session took a big step forward when it announced an ambitious decision to cut the number of Party cadres and government officials by 25 percent (9 million nationwide) within the next three years. Liu Jiang, "The Second Plenum." The first ninth NPC session (March 1998) overwhelmingly passed a proposal made by the Politburo that would cut by half the number of "civil servants," which in China included both cadres and officials. *MB,* March 11, 1998, p. A15. Although the streamlining of government is part of the administrative reform, its political significance should not be underestimated. The reduced size of the bureaucracy will create a smaller state and contribute to a more autonomous society. Congressional deputies should also profit from the new, largely zero-sum power game with cadres and officials.

6

The Three-Cornered
Power Game

According to the new political structure decided by the thirteenth Party congress, the Party-government separation and the expansion of congressional authority should begin at the top. This was important to the success of the overall political reform strategy in two ways. In the first place, given China's hierarchy of authority—that is, the vertical subordinate administrative relations—local government and Party organizations could not be practically separated unless the central Party Secretariat and the State Council performed distinct functions and separately issued directives to the local organs that were their direct subordinate units (local Party committees and local governments, respectively). In the second place, the reform at the central level was expected to provide an example for local institutions to follow. It was especially important for local congresses, which, albeit not branches of the NPC, needed it as a clear model for asserting authority over local affairs vis-à-vis Party apparatus.

But the triangular power relations at the central level were significantly different from those at local levels. The unique structure of authority and sources of power at the center made the Party-government separation less successful or meaningful. This chapter examines the clashes between the central Party Secretariat and the State Council over government affairs and the change in the status of the NPC and NPCSC in legislation, as well as its potential antagonism with the Party (the Politburo and Secretariat) over its control of the State Council and the policy agenda.

The Party Secretariat and State Council:
How Meaningful Is the Separation?

If the "government" at the central level definitely denoted the State Council (referred to as the "central government" in all kinds of Party-state documents), and it was similar to the cabinet in a Western parliamentary system, then what was its parallel Party apparatus? There were five Party bodies at the center: the Party congress, the Central Committee, the Politburo, the Politburo Standing Committee, and the Secretariat. In Zhao Ziyang's report at the thirteenth Party congress and relevant documents, the Party organ that seemed to be the closest counterpart to the State Council was the Central Committee, whose responsibility was defined as exercising "political leadership." But the Central Committee, along with the Party congress, was neither an executive nor a de facto decisionmaking organ.[1] Following the Leninist principle of "democratic centralism," it was usually used by the central leadership as an intra-Party rubber stamp to show the "consensus" of the Party on the decisions made by the Politburo.

The Politburo and its standing committee could not be involved in the separation either. Rather, theoretically justified by the Party's leadership position, they had to dominate and lead the State Council. This may be seen from the fact that the first three functions of the "Central Committee" (more precisely, the Politburo)—that is, to formulate political principles, to point the political direction, and to make major policy decisions—overlapped the functions of the State Council as provided in the 1982 constitution, which included (1) to adopt administrative measures, enact administrative rules and regulations, and issue decisions and orders; (2) to submit proposals to the NPC or its Standing Committee; and (3) to draw up and implement the plan for national economic and social development and the state budget. Since all these measures, rules, regulations, decisions, orders, or plans were supposed to be carried out nationwide, they in themselves constituted what could be defined as political principles or directions. Thus, the Politburo, in the name of the Central Committee, was fully "legitimized" to invalidate any policy proposals initiated by the State Council if they contradicted the Politburo's intentions.[2] But some major leaders (premier and vice premiers) of the State Council were either members of the Politburo standing committee or ordinary Politburo members.[3] It was hard to categorize them in terms of the Party-government dichotomy.[4] This integration of Party-government posts implied that any decision made by the Party center (the Politburo) should already incorporate the opinions of the State Council.

It is therefore clear that the separation at the top level did not involve decisionmaking, which was in theory the responsibility of the Central Committee (the Politburo and its standing committee) and the NPC. By contrast, the State Council in principle was not supposed to be a decisionmaking organ, even though its top leaders participated in the policymaking process. But the de facto Party-government fusion in terms of the formulation of political principles and major policy proposals at the center did not mean that the principle of separation could not be applied to the central level or was just a propaganda ploy. In fact, the separation did make sense when it came to the executive power of the State Council on government affairs. Among the five Party bodies at the center, the only one that might compete with the State Council for executive power or "unjustifiably" interfere in its work—and hence become the target of the separation—was the Party Secretariat.[5]

The Secretariat and State Council: A Zero-Sum Game

The Party Secretariat was the executive office of the Politburo and its standing committee, and was in charge of day-to-day Party operations. Its main task was to monitor the execution of decisions taken by its parent bodies on a daily basis through the central Party departments, bureaus, and committees.[6] As some scholars observed, the potential conflicts between the Secretariat and the State Council gradually took shape after 1955, when the Central Committee established departments that paralleled similar bodies that had been set up under the State Council to run the economy. Partly through these Party departments, the Party Secretariat became a key organ in the Party's exercise of power over the state bureaucracy.[7] As its head, Deng Xiaoping acquired a strong position from which to build a personal power base to rival that of the PRC president Liu Shaoqi and Premier Zhou Enlai.[8] Not surprisingly, when political reform restarted with the separation of Party and government in 1986, the only victim among the central Party organs was the Secretariat, particularly its head, the Party general secretary.

From an institutional perspective, the sole visible change effected by the separation at the center was the abolition of the cross-officeholding of some major leaders. During the terms of the twelfth Party congress (1982–1987) and the sixth NPC (1983–1988), several Party leaders, such as Wan Li, Yao Yilin, and Gu Mu, were both members (secretaries) of the Secretariat and vice premiers (or state councillors, the same rank as vice premiers). It was decided at the thirteenth Party congress and the seventh NPC that the leaderships of the two organs could no longer overlap. This separation was of symbolic importance because it at least formally rid the State Council of its image as a component of the Party center and established it as a central *government*—partially in the sense that it removed some of the ideological obstacles, under the supreme principle of Party domination, to its acceptance of legislative oversight (as the official theory went, the legislature could supervise only the government, not the Party).

After the decision was taken, the Party Secretariat was no longer justified in sending its directives directly to local governments but only to local Party committees, its "legitimate" subordinate units. Although local Party committees were required by Party discipline to obey the instructions from the Secretariat, local governments were not. And the latter could even defy the Secretariat on the grounds that it was now only the State Council whose decrees they, as its subordinate units in the state administrative hierarchy, had a legal obligation to follow. Since the major responsibility of the State Council was to direct China's socioeconomic development, the political principles and directions of which should already have been decided by the Politburo, the Secretariat was deprived of many of its excuses for impinging upon the State Council's administrative domain.

Although the Secretariat was obviously the loser and its authority and responsibilities were considerably diminished by the separation, its ordinary members had no reason to feel frustrated. These members did not stand higher in the Party hierarchy than the major leading members of the State Council.[9] Even before the separation, they were not in a position to dominate or interfere in the work of the latter in the name of party leadership. As later developments showed, the person who really suffered from the separation was none other than the Party general secretary, and the person who benefited most was the premier. To a certain extent, the separation of Party and government at the central level evolved into a power struggle between these two individuals.

Between the twelfth and thirteenth Party congresses, the most active advocate of the Party-government separation was Zhao Ziyang, who held the premiership during this period (au. int.). Zhao's enthusiasm arose partly from the relative open-mindedness he consistently displayed in the reform process. But presumably it also related to his collision with another reformer, Hu Yaobang. As mentioned before, Hu had raised the issue of the separation of Party and government in his report to the twelfth Party congress in 1982. But as the Party general secretary, Hu was not eager to put into practice a principle that would place restraints on his own authority—which could partly explain the nationwide failure of this policy prior to 1986. In May 1984 Premier Zhao wrote to Deng Xiaoping and complained that Hu, in the name of the Secretariat and also using his status as the Party general secretary, interfered too much in the work of the State Council.[10] At the meeting at the end of 1986 in which it was decided that Hu had to step down, Zhao allegedly made the same charge more strongly worded and criticized Hu of violating the principle of collective leadership.[11]

Although both Hu and Zhao were widely seen as liberal reformers in the central leadership circle, there is no doubt that when political reform returned to the agenda in 1986, with the separation of Party and government at its core, it was Zhao's camp rather than Hu's that was the major driving force behind it.[12] If Hu's attempt to dominate the State Council led to conflicts with Zhao, it was ironic that Deng's sudden and unexpected selection of Zhao as the new Party general secretary and his subsequent efforts to maintain his influence over the State Council made his working relations with the new premier, Li Peng, even worse. The refusal of the Party chief to take the lead in complying with the separation principle undoubtedly added to the difficulties with which this crucial step of reform was taken at local levels. In 1993, as Deng and other elders were passing away, Jiang Zemin broke the separation rule by taking over the PRC presidency in order to secure his position as supreme Party-state leader.[13] The separation at the central level was virtually abolished in 1995 when two Secretariat members (Jiang Chunyun and Wu Bangguo) were appointed as vice premiers through an NPC by-election (with record low positive votes).[14] At the ninth NPC session in 1998, two Secretariat members, appointed just five months before, entered the State Council (Wen Jiabao as vice premier and Luo Gan as state councillor). This cross-officeholding in the two central organs marked a restoration of the pre-1987 pattern.

Here is a puzzle: If the separation made the post of the Party general secretary less profitable and more vulnerable, why could it be proposed and implemented in the 1980s against the general secretary's (first Hu's, then Zhao's) own will—assuming he was a rational egoist—and to a lesser extent against the will of the Secretariat? To find an answer to this question, one must look at the unique power structure and sources of influence at the central level during the Deng period and distinguish between formal and informal power. As some scholars indicate, the personal authority of individuals within the leadership could not be judged only by their titles. Many central leaders, typically the younger ones, were handpicked by their patrons (Party elders) to succeed the formal posts the latter had quit because of senility or deteriorating health. But the patrons did not really transfer their power to their successors; they just used their clients as agents to handle the day-to-day Party-state affairs on their behalf while retaining the final say in decisionmaking.[15] This informal but truly formidable power in the hands of the Party elders not only made the actors on the political stage merely puppets but also enabled the elders to play a decisive role in choosing the actors.[16] Therefore, although Hu and Zhao occupied the top Party position one after another, they had no strong power bases of their own, and their formal posts were completely at the mercy of Deng and other "retired" Party elders who remained behind the scenes.[17] The separation of the Party from government was never designed to have any negative impact upon Deng's patronage politics at the center. On the contrary, by circumscribing the authority of the Party general secretary and making this post essentially superfluous, the separation only brought the nominal first leader under Party elders' tighter control.[18] As an insider indicated, this was the main reason that, on the eve of the thirteenth Party congress, Zhao was reluctant to assume the office of the Party general secretary, insisting that the premiership suited him better. As Party chief, his assigned responsibility for "political leadership" would be empty. But as premier, he would possess at least some concrete powers to decide on specific socioeconomic affairs as well as implement policies.[19]

The Politburo-NPC Relationship: Control and Anticontrol

As suggested by the above discussion, separation of the Party from government did not alter the unique central structure of authority in any significant way. If anything, it only placed the younger leaders of the Party (the Secretariat) and government (the State Council) under the firmer control of the Party elders because it created a competition or balance of power between the two major central institutions. But even so, this separation policy was still democratically meaningful on two accounts. By downgrading the Party Secretariat in relation to the State Council and denying it the administrative functions it used to perform, the separation eroded the foundation of the authority of professional Party leaders (those who did not hold any posts in the government) and would move the Chinese Party-state in the direction of what Max Weber described as a rational-legal system, especially after Party elders completely quit politics.[20] In addition, the separation paved the way for the NPC's assumption of genuine legislative functions as well as for its ascent as a balancing force in the central game of power. The legislative oversight of government became practicable and operational, as it would not do much damage to the Party's hegemonic image. Party elders intended this institutional innovation for their own purposes. They surely did not expect to have increasing difficulty constraining the NPC within the limits they desired.

Deng's "Rule of Law" and Its Significance

Post-Mao leaders had many lessons to learn from the Cultural Revolution. The weakness of intra-Party mechanisms for checking Party cadres' abuses of power and the lack of institutionalized channels through which to redress injustices in society resulted in the accumulation of popular grievances and their eruption through Maoist-style mass mobilization and participation in the Cultural Revolution. Reflections on the past social upheaval led the post-Mao leadership to appreciate the importance of the rule of law and the potential utility of the legislature. The restoration and innovations of the electoral system, combined with the Party-government separation, represented part of the Party center's broad efforts to strengthen people's congresses and, through it, to establish a workable legal system.

Although Deng and his colleagues came a long way to emphasize the rule of law as opposed to the rule of individuals as a top priority of political reform, they never showed an understanding of this concept as it was used in the West, as a governing system in which the highest authority is a body of law that applies equally to all, with individual political and economic liberties protected from arbitrary state encroachment.[21] Instead, they expected the legal system to play a more significant role in maintaining the new social order during the post-Mao period, when the Party's traditional control mechanisms had lost much of their effectiveness.[22] This intention may be inferred from the communiqué of the Third Plenum (December 1978):

> In order to safeguard people's democracy, it is imperative to strengthen the socialist legal system so that democracy is systematized and written into law in such a way as to ensure the stability, continuity and full authority of this democratic system and these laws; there must be laws for people to follow, these laws must be observed, their enforcement must be strict and law breakers must be dealt with.[23]

Another Party document (June 27, 1981) revealed a similar intent to use the rule of law as one of the Party's new instruments for control. It asserted that to prevent a recurrence of the kind of chaotic situation that obtained in the Cultural Revolution, it was necessary to make people's congresses at all levels and their permanent organs "authoritative organs of the people's political power."[24] Deng perceived a legal system operated by people's congresses to be better at cracking down on criminal activities and took this as a major task of political reform.[25] But even if laws and legislation were aimed mainly at citizens, to regulate societal activities rather than limit Party power, it demoted the Party's status in Chinese society in a quite remarkable way and jeopardized the legal base of Party authority.[26] Party policies were to be replaced by state laws that would become the new codes of social conduct as well as the basis of government policies. Moreover, concrete lawmaking was in theory no longer the Party's business but fell largely within the domain of authority of people's congresses.[27]

The post-Mao rule of law campaign to a large extent marked the resumption of China's state-building process. This process, interrupted after the late 1950s, propelled a transition from an undisguised rule of Party policy to a rule of state law that aimed to place Party policy under a constitutional and legal cloak. Indeed the campaign derived powerful impetus from the new CCP constitution (1982), which claimed to keep Party activities within the limits permitted by the constitution and state laws. Peng Zhen worked out a theoretical explanation of why law must replace Party policy in government. He argued that although the Party represented the people and served them wholeheartedly, Party members constituted just a tiny minority of China's 1 billion people. "What we have is not only the Party but also the state. . . . Only through legal procedures can Party policy become state policy."[28] One would see later that this transition, though it failed to shake Party dominance, strengthened legal procedures and paved the way for certain legislative checks and balances. Presumably because the perceived merits and necessity of a legal system outweighed its potential threat, the efforts toward legal reform, compared with some other aspects of China's political reform, appeared to be more purposive than expedient and thus proceeded more steadily and with less opposition. As a Western scholar observes, the increase in the scope, complexity, and sophistication of the legal environment and in the volume of activity within it "is not the fortuitous result of undirected evolution, but the product of a deliberate policy espoused by the leadership."[29]

The NPC in the 1982 Constitution

The first sign of the NPC's rise as a major actor in top-level politics could be found in the revision of the 1978 constitution. Following what Kevin O'Brien portrays as the "most open and lively legislative [NPC] session in the history of the People's Republic" in 1980, a Committee for Revision of the Constitution was set up.[30] In the two years and three months of revision that followed, the official press asserted that people of all nationalities were mobilized to participate in the discussion and contribute their opinions, whose influence was "unprecedented in the PRC history."[31] An official source implied that some revisions were insisted on against the instructions from the Central Committee.[32]

There had been different constitutional provisions regarding the legal status of the NPC. In the 1954 version, obviously as an expedient to maintain the "united front" for the new regime, the NPC was defined as the "highest organ of State authority in the PRC" (article 21). In 1975 this was revised to the "highest organ of state power under the leadership of the Communist Party of China" (article 16). In 1978 the NPC was once again named as the "highest organ of state power" with the original qualifications dropped (article 20).[33] But this provision in the 1978 version, not to mention the 1975 one, directly contradicted article 2, which maintained that the CCP should be the core of leadership for the entire Chinese people: "The working class exercises leadership over the state through its vanguard, the Communist Party of China." The 1982 constitution restored the ambiguous wording of the 1954 version concerning the relationship between the CCP and the NPC. On the one hand, the NPC was the "highest organ of state power" (article 57). On the other, party leadership was mentioned just as the "general guiding ideology" (in the preamble of the constitution).[34] The official explanation was that the constitution stipulated only the state system. The Party's functions and various activities did not belong to the state system and hence were not covered by the domain for which the constitution must have concrete provisions. It also alleged that it was inappropriate to write "party leadership" directly into the articles of the constitution, "because it will confuse the functions of the Party and state."[35]

A comparison of this new constitution with the documents passed by the twelfth Party congress during the same period seems to suggest that the separation of the Party from government was indeed under serious consideration. Even if "party leadership" as an abstract principle was still there, Party control of the government (the state) was, after all, constitutionally deempha-

Table 6.1   Changes in the Number and Percentage of NPCSC Members

	Number of NPCSC Members	Number of NPCSC Chairs and Vice Chairs	Percentage of NPCSC Members Among NPC Deputies	China's Total Population (millions)
First NPC (1954)	79	14	6.4	602.66
Second NPC (1960)	79	17	6.4	662.07
Third NPC (1964)	115	19	3.8	704.99
Fourth NPC (1975)	167	23	5.8	924.20
Fifth NPC (1978)	196	21	5.6	962.59
Sixth NPC (1983)	155	21	5.2	1,024.95
Seventh NPC (1988)	155	20	5.2	1,096.14
Eighth NPC (1993)	155	20	5.2	1,185.17
Ninth NPC (1998)	154	20	5.2	–

Sources: Wu Kaiping, "On the Composition of the NPCSC Members," in Zi Mu, ed., *Minzhu de Gousi*, pp. 212–224; *The PRC Yearbook, 1989, 1994*; *XHYB*, 641:4 (April 30, 1998), pp. 55–56.

sized. To a certain extent, government officials and people's deputies were provided with a constitutional base to assert their autonomy and establish their own institutional authority, which proved a significant turn of events in the changing political environment.

A second important revision in the 1982 constitution involved the delegation of some of the functions and powers that originally belonged to the NPC to the NPCSC, whose members were elected by NPC deputies in the same way state leaders were. These functions and powers included (1) enacting and amending statutes (laws) (in the 1978 constitution the NPCSC could enact only decrees); (2) supervising, jointly with the NPC, the enforcement of the constitution; examining and approving, when the NPC was not in session, partial adjustment to the plan for national economic and social development and to the state budget that proved necessary in the course of their implementation; and (3) deciding, when the NPC was not in session, on the choice of all the members (in contrast to "individual members" in the previous version) of the State Council except the premier, vice premiers, and state councilors. The NPC had close to 3,000 deputies and met in session only once a year. The infrequency of sessions and its unwieldy size, among other things, made it difficult for the NPC to discharge its functions efficiently. By contrast, the NPCSC had just over one hundred members and met every two months (Table 6.1). The expansion of the NPCSC's functions and powers had mixed effects on the NPC. Although it drew the national legislature more deeply into the political process and brought it out of its traditional state of inertia, the Politburo had one more instrument to keep the NPC in its grip.[36]

The NPC-Party Relationships: Some Theoretical Points

This chapter does not chronicle the NPC's activities and sessions since the late 1970s.[37] Instead, the discussion here addresses two questions: To what extent did the NPC authority expand at the cost of Party domination? And how were the apparent zero-sum power relationships between the NPC and the central Party apparatus handled in practice?

One has to approach these issues with China's general sociopolitical development in mind. China's political environment improved considerably after Mao's death to allow the expansion of an autonomous sphere of public discourse.[38] During most of the post-1949 period, various democratic principles, such as those defining the NPC as the supreme power organ, were explicitly written into the constitutions, laws, Party-state documents, and public publications. Under the Maoist reign of terror, however, very few people had the courage openly to question whether or not these principles were actually upheld. In the era of reform, the rule of law was more than rhetorically enshrined in the official ideology and deliberately made a hallmark of the Deng regime. Consequently, political terror was mitigated and freedom of speech increased. The repudiation of Maoism and the "fascist dictatorship" of the Cultural Revolution led Chinese society to take the democratic principles and legal procedures on paper more seriously. In 1987 and 1989, for example, university students took to the streets for democracy on the grounds that the right to demonstration was solemnly guaranteed by the constitution.[39] The Party center thus had to pay special attention to the theoretical elaboration of the "democratic" and legal reforms, lest citizens, liberal intellectuals in particular, exploit the loopholes or contradictions in the official ideology to challenge Party hegemony. But certainly not all NPC deputies reconciled themselves to a state of powerlessness. As the NPC rebellion of May 1989 showed, some of them had been searching for "legitimate" opportunities to assert legislative supremacy.

The communist regime proved unable to solve the theoretical dilemma that kept the reform from being structurally and democratically meaningful. In the Chinese case, this dilemma could not be seen more clearly than in the conflicting definitions regarding the authority of Party apparatus and the legislature. The Communist Party, given its "vanguard nature," must be the leading force, whereas the NPC should hold supreme power as the organ "through which the people exercise state power" (article 2 of the constitution). More perplexing, the alleged aim of political reform was to strengthen both party leadership and the authority of people's congresses, as if the two were identical.

After the 1982 constitution and Party constitution were adopted, the leadership made serious efforts to clarify some basic guidelines regarding the power relationships between Party apparatus and the legislature. First, the

Party was neither an organ of power nor an administrative organization. Party leadership meant the "political, ideological and organizational leadership" (1982) before it was further reduced to the "political leadership" (1987), which was specified in such a way as to prevent Party apparatus from exercising administrative power. Accordingly, state power should concentrate in the congress. But the Party center attempted to avoid making a comparison between the power positions of Party apparatus and congresses. In a speech of June 1986, Peng Zhen cautioned that it was not appropriate to raise certain questions, such as, Who is more powerful, the Party secretary, SCPC chairperson, or government head? These individuals "have different responsibilities, so their relationships are not competitive."[40] During the 1990s the priority regarding Party functions was switched to the Party's "organizational leadership," with the Party-government separation deemphasized. The status of the legislature remained legally unchanged, but its relations of authority with Party apparatus were made even more rhetorically equivocal.[41]

Second, all the parties and organizations, including the CCP, must abide by the constitution and state laws. This provision aroused controversy immediately. In response to the question which was more authoritative, the Party or the laws, Peng Zhen gave a vague response. "In my view," he argued, "this question can be answered by three sentences: The Party leads the people in drawing up the constitution and making laws; the Party leads them in obeying the constitution and laws; the Party itself must also conduct its activities within the limits permitted by the constitution and laws."[42]

What does "the Party leads the people" mean? Peng did not elaborate. But one thing was made unquestionable: Party leadership did not mean Party domination over the legislative process. In other words, the Party could not take it for granted that its policy or legislative proposals would be converted into state policies or laws. According to an official tract on China's legislature, the suggestions on legislation made by the Central Committee "do not count" unless they are formally adopted by the NPC. To be sure, the NPC and its Standing Committee should "respect the opinions of the Central Committee in making and revising laws. But they are not fettered by these opinions."[43] Quoting as an example the revision of the constitution in 1982, the author argued that the Party did not have the power of legal effect to examine and decide on legislation.[44] In an NPCSC pamphlet, the relationships between the Party and people's congresses were defined as those between the Party and the people: "If the Party does not respect the power of the people's congress, it does not respect the power of the people." This pamphlet made it unmistakable that party leadership over people's congresses was not the kind of leadership exercised by higher authorities.[45] Regardless of their motivations for making these statements, Party leaders, especially conservative ones, would soon see the results.

The Mechanisms for Politburo Control over the NPC

The central efforts to establish a legal system through the NPC produced a legislative explosion at the national level. As official sources disclosed, the total number of laws (including legal decisions) enacted by the NPC and NPCSC from 1979 to early 1997 exceeded 300, more than doubling the number made during twenty-nine pre-reform years (1949–1978).[46] They covered administrative, economic, criminal, and civil areas.[47] As part of the legal reform, a nationwide campaign of "learning and obeying laws" was carried out. In November 1985 the Central Committee and State Council jointly approved and issued the "Five-Year Plan for Spreading Legal Knowledge Among Citizens," demanding that leading Party cadres strengthen their sense of the rule of law.[48] By August 1986 forty-four ministries and commissions of the State Council organized more than 200 classes to teach laws, and 10,500 senior cadres attended.[49] During the Mao era, if Party members committed crimes, most probably only disciplinary action was taken against them. An *RMRB* commentator warned that the practice of substituting Party discipline for legal penalty had to be discontinued. Whoever violated the law must be punished by the state organs concerned: "The Party's interference is neither advisable nor proper."[50]

Notwithstanding the Party's major part in the process, the replacement of Party policies by state laws enacted by the people's congress provided chances for citizen participation in legislation and the policy process and imposed some structural restraints upon Party arbitrariness.[51] At the national level, even if the election of NPC deputies was removed from the reach of ordinary citizens and subject to massive Party influence, the Party center still faced the problem of how to control the NPC and at the same time expect it to play a constructive role in the political and legal reform. For that matter, the leadership had been haunted by the contradictions inherent in developing the functions of the national legislature and had to maintain a balance between the NPC's usefulness and recalcitrance. Although the negative votes and sharply critical comments at NPC sessions might embarrass the leadership, the control mechanisms of the Politburo made any collective rebellion in the NPC extremely difficult even during the most "liberal" period.

In the first place, most if not all NPC deputies had a political commitment to the regime. From Table 3.2 one can see that approximately two-thirds of NPC deputies during 1988–1998 were CCP members. After the 1982 constitution was adopted, the NPCSC became the core of the NPC and essentially seized much of its power. Of the fifty-five major laws promulgated during 1979–1986, thirty-three (60 percent) were enacted by the NPCSC and only twenty-two (40 percent) by the NPC.[52] Relevant information is not available for the post-1986 period, but a legal expert charged that the NPCSC impinged upon the authority of the NPC. For example, some "fundamental laws" (such

Table 6.2   Changes in "Partisan" Composition of the NPCSC

	CCP Members		Members of Satellite "Parties"		Members with No Party Affiliation	
	Number	Percentage	Number	Percentage	Number	Percentage
First NPCSC (1954)	40	50.63	25	31.64	14	17.73
Second NPCSC (1960)	40	50.63	30	37.98	9	11.39
Third NPCSC (1964)	67	58.26	33	28.70	15	13.04
Fourth NPCSC (1975)	129	77.25	25	14.97	13	7.78
Fifth NPCSC (1978)	153	78.06	35	17.86	8	4.08
Sixth NPCSC (1983)	113	72.90	32	20.65	10	6.45

Source: Wu Kaiping, "On the Composition of the NPCSC Members," in Zi Mu, ed., *Minzhu de Gousi*, pp. 212–224.

as the laws on agriculture, labor, and foreign trade) whose formulation should have been the responsibility of the NPC were "improperly" enacted by the NPCSC.[53] The laws passed by the NPCSC usually went into effect immediately upon the signature of the PRC president. They did not need to be approved by the NPC, although the NPC was empowered to "alter or annul inappropriate decisions of the NPCSC" (article 62 of the 1982 constitution). By contrast, the bills proposed by the NPC were normally submitted to its deputies for voting only after examination and approval by the NPCSC.

Thus, the NPCSC's political composition became particularly important. Since NPCSC members were elected by NPC deputies in the way state leaders were, the Politburo possessed enormous leverage over the election through its nomination of candidates. The deputies had few choices because of the small difference between the numbers of candidates and seats.[54] For example, the 135 members of the seventh NPCSC were chosen from 144 candidates.[55] In 1983 more than 70 percent of those in the NPCSC were also members of the CCP (Table 6.2). Information on the partisan composition of the NPCSC since 1983 is unavailable. I tried to check the backgrounds and experiences of eighth and ninth NPCSC members from publications in mainland China, Hong Kong, and Taiwan. Although the data are not complete, my approximate estimate is that the percentage of CCP members in the NPCSC since 1983 is not below 75. Among sixth NPCSC members, 104 (67 percent) were Party cadres and government officials ranking at or above the level of central deputy minister.[56] It seemed that two opposite tendencies offset each other in Party representation and domination in the NPCSC. To demonstrate "democratization" and the "rule of law," the Party had to quit the NPCSC or at least avoid a public impression of using it as a Party instrument. But as the NPCSC was granted more autonomy and authority, the Politburo managed to maintain a high percentage of Party members therein, on guard against its rebellion.

The second source of the Politburo's strength was some means at its disposal to control the lawmaking and voting of NPCSC members. Several scholarly works probe into this issue. Kevin O'Brien argues that the Party center controlled lawmaking through the Central Political-Legal Leading Group (CPLG).[57] Murray Scot Tanner specifies four dominant organizational forms of party leadership over lawmaking and the NPC.[58] But there have been few detailed analyses of the internal channels of communication, consultation, and consensus-building between the Politburo and the NPCSC that gave the Party soft but firm control. Within the NPCSC, there were two key dominant groups whose members partially overlapped. One was the "chair's meeting" (*weiyuanzhang huiyi*); the other was the Party group (*dang zu*). The "chair's meeting" comprised the chair, vice chairs (for the number of its members, see Table 6.1), and secretary-general of the NPCSC. Although some were incumbent Politburo members, most of them had retired from senior central Party or government offices but retained their status and titles as "state leaders" in public references. The "chair's meeting" was charged with handling the daily routine of the NPCSC and determined the agenda of the NPC and NPCSC.[59] The decisions taken by the "chair's meeting" partly resulted from and partly shaped the will of the NPCSC members through a process of discussion and persuasion.[60]

In terms of decisionmaking, the Party group was the real core of the NPCSC. For obvious reasons, the Party group always kept a low profile within the NPCSC after 1979. The tasks assigned to it were not clearly specified except for a general provision that the Party should exercise its "political leadership" over people's congresses through the Party groups in them.[61] As an official source suggested, the Party group was not supposed to demand that all people's deputies and SCPC members accept Party decisions. But it was justified in asking those with Party membership to do so because Party discipline required its members to abide by Party resolutions.[62] The source also argued that the resolutions or decisions of the people's congress should be preapproved in principle by the Party committee of the corresponding level (at the national level by the Politburo). No solution was suggested, however, concerning what to do if the Party committee refused to approve a decision. It is important to note the role of the SCPC Party group in connecting the SCPC and the Party committee of the corresponding level. In the next chapter, I examine this role at local levels; here my interviews with NPCSC members provided some details regarding how the game was played at the central level.

It was a confidentially stipulated rule that the content of any major law made by the NPC or NPCSC must be examined and approved by the Politburo.[63] But the Politburo usually did this quietly, to avoid the impression that it manipulated legislation. The Party group in the NPCSC thus played a double role, both as supervisor and bridge connecting the NPCSC and the Politburo. It directed and supervised the making of a draft law on the Politburo's behalf. It exercised this power implicitly rather than explicitly, as even the Party group was constitutionally forbidden from dominating the legislation that was supposed to be drafted autonomously by NPC deputies or NPCSC members. After an important draft law was completed, the Party group usually sent it to a meeting of the Politburo for discussion before it was submitted to a vote by the NPC or NPCSC.[64] As the secretary (head) of the Party group (also the NPCSC chair) was usually a senior Politburo member (such as Peng Zhen, 1983–1988, and Wan Li, 1988–1993) or even a member of the Politburo standing committee (such as Qiao Shi, 1993–1998, and Li Peng, 1998–), the draft law generally passed at the Politburo meeting. Although the Politburo sometimes demanded revisions, it did not always impose its will upon the NPCSC. If the issue was not appraised as critical or if it involved legal expertise, the Politburo might back down and defer to the opinions of the NPCSC majority. The adoption of the law on mass rallies and demonstrations by the NPCSC in October 1989 was such a case.[65]

Because China's highest-level politics is a closed-door, elitist game, it is hard to find out whether there were any substantial divergences of opinion between NPCSC and Politburo in the legislative process that might provide a base to test their relative strengths. Since the NPCSC mainly consisted of former senior Party cadres and government officials and was largely controlled by its Party group, any NPCSC resolutions or legislative proposals probably did not widely deviate politically and ideologically from the Politburo's spirit. Moreover, an examination of the content of the laws enacted by the NPC and NPCSC up to 1998 suggests very little macropolitics and few ideologically sensitive matters. The demonstration law was perhaps one of a few exceptions. The controversy, if any, revolved mostly around technical details and legal professionalism, and there was certainly no reason the Politburo and the NPC or NPCSC could not reach a consensus on these (au. int.).

If one assumes that cleavages might arise over the issues of reform, then some professional Party leaders were radical, liberal reformers. In fact, reform and antireform orientations went across the board, and conflicts in this regard could be more intense and substantial among top Party leaders (including Party elders) than between the Politburo and the NPCSC. Throughout the reform period, one could find only one case in which NPCSC members came into serious collision with the Party center. In May 1989, after martial law was proclaimed in Beijing, fifty-seven NPCSC members (more than one-third of the total number) signed a proposal demanding an emergency session.[66] This proposal was intended to revoke martial law and recall Premier Li Peng. Immediately after the massacre, reprisals were made against these members.

Hu Jiwei, who sponsored the proposal, was expelled from the NPCSC. Under pressure from above, some NPCSC members who signed the proposal claimed that their signatures were forged; some said they had been cheated by the sponsor.[67]

This case of NPCSC disobedience was illustrative of the most likely outcome if the NPCSC tried seriously to challenge the authority of the Politburo—more precisely, of Deng. It was a rare occasion indeed that brought to light the spurious "supremacy" of the NPC.[68] But this case was exceptional anyway. Given the intensified confrontation among Party leaders on how to handle the prodemocracy movement, one could hardly cite it as an example of the NPCSC's opposing the Party. It did demonstrate, though, that on what Deng and other Party elders considered to be crucial issues, they would not tolerate any disagreement on the part of the NPC, even if the NPC essentially did not go against the Party but just followed a Party faction that failed in the intra-Party policy or power struggle.

The NPC's Sources of Strength

For all the powerful Politburo domination, the prevailing perception of the NPC as little more than a tool of the Politburo needs revision. On broad systemic issues, without doubt, there was no substantial disagreement between the Politburo and the NPC. It was true, too, that if a political conflict did arise (such as it did in 1989), the Politburo did not have to take pains to subdue the NPC. But on many legal subjects or the issues concerning the pace and scope of market reform, the NPC and NPCSC did acquire influence and even an institutional capacity to contend with the Politburo. The Politburo displayed a certain respect for the NPC's legislative initiative and deferred to its "autonomy" from time to time. In that respect, the adoption of the state enterprise bankruptcy law in 1986 was a spectacular though somewhat ironic case.[69] It was seen by some observers as an example of how a conservative NPCSC acted rather successfully against a seemingly reform-minded Politburo.[70] Because of publicity in the official press, this case set a precedent for NPCSC defiance whose effects were to be felt for years to come.[71]

Although one must avoid exaggerating the meaning of this sort of defiance, it seems that a certain amount of rivalry has been developing between the NPCSC and the Politburo. Most of this rivalry did not originate from the NPCSC members, who wanted to establish a democratic system of checks and balances, but from the quarrels over the distribution of power resources within the Party leadership. Roughly half of the vice chairs of the NPCSC were forced to quit high Party and government offices.[72] Since these offices were traditionally more powerful, profitable, and prestigious than NPCSC seats, those who were turned out of them grasped at the chance offered by the Party emphasis upon the rule of law to attempt to augment their political weight in the name of defending the legal system.[73] Meanwhile, the leaders who disagreed with Deng on major issues and hence were elbowed out of the center of power found a forum for their views in the NPC or CPPCC.[74]

NPCSC chairman Peng Zhen was a typical example. In terms of revolutionary qualifications, Peng was Deng's equal. But in the twelfth Party congress of 1982, he failed to enter the Politburo standing committee.[75] Instead, Hu Yaobang and Zhao Ziyang, younger and much less "qualified," were "elected." Peng's efforts toward legal reform and the substitution of Party policy by law related to his personal stake, which combined with his ideological orientation as a hard-liner to shape his seemingly self-contradictory role in political reform. On the issue of "party leadership" he was a well-known conservative (but recall that as a senior Politburo member, he represented party leadership within the NPC). But he showed great zeal for bolstering the status of the people's congress to balance the Party apparatus. Peng often behaved like a staunch defender of the constitution. When he referred a Party resolution to the NPCSC, he made a deliberate show of placing the NPC above the Party, and to his self-addressed question whether or not this resolution "conformed to the spirit of the constitution," he answered yes. As one observer remarked, this statement contextually implied not just that any Party policy must keep in line with the laws to be lawful but, more important, that only the NPCSC chair's meeting had the legal authority to judge whether or not CCP documents and policies were constitutional.[76]

Regardless of his personal motivations, as a major Party elder Peng Zhen encouraged the NPC to exercise its constitutionally conferred authority and even deliberately connived legislative disobedience. And his example in effect removed many of the scruples for NPC deputies and NPCSC members who were politically risk-averse and tended to avoid any action that could arouse suspicions of anti-Party sympathies. In the 1982 constitution, among all the functions and powers the NPC and NPCSC were authorized to exercise, only three had the potential to make a difference in political terms. Except for the election of state leaders already discussed in Chapter 4, the other two were legislation and supervision of the State Council (cabinet).[77] Until 1986, all proposals submitted to the NPC and NPCSC for discussion and approval were, without exception, passed unanimously. At the sixth NPC session of April 1986, a few deputies unprecedentedly cast negative or abstention votes on the reports by the Supreme People's Court and the Supreme People's Procuratorate and made troubles for the appointment or removal of cabinet personnel.[78] At NPCSC sessions, the number of no votes and abstentions increased by a change in the voting method. In elections of people's deputies and government officials, a secret ballot was used immediately after the new electoral law and the local organic law were promulgated in 1979. But voting on legislative proposals had been conducted by a show of hands until March 1986, when electronic voting machines were installed for the NPCSC. Thereafter negative or abstention votes appeared on almost every proposal or draft law.[79]

The NPC session of March-April 1988 was described by Western observers as "unprecedented for its openness."[80] Outspoken Hong Kong reporters were surprised by "some new phenomena never seen before."[81] Three developments stood out: (1) sharp criticisms on the work report of the premier from the deputies,[82] (2) the large number of ballots cast against candidates for state leadership, and (3) adoption of more deputy proposals. In no previous session had the agenda changed so frequently following the suggestions of the deputies.[83] The NPC passed an amendment of the 1982 constitution that, allegedly built on the deputies' initiative, made two radical revisions to accelerate the privatization of economy.[84] Since the revisions offered some constitutional protection of capitalism, the observers from Taiwan predicted that the CCP might become the "first communist party [in communist countries] that changes its political nature."[85] The challenges from the NPC deputies were given a big boost by the official press, signaling less political risk in making critical remarks.[86]

In 1988 Peng Zhen retired, and a staunch reformer, Wan Li, was elected to succeed him. The new NPCSC leadership brought with it a more liberal atmosphere for NPC discussions. At a spring 1989 NPC session, many deputies suggested that the NPCSC should be dismissed and more professional committees established instead to prevent the NPC from being "alienated," or, to be blunt, rigged. It was also proposed that NPC deputies should be directly elected to make them more accountable to the people.[87] This session witnessed the first massive "rebellion" in the NPC: More than one-third (1,079) of the deputies voted to reject a State Council (more precisely, a Politburo) proposal to grant legislative power to the Shenzhen Special Zone.[88]

The 1990s: Toward Territorial Politics

The consequences the Tiananmen crackdown had on NPC-Party relationships must be analyzed from both political and legal perspectives. The expulsion of Hu Jiwei from the NPCSC as well as the repressive political climate following Tiananmen obviously frightened the outspoken deputies into silence.[89] In the case of Huang Shunxing, the Politburo once again exhibited its intolerance of any NPC deviation on "principled" matters. Huang came from Taiwan, where he used to be a member of parliament. He was selected by Beijing to "represent" Taiwan in the NPCSC. In the 1992 NPC session, Huang agitated against the Three-Gorge Dam project, and his opposition cost him his NPCSC seat.[90] If political and legal reforms once seemed to have brought China close to a breakthrough toward a Western-type democracy, Tiananmen thwarted the efforts in that direction and stifled the lively discussions that had prevailed during the late 1980s about the possibility of a change in the political system.[91] The political taboo persisted into the late 1990s. Insofar as it can be publicly voiced, any kind of political opposition within the NPC appeared farther away during the 1990s than during most of the 1980s.

China's political reform involved three major components: administrative reform, legal reform, and political structural reform.[92] (The last is what I and many Western China scholars refer to as political reform in its narrow sense.)[93] The Tiananmen bloodshed surely stopped the political restructuring from moving toward the political liberalization and democratization that once appeared possible. But perhaps for two reasons Tiananmen did not affect the legal reform, especially those aspects regarding NPC legislation and supervision, as much as might be imagined. For one, central authorities did not want to hurt their image as reformers as long as reform remained popular and the base of the leadership's legitimacy. Then, too, the Party center—Deng in particular—saw legal reform and the rule of law as a useful instrument not to promote democratic governance but to improve the means of Party control over society. They seemed to conclude that legal reform and the expanded authority of the congress should not be held responsible for the spread of "bourgeois liberalism" and could be continued without substantial harm to the one-party system.[94] In any case, there were no reports suggesting the presence of political intimidation of NPC deputies (au. int.). At least in official discourse, NPC authority and autonomy were still endorsed, and the inertia of NPC deputies following Tiananmen proved to be temporary.

The first eighth NPC session in 1993 restored the atmosphere that had characterized the 1987–1989 NPC sessions, with some differences. There were still several deputies who wielded the rule of law to question the legal justification of the Party committee's "leading" the people's congress. But most deputies tended to avoid any association with "bourgeois liberalism."[95] Instead, they used the session as a forum to bargain for more territorial or professional prerogatives. Deputies from several provinces appealed for the Party center's approval of their own special economic zones and demanded laws that would loosen central control over regional budgets. The army deputies petitioned for increasing military expenditures to improve military equipment and soldiers' livelihoods.[96]

In the 1994 and 1995 sessions, presumably as Deng's health worsened and Jiang had yet to consolidate his personal authority, regionalism further developed in the NPC, and several group discussions and legislative proposals were derailed. For example, the deputies from Inner Mongolia submitted bills requesting that the central government grant their region the same economic and foreign trade privileges as were enjoyed by Hainan Province. Hainan deputies proposed setting up red-light districts in the province's major cities to attract investors and tourists and increase government revenues.[97] What made the Politburo nervous was that the demands for more provincial autonomy turned out to represent not just the personal views of the deputies or regional congresses but concerted local efforts. They were endorsed by regional Party apparatus, which, to quote a Party leader's words, "placed regional interest above the Party interest."[98] Some regional leaders argued that they could not put all central decisions into practice indiscriminately but had to check first whether these decisions suited local conditions. Some local cadres threatened to fight the "central bureaucratism."[99] In a speech at the enlarged Politburo meeting right after the first ninth NPC session (March 1998), Jiang Zemin condemned some local leaders for demanding more territorial power, more legislative authorization, and a larger share of the national budget. Admitting that central policy and resolutions were not being carried out in many areas, Jiang exclaimed that regionalism was ruining the country's future and combating it had become an urgent task for the whole Party.[100]

Confronting the prospect of losing its authority over regional authorities and the national legislature, the Politburo abandoned its "democratic" pledge and instead explicitly demanded that NPC deputies stand by the central decisions. At the March 1998 session, the Politburo tried two levers to control NPC deputies. Through the meetings of provincial NPC delegation heads, the Party leaders communicated their messages to the deputies. Special directives were issued for the deputies with CCP membership that they should vote for the "Party decisions." Another method was to censor session bulletins and minimize the publication and spread of harsh remarks or those on forbidden topics. To prevent negative votes for Li Peng, a candidate for the NPCSC chair, the deputies were informed that Li, once elected, would strive for more NPC authority and autonomy rather than place the NPC under the tighter Party center control.[101] Even so, this session made history for the largest number of negative votes on record on the government's work performance. The work report of the Supreme People's Procuratorate, normally approved by the Politburo, was passed with only 54 percent of the vote. Such a low percentage of congressional support was quite unusual in the legislature of a communist state (Table 6.3). Some deputies cast their votes for deceased leaders to express their grievances against the incumbent leadership.[102]

At the end of the twentieth century, one may identify two tendencies of NPC development. It seems that many NPC deputies and NPCSC members are consciously trying to push the national legislature in a Western parliamentary direction and more seriously treat their constitutionally conferred powers, duties, and rights. The emergency proposal jointly made by thirty-five NPCSC members in June 1998 is a recent indicator of increasing NPC independence.[103] Another tendency is represented by the kind of legislative activity aimed at pursuing regional, group, or professional interests. Michael Mezey divides legislatures into three models—policymaking, representation, and system-maintenance—according to their authority and role in the lawmaking process.[104] The late 1990s witnessed the beginning of the NPC's departure from its previous sole system-maintenance function and a move in a

Table 6.3   Voting on Reports and Proposals at the First Session of the Ninth NPC, March 1998

	Pros	Cons	Abstentions	Absences
Report of government (State Council) work	2,885	7	9	6
Plan for economic and social development	2,840	29	29	9
Budgets for the central and local governments	2,736	83	76	12
Report of NPCSC work	2,837	29	24	17
Report of Supreme People's Court	2,169	399	324	15
Report of Supreme People's Procuratorate	1,601	845	447	14

Source: MB, March 20, 1998, p. A5.

more representational direction. As the NPC gradually evolves into a battlefield for redistribution of resources and central-local bargaining, and as it bares its sharper teeth to Party authority, some fractures seem to have developed within the central leadership circle. Tian Jiyun, a senior Politburo member, sided with resentful NPC deputies who agitated for the transformation of the NPC into a more independent institution. In his speech to the Guangdong NPC delegation, Tian overstepped the Party line and argued in favor of campaigning in elections.[105] But Qiao Shi, on behalf of the Politburo, criticized many deputies for their ideas of Western parliamentarianism as well as their "attempt to place the NPC above the Party center."[106] All these vertical and horizontal contradictions converged to create a delicate situation the Politburo (or more exactly, the dominant faction within it) has to face up to. The "bourgeois liberalism," such as the appeal for a multiparty system, does not seem to loom as a serious problem, but NPC threats to the Party center are intensifying in a different form and perhaps with different consequences.

Conclusion

The political game at the central level was different from that at local levels. First, at the center the sole source of all powers in policymaking and in the nomenklatura was Deng Xiaoping and his elderly group, almost all of whom had quit their Party and government offices and had no formal titles. Any political reform aimed at establishing checks and balances among the central Party apparatus, the cabinet, and the national legislature would not affect this unique structure of authority, that is, Deng's supremacy. Second, the central pattern of institutional arrangement would determine the nature of China's political system and have a decisive influence on local politics. Thus, Deng and his follow-ers showed considerable caution, particularly in granting greater authority to the NPC, over which they were afraid they might lose control.

But political and legal reform at the central level made some headway. The separation of the Party from government deprived the Party Secretariat and professional Party leaders of their justification for interfering in govern-ment (State Council) work. It strengthened the power position of the premier at the cost of the Party general secretary (until Jiang took over the PRC presi-dency in 1993). This balance of power (or competition for power) between the two individuals only more conveniently put both at the mercy of Deng and other Party elders. At the same time, Deng allowed a more constructive and assertive role for the NPC both in legislation and in supervision of the State Council. The latter was made more feasible as the Party—the "leading force" that could not become the target of legislative oversight—had been "sepa-rated" from government work. The strengthened supervisory role of the NPC was manifested in the rapid rise in NPC deputies' critical remarks about gov-ernment work and the incorporation of more deputy suggestions into govern-ment policy.

Deng's motivations for this institutional arrangement could hardly be as-sociated with any Western democratic values. He pragmatically expected the NPC to be functional in promoting what he understood as the "rule of law." A powerful NPC check upon the State Council would also help improve and ra-tionalize China's socioeconomic development programs. But Deng and his cronies soon found that it was not always easy to balance the NPC's construc-tive and disruptive roles. In other words, when the NPC and, to a lesser extent, the NPCSC—as Deng more or less sincerely wished—struggled to get rid of their rubber-stamp image, the Party center felt the impact uncomfortably.

It would be misleading to exaggerate the antagonism between the NPC and the Politburo or the former's institutional capability of defying the latter. The political or "partisan" composition of both the NPC and NPCSC may guarantee no substantial disagreement on important and sensitive issues be-tween the two institutions. Also, the chair's meeting and the Party group of the NPCSC maintained powerful influence, if not control, over NPC deputies and NPCSC members. Tiananmen provided us with a rare glimpse at how vulnerable the NPCSC would be in a showdown with Deng and his Politburo. The military crackdown of 1989 also successfully expelled the "bourgeois liberalism" from NPC and NPCSC sessions and made political opposition even more remote in the national legislature.

Nevertheless, the NPC has developed its own bureaucratic interest and evolved into an institution that is both more authoritative in terms of legislation and supervision of government and more representational. As regionalism and interest-group politics have gradually entered the NPC and influenced its agenda since the 1990s, NPC deputies have become more assertive in a way that minimizes ideological and political implications. Meanwhile the Party center has seen its authority over regions greatly weakened by the passing of Party elders. This development may augur well for constitutional evolution in a democratic direction.

Notes

1. Not to mention the fact that the Party congress was regularly held every five years and the Central Committee, whose members were dispersed across the country, usually met only once a year.

2. It was theoretically so. As indicated later in this chapter, the relationship between the two bodies was made tricky by the manipulation of the Party elders behind the scenes.

3. During the term of the seventh NPC (1988–1993), there were three vice premiers and nine state councillors (equivalent to vice premiers). Premier Li Peng and Vice Premier Yao Yilin were members of the Politburo standing committee, and the other two vice premiers (Tian Jiyun and Wu Xieqian) and two state councillors (Li Tieying and Qin Jiwei) were ordinary Politburo members. During the term of the eighth NPC (1993–1998), among the premier and twelve vice premiers and state councillors, Premier Li Peng and Vice Premier Zhu Rongji were members of the Politburo standing committee, and the number of ordinary Politburo members dropped to three (Li Lanqing, Li Tieying, and Qian Qichen).

4. Perhaps the only major exception was the election of Rong Yiren, nominated by the Politburo, as vice president at the seventh NPC in March 1993. Rong was not a CCP member but leader of a satellite party. His election had hardly any political significance but was generally seen as part of a typical communist "united-front" show. So strictly speaking, Rong could not be regarded as one of the "state leaders."

5. A concise discussion of central Party organs may be found in Richard Baum, "China's Political Institutions: A Forty-Year Appraisal," in Kallgren, ed., *Building a Nation-State,* pp. 65–97.

6. See Allen S. Whiting, "Political Dynamics: The Communist Party of China," and Committee on Government Operations, U.S. Senate, "Staffing the Party," in Jan, ed., *Government,* pp. 129–178.

7. Lieberthal, *Governing China,* pp. 208–209.

8. Whiting, "Political Dynamics."

9. For example, among the secretaries of the Party Secretariat appointed by the thirteenth Party congress, only two were concurrently members of the Politburo standing committee (Hu Qili and Qiao Shi). During the same period in the State Council, two members had posts in the Politburo standing committee (Li Peng and Yao Yilin), and four were ordinary Politburo members.

10. See Wu Jiang's memoir, *Shi Nian De Lu,* p. 198. When Hu Yaobang was the Party general secretary (1982–1986), Wu was one of the leaders of the central Party school. He was also Hu's close friend and policy adviser.

11. Wu Jiang, "Some Supplements." Wu's memoir (see the previous note) reportedly made Zhao Ziyang very angry. In a private interview in 1997, Zhao denied any role in Hu Yaobang's resignation. But Zhao did admit that he did not defend Hu at that critical meeting because he was at odds with Hu over the latter's interference in the work of the State Council. See Zhang Feng, "History."

12. Wu Jiang, *Shi Nian De Lu,* pp. 208–209; Chen Yizi, *Zhongguo,* ch. 5. Wu's memoir obviously defended Hu against Zhao. Although he implicitly acknowledged that Hu Yaobang was not active (he used a commendatory term, *wenjian,* meaning "steady" or "prudent") in political reform, he blamed Zhao for usurping part of Hu's power when Zhao instructed his own people to study the issues of political reform and prepare reform proposals for the Politburo. Wu also asserted that Zhao did so mainly to consolidate his personal base of power.

13. The PRC presidency would provide Jiang with a more justifiable excuse to "interfere" in the work of the State Council. But this justification was not indispensable for Jiang. The Tiananmen crackdown created a context that enabled Jiang to use his Party position to interfere more "legitimately." Jiang was reelected to the top posts in both the Party and state at the fifteenth Party congress (October 1997) and at the first session of the ninth NPC (March 1998).

14. *SJRB,* March 17, 1995.

15. A more detailed analysis is found in Dittmer, "Patterns"; Lieberthal, *Governing China,* p. 224.

16. See Shirk, *The Political Logic,* ch. 4; Lieberthal, *Governing China,* ch. 8. The actors here included both professional Party and state leaders. They were elected by the exact-number method by the Party congress and NPC, respectively. This meant that despite the possible occurrence of a negligible number of negative votes in elections, the Party elders, by keeping a firm grip on the power of recommending candidates, actually controlled the selection of nominal Party-state leaders. But patronage politics was not the sole source of Party elders' influence. Personal prestige could also play a critical role.

17. The fall of Hu and Zhao best illustrated this. They were ousted almost in the same way. At first, the Party elders reached consensus among themselves to depose Hu and Zhao. Then they held a Politburo meeting and declared Hu and Zhao's dismissal. Finally, they submitted their dismissal as a fait accompli to the Central Committee for approval. In May 1989, having lost the support of the elders, Zhao became powerless and isolated.

18. As some scholars indicate, communist politics under Mao was characterized by its irregularity or lack of institutionalization, which contributed a great deal to the differences between China and the Soviet Union. Harding described these differences as follows: Stalinist totalitarianism was fundamentally conservative and elitist and thus created relatively stable political institutions, whereas the Maoist variant was radical and populist and therefore tended to undermine political stability. See Harding, "Political Development." Also see Starr, *Continuing the Revolution.* In contrast with Chinese attempts, Soviet efforts to promote legally regulated mass participation to strengthen the legislative branch went back several decades, paralleling similar Eastern European initiatives. See White, "The USSR Supreme Soviet"; Welsh, "The Status of Research." Part of the anti-institutional legacy of Mao's politics was inherited by the Deng regime. In 1988 Chen Yizi headed a delegation to visit the USSR. He concluded that the Soviet Communist Party far excelled the CCP in its members' education and quality, as well as in complying with the formal rules and procedures in intra-Party life. See Chen Yizi, *Zhongguo,* pp. 137–138. This political feature seems to be more Asian than communist. McCormick argues that extensive patrimonial networks are powerful impediments to the implementation of any reform in China and particularly to reform that seeks to promote rational-legal authority. He calls China's democratic reform "institutionalized patronage." See McCormick, "Leninist Implementation." Nathan applies a factionalism model to the analysis of CCP elite politics and

suggests that clientelist ties were more important in political conflict than formal organizations. See Nathan, *China's Crisis,* ch. 2.

19. Chen Yizi, *Zhongguo,* p. 124.

20. According to Max Weber, this "ideal type" of bureaucracy possesses ten major characteristics, including the following: The bureaucrats are organized in a clearly defined hierarchy of offices; each office has a clearly defined sphere of competence in the legal sense; and the office must be the bureaucrat's sole or at least major occupation. See LaPalombara, ed., *Bureaucracy,* ch. 2; Gross, *The Managing,* pp. 136–142.

21. Deng's view of the rule of law was also shared by local Party cadres. See Baum, "Modernization."

22. The expected utility of the rule of law was of course not limited to maintaining social order. Shiping Zheng identifies four reasons for the post-Mao legal reform: revulsion against the Cultural Revolution, need for new sources of legitimacy, concern about social order and stability, and economic imperatives. See Zheng, *Party vs. State,* ch. 7.

23. *Beijing Review,* no. 52 (December 29, 1978), pp. 6–16.

24. See "On Questions of Party History."

25. In a June 1986 speech to senior Party leaders, Deng mentioned that China "has no tradition of observing and enforcing laws." "It is not appropriate for the Party to concern itself with matters that fall within the scope of the law," Deng argued. "The Party should concern itself with inner-Party discipline, leaving problems that fall within the scope of the law to the state and the government." Deng Xiaoping, *Fundamental Issues,* pp. 145–148.

26. As Alford puts it, the greater the regime's instrumental use of legality to consolidate its hold on power, "the more vulnerable it ultimately is to the use of this weapon against it." Alford, "Double-edged Swords."

27. A more complete account of the post-Mao rule of law and its implications and consequences may be found in Keith, *China's Struggle,* chs. 1, 2.

28. Gu Angran, "The Socialist Legal System and Legislation," in QRCBY, ed., *Lun Woguo,* pp. 26–50. Peng contended that before the communist takeover, the legal system was reactionary and had to be destroyed rather than respected. "The people's revolution relied on the Party's leadership and policies. After the founding of the PRC, the people took over national power. It wouldn't do without a legal system. So our way of governing must gradually evolve from relying on [Party] policy to relying not only on policy but on laws and a solid legal system."

29. Dicks, "The Chinese Legal System."

30. See O'Brien, *Reform Without Liberalization,* ch. 6. As O'Brien observes, this was a period during which reform was riding high, and the reformers led by Deng Xiaoping were involved in a critical power struggle with Hua Guofeng and other Mao loyalists. The NPC became a battlefield both for power and policies. The reformers tried to use a revived NPC to weaken the position of Hua and his group and press ahead with their own reform programs.

31. QRCBY, ed., *Renmin Daibiao Dahui Zhidu Jianshe Sishinian,* p. 171.

32. Ibid., p. 172. According to its account, the leadership gave high priority to the revision, and the Politburo and the Secretariat held eight discussions specifically on it. The draft was revised many times. "Every draft was approved in principle by the Central Committee. Can the draft approved be further revised? As the fact manifests, the answer is yes."

33. For the full English texts of the 1954, 1974, and 1978 constitutions, see Q. Xin, *China's New Democracy,* pp. 152–228.

34. "Under the leadership of the Communist Party of China and the guidance of Marxism-Leninism and Mao Zedong Thought," it read, "the Chinese people of all nationalities will continue to adhere to the people's democratic dictatorship and follow the socialist road." According to official interpretation, the preamble of the constitution represents just the "general guiding ideology" and should have no binding force. Xu Chongde, ed., *Renmin*, p. 336. For the full English text of the 1982 constitution, see *Beijing Review*, vol. 25, no. 52 (December 27, 1982), pp. 10–29.

35. Xu Chongde, ed., *Renmin*, p. 336.

36. In his report to an NPC session in November 1982, Peng Zhen, vice chairman of the Committee for Revision of the Constitution, argued that the expansion of NPCSC power served just this purpose. "The NPCSC is the permanent body of the NPC," he claimed, "and all those on the NPCSC can be described as executive deputies to the congress. Being few in number, they can meet frequently and carry a heavy load of legislation and day-to-day work." *Beijing Review*, vol. 25, no. 50 (December 13, 1982), pp. 9–23.

37. O'Brien has undertaken this task. In his *Reform Without Liberalization*, he presents an excellent comparative analysis of the NPC's role in China's political life in different historical periods.

38. This notion comes from Jürgen Habermas's discussion of the transformation of the public sphere during the rise of the bourgeoisie in Europe. McCormick applies it to his analysis of the origins of change in a Leninist system. As he and other scholars point out, even small cracks in the Party control of the public sphere could have enormous consequences. Habermas, *The Structural Transformation;* McCormick, "China's Leninist Parliament."

39. Alford's study quotes five cases to describe how the Deng regime, in seeking to deploy formal legality, "unwittingly handed its opponents a keenly honed instrument through which to seek to accomplish their own, very different ends." Alford, "Double-edged Swords."

40. Peng Zhen, *Lun Xinshiqi*, pp. 328–329.

41. The rhetoric of the leadership and the propaganda machine has to be read between the lines to discern the delicate changes in the "central spirit." To maintain an image of policy continuity, no radical measures were proposed to reverse previous reforms after Tiananmen. But in a speech after the crackdown, Jiang Zemin—along with giving much talk about the importance of the "rule of law"—stressed that the people's congress must accept party leadership. *RMRB,* July 1, 1990. This kind of fuzzy statement, to be read and understood by different people in different ways, became typical in the post-Tiananmen propaganda. Presumably, Beijing hoped local authorities would read the message correctly but at the same time left itself sufficient room to back down or initiate a new policy reversal.

42. *MYF,* no. 4 (April 1986), title page.

43. Guo Daohui, *Zhongguo Lifa Zhidu,* p. 157.

44. Ibid. The quotation implies that since the draft approved by the Central Committee (Politburo) was revised, its opinions could therefore be vetoed.

45. Wu Wentai, "Some Issues Concerning the Relationship Between Party Organizations and People's Congresses," in QRCBY, ed., *Lun Woguo*, pp. 195–209.

46. Guo Daohui, *Zhongguo Lifa Zhidu,* p. 7; *FZRB*, March 13, 1997. This number includes the laws made under the Mao regime but carefully screened.

47. An examination of some of these laws can be found in Lubman, ed., *China's Legal Reform*; also in Keith, *China's Struggle*.

48. *Bulletin of the State Council.*

49. *RMRB,* August 23, 1986.

50. *RMRB,* August 18, 1986.

51. Of course the significance of the legal reform was not limited to that. In the Chinese context, as O'Brien puts it, laws would stabilize reform and protect it with coercive state power. O'Brien, *Reform Without Liberalization,* p. 159.

52. Guo Daohui, *Zhongguo Lifa Zhidu,* pp. 179–182.

53. Hu Tugui, "The NPC."

54. Ge Shufan, "Is the NPC Still a Rubber Stamp?"

55. As an NPC deputy from Hong Kong recalled, the nine candidates lost the election simply because they were too old (over the age of seventy). No political factors were implicated. See Wu Kangmin, *Renda Huiyilu,* p. 195.

56. Guo Daohui, "Legislation of Democratization and Legislated Democratization," in Zi Mu, ed., *Minzhu de Gousi,* pp. 103–134. In China's nomenklatura system, the "central minister" (*zhongyang buzhang*) refers to the ministers of both the State Council and the Central Committee. The latter had some powerful ministries, such as the Central Ministry of Organization and the Central Ministry of Propaganda, which were under the direction of the Party Secretariat.

57. O'Brien, "Legislative Development."

58. They are preapproval of draft laws by the Party center; involvement by the Central Political-Legal Leading Group (its name has since changed to the Central Political-Legal Commission); organizational control over key appointments; and control over meeting agendas. Tanner, "Organizations." According to Tanner, the CPLG's role in lawmaking had declined steadily after 1979 and was mainly limited to criminal law. I would argue that the role of the CPLG in relation to the NPC was quite delicate, particularly during the eighth NPC (1993–1998). Theoretically, there was no direct organizational relationship between the CPLG and the NPC. The officially defined responsibility of the CPLG was to direct the work of public security, state security, judiciary, civil administration, law court, procuratorates, and armed police. As such, it was heavily involved in the implementation of laws. During the eighth NPC, when Qiao Shi was both the NPCSC chair and its Party group secretary, he also presided over the CPLG, one of the responsibilities assigned to him as a Politburo standing committee member. He Ping, "The Execution."

59. See Tao Jun, "An Analysis."

60. An example was the adoption process of the enterprise bankruptcy law, discussed later.

61. Wu Wentai, "Some Issues."

62. Ibid. The NPC delegates with Party membership enjoyed the privilege of being informed of the Party center's "suggestions" prior to each NPC session, aimed to win support from those delegates and prevent any substantial NPC deviation from the central line. Tanner, "Organizations."

63. As Tanner argues, this examination was hardly detailed as Party leaders tended to concern themselves "only with whether or not the draft law's basic thrust fits in with the 'general direction' of current Party policy." Tanner, "Organizations," p. 61.

64. I disagree a bit with Tanner, who thinks that the legislative proposal was reported to the Secretariat for approval. Tanner, "The Erosion." My findings suggest that the proposal was usually directly sent to the Politburo. The Secretariat was a subordinate unit of the Politburo. Because the leading members of the NPCSC Party group were senior Politburo members, the Secretariat clearly did not have enough authority to approve NPCSC proposals. So when the proposal was sent to the Secretariat, it was most probably for the record (*bei'an*) rather than for approval (*pizhun*).

65. The adoption of such a law soon after Tiananmen was obviously intended to use the rule of law against democratic demonstrations. Despite the political repression

in late 1989, the Politburo failed to persuade the NPCSC to accept its will wholesale. According to my interview with a participant in the process, the passed law was less harsh than the Politburo expected. For one thing, the Politburo instructed that the activities prohibited in mass rallies and demonstrations should include *chuanlian,* or "ganging up" and "collaboration." But this instruction was rejected by the NPCSC on the grounds that this term was legally improper and could also lead to misinterpretation and abuse of power. The official report on the law may be found in *Beijing Review,* vol. 32, no. 46 (November 13–19, 1989), p. 4. My interviewee agreed that on issues the Politburo perceived as critical, NPCSC rejection was extremely unlikely.

66. This proposal was published in *WHB,* May 25, 1989.

67. Wang Kejia, "Hu Jiwei."

68. During the Tiananmen demonstrations of 1989, a rumor was widely circulated in Beijing that there had been a secret decision that any NPC and NPCSC session must be approved in advance by the Politburo. See Hu Nan, "The Lobbyist." Although it was inconceivable to hold an NPC or NPCSC session without Politburo approval, such a written stipulation had never been confirmed by the authorities.

69. The implementation of the enterprise bankruptcy system was perhaps one of the most capitalistic measures adopted in economic reforms until 1997. In early 1986 the State Council submitted to the NPCSC a draft bankruptcy law, which allowed unproductive enterprises to go out of business. This draft was apparently favored by the Politburo. *RMRB* (August 22, 28, 1986) repeatedly and strongly urged the NPCSC to pass it as soon as possible. But this law was rejected by the NPCSC in June 1986 on the grounds that it was premature. In September the revised draft was submitted to the NPCSC once again and was heatedly debated by its members. Among those who opposed the law, some thought that if the law were introduced, the superiority of Chinese socialism could not be given full expression; some argued that workers' right to work would be threatened (for a detailed discussion of different viewpoints on this law among the NPCSC members, see *FBIS Daily Report: China,* December 2, 1986, pp. K9–K11). The opponents forced this session to postpone its adoption. The law was further revised and passed in December 1986. *FBIS Daily Report: China,* December 2, 1986, p. K8.

70. Ai Kesi, "The Conservatives." O'Brien also saw this as an example that the conservative NPCSC headed by Peng Zhen tried to block radical reform. See O'Brien, *Reform Without Liberalization,* ch. 7. It was true that a number of retired senior cadres, a big proportion of whom were hard-liners, sat in the NPCSC. The NPCSC appeared hesitant and cautious in legislation on not a few occasions. But one has to take care in describing the NPCSC as a politically conservative institution. My interviews found that many NPCSC members did take their lawmaking role seriously, and their prudence in legislation was quite understandable. They believed that since laws differed from policies and afforded no frequent changes, the NPCSC had to bear the sole responsibility if anything went wrong. The villagers' committee law was another similar case. See *FBIS, Daily Report: China,* April 7, 9, 14, 24, 1987, section K; Wang Zhenhai and Han Xijiang, "On the Organizational Building."

71. An influential newspaper applauded: "This [the discussion of the bankruptcy law] gives us an idea of how democratically and seriously the country's highest organ of state power makes decisions on proposed laws." Gu Ming, "Why Is It Necessary?" Also in *FBIS Daily Report: China,* December 2, 1986, p. K12.

72. This was also the case for many NPCSC members. Hu Jiwei, for example, was *RMRB* head before entering the NPCSC.

73. Some observers thought this situation could be blamed on Deng. Deng himself did not pay much attention to the NPC in the early 1980s and so let the senior

leaders he considered to be antireform conservatives enter the NPCSC. Ai Kesi, "The Conservatives."

74. The views conflicting with Deng's were not necessarily against his reforms. Lu Dingyi was a case in point. Lu used to be a Politburo member and head of propaganda. After the Cultural Revolution, Lu's political qualifications justified his return to the Politburo. But Lu disagreed with Deng on the evaluation of Mao, and he insisted that Mao be condemned. Deng forced him to "retire" into the CPPCC (au. int).

75. Peng's candidacy for the Politburo standing committee was seriously considered. Luo Bing, "The Change of Personnel." The reasons for his failure to be elected were not clearly known. Hu Yaobang allegedly objected to Peng's election because of Peng's reservations on market reform. Peng's active role in deposing Hu in early 1987 seemed to prove the animosity between them.

76. Ai Kesi, "The Conservatives."

77. In the 1982 constitution, the functions and powers of the NPC and NPCSC partially overlapped. The president and vice president of the PRC, chair of the Central Military Commission, president of the Supreme People's Court, and procurator-general of the Supreme People's Procuratorate were to be elected by the NPC. Premier, vice premiers, and state councillors, nominated by the PRC president and the premier, had to be approved by the NPC through voting. On the supervision of the State Council, there were no substantial differences between NPC and NPCSC functions. The NPC's functions were "to examine and approve the plan for national economic and social development and the reports on its implementation" (item 9, article 62) and "to examine and approve the state budget and the report on its implementation" (item 10, article 62). The NPCSC's functions were to be performed on a more daily basis: "to supervise the work of the State Council, the Central Military Commission, the Supreme People's Court, and the Supreme People's Procuratorate" (item 6, article 67) and "to annul those administrative rules and regulations, decisions, or orders of the State Council that contravene the Constitution or the statutes" (item 7, article 67). The NPC and NPCSC shared the supervision of the constitutional enforcement.

78. Li Zuxing, "The Voting System of the People's Congress and the Relevant Issues," in Zi Mu, ed., *Minzhu de Gousi,* pp. 254–260. Ironically, this history-making event was not reported in China but published in Hong Kong's newspapers as "shocking" news. Guo Daohui, "Legislation." Abstention votes occurred in 1982 for the first time; three NPC deputies abstained from voting on the new version of the constitution. Xiao Tie, "On the Institutional Guarantee."

79. Guo Daohui, "Legislation." The electronic voting machine was used only at NPCSC sessions until March 1998, when it was also installed for NPC sessions. A show of hands in voting on legislation might have greatly reduced the number of negative votes. At a sixth NPC session of 1987, there were seven negative and sixteen abstention votes on a proposal. Zeng Tao, the NPC spokesman, estimated that negative votes might have increased to seventy if secret balloting were adopted. "I think you know the [Chinese] popular mentality," he said. "It is not easy to raise your hand to show your opposition when you face several thousand people." See Feng Hui and Hu Shengsheng, "A Demonstration." At an NPC session in early 1989, many NPC deputies demanded that electronic voting machines be installed in the Great Hall of the People and that voting on proposals be made confidential. Zhang Weiguo, "Watch the Two Congresses." It took the authorities nine years to respond favorably to this demand.

80. *Asian Wall Street Journal Weekly,* April 4, 1988.

81. "Right and Wrong."

82. Sharply critical remarks were voiced on a series of issues, ranging from the limited budget for education and underpayment of intellectuals to corruption of officials. Several deputies appealed for the protection of freedom of the press through legislation. Liang Xiang, an NPC deputy who had been internally designated as governor of Hainan, declared that he would permit privately owned newspapers and magazines in his province. *JSND,* 220 (May 1988), p. 69.

83. But none of these changes involved political principles. For example, the State Council proposed that the Bureau of Civil Aviation, Railway Ministry, and Ministry of Communications merge into a transportation ministry. The proposal was vetoed by NPC deputies. This was cited by the authorities as evidence of the respect for the deputies. See Xu Minhe, Hu Guohua, and Shao Quan, "Watch."

84. Article 10 of the 1982 constitution provides that no organization or individual may appropriate, buy, sell, or lease land or unlawfully transfer land in other ways. The revised clause endows peasants with the right to "transfer the possession of the right to use land." In other words, they are free to auction land. The second revision legalizes and protects the status of private economy. These two revisions touched on the sensitive issues of state ownership of land and socialist economy, which until then had been a political taboo.

85. Guo Sheng, "The Anti-Mao Tendency."

86. *HQ* hailed it as a "new democratic wind," saying the NPC's image as a rubber stamp or voting machine had "passed into history." Wang Jue, "The New Wind."

87. Zhang Weiguo, "Watch the Two Congresses."

88. Yan Jiaqi, "A Commentary."

89. Wu Kangmin was a veteran NPC deputy "elected" from Hong Kong from 1975 to 1998. As he recalled, at the 1990 NPC session, the feeling of depression was quite obvious among the deputies. Many group discussions proceeded in silence. Several group leaders simply canceled discussions. Wu Kangmin, *Renda Huiyilu,* pp. 257–262.

90. The Three-Gorge Dam project became politically explosive largely because it invited international criticism for its possible damage to the environment. Tu Li, "The Hong Kong"; also, my interviews.

91. As Wu Guoguang recalled, the topics Zhao Ziyang discussed with his advisers for the next stage of political reform during 1987–1988 included a free press, independent labor unions, the Solidarity style, and a multiparty system. Yan Mingfu, the head of the central Ministry of United Front, even proposed drafting a law to allow (opposition) parties to register legally. See Jin Zhong, "Zhao Ziyang."

92. "Administrative reform" refers mainly to the reform of personnel management and public finance. I do not include it in this book because it does not have enough political relevance. A detailed discussion on this subject may be found in Mills and Nagel, eds., *Public Administration.*

93. Scholars are fully justified in incorporating the legal reform into their discussion of political reform. For my analytical purposes, however, it is useful and necessary to separate the two.

94. The first signal Deng sent after the massacre concerning the fate of political reform was embodied in his speech of June 9, 1989. "There is one thing with political reform we are sure of," he claimed. "We must stand firm with the people's congress system." *Deng Xiaoping Wenxuan,* pp. 302–308.

95. Luo Bing and Li Zijing, "The Noise."

96. Ibid.

97. Luo Bing and Li Zijing, "Why So Many Shells?"

98. Li Zijing, "The NPC Turmoil." A typical case was the strategy some provinces took against Beijing's application for the 2000 Olympic games. Several provinces did not want to share the financial burden for the games because all of the glory and benefits associated with it were to be monopolized by the city of Beijing. The provincial Party and government leaders managed to put the issue on the agenda of provincial congresses and instigated the deputies to veto it. Then they used the congressional veto to refuse the Party center's call for "nationwide coordination" for the games. Yue Ming, "Regional Leaders."

99. Luo Bing, "Jiang Zemin."

100. Ibid.

101. Chen Zhinong, "The CCP."

102. Li Zijing, "Mao and Zhou."

103. This proposal criticized the Party leadership for its violation of the constitution and the law on labor by allowing too many employees to lose jobs. It warns that the current high rate of unemployment is threatening social stability. Luo Bing, "Jiang and Zhu."

104. Mezey, *Comparative Legislatures*, ch. 1.

105. Luo Bing, "Tian Jiyun's Speech."

106. Li Zijing, "The NPC Turmoil"; Li Zijing, "Stick and Carrot." As a Politburo standing committee member, Qiao had to keep in line with its dominant opinions. But he was personally well known to be an open-minded reformer. In a tour to Guangdong in January 1998 (at that time he had quit the Politburo and was going to retire from the NPCSC), he advocated further political reform and attributed rampant corruption to the "backward" CCP governing system and ineffectual supervisory mechanisms. Luo Bing, "Qiao Shi."

7

Restructuring Authority in Local Politics

In a state whose political power is highly centralized in its capital, local politics may not matter very much in the sense that any local change, for good or bad, would less likely have a significant impact upon the political system or produce nationwide effects.[1] If anything goes "wrong" in local government, central authorities would be powerful enough to get it "corrected." This is perhaps one of the most important factors in explaining why the Party leadership appeared to be more "democracy-oriented" and more resolute in its steps toward the institutionalization of citizen participation in the local political process through legislative channels. But local institutions are, after all, responsible for the execution of central policy guidelines in local affairs. Without reliable local agents, the Party center would have much difficulty carrying its decisions through to the bottom of Chinese society and across the country.

Even in China, a country with a 2,000-year history of centralized state power, local obedience to central authorities, or central-local harmony, can never be taken for granted. It is, of course, not just a contemporary problem. Some scholars indicate that politics in imperial China was characterized by a mutual tension between throne and officials.[2] A popular couplet in China's officialdom accurately portrays how local Party-state bureaucracies may distort the central policy and turn it to their own advantage under the communist regime: "the center decides policy, whereas local authorities devise countermeasures" (*shangyou zhengce, xiayou duice*). The local defiance of the center became an even more serious problem after the post-Mao leadership launched a reform campaign in late 1978.[3] This problem originated from the profound political distrust, if not hostility, between Deng's Party center and local Party cadres. Adding fuel to the conflict was that Deng's reform programs from the very beginning aimed to transform the existing economic structure in which local Party cadres had a vital personal stake.

Maoist cadres' survival of post-Mao purges posed an enormous potential threat to the successful implementation of reform and made local political insti-

183

tutional shake-ups urgent. But the Party center faced a fundamental dilemma. For all the local cadres' opposition to Deng's reforms, their commitment to communist rule remained firm. And they constituted a base the leadership would perhaps eventually fall back upon to maintain control over the subordinate population. This control seemed to be particularly necessary during a period when the economic reform, given its nature as, in Deng's words, "crossing the river by feeling for the stones underfoot," was expected to produce unpredictable social consequences. Nevertheless, the Party center must keep local cadres under control as well, not just because the widespread cadre abuse of power, corruption, bureaucratism, and so on had tarnished the Party image and shaken the social foundation of the regime. For the conflict of interests involved in reform, the continuous wholehearted dependence upon local cadres as ruling instruments would make any meaningful changes impossible. Simply put, as Deng circumscribed the reform efforts within the communist hegemony, the Party center could neither get rid of Party cadres nor trust them with reform.

To solve this dilemma, local political reform was intended to create certain institutional mechanisms with the purpose of pressuring local cadres into implementing the central reform programs at their own cost. This chapter provides a microanalysis of the changes in local relations of authority. It discusses the major measures taken in local reform and examines its political meanings and structural consequences. We will see that the separation of the Party from government at local levels was carried out more effectively than at the central level. It broke up the traditional power monopoly of Party committees by depriving them of administrative power and reducing their influence over local legislation and policymaking. At the same time, local people's congresses (LPCs) carved out an increasingly prominent institutional role in both local legislation and supervision of government. In many locations LPCs emerged as one of the three major powerful actors, along with Party committees and governments, in the local policy process. But as a top-down process sponsored by the Party center, local power restructuring has been placed under considerable central manipulation and has proceeded largely according to the central blueprint. Unlike the reform at the central or grassroots levels, Beijing had to make greater efforts to strike a balance of power between local Party committees and LPCs to prevent either side from gaining a monopolistic position in local politics or slipping out of central control.

Understanding Local Political Reform

To understand the efforts for local political reform and what it attempted to achieve, an analysis of the political relationships between the Party center and local cadres is helpful. To the extent reform is relevant, the relations between the central elite and local (government-level) cadres differed both from those between Deng (and his elderly group) and his handpicked younger leaders and from the center-grassroots relations. At the central level, as Hua Guofeng and his allies were removed from the core of power, Deng and other Party elders—who managed to forge a united front against Hua and also reached a consensus on the repudiation of Maoism and on the necessity of reform—immediately placed their clients, such as Hu Yaobang and Zhao Ziyang, in all the key positions. The main responsibility of these younger leaders was to translate Deng's doctrine of reform into specific policies and implement them as well. For the long-standing patron-client ties and their own reform orientation, they had no such problems as defying or betraying Deng's reform ideas. Furthermore, the negative impact of reform upon the power and privileges of central leaders did not reach such a magnitude as to incur strong opposition.[4] Therefore, the reform of the central political structure was not motivated so much by a desire on Deng's part to constrain younger leaders as by an attempt to rationalize the policymaking process as well as set examples for local authorities. This reform did, however, create a certain amount of rivalry among the Party Secretariat, the State Council, and the NPC.

To the Party center, local (regional) and grassroots cadres were not alike in some major respects. In the bureaucratic hierarchy, local cadres were located more highly and hence had a wider sphere of authority than grassroots cadres. When reform started around 1979, many Party-state offices at subcentral levels were occupied by fanatical Maoists who had ideological instincts against any moves toward what they perceived as capitalism.[5] Although post-Mao purges were carried out in a highly inefficient way, they did result in a shake-up of the leadership at the provincial level. In provinces and major cities, top offices were taken by the protégés of the central elite, and their political adherence to the new Party center was not problematic. As the purge came down to the municipal, county, and township levels, the central clientelist ties tended to thin, and more Maoists survived through the protection of their personal network in local government, characterized as *guan guan xiang hu* (cadres shield and protect one another). But even so, since the Party center kept a close watch on the performance of government-level cadres and also maintained tight organizational control over them, few could stay in office for long if they displayed any public animosity toward Deng or his reform. As a matter of course, one should not treat all the cadres of the four ranks as an undifferentiated aggregate in the analysis of their ideological orientations and political commitment. In any case, collectively these cadres constituted a cornerstone of the Deng regime that, given the nature of its reform, could neither find nor create an alternative institutional force. Thus, any central reform decisions must let stand at least some of local cadres' privileges so as to win their cooperation.

By contrast, in the workplace, such as industrial enterprises, the leadership personnel of Mao's era was largely untouched by the purge. Grassroots cadres were the most immediate rulers of the masses and interacted with them on a daily basis. Their relations of power with citizens were therefore a typical zero-sum game. They could be made the scapegoat for all the Party policy failures or placed on the altar of reform without eroding the structural support of the one-party system to any substantial degree. These cadres, as indicated in Chapter 2, constituted the (largest) portion of the Party who had the least education. Although many of them were well known as local despots, the Party lacked strong levers to control them. All these factors combined to account for the fewer scruples of the Party center to do away with grassroots cadres in exchange for reform success and public support.

Yet economic reform per se entailed different sacrifices for cadres at government and grassroots levels, at least at a certain stage. As previously mentioned, China's urban reform took off from the overhaul of enterprise management structure in late 1978. It could not move a single step without altering the relations of power in enterprises. As a system of profit retention was tried and the status of enterprises transformed, Party cadres were either voted out of office by the workers or faced dismissal for failure to improve enterprise productivity. Not surprisingly, enterprise cadres desperately resisted change and struggled to retain their positions and influence. To jumpstart urban reform, the leadership simply could not compromise but had to take further actions to demote enterprise cadres.

But the blows to cadres at government levels were indirect and cushioned. Before the 1984 Central Committee decision for urban reform, the governments (more accurately, Party committees at the corresponding levels) were instructed to give up administrative means to command enterprises directly. In addition to a heavier emphasis on this hands-off policy, the 1984 decision also demanded the reduction of the scope of mandatory planning and advocated technocracy. Although these reforms would lead to the diminution of governmental authority at all levels and undermine some of its traditional profitable functions, they did not immediately endanger the offices of senior local cadres. Given the Party's totalitarian control (though it had loosened) over all aspects of social life, local cadres could still retain much of their power even if they kept their hands off subordinate enterprises and some economic matters. Stated another way, if local cadres had every reason to lack enthusiasm in implementing reform, they would not risk their jobs, which ranked higher than those in enterprises, by boycotting it. It was therefore possible for the Party center to allow local cadres to stay in offices but to co-opt or coerce them into submission to the Party's reformist line by establishing some institutional checks and balances.

Reduced Party Role in Policy Implementation

The local political restructuring placed the government under a double domination. As the Party documents demanded, the government must accept the

Table 7.1   Changes in the Number of Party Institutions in Heyuan and Qingyuan, Guangdong Province

	Before 1988	After 1988
Offices of municipal Party committees	53	40
Organizational departments	44	26
Propaganda departments	24	8
Departments for "united front"	23	8
Commissions for discipline inspection	29	16
Bureaus for veteran cadres	11	0
Judicial commissions	12	0
Departments for rural work	15	0
Institutions for policy study	11	0
Offices for Party history study	12	0

Source: Liang Yukai, Chen Ruilian, and Wen Wenfei, "Clarify Major Functions of Municipal Party Committees," in Zhao Baoxu, ed., *Zhengquan Jiegou,* pp. 67–79.

"political leadership" of the Party committee (of the corresponding level). According to the constitution and laws, the government should also function as the executive body of the people's congress. Above all, the government was required to be responsible for the "autonomous" implementation of policy. Yet there were supposed to be no direct dealings between the people's congress and the Party committee, that is, the former was not authorized to command the latter and vice versa. So to assess the extent to which local legislatures influenced the governmental process, one must first of all take a look at whether or not Party committees truly pulled out of the process of policy implementation.

A number of empirical studies show that there was indeed a movement in that direction. In 1988 some research groups conducted investigations in Shaanxi and Guangdong Provinces and in several cities such as Ha'erbin, Weifang (Shandong), and Zigong (Sichuan). Their reports showed that political reform effected three visible changes. First, the posts of government chief and Party chief were assumed by two persons rather than one. Second, whereas the Party committee used to have departments that paralleled those of the government and took over their functions, as a result of reform these Party departments were dismantled to let the government assume sole responsibility for its work. Third, to reduce improper interference through vertical intra-Party channels, Party groups (*dang zu*) within government departments ceased to exist.[6]

Some statistics serve to illustrate the institutional changes. In Heyuan and Qingyuan (Guangdong), 45 percent of the departments in the municipal Party committees were abolished (Table 7.1). The number of professional Party cadres was cut by 57 percent.[7] In Zigong the municipal Party departments were reduced from thirteen to seven.[8] In Ha'erbin, as most municipal Party departments ceased to exist, the number of Party cadres dropped from 607 to 407.[9] The Party committees in twenty-one major municipal-level government bureaus, whose principal function was to exercise direct "party leadership" over enterprises and some other grassroots work units, were dismissed to guarantee the latter's "autonomous" operation.[10] But developments in that regard appeared quite uneven. In a survey conducted in urban Xicheng and Haidian Districts of Beijing in 1988, only 7 percent of those surveyed said that in their workplace (excluding enterprises) the number of professional Party cadres decreased by a big margin, 36.7 percent a little bit, 38 percent no changes, and 7 percent found that it actually increased.[11] The movement to curtail the scale of local Party apparatus set off by the 1987 Party congress reached a peak in 1988. Unlike some other aspects of political reform, this trend did not seem to have been much affected by the 1989 crackdown in Tiananmen, particularly at the county and township levels.[12] During the 1990s, although the surviving departments of local Party committees in some regions attempted to overstep the limits of authority with the excuse of strengthening party leadership, there were no reports about the restoration of any dismantled Party apparatus (au. int.).

In the 1988 nationwide election following the thirteenth Party congress, the chief Party and government posts were as a rule taken by different persons to highlight Party-government separation. This aspect of separation was no longer emphasized in 1992. Even so, only in a few regions did the pattern of one person for two posts return during the 1990s. Up to April 1, 1998, of China's thirty-one provinces (including four province-rank cities), only in three (Beijing, Tianjin and Henan) were the top Party and government offices occupied by one person. But in seven provinces (Hebei, Jilin, Zhejiang, Hunan, Hainan, Sichuan, and Qinghai) the provincial Party secretary was chair of the standing committee of the provincial people's congress.[13] A typical county Party committee had one secretary and three deputy secretaries. After 1988 it was rare for a Party secretary simultaneously to serve as county government head. Among the deputy secretaries, the first was almost certainly also the government head and gave priority to government work (in some counties the first deputy government head was also deputy Party secretary). The others were usually professional Party cadres in charge of Party routines, including organizational building, ideology, and propaganda (au. int.).

But what difference did this institutional overhaul make in policy implementation? How effectively did it keep Party committees out of government affairs? In the early 1990s, some scholars conducted a survey on this subject in four counties under the jurisdiction of different provinces (Anhui, Hebei, Hunan, and Tianjin). Despite some variations, a general pattern emerged: In the county-level relations of authority, Party committees largely still occupied a dominant position, though the challenges from people's congresses were rising. In the making of policy proposals, there was essentially no separation between Party committees and governments (a subject discussed in greater length in the next section). But in policy execution a rough division of labor developed after 1987. Party committees were devoted mostly to Party affairs, such as personnel management (of both Party and government apparatus), routine Party activities (such as organizing Party members for the study of Party documents and recruiting new Party members), propaganda (including mass media), political and ideological education, and directing the work of "mass organizations" like the Communist Youth League, trade unions, and women's federations. The government concentrated on the implementation of the policies and programs connected with local socioeconomic development. In matters that could be categorized as either Party or government affairs, such as culture, school education, and the rule of law (*zheng fa*), either the traditional overlap of work remained or Party and government apparatus cooperated and took joint actions. Only in one of the four counties did the Party committee still interfere heavily in what was strictly defined as government affairs. Even in this county, nonetheless, the authority of the Party committee had reportedly diminished a great deal compared to the power monopoly it held prior to 1983.[14]

Although we still lack enough persuasive evidence to assess the extent to which this pattern prevailed across the country, it is perhaps reasonable to gather that after 1987 professional Party cadres and Party committees found real institutional restraints upon their habitual attempts to exercise executive power. This observation was indirectly confirmed by deteriorating personal relations between the Party secretary and government chief in many areas[15] and also somewhat supported by a popularized description of China's interinstitutional relations: "The Party waves its hand (to point the direction); the government uses its hand (to implement policies); the people's congress raises its hand (to approve the decisions); and the CPPCC claps its hands (to applaud)" (*dang hui shou; zhengfu dong shou; ren da jiu shou; zhengxie pai shou*).[16] Chinese scholars had their own synopsis of the policy process: "The Party directs, the government performs, and the people's congress comments."[17] If some Western scholars saw this as an indication of continuous Party supremacy or false democracy,[18] it could instead be taken from a historical-comparative perspective as evidence that the local Party committee had lost its function to "perform" (execute policies). A county Party secretary openly warned against the harm this loss meant for "party leadership," claiming that the Party-government separation left his Party committee an "empty entity," and it was consequently "harder to put the Party will into effect."[19] This model was certainly not limited to the county level. A municipal Party secretary also wrote to highlight the decline of the Party committee's influence in government affairs.[20]

A look at China's local political structure suggests the significance of the loss of administrative privilege. Party cadres usually had much more of a personal stake in the exercise of executive power than in policy formulation. In the latter case, they could share power with the legislature. The "democratized" intra-Party decisionmaking mechanisms further reduced the possibility that a policy could be made specifically to any individual's advantage. Right after Deng consolidated his position as paramount leader, he established the principle of "collective leadership" allegedly as a corrective measure to past Party mistakes. Although Deng himself was not well known for his respect for this principle at the Party center, he appeared to be deadly serious in enforcing it in local politics.[21] But Deng's interpretation of "collective leadership" applied this principle only to decisionmaking, not policy implementation. "Major issues must certainly be discussed and decided upon by the collective," Deng demanded of Party committees at all levels. "In the process of taking decisions, it is essential to observe strictly the principle of majority rule and the principle of one-man-one-vote, a Party secretary being entitled only to his single vote. That is, the first secretary must not take decisions by himself." But when Deng came to the issue of how to get things done, he emphasized "individual responsibility."[22] In contrast with the collective or impersonal nature of policymaking, the power for policy implementation offered more opportunities and richer administrative resources for expanding personal influence and clientelist ties, and it could also be exploited more conveniently for private material gains.

The enforcement of Party-government separation generated a modest amount of competition between local Party and government chiefs, particularly at submunicipal levels. In some regions where presumably the principle of separation gained sufficient emphasis, the most profitable and attractive post was no longer the Party secretary but government head. Two explanatory notes should be made here, though. First, according to the official ranking system as illustrated by the order of names in mass media, the Party secretary still came first, followed by the government head. Second, that model did not apply to the provincial level. Perhaps one of the reasons was that as many examples showed, provincial Party secretaries were more likely to be promoted to the Party center than governors, partly because as senior Party cadres they were organizationally closer to the Politburo.[23]

For those Party cadres who could neither resist the tide nor transfer to top government positions, the separation seemed to be a real disaster. The widespread grievances among local cadres reached central Party publications. *Liaowang Zhoukan* (*LWZK*) quoted them as grumbling, "There is now little work left for us to do and hence we have a sense of loss."[24] Departing from their normal political discreetness, many disgruntled cadres protested openly against the separation on the grounds that it weakened party leadership. A survey showed that the opponents constituted a majority of local cadres. Among the cadres surveyed, 80 percent were under the age of forty-five, and 72 percent had received higher education. They had been expected to be the backbone of reform.[25] Obviously, the opposition to local political restructuring from within Party organizations went beyond isolated individuals. Rather, it represented an institutional reaction based upon its bureaucratic interest and hence could hardly be eliminated by a reshuffle of cadres.

Local cadres' sense of frustration and sagging morale is even less surprising if one takes into account the eruption of accumulated social animosities against cadres. "Professional Party cadres" (*zhenggong ganbu*) became a pejorative term and from time to time a joke in popular culture. *LWZK* quoted some prevailing and "representative" views in that regard. Some citizens attributed all the maladies of the political system to the role of Party cadres. Some poured ridicule on cadres and perceived them as able to do nothing but show off their eloquence in empty talk. Some regarded cadres as representatives of the old system and an obstacle to the establishment of a new system; others contended that the reform of political structure should just aim at casting aside Party cadres. Obviously upset with this strongly anticadre sentiment permeating Chinese society, the leadership warned that these views were "neither correct nor fair."[26]

Local Policymaking Process:
Party-Government Integration

For all its losses in reform, the local Party committee still played a significant if not dominant role in the formulation of government policy. To study the local policymaking process and the Party role, it is necessary to analyze the two stages of the process: with whom the essential legislative and policy initiatives lay and how they were converted into local laws or official policies. Theoretically, all the policies carried out by the government must be either initiated or approved by the people's congress at the same administrative level. But in reality the initiative of the LPC for legislation and policymaking was much weaker than its function to ratify decisions taken elsewhere by the Party committee and government. Although many LPCs, along with the NPC, struggled hard to get rid of their image and status as a sheer legitimizing machine, it accepted far more proposals than it vetoed. The first stage, then, was particularly important. As with its nomination of candidates for government offices, if the Party committee could take policy initiatives into its own hands, it would to a large extent dominate the local policymaking process.

Party Control of Government in Policy Formulation

One of the main responsibilities of local Party committees was to propose policy decisions on important local issues. For lack of a legal basis for direct interactions between the Party committee and the LPC, the former submitted proposals not to the LPC but to the government. And it was never implied in Party-state documents that the government had no role in policymaking. Instead, the government was authorized to "issue decisions and orders" (article 107 of the constitution; article 59 of the local organic law). As one might reason, the government as an executive body should be more suitable to exercise legislative and policy initiatives than the Party committee.

In late 1988 a group of Chinese researchers conducted a nationwide investigation regarding the practical effects and consequences of the Party-government separation, with the emphasis on policymaking. It discovered that although desired changes were evident and even conspicuous in some areas, the substitution of the Party for the government was still widespread. The Party committee's takeover of government functions relating to policy issues and its excessive interference in administrative affairs had not changed fundamentally.[27] In some areas Party committees often took decisions on government-related issues based on the instructions of the next higher-level Party apparatus. Thereafter, they called together government and congress officials. If no opposition was voiced, the Party cadres urged the governments to implement the decisions immediately. Some cadres even treated LPCs as the Party's executive bodies and assigned them certain tasks.[28]

An investigation among five townships of Anhui Province showed that this pattern in which "the Party committee decides and other bodies implement" was especially widespread at lower government levels. The investigators examined the minutes of the meetings the Party committees in three townships convened from 1986 to 1987. During this period, 594 issues were discussed and decided at these meetings, and 274 (46.1 percent) of them focused on administrative and economic affairs that should have been none of the Party committees' business. And only a few of these issues sounded genuinely important and thus fell within their legitimate authorization. This unjustifiable Party committee interference became even more rather than less serious after the thirteenth Party congress.[29] At higher administrative levels, the Party committee control of government agenda seemed to be more delicate and skillful. In Hubei the provincial Party committee, sometimes jointly with the provincial government, annually issued dozens of documents concerning administrative work.[30] During the 1990s, local Party apparatuses continued to issue joint Party-government documents, that is, to confuse Party and government policies deliberately, in order to meddle in government affairs. As a researcher commented, this was a tactic local Party committees used to bypass congresses, as the latter were not authorized to check Party policy.[31]

The Sources of Party Committee Strengths

In the Western parliamentary system, as Smith argues, it is executive administration that is "widely regarded as providing the mainspring for political initiative, implementing party policy by settling priorities."[32] When a local Party committee was stripped of its monopoly on power and instead became a decisionmaking body (more precisely, a body with the de facto policy initiative), its interactions with the government resembled the Western legislature-cabinet relations in some aspects. But with fundamental structural dissimilarities, one could hardly apply the rationale of executive dominance to Chinese Party-government relations.

The reform was designed to push government officials into a central position in the local policy process and endow them with considerable autonomy in executive administration. Their readiness to accept Party committee interference or allow it to dictate the policy agenda, particularly on issues that neither involved controversy over political principles nor were important in some other respects, was a departure from the reform goal. It may be explained from a structural perspective that explores the inherent vulnerabilities of the government in relation to the Party committee by turning to the basic organizational means of control typical of a one-party polity.

One critical element was Party cadres' capacity to bear heavily on, albeit no longer completely control, the nomination of candidates for major government offices (a subject treated in greater length in Chapter 4). Even if government officials desired to defend their legitimate authority, they needed to be extremely cautious not to show disrespect for or disobedience to Party cadres for fear of losing their jobs. A deputy county head put it bluntly: "Since the county Party committee holds my *wu sha mao* [a hat worn by officials in ancient China that has become a symbol of office] in its hands, how could I dare to defy the Party secretary?"[33] Another deputy county head complained that he was hierarchically boss of the director of the finance bureau, a government department, but this director always asked for instructions directly from the county Party committee. The deputy head dejectedly expressed his understanding: "No wonder: Their *wu sha mao* was given by the Party committee. . . . A view was epidemic among government officials: It does not matter whether you have done your work well or poorly. The important thing is to cultivate good [personal] relations with the [Party committee's] department of organization." As a rule, it was this department that took charge of nominating candidates for government offices.[34]

The number of posts within Party committees held simultaneously by government officials was another factor. After the separation, the Party secretary typically quit the government of the same administrative level.[35] As mentioned above, the head of government usually held the post of the first deputy Party secretary. And the number-two official (such as first executive vice governor or deputy mayor) was usually an ordinary member of the standing committee of the Party committee.[36] Usually, the standing committee of a local Party committee comprised seven to ten members, among whom were one Party secretary and three deputy secretaries.[37] This was the most common organizational arrangement in local power structures across the country, although it was not dictated by explicit written rules in any Party documents or state laws. The expansion of LPC authority posed a potential threat to this arrangement because in principle it was the people's congress, not the Party committee, that had the final say in the selection of top government officials. It was therefore theoretically likely for a non-Party member to be elected the head of government. If this occurred, the Party committee would be in danger of losing its organizational grip on the government, since the government head was not politically qualified for membership in the Party committee, let alone its standing committee. But in practice, at least up to early 1998, this kind of uncontrolled election rarely happened thanks to the Party committee's efforts to rig the nomination process. In most areas government chiefs were elected by the exact-number method to guarantee the election of Party nominees.

Arising largely from the Party posts of top government officials, the local Party committee–government relationship operated in an interlocking system that made any intense confrontation between the two bodies either highly unlikely or destructive. In fact, the system's operation depended upon consensus and cooperation between the Party committee and the government. Each side fostered agreement with the awareness that any failure to do so would only result in the paralysis of government and eventually the dismissal of either Party cadres or government officials, depending upon who was held responsible by higher authorities (au. int., 1996). So it is not hard to understand that when Party cadres attempted to make inroads into the government's domain, the officials, albeit unhappy, would tend to tolerate it unless critical personal welfare were involved or the interference went far enough to damage the face or "dignity" of the government (au. int.).

As far as policy initiative was concerned, it is not entirely appropriate to describe the Party committee as "dominating" the government. In fact, in this interlocking system neither side could act on its own or make any (government) policy merely based on its institutional preferences. To a large extent and in most cases, the preparation of policy proposals was of a truly collective nature: Neither side could afford to ignore the other. A case study may serve to illustrate the situation. In Wuxi (Jiangsu) all proposals for important policy issues were discussed and decided at the meetings of the standing committee of the municipal Party committee. The standing committee had ten members: one Party secretary, three deputy Party secretaries, and six ordinary members. In addition to professional standing committee members, these meetings were attended by the mayor (concurrently the first deputy Party secretary) and the first deputy mayor (an ordinary member of the standing committee).[38] After the meetings, the proposals were submitted, in the name of the government, to the municipal congress for examination and approval. Since congressional approval, whether conditional or unconditional, was normally not problematic, it was the meeting of the standing committee of the municipal Party committee that was widely regarded as the highest decisionmaking body in Wuxi. In this process the Party committee prevailed over the government in two ways. First, the Party secretary presided over the meetings and was in a position to decide the direction of discussions, though he was in theory just the "first among equals" and had one vote like everyone else. Second, if a decision had to be passed by a vote, professional (Party) standing committee members constituted an overwhelming majority (eight vs. two). As a matter of fact, the issues were seldom decided by a majority principle but were based on consensus. On controversial matters, the meetings would continue until a solution acceptable to all participants was worked out.[39]

Some findings show that this pattern was also dominant at the provincial and submunicipal levels.[40] At the county level, along with this regular arrangement there existed some subtypes to the greater advantage of the government. In some counties the standing committee of the county Party committee convened enlarged meetings (*kuoda huiyi*) or joint meetings (*lianxi huiyi*) (with the government) to invite more government officials in charge of specific affairs, such as bureau directors, to attend. In some others it was usually the county government that provided original texts of proposals. Then the government head requested a county (Party) standing committee meeting to discuss and decide. In all these cases, the personal coordination between the Party secretary and the government head was crucial to ensure a smooth process. Only if the two agreed could any decision be passed.[41] But if they disagreed, what would happen? If the LPC were excluded from the process, to raise this hypothetical question would make no sense, as the Party secretary was hierarchically superior to the government chief. As the accountability of the government to the LPC was stressed, the possibility was enhanced that the government might seek an alliance with the LPC against the Party committee. Insofar as this study can conclude, it remains a topic for speculation since such an alliance, where it did exist, tended to rest on sensitive and highly confidential personal interactions that sometimes affected the LPC's attitude toward the proposals in question. This united front, in whatever form, would be so provocative to Party cadres and ultimately so destructive to the base of mutual trust and cooperation that it could never be documented. As a rule, in case of debate it was the government head who, deterred by the party leadership principle, gave in (au. int.). In short, behind the appearance of "consensus" stood Party cadre dominance.

To do justice to local Party committees, their frequent intrusion upon the domain of government was not always a phenomenon that may be simply explained away by ambition for power. Although it was certainly true that many cadres would not resign themselves to loss of power and privileges, some factors pertaining to the vertical relations of authority within the complex Party-state hierarchy need to be taken into consideration. At the Party center, Deng and other elders manipulated the Politburo and the Secretariat in the determination of "political principles." Many of these principles could not be easily distinguished from the policy guidelines concerning the nation's general socioeconomic development whose formulation should have been the responsibility of the State Council. This confusion of the Party and state functions at the central level, in the first place, gave rise to some degree of struggle for executive power between professional Party leaders (all those who did not hold any government posts) and the leaders of the State Council, particularly between the Party general secretary and the premier. Despite its relatively modest nature, this power contest greatly complicated the local separation of the Party from government.

On the one hand, to win more "respect" and followers among local cadres (of course not only cadres but also government officials), professional Party leaders and central Party institutions such as the Secretariat had to demonstrate their position of authority at the center. They did not want to be ignored when local leaders came to Beijing for solutions and directives regarding regional problems. But between professional Party leaders and local government officials, there were no legitimate vertical relationships of the kind that usually existed between superiors and subordinates. These Party leaders, then, had to keep local politics under their control through intra-Party channels, that is, by relying on local Party cadres. For their part, local cadres needed big opportunities to display their competence; visible accomplishments would win their bosses' grace, a primary requisite for job promotion (au. int.). They would therefore willingly carry out any instructions from the higher-level Party apparatus and attempt to make substantive "contributions" to local socioeconomic development. The reciprocal reliance and support between Party cadres at different levels extended from the top right down to the grassroots to create a vertical political symbiosis. This "embarrassing" situation for Party cadres was elucidated by a county Party secretary who grumbled to an official investigator: "If you ask us to separate the Party from government, you must do so at the higher level first." The provincial Party committee issued documents to him and asked about plans of production, grain quotas, family planning, the enrollment of students, and so on. (all of which were strictly government work). "If the tasks are not accomplished," he claimed, "as the Party secretary I am the first in line for blame. How can I ignore these [government] affairs?"[42]

Another county Party secretary contended that not only higher authorities pressed him but lower people also counted on him. "For a long time," he lamented, "people have had a fixed perception that the Party is paramount and almighty. Both cadres and the masses think that the Party secretary represents the Party. So once problems, big or small, occur, they ask me for a solution. . . . A slogan popular among the masses says: 'It is hard to handle matters unless number one (*lao da*) comes forward.'"[43] A certain awe of the Party, in part a historical residue, was thus a basic aspect of political life, even under its democratic guise during the reform years. Unlike the power wielded by the government or people's congress, the Party's power was never legally and concretely specified. Although the Party's direct control of state affairs had been a prominent character of China's political system, the provisions in the constitution and laws concerning the nature of the relationship between the Party control and the authority of organs of state power (congresses) were either unavailable or too ambiguous to serve as a guide. As some Chinese scholars observed, no matter how the Party role was legally defined or specified, Party supremacy had long been taken for granted by cadres and ordinary citizens alike.[44]

Local Policymaking Process: The Legislatures and Triangular Power Relations

Policymaking mechanisms became more sophisticated as the LPC assumed increasing prominence and the hegemony of the Party committee declined in local politics.[45] From an institutional perspective, the LPC worked only with the government, its two main functions being legislation and supervision of the government. Given the local Party-government integration in proposing policy and legislation, any lawmaking or policymaking activities necessarily involved three-cornered interplay. Furthermore, the Party committee had to fulfill its responsibility to maintain "political" oversight of the government, a requirement aimed to guarantee that the local governmental process remained in line with the central spirit. But how to coordinate the "political" and legislative oversight was a sensitive issue and a difficult task as well. Since it was an open secret that the Party committee stood behind the government and was closely associated with its performance, to supervise the government would bring the LPC into potential collision with Party cadres. One may imagine that the Party committee and LPC were essentially playing a zero-sum game: Each had to increase its influence over government at the sacrifice of the other.

The "Consensual" Nature of Party Committee–Congress Relations

Then again, under China's local political circumstances, this game was not always zero-sum. Any decision on government issues taken at the meetings of the standing committee of the Party committee had to be approved by the LPC or its standing committee by a vote before it could be legally converted into local government policy or law. In that process Party cadres needed to demonstrate respect for the will of congressional deputies, a much-highlighted democratic progress that was supposed to have been made where reform was not blocked. So if deputies aspired to assert their rights, they were in a legal position to veto any proposals and hence nullify any decisions. As one may conceive, such a veto might create a situation in which a test of strength between the Party committee–government and the LPC could not be avoided. But in practice, this kind of straightforward veto was infrequent.

The Party committee–government's de facto possession of legislative and policy initiative partly explains the apparent impotence of the LPC. But this was not a unique Chinese phenomenon. As Yves Mény indicates, nearly everywhere in the West the "executive plays an essential, if not dominant, role in the elaboration of laws."[46] In China the LPC's less assertive role in legislative activities had a more basic cause deeply rooted in China's one-party system. Even though parliaments in Western democracies "nowadays sometimes seem to be hardly more than rubber stamps,"[47] they still differed fundamentally from their Chinese counterparts.

The bottom line was that in legislation and formulation of regional policies, substantial divergence of opinions among Party cadres, government officials, and deputies seldom occurred, at least on the table. The materials available as well as my fieldwork show that it was unusual for deputies and Party cadres to diverge so widely as to fail to reach a compromise on a policy issue. It was even more rare for a dispute to be solved by compulsory means, often denoting a vote with a majority principle. Put another way, if one takes the Party committee and government as a single policymaking unit, then this unit and the legislature interacted, to a lesser extent, in another interlocking system in which each side had to know the limits of its autonomy and be ready to accept mutual constraints.[48] The decisionmaking process on policy stood in contrast with the election of government officials, in which the collision between Party cadres and congressional deputies was more common and frequent and the cadres did not always prevail.

The relatively impersonal nature of law- or policymaking was surely among the elements that underlay the building of consensus. More decisively, in the Chinese system, which prohibited political opposition, people's deputies had no real constituency in the sense that they did not represent any ideology except the official one, distinct political-economic platforms or any particular social class, or even interest groups (which began to make their way into legislative politics slowly and incrementally after the late 1980s).[49] Although one might assume that cadres and deputies would be diametrically opposed on the issue of reform, this was not the case, as the debate on the enterprise bankruptcy law suggests. Not all deputies were more pro-reform than all Party cadres on all relevant issues.

But if the policymaking process was more harmonious than conflictual, the consensus building could hardly exclude the use of coercion. That the Party committee was in a more advantageous and authoritative if not dominant position in that process was beyond dispute. Even after all the reform measures, it still held powerful political means to pressure weaker LPCs into "consensus" in case of disagreement. First, since Party cadres possessed some privileges to manipulate the selection of candidates for congressional seats, the deputies tended to be risk-averse and avoid provoking Party cadres except under exceptional circumstances. Congressional leaders needed to be even more careful, for cadres had stronger leverage over their offices. Second, Party discipline required local Party apparatus to monitor the behavior of its members, including those working in the legislature. As the official explanation went, this would guarantee party leadership over local legislation because most of the legislators were Party members.[50] Given the Party committee's authority as the enforcer of Party discipline, as well as its "legitimated" responsibility to ensure that local legislation did not deviate from the will of the CCP as the "governing party," it could persuade—though it was not authorized to force—congressional officials and deputies with Party membership to accept what it interpreted as the Party will. True, these officials and deputies might just as legitimately reject any Party committee instructions by calling attention to the legal status of the congress, and they had a good chance of getting the leadership's endorsement in doing so. But the foundation of the congressional confrontation was feeble anyway because, among other things, it was not always easy to distinguish between the Party committee's "reasonable" control and its unjustifiable interference. The strong tradition of Party supremacy among both Chinese officials and citizens would lend confidence to the Party committee in a potential showdown (au. int., 1989, 1996).

Third, despite the lack of direct working relations between the Party committee and the LPC, the organizational channels for communication and consultation did exist. Presumably afraid that the refusal of the two institutions to cooperate would bring government into a stalemate, the Party center "suggested" that in preparing bills or proposals on important issues or before presenting them for a vote in LPCs, the secretary of the SCPC Party group (who as a rule was concurrently SCPC chair) should report (*tongbao*) the bills or proposals to the Party committee at the same administrative level.[51] After Tiananmen, Jiang Zemin gave further instructions that discussion and *approval* of the Party committee were necessary for all bills and proposals concerning major policy or legal issues, implicitly including those arising from the legislature. He also demanded that the Party group of the SCPC be responsible to the Party committee at the same level.[52] If the Tiananmen crackdown did reverse local reform, it was in the more explicit application by the Party center of the party leadership principle to local lawmaking and the strengthened connections between the Party committee and the local SCPC Party group, although the latter's influence within the LPC or SCPC was limited. In some areas the Party group of the SCPC attempted to tighten control over the LPC and SCPC in collaboration with the Party committee. They decided the agenda of the SCPC or LPC and drafted the bills entirely in accordance with the "intentions" and preferences of the Party committee.[53] The chair of one municipal SCPC even remarked that congressional work was just

Party work and the congress should take the initiative to "seek Party committee leadership."[54]

The Rise of Local Legislatures as a Counterweight

In spite of local Party committees' obvious advantages, their efforts to dominate the local policy process met with tougher challenges from the legislatures. After all, the propaganda machines had extolled the breakup of the
overconcentration of power in the Party committee and expansion of the LPC
authority as a spectacular achievement of Deng's "democratic" reform. In a
showdown between the Party committee and the LPC, therefore, it could no
longer be taken for granted that the Party center or the Party organizations of
the next higher level would side with the former.[55] On the contrary, any attempt on the part of the Party committee to hold back or bully the legislature
could be interpreted by the Party center, especially reform-minded central
elites, as an act of hostility toward reform. By the same token, at least as a
public gesture the Party center commended the assertiveness of LPCs, mainly
as demonstrated in their veto of Party-government proposals or Party nominees.[56] In addition, although congressional leaders tended to accommodate
Party cadres, they had neither legitimate authority nor effective means to control the voting behavior of people's deputies. Under normal circumstances
congressional leaders had to comply with the legislative procedures in which
the majority of deputies had a final say.[57] The complete absence of political
opposition only enhanced the likelihood that the legislature would defend its
dissenting views, as its "confrontation" would appear less politically motivated but more "reform oriented" (au. int.).

Since the late 1980s, China's LPCs have slowly but steadily moved away
from what Michael Mezey defines as the "minimal legislature."[58] The rise of
the legislature as one of the major actors in the governmental process and the
shaping of triangular relations of authority have transformed the local policy
process from a unidimensional to a multidimensional one. To examine the extent to which the role of local legislature was politically meaningful, one
should discuss legislation and policymaking separately. Local legislation
meant the making of local laws, statutes, ordinances, and so on, which—as
rules governing the behavior of all citizens—involved lower individual stakes
and fewer regional favors than the formulation of policy that dealt with more
particular problems and public concerns.

From 1979, when local lawmaking was revived, to the end of 1997, more
than 5,300 local laws were passed by people's congresses at subnational levels.[59] The overwhelming majority of these laws were virtually enacted by the
SCPCs.[60] Of these laws, 80 percent were initiated by government (and Party)
departments.[61] Presumably because the enactment of laws involved many
technical details and entailed legal knowledge, government officials and con-

gressional deputies rarely complained that Party cadres imposed their will and thus triggered conflicts (au. int.). Instead, the common view was that many SCPC members previously had worked in Party or government apparatus and lacked professional training and expertise required for their new jobs, so they were unfamiliar with the legislation procedures.[62] The number of bills that originated from people's deputies who engaged in relevant professions was perhaps a little larger than the number of policy proposals they made.[63] In any case, it seems that the Party committee kept quite a low profile in lawmaking activities.

Policymaking—more exactly, examination and ratification of policy proposals—was a major task on the LPC agenda.[64] It addressed government plans or courses of action, two-thirds of which related to local social and economic development.[65] Regardless of the consensus on general principles, dissenting opinions on specific issues were voiced more frequently. The veto of a Party committee–government policy proposal provided an opportunity to measure the real weight of the LPC.

With great regional variations, the number of cases in which the local legislature rejected Party-government proposals increased rapidly at all levels. For all the caution with which this kind of event was publicly reported, a number of examples appeared in the press.[66] In Guangxi Province the provincial Party committee and government issued a joint document to announce measures to punish cadres who used public funds to build private houses. To preempt the congress, before sending the document for legislative approval they published the measures in the newspaper as a fait accompli and started to put them into effect. The provincial congress vetoed these measures on the grounds that they violated the law, forcing the withdrawal of the document for major revisions.[67] This case of direct confrontation between the Party committee and the legislature with a humiliating defeat for the former was perhaps not typical. A more common form of challenge from the legislature was to take the government as the target without directly or publicly touching the Party committee, which usually stood behind. In Minqing County of Fujian Province in March 1994, the county congress vetoed a government decision regarding the price of tap water. The county government, encouraged by the Party committee backstage, did not accept the veto and decided to proceed with its decision. Provoked by this contempt for its authority, the congress openly condemned the government for its "irresponsible" behavior and forced it to cancel the policy.[68] At a 1995 session, the municipal congress of Xiangfan, Hubei Province, vetoed the government's budget plan in defiance of private calls from Party cadres, claiming that the increase of expenditure for education in this budget plan was too small and failed to conform to central policy.[69]

As a rule, major policy proposals on regional socioeconomic development, drafted by the Party committee and government, were annually submitted to the LPC or local SCPC in the form of the "report on government work." This kind of report typically contained government plans for the future and reviewed the implementation of the programs adopted during the previous year. The critical scrutiny of the report, as a provincial congress official put it, was "the most basic form of [legislative] supervision of government work."[70]

Contrasting with the symbolic discussion and ceremonial approval characterizing communist legislatures, critical comments and constructive suggestions by people's deputies became increasingly frequent and fashionable after the late 1980s.[71] Many deputies exhibited considerable enthusiasm in their critique of the annual report and took it as a chance to show their commitment to the rule of law, cultural quality, and governmental ability, particularly during the 1990s, when the competence of deputies for "participation in governance and discussion of policy issues" (*canzheng yizheng*) was heavily emphasized (au. int.). By hindering passage of the report (forcing revisions) or deliberately making life difficult for the government, deputies (though not necessarily including congressional leaders) demonstrated their power at minimum risk (au. int., 1996). In Shandong Province, at the demand of the congress, the provincial government must submit its report draft and its agenda for major policy issues to the people's deputies one month before the annual session of congress, so that the deputies have enough time to conduct social investigations to verify whether government plans are appropriate and popular.[72] In Tianjin (a province-rank city) as of 1990, professional inspections by deputies must be organized before each annual congressional session, and data and evidence are to be gathered as the basis of their critical review of the government report.[73]

The review of the "report on government work" was an annual event for the LPC plenary session that convened only once a year for a few weeks, usually in March and April. Of limited length, this report had to address general issues and actually only offer an outline of government plans. During the rest of the year, many more reports on specific affairs would be delivered by various government departments to the local SCPC, which held six sessions each year (once every two months).[74] SCPC sessions were typically held behind closed doors. Although it would seem likely that SCPC members would be more accommodating because they were higher in rank than ordinary deputies in the congressional hierarchy, in fact, as some evidence suggests, the SCPC could be very defiant and aggressive. The Wuxi SCPC proceedings, circulated only internally, provide a glimpse of the matter.

On March 28–30, 1989, the tenth municipal SCPC of Wuxi held a regular (its ninth) meeting. The agenda was to examine seven reports and policy proposals: Deputy Mayor He Zhengming's report on the production of agriculture and supply of vegetables in the city; vice chairman of the municipal Commission of Agriculture Zhou Wei's proposal on the increase of investment into agriculture; director of the Bureau of Land Management Xie

Bendu's recommendations on preventing urban construction from encroaching upon arable land; vice chairman of the Commission of Economic Planning Xu Ji'an's report on liquidation of fixed capital; director of the Pricing Bureau Zhu Bingnan's proposal on controlling inflation; secretary-general of the tenth municipal SCPC Xu Shiqing's report on "deepening legal education and ruling the city by law"; and Zhu Bingnan's suggestion on the punishment of a transportation company that had raised ticket prices without authorization.

It was known to the SCPC members that except for Xu Shiqing's report, all the reports were either drafted or already approved by the municipal Party committee. But the SCPC rejected two of the reports (those by Zhou Wei and by Xu Ji'an), deciding that the departments concerned must reformulate their proposals. It conditionally accepted Xie Bendu's recommendations, pending revisions. Wang Liandao, vice chairman of the SCPC, warned in his concluding speech that the government should have prepared these reports more responsibly and submitted them in time: "The government had its difficulty indeed. But the main problem lies in an incorrect understanding and neglect of its duty."[75]

Why Party-Government Proposals Are Rejected

Legislative rejection of proposals reached a frequency unusual by Chinese or communist standards. Analyzing the causes and political implications of the phenomenon and assessing its long-term consequences are important to our study of the role of the LPC as a representative institution in China's democratic transition. As indicated above, it was the meeting of the standing committee of the Party committee that made policy or legal proposals on regional issues. In many areas the LPC head (i.e., the chair of the local SCPC, who was most likely its Party group head as well) had a low post or none at all in the Party committee of the same administrative level. In most provinces, the provincial SCPC chair was not even an ordinary member of the provincial Party committee.[76] As a gesture of respect to the legislature, the SCPC head was often invited to the meeting of the standing committee of the Party committee but was denied the right to vote.[77] So though SCPC heads attended the meetings, they were not responsible on behalf of the legislature for the decisions made there, nor did they even try to persuade deputies to ratify these decisions. In effect, a more critical and recalcitrant congress only strengthened the importance of the SCPC head as a nonvoting participant, although instigating the deputies to rebel was hardly a good strategy for political survival (au. int.).[78]

Since the government as a rule submitted proposals to the LPC in its own name, it actually functioned as a buffer zone to prevent the LPC from coming into direct collision with the Party committee. When government officials explained bills and proposals to LPC deputies, they usually deemphasized the role of the Party committee and highlighted the government's initiative, partly because Party cadres were discouraged from intervening excessively in government affairs. This arrangement gave further encouragement to unyielding deputies. In the first place, secret ballots made it impossible to tell how individual deputies had voted. In the second place, deputies were not quite sure how seriously the Party committee cared about the fate of the proposals in question until they were vetoed. One should also note that the proposals were normally not vetoed entirely in the Western sense. Since they did not involve conflict on ideology or political platforms, rejection just meant, as the case of Wuxi illustrates, that the proposals were to be returned to the government for revisions before being resubmitted to the congress. In other words, the consequences of any veto were under complete control, with the expectation on both sides that at the end of the day a compromise would be worked out. In that process, if the Party committee flew into a fury over the veto or displayed an obvious inclination toward intolerance, deputies would most likely back down. But to avoid any charge of attempting to revert to the overconcentration of power—a charge that might be referred to the higher authorities and invite reprimand—the Party committee had to handle the veto very carefully and show that it held the legislative authority in high esteem (au. int.).

During the 1990s the legislative veto of proposals took on a new feature. Albeit not politically motivated, the veto seemed to reflect a conscious effort on the LPC's part to develop its distinct bureaucratic interest in local politics. Two major factors presumably contributed to this increasingly discernible trend. The first was the improvement of the quality of congressional leadership. Chairs and vice chairs of the SCPC were not permitted to treat deputies or SCPC members as subordinates or to rig their voting, but these leaders could certainly take advantage of their standing as well as usually cordial personal relations with deputies to exert considerable influence. For instance, before a vote on a bill they would stress either party leadership or the legal status of the congress as the highest organ of state power, depending on their own preferences, to hint which way the deputies or SCPC members should vote. Recognizing their common welfare, deputies or SCPC members might take the cue and vote accordingly (au. int.).[79] In the 1980s many leadership positions in LPCs were filled by veteran cadres who had retired from Party-government posts.[80] This was a face-saving arrangement before their phasing out.[81] Aware of the Party center's intentions, these LPC leaders (most of them over seventy) had neither the energy nor the enthusiasm to transform the LPC into a genuine organ of power to contend with the Party committee.[82]

This scenario has changed substantially since the late 1980s, when more younger local leaders were ushered into the LPC. In provinces such as Anhui, Hunan, Hainan, and Hebei, provincial SCPC chairpersons were under sixty when they took over the posts.[83] In thirty-two municipal SCPCs, many chairpeople were in their early fifties when they got the job in the 1993 elections.[84] Many of these local younger SCPC leaders had experience with Party or government chiefs or deputy chiefs. The reasons they quit—or were forced to quit—Party or government posts were not always clearly known. But one thing seems to be certain: Whereas the practice of treating the LPC as a last stop for retirement continued to a lesser extent in many regions, more and more local leaders were elected into SCPCs because it was not appropriate to occupy a Party or government position too long.[85]

In many areas rising political stars were purposely landed in SCPCs as kind of a testing ground, a preliminary phase in the career upswing.[86] Tian Jiyun, a Politburo member and the NPCSC's executive vice chairman, suggested that the people's congress should recommend its officials for major government offices once they had accumulated enough knowledge of law and legislative procedures. "This may become an important method for us to train cadres (officials)," he said.[87] In short, to transfer from Party or government posts to leadership positions in the SCPCs was no longer seen as a loss of face or grace or the downslope of a political career. At the center, the powerful political figures took the NPCSC chair as a symbol of the noble status of the legislature.[88] Many local SCPC leaders were not just relatively young, energetic, and well educated but had a strong incentive to develop the LCP as their base of power and aspired to make tangible achievements that would lead to promotion.[89] Maintaining cooperative working relations with Party cadres, however, was usually just as if not more crucial to their career goals.[90]

Along with the replacement of the LPC leadership, the composition of deputies underwent some important changes as well. During most of the 1980s, as LPCs remained impotent, many deputies were passively recruited: Without taking the initiative, they did not refuse their recommendation and appointment as candidates. It was no wonder, then, that they had a strong tendency to regard the election as an honor rather than a responsibility.[91] As the cultural quality and competence of deputies were stressed after the late 1980s, their participation in government became more substantial than ritualistic. There were three trends that reinforced one another. Since 1979 China's political macroenvironment and general atmosphere have been quite favorable to LPCs' development. The expansion of the LPC authority represented China's progress toward what Deng allegedly looked forward to as a "rule-by-law" society. Any hostility to or contempt for LPCs—particularly in cases involving cadre corruption or other misdoings—could be taken as evidence of antireform sentiment that by extension would come to mean opposition to Deng and the Party center. For ambitious cadres, its risk under certain specific circumstances was not much less than the counterrevolutionary behavior of an ultraleftist Gang of Four follower or a typical dissident. Although it served propaganda purposes as well, the heavy official emphasis on the people's congress over time cultivated a "democratic consciousness"—or more precisely, a sense of importance—among deputies and spurred them to take their constitutional rights and powers more seriously. Because of this and because deputies were better informed and better educated, the LPC gradually moved into the limelight in local politics. In turn, more proactive and better-qualified citizens were recruited into LPCs. The attraction to citizens of the office of people's deputy increased also as a result of more visible benefits.[92] My findings in Wuxi unmistakably showed that as LPC deputies came to taste real power and all its accompaniments, the number of passively elected deputies dropped by a big margin. More candidates now believed that people's deputies could make a difference regarding many local policies if only they wanted to do so.

Legislative Oversight of the Government

Since Party cadres were deeply implicated in making proposals, any veto or delay might be seen as a confrontation with the Party committee and, if not well handled, could erode the foundation of continuous cooperation between the Party committee and the LPC. Therefore, the LPC's adoption of a discreet and conciliatory approach would not necessarily indicate its timidity or impotence. From the above examples, we may indeed recognize some of the legislature's impact on the selection of preferred courses of action. But the difficulty for our research lies in the lack of sufficient cases that can provide a satisfactory basis to gauge the real strengths of the LPC against the Party committee. By contrast, it seems that the LPC fulfilled its responsibility of supervising government implementation of policy in a more forcible and aggressive way. The Party committee appeared to keep out, leaving the government and LPC as the two main players in this particular game. Perhaps because the supervisory role could be played at a safe distance from Party apparatus, LPC domination over the government may leave a sharp impression on the minds of Western observers preoccupied with the conventional wisdom concerning the rubber-stamp metaphor under a communist system.[93] Before we analyze its implications, we should look at some meaningful mechanisms of the legislative oversight.

Inquiries and Interpellations

During most of the 1980s, a frequently used method for legislative supervision was to address inquiries to government officials at LPC sessions. After 1987, congressional inquiries and interpellations intensified and became more hostile. A striking event was the recall of Yang Huiquan, vice governor of Hunan Province, for his failure satisfactorily to respond to deputy inquiries in 1989. Unlike some other cases of legislative recall of government officials that resulted from the initiative of Party cadres, evidence suggests that Yang's recall was the deputies' spontaneous action without or regardless of any in-structions from the Party committee or higher authorities.[94] When the case was referred to the central leadership, deputy initiative was endorsed. As the Yang case brought to national attention a potentially formidable weapon wielded by congressional deputies against government officials, deputies came to use inquiries and interpellations during the 1990s "to see how greatly their authority [was] respected."[95] Many reports are striking in their depiction of a typical scene during deputy inquiry at LPC sessions: Government offi-cials summoned to respond kept apologizing to the deputies, expressing their "humble acceptance of criticisms."[96]

However, these reports may lead to an overestimation of the legislative capacity to recall or penalize government officials. This capacity seems to de-pend on the operation of specific local networks of personnel, into which an outsider would have much difficulty gaining insight. Some evidence shows that it could be highly risky for deputies, without the institutional backing from the Party committee or higher authorities, to propose the recall of power-holders. The Yan Yueming case illustrates the risk.[97]

Appraisal of Government Officials

In the past several years, LPCs have developed more methods to torture gov-ernments. A major innovation was the so-called appraisal (*pingyi*), recom-mended by the central leadership and adopted by LPCs across the country af-ter 1991. Two practical types can be identified. One addresses the work of various government departments; the other, individual officials' performance. In some large cities such as Ha'erbin and Xi'an, the municipal SCPCs passed a resolution stipulating that each government department submit reports on the implementation of policy in its functional field. At the same time, the deputies made special inspections, organized seminars among the con-stituents, and collected comments on whose basis to evaluate government work in specific policy areas. Finally, deputies would present a report to the SCPC indicating problems and suggesting improvements.[98]

The second type of assessment, called self-evaluation of performance combined with (deputy) appraisal (*shuzhi pingyi*), targeted individual govern-ment officials rather than the government as a collective. These officials were usually heads of government departments, such as bureau directors, whose appointment had to be approved by the LPC; this provided the legal basis of the legislative appraisal. The typical procedure, as adopted by the Hainan provincial SCPC since 1993, looks like quite an ordeal. Each SCPC session summoned two government officials to report on their work performance and receive critical review. Prior to the session, the SCPC sent a team to collect feedback, through opinion polls, citizen meetings, and private visits to the workplace, relating to the officials' execution of policies the legislature had ratified (sometimes also administrative decrees issued exclusively by the government), their leadership ability, integrity, diligence, and so on. All officials who were either elected or approved by the legislature had to go through this torture at least once during their term.[99] This type of appraisal could be vital to the officials' political life; the results and materials it produced were kept in their personal files and used as references for later appointments. In many areas officials who failed to pass the appraisal lost their jobs.[100] The central Party newspaper *Fazhi Ribao* (*FZRB*) claimed that this harsh appraisal enhanced officials' consciousness of "crisis"—or lack of job security—and hence sense of responsibility.[101]

Examination of Law Enforcement

From the start of the legal reform, preparing and reviewing bills and converting them into laws dominated the LPC agenda. Pushed by widespread complaints that laws failed to be forcefully executed, the LPC's role extended from lawmaking to examining law implementation during the 1990s, with Hebei Province taking the lead.[102] From 1991 to early 1994, thirty provincial SCPCs organized 719 inspections in which nearly 70,000 people's deputies and government officials (the latter invited) participated. During the same period, the seventy-six county SCPCs surveyed conducted 1,174 investigations into how the law was executed in their areas.[103] Supervision included two aspects: (1) how effectively government departments enforced law in practice and (2) whether there was any illegal behavior among the officials.[104] This task often required special inspection teams who could become the bane of the government, since it was held accountable for any failure to apply legal provisions literally and forcibly. In provinces such as Guangdong and Hubei, if any shortcomings were found, the SCPC would send the government an ultimatum—called the "law supervision paper" (*falü jiandu shu*)—in which a deadline for corrective measures was set.[105] In some areas if the responsibility was clear, the government head concerned was immediately punished.[106]

The second aspect of law inspection was initially intended to check political corruption of officials; later it covered any misconduct. If an LPC was bent on demonstrating its power, it could ruin the political career of any official who made a simple slip. In Wuxiang County, Jiangsi Province, it was discovered that a bureau director gambled at home. Although gambling was forbidden by law, very few people in Chinese society took the law seriously, considering petty gambling just a form of amusement. Perhaps for this reason, the county government (most probably after consultation with the Party committee) did not act upon the report. But this inaction irritated the county SCPC, which openly condemned the government for failing to penalize the director, a law violator. After the SCPC put the proposal of his dismissal to a congressional vote, his removal was decided.[107]

It would be a mistake to conclude from this discussion that LPCs had reached an institutional magnitude comparable to the Party committee in the local governmental process. Indeed, in numerous cases the Party committee was hardly visible in the governmental activities that required the legislative oversight. It was not known exactly what role Party cadres played behind the scenes when the legislature penalized officials. Thus, there was no definitive way to measure legislative power. In some areas the tendency of LPCs to ingratiate themselves with Party cadres or come to a consensus with them before taking any action was obvious. In Ha'erbin the municipal SCPC reported the results of every appraisal to the municipal Party committee and "listen[ed] to its instructions."[108] In Qingdao the municipal Party committee usually approved the measures for legislative oversight before they were adopted by the SCPC.[109]

But equally important in the Chinese cultural context, with its emphasis on face-saving, was how much substance this apparent "respect" for party leadership contained. Given the need for publicized unity and cooperation, both the legislature and Party committee would stand to lose if consensus-building efforts failed. But the legislature had a great advantage in that it could effectively force government officials out of office. If the legislature gathered hard evidence against an official, Party cadres would find themselves in an embarrassing position if they tried to protect the official. To say the least, this protection could be extremely risky, as it could be rejected or reported to the higher authorities as a likelihood that the cadres were implicated in the crime or misconduct (au. int.). Because of the high degree of integration of the Party committee and government, few local senior officials could be penalized without touching the Party committee.

In Xiong County, Hebei Province, and Wufeng County, Hubei Province, the county government head and deputy head fell victim to SCPC supervision. As a rule, the head concurrently holds the second-ranking post in the county Party committee, but the Party secretary obviously failed to shield him.[110] What made it even harder for the Party committee to control the situation, as in the case of Dalian, Jiangsu, was that people's deputies who participated in the inspections could spontaneously propose to dismiss officials. Their motions were presented for a vote by secret ballot among the deputies according to the majority principle.[111] Whether or not the SCPC leaders hoped to accommodate the cadres, any attempt to intimidate the deputies, manipulate their voting, or tamper with the legal procedures in favor of the accused would invite as many troubles for them as for the Party cadres.

A number of documented cases suggest that the legislature's readiness to hurt the career prospects of government officials through its authorized legal supervision, combined with its increasing say in officials' election and appointment, provided it with tremendous deterrent power. This power was made more formidable by the explicit encouragement from the leaders in Beijing, who rarely let any opportunity slip to publicize their alignment with the LPC in pushing through legal reform and punishing corrupt cadres and officials. Consequently, the government became doubly accountable, to the Party committee and the LPC, with the scale seeming to tip to the LPC's side. The government's grievances about "too much" interference from the legislature were also widespread (au. int.).[112] The legislative authority over government brought about a noticeable change in the attitudes of officials in dealing with LPC deputies. The government head of Kaifeng, his eyes "brimming with tears," complained to the surveyors that the municipal congress "treats us as if we were children. They [deputies] order us to report our work twice a week and reprimand us like our masters even if they feel a little dissatisfied."[113] Some officials were found to "tremble out of fear" before the legislative appraisal.[114] In Wuxi the city government responded to every suggestion made by the deputies, asking the deputies to grade each response as either satisfactory or unsatisfactory. They would not leave until they had received a satisfactory grade (au. int., 1996, 1998).

Political Weakness of LPCs

Given the vast size of China and the huge regional disparities in social, economic, and political conditions, any generalization about the development of LPCs, based as they would be upon fragmentary evidence, would be misleading. Despite signs of the rising importance of LPCs in the local political process since the late 1970s, an equal—if not larger—amount of evidence points to the fact that at least in some areas the LPC's role remained ornamental and largely perfunctory, characterized by mere ceremonies of ratification and unanimous acceptance of legislation. These LPCs were far from maximizing their powers in a politically safe way. Party cadres' disrespect for them was allegedly widespread and has become the focus of considerable criticism.[115]

In Xinzhou, Shanxi, the chairman and five vice chairmen of the municipal SCPC, who were elected by the congress, were removed from office simply by a document issued by the municipal Party committee.[116] In a region of Hubei, the congress asked a Party chief who was also the government head to attend its session and respond to inquiries about his government work. At the session he told the deputies that as government chief he accepted their supervision. "But as the Party secretary," he said, "I would caution you that your criticisms were inappropriate."[117] Party cadres' contempt for LPCs inevitably spread to government officials. In a county adjacent to Wuhan, the government never reported work on its own initiative to the county SCPC. When a county head had to attend an SCPC meeting and listen to the criticisms, he "arrogantly" gave the body "instructions."[118] Not a few people liked to joke that the people's congress was the "elderly gentleman [*lao tou zi*], grand billboard [*da pai zi*], and empty skeleton [*kong jia zi*]."[119]

When Party cadres and government officials treated the people's congress with disdain and encroached upon its legal authority, timid legislative reaction appeared to be the rule rather than exception in many areas. Such weakness was unquestionably related to the role of the Party committee in the election of congressional deputies, especially SCPC members. But this did not seem to be the whole story.[120] An overwhelming majority of proposals and bills were prepared jointly by the Party committee and government; most of these the legislature accepted. The unlikelihood of a challenge from the legislature resulted to a certain extent from the deputies' lack of technical expertise (au. int.). Despite the notable increase in the number of full-time SCPC members at the provincial and municipal levels during the 1990s, nearly all ordinary deputies at all levels remained nonprofessional legislators. Preparing viable bills or policy proposals, as opposed to merely submitting criticisms and suggestions, requires some professional training and appropriate understanding of policy issues. But deputies were usually preoccupied with their own jobs and had little time to study the issues. Not surprisingly, the government threw out many of the deputies' proposals as either impractical or "unscientific." A study of LPCs at the county and district levels in Nanjing showed that the government invalidated more than 70 percent of deputy proposals on the grounds that their execution would far exceed its financial capacity.[121] In another survey, the government complained that proposals originating in the LPC were (1) simplistic repetition of the "Party committee's opinions" (that is, no new ideas), (2) based on incorrect information, or (3) utopian and inappropriate given local conditions. Those who conducted the survey concluded that the government's grievance was "fair and justifiable."[122]

For all the compelling evidence of the increasing importance and autonomy of LPCs, it is difficult to identify any signs heralding the approach of political opposition. Advocacy of political freedoms was completely absent in deputy activities. Instead, deputies were usually extremely wary of questioning the "political principles" imposed from on high and were particularly careful not to touch any taboos relating to the communist one-party dictatorship. Understandable though this caution was, it must disappoint scholars who hope to assess the depth and breadth of the potential political opposition in Chinese society and explore its development in LPCs. Any conflict over more basic issues associated with ideology or macropolitics might result in substantial institutional antagonism between the legislature and the Party committee and hence undermine the consensus-building process. Since no such conflicts have been recorded, efforts to explore any emergent opposition would lack a solid basis.

The behavior of deputies and their aversion to any involvement in political trouble may not be attributed exclusively to a repressive communist regime, as the totalitarianism model quite popular in Western scholarship would have it. Although thriving social democratic forces and dictators' tendency toward democratization present a classic chicken-and-egg issue in the study of democratic development, the causal relations between them are more complex than a one-sided, systemic approach would assume. There is no denying that under Deng political terror and coercion (which never entirely disappeared even during the regime's most enlightened years) frightened most of the population into submission or silence. Any challenge to the theoretical justifications of the regime involved high risks. One has to add as well that the prohibition on the free exchange of information impedes the creation of a strong popular consciousness regarding political rights, particularly in China's cultural and historical context. To some deputies, challenging the regime may be just a problem of political courage. But for more, the notion that democracy means a multiparty system and elections based upon freedom of political competition was either quite blurred or unacceptable. After twenty years of reform, many local congressional deputies still reject, at least in their rhetoric, this idea as foreign and unsuitable to Chinese circumstances (au. int.).

Legislation hardly occupied a prominent place on most deputies' agendas, and few thought it should. Those deputies who were keen to represent the interests of a specific constituency understood the larger part of their duty as doing concrete "good things" on a daily basis. Such an understanding is hardly unreasonable or inappropriate, especially for local legislators. It is justified in Western democracies, too.[123] But during the Deng period, that notion was still shaped by the Maoist interpretation that denies any links between the people's welfare and political democracy. Put another way, political liberty and human rights—though solemnly guaranteed by the constitution and laws—were not perceived by deputies as the "public goods" they were supposed to offer, defend, or address in their investigation into law enforcement.

And yet to the extent they were allowed to be publicly voiced, citizen expectations seem to justify deputy performance. Since the late 1980s, the people's congress has developed into a more representative institution as a result of closer interactions between deputies and constituents. Heightened authority of LPCs and the greater privileges for deputies that went along with it noticeably raised deputy status in the public opinion. Consequently, it made deputies become more active in collecting citizen comments, complaints, and feedback and bringing citizen concerns to the attention of the government or to the LPC agenda.[124] Since 1991 a new system has gradually been set up in LPCs across the country to allow deputies to report their activities to their constituents on an annual basis. The report typically includes a list of "good things" they have done and stresses how earnestly they have incorporated voter opinions and suggestions into government policy. Constituents are then asked to grade the deputies' performances.[125]

There is little doubt that the transformation of the role of deputies from regime agents to remonstrators (to use O'Brien's terms) has been accelerated as a result of the reporting system and similar measures in recent years.[126] As deputies were compelled to make greater efforts to curry favor with the voters, citizen expectations influenced deputy behavior. From two cases (in Qingdao, Shandong) of what constituents reportedly called "superb deputy service," one may gain some idea of how citizen needs might shape deputies' agenda.

First, when a high school erected a laboratory building, questions arose concerning its quality. The school looked to the people's deputies for help, and the deputies in turn persuaded the appropriate government departments to help solve the problems. Second, the 273 families in a particular residential compound suffered from pollution of industrial smoke (probably caused by a nearby factory). They appealed to their deputies, who collected data on the environment of the compound, drafted a report, and demanded that the government find an immediate solution. [127]

Although these examples largely illustrate the essence of the "good things" congressional deputies did in the late 1980s, deputy responsiveness rose in the 1990s to relate everything to the defense of the "rule of law." Deputies tended to be more ready to stand up to the Party committee and government for their failure to enforce law that allegedly hurt or neglected the interests of the people. Two examples were favorably introduced in a central publication as reflecting a nationwide tendency. In its law inspections, the Hunan provincial congress picked out more than 6,700 government documents whose content did not entirely conform to relevant legal provisions. The legislature canceled over 3,000 illegal or "unreasonable" items that taxed the peasants. In Anhui Province deputies found out that in some areas the government delayed payment of teachers' salaries, in violation of the law. Under legislative pressure, the government soon paid the teachers.[128]

If at the end of the 1980s the Chinese regime, as Burns argues, "still failed to institutionalize a formal system of popular participation that is valued by the people," remarkable improvement was made in that regard in the 1990s.[129] Citizen participation and representation in the governmental processes connected to their material benefits reached a higher degree of institutionalization through the LPC and the constituency-serving activities of congressional deputies. Empirical studies show that citizens have quickly learned how to utilize legislative channels to serve their purposes. As one legal scholar points out, when citizens met with injustice, they used to appeal to the Party committee and government. Now, with enhanced confidence in the competence of the LPC, they look to people's deputies.[130] In recent years the NPCSC department in charge of citizen complaints has received nearly 100,000 letters annually. And the number of grievances addressed to the LPCs is even higher.[131] Insofar as their publicly voiced preferences suggest, many citizens at this stage seem to approve of this essentially "depoliticized" participation and representation, and they expect their representatives to look after their material welfare rather than take a broader political perspective.[132] It is highly likely, though, that political debate and opposition will sooner or later emerge in LPCs when apolitical representation reaches its structural limits.

Conclusion

In a communist one-party system, local legislature can never become a truly representative institution, primarily because the prohibition of political competition and free expression of ideology sharply circumscribes citizen representation. Although the Deng regime remained firmly within the one-party tradition, it did make efforts to maximize the representative function and institutional capacity of the LPC while leaving intact the hegemonic appearance of the Party. Since political and legal reform was launched in 1979, LPCs have enjoyed some advantages that provide them with the potential to expand their institutional authority. These advantages arose from the Party center's move to create certain checks and balances in the local governmental process, with the purpose of ensuring the faithful implementation of the central reform line at subnational levels. From the large number of official and central publications and policy documents that recommended and brought to nationwide attention the examples of legislative "domination," one could identify an amorphous alignment between the central elite and the local legislature in the local power game during most of the reform years. Indeed the central decisionmakers found the LPC quite useful in handling local Party cadres whose loyalty to Deng and his reforms was highly questionable. Many findings suggest that at lower administrative levels the central leadership seemed to side with the LPC more firmly.

There were a few other factors that reduced the central reliance upon local cadres and hence favored the formation of the center-LPC alliance against the local Party apparatus. First, as market reform was accelerated, the orthodox Party ideology underwent a noticeable transformation, becoming more flexible to accommodate more social groups and economic interests. The local Party apparatus lost its status as the most authoritative interpreter of the political principles (which it had tended to abuse to oppose reform and retain power).

Yet the Party center counted on local cadres to nip political opposition in the bud or, as a last resort, control the unpredictable consequences of reform. But with a brief exception in 1989, no substantial threats to the regime seem to have emerged. Deng and his colleagues could rest particularly assured of the highly depoliticized role of LPCs and deputy activities that served to make macropolitics, such as the multiparty system and claims for political freedoms, appear almost completely irrelevant to citizens' private concerns. Thus, the utility of the local Party apparatus diminished in the reform process. With the administrative power highly centralized in Beijing, local government, especially at the county and township levels, did not produce an impact upon the political system or national politics anyway. The Party center's seemingly generous endorsement of local legislative power was not surprising for all these pragmatic considerations.

The considerable decline of local Party (committee) hegemony was quite identifiable as compared with the pre-reform overconcentration of power. Party supremacy remained in principle, but the concrete content and forms of party leadership as applied to a more complex society significantly changed. Yet one must be careful not to make any simplistic generalizations, and not just because of regional variations: As a result of the separation of the Party from government and the rise of the legislature, local institutional politics was much more complicated than a who-controls-whom approach would suggest. For analytical purposes, one must divide the local policy process into two stages: (1) the preparation, deliberation, and ratification of policy proposals or bills and (2) policy or law implementation. At the first stage, it is especially difficult to identify a pattern by which one may assess reliably the relations of dominance among the three institutions. The triangular relationships of power among the Party committee, the government, and the LPC were characterized by two separate interlocking systems that operated within a framework of general agreement on major principles as well as on a consensus-building and cooperative basis. In each of the interlocking systems, neither could make any (government) policy decision autonomously, that is, merely based on its own institutional preferences and in defiance of the other. Any substantial confrontation between the Party committee and the government at the drafting phase or between the Party committee–government and the legislature at the ratification period is highly unlikely, as both sides recognize that any failure to achieve compromise would result only in the paralysis of government and eventually, perhaps, penalty for either or both sides.

Therefore, no hard evidence is available for a precise conclusion concerning the decline and growth of the relative strengths of the local Party apparatus and LPCs. From well-documented cases and my personal fieldwork, we may speculate that for all its apparent "modesty," the Party committee retained its dominant position in local politics, although the degree of its dominance seemed to decrease progressively as the administrative level moved down from the province to the lowest township. The supreme party leadership principle, the Party committee influence over the election of congressional deputies (SCPC members in particular), and its integration with the government in making bills and policy proposals, as well as the strong tradition of Party domination, all combined to give the Party committee an unparalleled capacity to compel the legislature into "consensus" in case of the divergence of opinions. The main problem with the Party committee was, however, that it needed to be extremely careful not to abuse its status; such abuse could be persuasively interpreted, as well as referred to the Party center, as an antireform attempt to revert to the overconcentration of power, a charge that might bring big trouble to Party cadres.

The supervision of the government in its implementation of policy and laws was the function the LPC seemed to perform best in its newly expanded role. But the LPC's success should not be taken as an indicator of its superiority to the Party committee in terms of power. Instead, as local Party committees were pressed to withdraw from the process of policy execution, the legislative oversight of the government could be carried out with less Party committee involvement. In any case, the LPC in many areas took advantage of the provisions in the Party-state documents and laws that deny Party cadres' interference in policy execution and guarantee legislative supremacy. Many LPCs established genuine authority over the government by displaying their willingness and capacity to ruin the political career of irresponsible or incompetent officials. As a result, a double responsibility system took shape, in which the government, as the executive body, was placed in quite a vulnerable position, as it must be accountable to both the Party committee and LPC. In the local institutional rearrangement, whether in policy formulation or implementation, the government served well as a buffer zone between the Party committee and the LPC.

Notes

1. In this study Chinese politics is vertically divided into the central, local, and grassroots categories. Local politics, discussed in this chapter, comprises four ranks or levels in China's political administrative hierarchy: province, municipality (city), county (also urban district in large and medium-sized cities), and township. Most counties accept the direct administrative leadership of the respective provincial governments, whereas large and medium-sized cities have suburban counties under their jurisdictions. See Lieberthal, *Governing China,* ch. 6. (But in his discussion of China's territorial layers of state administration, Lieberthal drops the township, which represents the lowest rank of government.) Since the 1980s more counties have come under the direction of the governments of their adjacent cities. See Pu Xingzu et al., *Zhonghua,* pp. 238–240.

2. See Wakeman, "A Note."

3. For a discussion of central-local conflicts before the Cultural Revolution, see Schurmann, *Ideology and Organization,* pp. 214–216.

4. As some scholars indicate, in the early 1980s economic reform did cause conflicts among economic sectors because it reallocated resources and capital. See Solinger, "The Fifth"; Shirk, "The Politics." In China's nomenclature, central ministers do not officially rank as "Party-state leaders." Even though some central ministries suffered from reform, they failed to constitute a substantial opposition, as they were under the close control of the premier (and the Politburo). The central authority was

indeed affected by the administrative reform that was aimed at redefining central-local relations and resisted by various central departments. For a more complete discussion of this issue, see Jia and Lin, eds., *Changing*. But this is basically a different matter, with less relevance to the horizontal structural reform that is the focus of this study.

5. Of course it was not necessarily a simple ideological problem. As MacFarquhar indicates, the long-standing tension within the CCP between the demand for "redness" (political fervor) and the demand for "expertise" (professional skills) settled in favor of the latter as required by the modernization drive. It came as a potential blow to the "roughly 50 percent of Party cadres who had been recruited during the Cultural Revolution" and who were inappropriately equipped for the new era. See MacFarquhar, "The Succession to Mao and the End of Maoism, 1969–82," in MacFarquhar, ed., *The Politics*, pp. 336–337.

6. The investigation reports quoted are Liang Yukai, Chen Ruilian, and Wen Wenfei, "Clarify the Main Functions of the Municipal Party Committee" and Zheng Zhibao and Cai Shizhong, "The Investigation on and Thinking over the County-level Separation," both in Zhao Baoxu, ed., *Zhengquan Jiegou*, pp. 67–79, 127–140; Chen Jing, Wang Longjiang, and Wei Xiaodong, "The Effects"; Ning Yongkang, et al., "The Procedures"; SSDWSDLD, "Focus on the Changes." For the "Party group," see Chapter 5, notes 72, 77.

7. Liang Yukai, Chen Ruilian, and Wen Wenfei, "Clarify the Main Functions."

8. Ning Yongkang, et al., "The Procedures."

9. Zu Boguang, "The Separation."

10. Ibid.

11. Hao Wang, "A Report."

12. After Tiananmen Deng Xiaoping asserted that he would not allow any changes in the reform line of the thirteenth Party congress: "Whoever opposes it has to step down." *Deng Xiaoping Wenxuan*, pp. 324–327, 370–383.

13. *GJJ*, 307:4 (April 16, 1998), p. 33. Just note the changes taking place between the fifteenth Party congress of October 1997 and the ninth NPC of March 1998. Up to November 1, 1997, in four provinces (Beijing, Tianjin, Liaoning, and Hainan) the top Party and government offices were occupied by one person. Only in two (Zhejiang and Henan) did the provincial Party secretary hold the chair of the standing committee of the provincial people's congress. *GJJ*, 302:11 (November 16, 1997), p. 45.

14. Xie Qingkui, et al., *Xian Zhengfu Guanli*, ch. 3.

15. At the ninth NPC session, some deputies proposed that since the disunity between top local Party and government leaders had become an outstanding problem, political reform should be further implemented to put an end to all excuses that allowed Party cadres to interfere in government work. They suggested a theoretical change from the Party's direct leadership to its "indirect leadership." Bai Dehua, "The (NPC) Deputies."

16. The Chinese People's Political Consultative Conference is a largely honorary national institution that bears some resemblance to the British House of Lords. It is structured in the same way as the people's congress and has branches at all levels. As Townsend and Womack describe it, the CPPCC occupies an ambiguous halfway position between the citizen-based interest articulation of the people's congress system and the clearly delineated constituencies of other mass organizations. For more discussion, see Townsend and Womack, *Politics*, pp. 272–273. Some Chinese scholars suggest that the CPPCC could be turned into an upper house in the future bicameral system. See O'Brien, *Reform Without Liberalization*, pp. 137–140. The role and influence of the CPPCC in Chinese politics—even during the period of political reform—have been too negligible to deserve inclusion in our discussion of democratization here.

17. Tang Tingfen, "On the Party's Exercise."

18. McCormick, "China's Leninist Parliament," pp. 44–45.

19. He Daquan, "Some Difficult Problems."

20. Meng Xiangxi, Party secretary of Anyang, Anhui, asserted that after the separation the power of the municipal Party committee for direct management of personnel, materials, and finance was drastically curtailed in his city: "Some comrades have a sense of losing power and think that nobody is listening to the Party committee anymore." Meng Xiangxi, "The Thinking."

21. Deng's emphasis on the Party's "collective leadership at all levels" can be found in several speeches made soon after his rehabilitation in 1977 and may be taken as one of his first ideas about political reform. In a 1980 speech, he listed it as one of the five major measures in reforming the leadership system. Deng Xiaoping, *Selected Works,* pp. 302–325.

22. Ibid., p. 323.

23. As regards submunicipal levels, I came upon an interesting example. In November 1989 I interviewed Pan and Hua, two leaders of a township of Wuxi County, Jiangsu Province. Pan was then secretary of the township Party committee, while Hua was the township government head and deputy Party secretary. In the interview Hua appeared to be much better informed, more ambitious, and more assertive than did Pan. Before the Party-government separation, Hua had been the Party secretary and Pan the government head and deputy Party secretary. They exchanged their posts after the separation was enforced. Later I asked a county official accompanying me why they exchanged posts. His answer was simply that Hua was more competent than Pan.

24. Hua Ding, "Cast Away the 'Sense of Loss.'"

25. This survey was made among 373 Party cadres of Shaanxi Province. According to the survey, 210 of them (56.3 percent) claimed that the Party's leading role (at the county level) had been undermined by the separation; 186 (49.8 percent) argued that the separation had reduced the power and prestige of Party organizations and would make their work very difficult. Only two (0.05 percent) thought otherwise. In the view of 169 (45.3 percent), the separation did not yield positive effects and just led the people to distrust the Party. When asked what they worried about after the separation, 79 (21.1 percent) replied: "The Party is losing its leadership position because its decisions on major issues may not be accepted by the people's congress or government"; 107 (28.9 percent) asserted that since the Party had "given up" its power of direct appointment of officials, "its leadership has lost the organizational guarantee"; 24 (6.4 percent) said: "If the people's congress or government acquires too much power, it would be unfavorable to the political stability of the country"; and 51 (13.4 percent) warned that the separation might cause nationwide political upheaval and lead to the capitalist road. See Wang Yukai, "Some Problems Must Be Studied and Solved Concerning the County-level Separation," in Zhao Baoxu, ed., *Zhengquan Jiegou,* pp. 1–12.

26. Hu Quan, "To Be Fair."

27. Zhao Baoxu, ed., *Zhengquan Jiegou,* preface.

28. Jiao Shiying, "A Study."

29. Cheng Lishun and Chen Gang, "The Status Quo."

30. Zhu Geng, "Some Issues Concerning the Exercise of Supervising Power by Local SCPCs," in QRCBY, ed., *Lun Renda Jiqi Changweihui,* pp. 169–174.

31. Lu Jindong, "Analyze the Issue." This view was shared by Yu Hanqin, chair of the Chongqin municipal SCPC and its Party group secretary, who openly complained that in his city the Party committee and government very often took joint decisions and issued joint documents. This practice made legislative oversight quite difficult. See Yu

Hanqin, "Strengthen the Consciousness, Improve the Quality and Increase Effectiveness," in Li Shenkuan, ed., *Qianjin Zhongde Shiji Renda,* pp. 317–332.

32. Smith, *Politics,* pp. 220–221.

33. Cao Wenguang, "Understand the Status Quo of the Party-Government Relationship," in Zhao Baoxu, ed., *Zhengquan Jiegou,* pp. 104–114.

34. See Zhang Anqing and Li Hezhong, "A Study of the Models for Separation of Party and Government Functions at the County Level," in Zhao Baoxu, ed., *Zhengquan Jiegou,* pp. 39–66.

35. A major exception was Tianjin (a city with province rank). Li Ruihuan, secretary of the municipal Party committee, also held the post of mayor from 1987 to 1989. After the 1989 crackdown, he was promoted to the Politburo standing committee and became the fourth-ranking nominal Party leader.

36. The official source confirmed this arrangement as a general pattern in local politics. See Wu Wentai, "Some Issues."

37. See Liu Yingxing, "An Important Issue." The author suggested that the SCPC chair should concurrently hold the position of deputy Party secretary. Given the "high prestige" of the Party, so doing would strengthen the authority of the people's congress. The SCPC chair was usually just an ordinary member of the Party committee.

38. For a period, the second deputy mayor was also an ordinary member of the standing committee.

39. Based on my fieldwork in Wuxi.

40. For the provincial level, see Yang Fengchun, ed., *Zai Shengji Renda.* This book covers the performance of twenty-seven provincial congresses until 1996.

41. Xie Qingkui, et al., *Xian Zhengfu Guanli,* pp. 85–89.

42. Zhang Anqing and Li Hezhong, "A Study."

43. Ibid. Citizens ranked them in this order: The Party committee was number one (*lao da*); the government number two (*lao'er*); the people's congress number three (*lao san*); the CPPCC number four (*lao si*) (au. int).

44. Li Zhuxing, "The Voting System."

45. Some historical comparisons may be useful to appreciate the changes in LPCs' role in policymaking in relation to Party apparatus. For the functions and status of LPCs during the Mao period, see Townsend, *Political Participation,* ch. 5; Barnett, *Cadres,* part 2.

46. For example, in West Germany from 1983 to 1987, 70 percent of the laws were proposed by the government. In Britain over 95 percent of the bills proposed by the executive are adopted and 82 percent of all laws are initiated by the government. In the Fifth French Republic, 95 percent of the laws are government bills. Mény, *Government and Politics,* pp. 196–197.

47. Ibid., p. 193.

48. Without question this three-cornered, consensus-oriented lawmaking process also existed at the central level. As Tanner's research shows, the central lawmaking activities during Deng's regime, in contrast to those of the late Maoist period, were influenced by "a strong norm of incorporating all or most of the major concerned parties during the early stages of drafting." Tanner, "How a Bill Becomes a Law."

49. This issue is briefly addressed by Benewick in his "Political Institutionalisation." According to Benewick, the economic reforms encouraged the formation of interest groups at local and basic levels of government that would seek to promote their interests through the people's congress. When explaining why they turned to an institution "whose effectiveness is no match for the Party," he argues that it was likely because the "majority of delegates are expected to participate as part of their Party careers." Although this might have been true during the 1980s, the strength of LPCs no

longer derives to the same extent from the Party influence. In any case, in the 1990s group interests and their articulation and representation in China increasingly took on forms and channels differing from the more traditional ones discussed in great length in Falkenheim, ed., *Citizens and Groups.*

50. Liu Hailiang, ed., *Zhongguo Difang Fazhi Jianshe,* pp. 307–308.

51. This demand was seldom publicly or explicitly mentioned. A most definite expression appeared in a speech of November 30, 1987, by Chen Pixian, vice chair of the NPCSC and a Politburo member. But the word he used, *tongbao* (report), was very ambiguous regarding whether or not Party committee approval was required. He stressed that though the Party committee should "lead" the congress, the latter was "not subordinate" to the former. QRCBY, ed., *Zhonghua Renmin Gongheguo,* pp. 612–614.

52. Jiang's speech on December 29, 1989 (*RMRB,* July 1, 1990). But the message from the Party center was not always clear and uniform. In a manual endorsed by the second-ranking NPC leader and Politburo member, Tian Jiyun, two points were stressed: (1) the Party committee could not issue directives to the people's congress of the same level, and (2) the SCPC Party group could not "instruct" the SCPC to do anything; that is, the SCPC was not under the "leadership" of its Party group. See Wu Changqi and Chen Jiyu, eds., *Difang Renda Zhidu,* pp. 10–11.

53. This was the case in Leshan and Deyang, Sichuan Province. See Yin Zhijun, "Strengthen the Effects of the People's Congress Work" and Yan Rugao, "Seriously Do the Duties and Keep Promoting the People's Congress Work" (both authors were municipal SCPC chairmen), in Li Shenkuan, ed., *Qianjin Zhongde Shiji Renda,* pp. 96–106, 127–141.

54. See Feng Xianzuo, "The Practice and Thinking of Municipal-level People's Congress Work," in ibid., pp. 68–81.

55. A study by O'Brien and Luehrmann suggests otherwise. They found that when local Party committees faced opposition from the legislature, they could successfully mobilize their intra-Party superiors against their opponents. O'Brien and Luehrmann, "Institutionalizing Chinese Legislatures." I would think of this as one of regional differences rather than a prevailing pattern.

56. A major legal journal pointed out that more votes against Party-government proposals or nominees in the legislature "reflect the higher degree of democracy." This kind of publicized praise seemed to reflect an embarrassing position of the central decisionmakers, who attempted to use negative votes in congresses to serve propaganda purposes while fearful of losing control. See Shen Jiali, et al., "Re-create Brightness." As McCormick persuasively argues (though it was not entirely so in the Chinese case), the hypocrisy inherent in the communist claims of more advanced democracy could be a costly political liability, because "citizens could criticize and reject the Leninist state in the name of its own ostensible values." McCormick, "China's Leninist Parliament."

57. Unlike the practice in Western democracies, where the votes of members of parliament are made known to the public to highlight their accountability to their constituencies, the secret ballot was adopted in China's local congresses in both elections and, according to an official source, votes on any bills or policy proposals. Liu Hailiang, ed., *Zhongguo Difang Fazhi Jianshe,* p. 217. But my interviews suggest that this was not a uniform pattern. At least in Wuxi up to 1997, deputies still voted on bills by raising their hands.

58. Mezey, *Comparative Legislatures,* chs. 2, 7. Mezey uses this term to describe the legislatures under dictatorial regimes. He argues that this type of legislature can neither reject nor amend policy proposals put before it: "Situations seldom arise when

executive-centered elites are compelled to deal with or to accept dissenting views articulated in legislative arenas" (pp. 42, 132).

59. Cai Dingjian, "Are China's?"

60. QRCBY, ed., *Renmin Daibiao Dahui Zhidu Jianshe Sishinian*, p. 216. If the people's congress thought inappropriate any laws and regulations enacted by its standing committee, it was constitutionally empowered to revise or cancel them.

61. Liu Hailiang, ed., *Zhongguo Difang Fazhi Jianshe*, p. 12.

62. Zhang Yongtao, et al., "An Investigation Report on the Jiangsu Provincial SCPC," in Zhao Baoxu, ed., *Minzhu Zhengzhi*, pp. 45–69.

63. In December 1989 I interviewed a deputy of the Wuxi municipal congress, a renowned physician. He and fellow physicians in the legislature proposed several bills concerning local sanitation statutes. As he told it, in an effort to show a sense of responsibility, many intellectual deputies were enthusiastic about proposing bills in their professional fields. But there was a common feeling that people's deputies in general (the SCPC in particular) paid more attention to government bills. In the municipal congress of Chengdu (Sichuan), the number of bills proposed jointly by ten or more deputies (a requirement for proposing bills in the organic law, article 18) at recent annual sessions was large, sometimes as many as 200. But the SCPC treated most of them as just suggestions, criticisms, and opinions and refused to place them on the lawmaking agenda. The deputies bitterly resented this "neglect of their initiative." Duan Weiyi, "Accelerate Lawmaking and Promote Socioeconomic Development," in Hangzhoushi Renda, ed., *Zhongxin Chengshi Renda Gongzuo de Xinjinzhan*, pp. 17–28.

64. Local policymaking functions used to be very weak. Until the early 1980s, as McCormick argues, the primary role of the people's congress system was "the mobilizing of lower levels to implement decisions made at higher levels." See McCormick, "Leninist Implementation." But starting in 1987, as local authorities acquired more autonomy, much of the policymaking for the affairs of a given administrative level was delegated to the local government of that level. Also, within the limits permitted by the general guidelines, local policy was no longer a simplistic imitation of the decisions taken by the higher levels.

65. Li Shenkuan, ed., *Qianjin Zhongde Shiji Renda*, p. 187.

66. In my fieldwork in China, this was a delicate topic of inquiry because it involved highly sensitive interinstitutional and personal relations. The Party committee and government were usually disgusted with efforts to publicize the legislature's veto of their proposals. As one congressional official put it, the legislature's boasts about its use of veto power would erode the base of continuous cooperation between it and the Party-government.

67. QRCBY, ed., *Difang Renda shi Zenyang Xingshi Zhiquande*, pp. 128–129.

68. QRCBY, ed., *Difang Renda Xingshi Zhiquan Shili Xuanbian*, pp. 92–93. Similar cases were also widely reported in *FZRB*.

69. *FZRB*, March 6, 1997.

70. Liang Yubei, "On the Supervision of the Government, Court and Procuratorate by LPCs," in QRCBY, ed., *Lun Renda Jiqi Changweihui*, pp. 139–148.

71. Cao Qirui, Huang Shixiao, and Guo Dacai, eds., *Difang Renda Daibiao shi Zenyang Kaizhan Gongzuo De*, part 1; QRCBY, ed., *Difang Renda Xingshi Zhiquan Shili Xuanbian*, parts 2 and 3. In some areas deputies tended to vie with one another in attacking the government and carefully recorded the number of criticisms they made. From his first election as a Jiangsu provincial deputy in 1983 to 1996, Zhu Siming alleged that he submitted as many as 631 criticisms, suggestions, and opinions and proposed more than thirty bills. He was selected by reporters as the "national champion"

in that regard. Zhu Siming, "How to Be a Good People's Deputy." Presumably because he had hard evidence of his "strong sense of responsibility" and competence, his career as deputy was unusually long.

72. Li Zhen, "Equip the Minds with the Party's Basic Theory" (the author was former head of the Shandong provincial SCPC), in Yang Fengchun, ed., *Zai Shengji Renda*, pp. 278–295.

73. QRCBY, ed., *Difang Renda shi Zenyang Xingshi Zhiquande*, pp. 120–122.

74. For example, there were forty-six items on the agenda of the Hubei provincial SCPC session in 1987. Among them, thirty (65 percent) involved listening to and examining the reports submitted by the government departments. The proportion was even larger at the county level. Zhu Geng, "On Some Issues."

75. The proceedings (*hui kan*) of the standing committee of the tenth municipal people's congress of Wuxi, nos. 8–9, printed on April 20, 1989.

76. Wu Changqi and Chen Jiyu, eds., *Difang Renda Zhidu*, p. 11. In a few LPCs, the secretary of the Party committee at the same level or his deputy concurrently held the SCPC chair, but his office was usually located in the Party committee building rather than in the SCPC building, an indication of which post took priority.

77. The official source indicated that this was the common arrangement of local power relations after the late 1980s. Not a few people thought such an arrangement inappropriate. There had been four suggestions regarding the adjustment of relations of personnel between the Party committee and the congress: The SCPC chair should simultaneously be (1) a member of the standing committee of the Party committee, (2) the first deputy Party secretary, or (3) the Party secretary, or (4) the SCPC chair should be held by the Party secretary, and all the members of the standing committee of the Party committee—except those who held government office—should be nominated as candidates for SCPC membership. If they failed to be elected, they should quit the standing committee of the Party committee. All these suggestions aimed at using the Party's prestige to enhance congressional clout over legislation, policymaking, and supervision. See Wu Wentai, "Some Issues."

78. How much the SCPC chair would be respected at the meetings of the standing committee of the Party committee hinged upon his own qualifications and prestige. Take Wuxi as an example. Wu Zhao held the municipal SCPC chair for an exceptional three terms (1986–1998). He maintained amicable relations with and was highly respected by the Party cadres and government officials. Part of the reason was that he joined the communist revolution much earlier and had an excellent work record (au. int.).

79. Very often, particularly when he felt despised or bullied by Party cadres, an SCPC chair's perception that he had no weight at the meetings of the standing committee of the Party committee would spur him to take a hostile stand. He was well aware that if he complained to his colleagues in the congress that he, as congressional leader, was not respected, more negative votes would follow. Sometimes the divergence on policy proposals on the part of the congress was nothing more than an expression of negative personal sentiments (au. int.).

80. For example, in the administrative districts and counties under the jurisdiction of the Shanghai municipal authorities, 60–70 percent of the SCPC members and 80–90 percent of the SCPC chairs and vice chairs were former Party cadres or government officials. Sun Chao and Xu Xianghua, "Eliminate."

81. Peng Zhen made it clear in the 1983 election that many former regional and local Party and government leaders retired into SCPCs because they were too old for the strenuous routine Party-government affairs. Peng Zhen, *Lun Xinshiqi*, pp. 199–200. But a survey conducted in four counties of Guangdong indicated that there

were also some congressional leaders who were virtually squeezed out of the Party committees and governments against their own will. In other words, they entered the SCPCs as a consequence of the failure in power struggle. Liang Yukai, Liu Yuelun, and Li Shaoxing, "A Report on Further Improvement of the Functions and Organizations of County-level SCPCs," in Zhao Baoxu, ed., *Minzhu Zhengzhi*, pp. 150–165.

82. The tendency of many congressional leaders (SCPC members) to shirk their duties might be seen from a quantitative analysis of the attendance rate of the sessions of fifteen provincial SCPCs from 1980 to 1986. The absence rate at these sessions was as high as 30–39 percent. The percentage of those who made speeches at the sessions of some local SCPCs was only 50 to 60. Some SCPC members never spoke during their three to five years in office. Sun Chao and Xu Xianghua, "A Thought." The inadequacy of the staff size of the local SCPC also added to the difficulties in performing its functions. In Hebei in each of the county-level SCPCs, there were only seventeen or eighteen staff members. Among them were six or seven SCPC chairs and vice chairs and two or three chauffeurs, typists, and accountants. Very few people were left to do routine SCPC work. In a county there were just eight SCPC staff members. They included one chair, five vice chairs, and one driver, who escorted the chair and vice chairs to the hospital. Wang Feng and Zhao Shuhuai, "Some Problems with the Supervisory Function," in QRCBY, ed., *Lun Renda Jiqi Changweihui*, pp. 183–191.

83. For example, Liu Fusheng was fifty-six when he was elected chair of Hunan provincial SCPC in 1988. At the age of forty-six, Du Qinglin took over the chair of Hainan provincial SCPC in 1993. Yang Fengchun, ed., *Zai Shengji Renda*, pp. 330, 388.

84. Li Shenkuan, ed., *Qianjin Zhongde Shiji Renda*.

85. For government chiefs, including the premier, the legal maximum number of terms is two (amounting to ten years). At subcentral levels, government chiefs held only one term in most cases. The lower the administrative level, the more frequent the change of government chiefs. In Hailongjiang and Sichuan Provinces, half of the township government heads could not even complete one term. Cai Dingjian, Gao Guozheng, and Chen Hanlan, "A Study of the Terms of County- and Township-level People's Congresses and Governments," in QRCBY, ed., *Renmin Daibiao Dahui Zhidu Luncong*, pp. 206–209. There are no definite written stipulations for term limits of Party posts. It was not very common, though, for Party chiefs to remain in their posts for more than five years after 1978. It seems that no uniform rules have been followed for frequent changes in the posts of Party cadres—some retired, some were transferred to another area, and some were promoted to the next higher level.

86. QRCBY, ed., *Difang Renda shi Zenyang Xingshi Zhiquande*, p. 297.

87. Tian's speech to the Guangdong delegation of NPC deputies on March 16, 1995, in *QB*, March 17, 1995, p. 5.

88. Wan Li, chairman of the seventh NPC (1988–1993), was a senior Politburo member and Deng's protégé. Qiao Shi, who presided over the eighth NPC (1993–1998), ranked third in the Politburo standing committee. In the 1998 election, the second highest Party leader and former premier, Li Peng, took the top NPC post.

89. A good example was Du Qinglin, who was promoted in February 1998 from the chair of the Hainan provincial SCPC to the post of the provincial Party secretary, widely considered the first leader in a province.

90. The cooperation between the Party apparatus and the legislature in the 1990s differed from that during the early development of people's congresses, whose success, as O'Brien argues, "hinged on minimizing conflict with party committees and other executive organs." See O'Brien, "Chinese People's Congresses." But even throughout the 1980s, LPCs actually never depended on Party committees to thrive. In

that regard, I do not entirely accept O'Brien's argument that relations between the executive (Party-government) and legislature had a positive-sum nature during that period. Instead, my findings suggest that Party committees never welcomed but just tolerated a stronger legislative role. This tolerance had to be understood in light of the differences on reform between Party leaders and cadres.

91. For a more detailed discussion of the "honorary deputies" in congresses, see O'Brien and Li, "Chinese Political Reform."

92. Under pressure from deputies and also as a gesture of respect, each deputy is issued an identification card, whose utility was greatly enhanced during the 1990s. By showing their cards, deputies can enjoy many privileges. For example, they can visit an enterprise or any workplace to inquire into anything relevant and expect to be entertained by workplace heads, who either hope they will help secure special favor from the government or at least not be troublemakers (au. int.).

93. It may be interesting to compare China's three-cornered relations with those in communist Eastern Europe and the former Soviet Union. Some studies show that in the latter the influence of representative institutions over policy implementation by the state apparatus "appears to have increased substantially." Unlike the Chinese case, however, this legislative "oversight" (not exactly supervision) was used by the Party apparatus as a means to control the bureaucracy. See Welsh, "The Status of Research."

94. To have such a high-ranking official removed from his position by deputies was very unusual indeed in a communist context. On May 5, 1989, at a session of the seventh Hunan provincial congress, the deputies complained about the inadequate punishment some state-run companies had received for corruption. The congressional presidium asked Yang Huiquan, who was in charge of this matter, to respond to the deputies' inquiries. His response failed to satisfy the deputies and in fact impressed them with his "incompetence and dishonesty." At the same time, some deputies exposed Yang's own corruption. This charge, combined with the deputies' disgust with him, stirred up bitter sentiments against him, and 177 deputies jointly proposed his dismissal. Since the case involved a vice governor, the congressional presidium suggested that a committee be formed to investigate the alleged corruption before any further action was taken. The presidium also reported the case to the NPC and asked for its "opinions." But the NPC's response (which should have involved consultation with the Politburo, given the political gravity of the case) was favorable to the deputies' initiative, suggesting that its handling depended on the majority of the deputies. It turned out that the deputies vetoed the presidium's proposal to investigate in a first vote. In a second vote by secret ballot, with 506 pros versus 162 cons and 98 abstentions, Yang was recalled. Then the presidium officially announced Yang's dismissal. See "Report on the Dismissal." Ironically, the process of recalling Yang, though perhaps democratic, appeared hasty and flawed to outsiders. One criticized the deputies for abuse of power. Citing the recall proposal, which used phrases such as "it is said" and "be suspected of," the critic charged that the recall of Yang was essentially based on rumors. But the officials refuted this doubt as a "lack of deep understanding of the laws." See Huang Zexiao, "Objection"; Xiang Ping, "Legal Recall."

95. Cao Qirui, Huang Shixiao, and Guo Dacai, eds., *Difang Renda Daibiao,* pp. 54–55. The local organic law (article 39) empowers the SCPC, when the people's congress is not in session, to recall officials who rank under government chiefs, such as vice governors and deputy mayors.

96. Over forty cases of this kind are reported in Cao Qirui, Huang Shixiao, and Guo Dacai, eds., *Difang Renda Daibiao;* QRCBY, ed., *Difang Renda Xingshi Zhiquan Shili Xuanbian;* and QRCBY, ed., *Difang Renda shi Zenyang Xingshi Zhiquande.*

97. This was a highly publicized case and was reported by several influential central newspapers, such as *FZRB, JJRB,* and *GMRB.* Yan Yueming was director of a municipal government bureau and also a deputy of the municipal congress in Loudi, Hunan Province. In other words, he could be regarded as a local senior official. In April 1992 Yan, seconded by twenty-three deputies, proposed a bill to dismiss the mayor, Zhao Bodong. Although the whole process conformed perfectly to legal procedures, Yan was soon after detained by the judicial organ (on Zhao's order) on the charge of "corruption." Yan appealed directly to the Party center. The Politburo instructed the Hunan provincial Party committee to handle the case, but in the end the committee "failed to uphold justice." Zhong Xingzhi, "Cries."

98. Wang Rensheng, "Some Measures We Adopt to Strengthen the Supervisory Function" and Lu Jianguo, "Improve the Quality of the Supervisory Work," both in Hangzhoushi Renda, ed., *Zhongxin Chengshi Renda,* pp. 66–75, 76–86.

99. *FZRB,* March 6, 1997. It was reported that the relevant "evidence" concerning officials' performance came mainly from comments by citizens. In Zhuhai (Guangdong) the municipal SCPC allegedly invited ordinary voters to listen to and grade the officials' self-evaluations. Li Nanhua, "Appraisal."

100. Two cases, one in Hunan and another in Guangdong, were quoted in *FZRB,* presumably as a warning to government officials. *FZRB,* May 29, 1997, p. 6; March 13, 1997, p. 1.

101. *FZRB,* May 29, 1997, p. 6.

102. This pattern was adopted nationwide after Wan Li, the chair of the seventh NPCSC, demanded in a speech of December 1991 that people's congresses place equal emphasis upon law formulation and implementation. *FZRB,* April 10, 1997.

103. Ibid.

104. But a weak aspect of local legislative supervision regarded the budget. In Western democracies the crucial step in the development of parliaments was gaining control over the budget. The U.S. Congress is so powerful mainly because it holds the purse strings. A study indicates that although the NPC was relatively effective in that regard, the government budget at local levels was almost out of the legislature's control: Approval was a formality and there was no follow-up check on its implementation. And this constituted one of the major sources of corruption. Cai Dingjian, "The Legislative Supervision."

105. Cheng Xiangqing, "We Must Summarize the Experience." Cheng was a senior official in the NPCSC staff, and he recommended *fulü jiandushu* as a model for all LPCs to follow.

106. QRCBY, ed., *Difang Renda Xingshi Zhiquan Shili Xuanbian,* pp. 293–294. Presumably because of this threat to government officials, they invited deputies to implement laws jointly in some areas. In Taiyuan (Shanxi) a government bureau appointed nineteen municipal people's deputies as "supervisors" so that responsibility for any "mistakes" would be shared. Hu Manhong and Zhang Hong, "To Accept the Supervision."

107. *FZRB,* May 11, 1997. The question here is only whether or not that director should be dismissed from office. What role should LPCs play if government officials commit crimes? There has been much controversy over this issue in both theory and practice. Theoretically, legislative supervision in China should cover all judicial departments. But some legal experts thought that LPC oversight of the judiciary could not involve concrete cases because it would impede "judicial independence." Others favored legislative involvement. Wang Youqun, "Can LPCs Supervise Concrete (Legal) Cases?"

108. Wang Rensheng, "Some Measures."

109. Qingdaoshi Renda Changweihui (the Qingdao municipal SCPC), "Let Us Do the People's Congress Work Well in the New Period," in Hangzhoushi Renda, ed., *Zhongxin Chengshi Renda,* pp. 135–144.

110. QRCBY, ed., *Difang Renda Xingshi Zhiquan Shili Xuanbian,* pp. 292–294.

111. Cao Qirui, Huang Shixiao, and Guo Dacai, eds., *Difang Renda Daibiao,* pp. 75–76.

112. There was one county Party secretary who had to go study in a Party school for a period. During his leave of absence, he let the government head, who was also a deputy Party secretary, preside over the county Party committee. This government head made use of his status as acting Party chief to do government work. He described his experience this way: "As the Party chief, I can work unrestrainedly. But as the government chief, I always feel impeded and tied up [by the people's congress]." Zhang Anqing and Li Hezhong, "A Study."

113. Cao Wenguang, "Understand the Status Quo."

114. *FZRB,* March 12, 1997.

115. Of course a historical comparative approach is helpful. The "disrespect" here was not measured by past standards but by the claimed legal authority of LPCs. Even such "disrespect," then, represented a sort of progress, let alone the fact that the behavior is often publicly condemned.

116. Zhou Runhong, "Let LPCs Exercise."

117. Zhu Geng, "On Some Issues."

118. Wuhanshi Renda Changweihui Yanjiushi (Research Institute of the Wuhan Municipal SCPC), "Strive Hard to Build Up an Authoritative Local Organ of State Power," in Zhao Baoxu, ed., *Minzhu Zhengzhi,* pp. 113–137.

119. "Elderly gentleman" referred to "respectability," "grand billboard" authoritative appearance, and "empty skeleton" no actual power. See Wu Wentai, "Can People's Congresses and Their Standing Committees Supervise Party Organizations?" in QRCBY, ed., *Lun Renda Jiqi Changweihui,* pp. 114–125. But among those voters who thought lightly of the people's congress, many reportedly had a "misunderstanding" of its functions. They believed that it would be more helpful to look directly for government officials if they met with any problems. These officials were in a position to solve the problems "efficiently and immediately." *MB,* January 4, 1998, p. A6.

120. Tian Jiyun blamed many local congresses for their lack of courage (to stand up to Party committees). He mentioned the "problems" with congressional leaders who could not accept "more progressive ideas" and had a weak sense of the rule of law. *ZYRB,* March 17, 1995, p. 4.

121. Diao Zhenfei and Zhou Qingnian, "An Investigation on People's Congresses," in Zhao Baoxu, ed., *Minzhu Zhengzhi,* pp. 138–150.

122. Jiao Shijia, "On the Improvement of the Functions of LPCs," in ibid., pp. 310–324.

123. When Morris K. Udall summarized his experience as a U.S. congressman, he argued that a congressman is not only a legislator but "also an employment agent, passport finder, constituent greeter, tourist agent. . . . His typical day will be far more concerned with these problems than with national defense, foreign aid, or appropriations for public works." Tacheron and Udall, *The Job of the Congressman,* ch. 3.

124. Of course there has been a countertendency in that regard. As O'Brien and Luehrmann suggest, some congressional leaders and deputies perceived the strengthening of ties with superiors—legislatures at higher levels and other established authorities—to be more important than strengthening ties with constituents, because the former could help protect a legislature's jurisdiction and increase its capacity. See

O'Brien, "Chinese People's Congresses"; O'Brien and Luehrmann, "Institutionalizing Chinese Legislatures." Although this observation is quite true, making the legislature more representative or responsive did not always contradict the goal of increasing its institutional capacity. I would argue that the popular base of the legislature could be its greatest asset if leaders and deputies would learn how to play the power game in the era of reform. All in all, it depends upon regional conditions.

125. Cao Qirui, Huang Shixiao, and Guo Dacai, eds., *Difang Renda Daibiao,* pp. 193–221.

126. For a discussion of the double role of deputies during the Deng period and its strain, see O'Brien, "Agents and Remonstrators."

127. See Feng Weitian, "They Are Worthy of the Envoys."

128. *FZRB,* March 12, 1997.

129. See Burns, "China's Governance."

130. Cai Dingjian, "Are China's?" A recent case would support this argument. At the first ninth NPC session, a number of citizens traveled to Beijing to appeal to NPC deputies to solve their local problems. They made the same attempt when the fifteenth Party congress convened in October 1997. After they were ignored, they reportedly placed their hopes on the national legislature. *MB,* March 3, 1998, p. A15.

131. Cai Dingjian, "Are China's?"

132. As far as political awareness or political cultural tradition is concerned, Chinese citizens obviously differ from their Western counterparts. But it may be improper to exaggerate such differences. As Schumpeter describes it, what typical citizens (in the West) really care about are family and job rather than national and international affairs that lack a direct and unmistakable link with those private concerns. See Schumpeter, *Capitalism,* p. 261. I would agree with Nathan and Shi, who contend that when compared to residents of some long-established democracies, the Chinese population scored lower on the variables that contribute to democracy, "but not so low as to justify the conclusion that democracy is out of reach." Nathan and Shi, "Cultural Requisites."

8

Conclusion: A Constitutional Path to Democracy?

Since the 1970s three forces interacted with one another to determine the route of China's political reform: the central elite, local Party cadres, and the subordinate population. Under Mao the border between the Party and the people was clear-cut, and the CCP, as the sole hegemonic party, maintained totalitarian control over Chinese society through its organizations at all levels. With the exception of a brief period during the Cultural Revolution in which Mao used students and workers as tools against his intra-Party rivals and their local followers, the role of local cadres as devoted agents of the Party center remained unquestionable. During most of the Mao years, endless conflicts over policy and power among central leaders never shook the foundation of vertical Party unity vis-à-vis what the regime referred to with contempt as *qunzhong* (the masses).

After Deng Xiaoping emerged as the paramount leader and expelled Maoists from the center of national power at the end of the 1970s, intra-Party relations underwent a significant transformation. Although the central leadership seemed to enter a more harmonious than antagonistic period, Party disunity was developing along a vertical dimension, originally as a legacy of the Cultural Revolution. The economic reform caused further alienation between Party leaders and cadres and tended to disintegrate the Party as a monolithic political organizational force. In fact, this tendency was little more than the logical development of the contradictions inherent in the Party-sponsored reform. When Deng launched his reforms, he found himself in an enormous dilemma. In the face of the rising social protest against economic stagnation resulting essentially from the inefficiency of central planning, market-oriented reform was necessary to generate public support for the regime. But to the extent it could make any real progress, this reform required a change in the system and hence had to hurt Party cadres who benefited from the status quo. Deng could afford to abandon neither Party cadres nor reform. To get out of this dilemma and mainly to overcome the opposition to reform from Party cadres, the central elite attempted to create a countervailing institutional force, not to replace Party apparatus but to supervise and constrain them through some structural means of checks and balances. This restructuring of political power was aimed to compel Party cadres, well entrenched in Party apparatus, faithfully to carry out the central reform programs against their own preferences. To make the new system operational and efficacious, the Party center managed to bring in a certain degree of citizen participation and representation.

Increasing Citizen Representation and Decay of Party Influence

The structural problem created by the market reform turned out to be the main dynamics of the (second-stage) political reform that took on some democratic features by increasing popular influence over the governmental process. As we have seen in the previous chapters, the restructuring of relations of authority started earliest in industrial enterprises. The elections of enterprise chiefs, the revival of the workers' congress and its share of decisionmaking power, and the director's assumption of supreme authority together squeezed professional Party cadres and Party committees out of management in a large number of state-owned enterprises. At government levels the political reform—after a seven-year hiatus and extant basically on paper only—was once again jump-started in 1986 when it became increasingly obvious that the economic reform had reached a political structural impasse. Widespread Party cadre resistance to the leadership's efforts to overhaul the economic structure highlighted the nature of the communist system as fusing politics and economics, such that partial reform could not go far. The stalemate of economic reform strengthened the determination of the central decisionmakers to destroy the overconcentration of power in (local) Party apparatus, a goal that Deng pledged as early as 1980 but failed to attain.

The major political reform measures, which were finalized at the thirteenth Party congress of 1987 and thereafter enforced across the country, transformed China's structure of government and shaped a new triangular relationship of power quite unusual for a communist state. Two key institutional changes came about because of the reform: the separation of the Party from government and the enlarged legislative authority. Specifically, the Party committee at all government levels (the relevant organ at the center was the Party Secretariat) was legally removed from the process of policy execution, a profitable function it traditionally performed and monopolized. Its "legitimate" authority was limited to the exercise of highly abstract "political leadership," as well as the making of policy proposals on "important" issues. Correspondingly, the government grew out of its status as a sheer Party appendage and was established in many areas as a genuine executive body with a certain amount of autonomy in its handling of government affairs. Related to this development, the legislature became a decisionmaking organ, potentially on an equal footing with the Party committee, and in many areas played a powerful supervisory role in policy implementation. What added some democratic elements to this three-cornered policy process was more substantial popular impact upon elections of people's deputies and government officials. Stated in brief, the new institutional arrangement went beyond an intra-Party system of checks and balances. Party power began to feel the structural constraints of people power.

Legislative authority is not perfect but is the only feasible measure to gauge the political magnitude of citizen participation and representation in the Chinese context. In many aspects the importance in the Chinese power structure of the legislature (i.e., the people's congress) at all administrative levels has exceeded its counterparts in the former Soviet Union and communist Eastern Europe in terms of both power-related functions and representativeness. Many scholars hold a low opinion of communist legislatures, dismissing them as mere rubber stamps.[1] But since the 1970s, people's congresses in China have moved away from the typical communist legislative pattern. In many regions the legislature rejected Party nominees for government offices and parliamentary seats and vetoed bills drafted by Party apparatus. Critical inquiries and harsh comments have become the rule among deputies, who increasingly tend to use challenges to prove their sense of responsibility, competence in governance, and commitment to a better government.

And as more and more government officials were penalized or recalled by congresses with or without the Party committee's endorsement, the government became accountable not just to the Party committee but also to the legislature. Given the inherent structural connections between the Party committee and the government, any legislative veto of government proposals or any reprimand of government officials represented an implicit challenge to the Party committee. Since the government served as a buffer between the Party apparatus and the legislature, the legislative supervision of government could proceed in a way that kept its damage to the Party's hegemonic appearance to a minimum. Thus, if one uses Deng's own criteria and purposes to evaluate the consequences of political reform, it seems to be a remarkable success.

But this success by no means suggests that Deng and his fellow leaders could completely control the consequences of the reform process, particularly its long-term impact on party leadership. Compared with the pre-1978 Party cadre monopoly of power at every level, the decline of Party hegemony in almost all aspects of Chinese society was a prominent feature of Chinese politics in the reform years. But the democratic significance of the structural aspects of this decline—embodied foremost in the expanded authority and strengthened institutional muscle of increasingly recalcitrant people's congresses—far exceeds that of the loosened Party control over individual socioeconomic activities. Indeed, Party apparatus and professional Party cadres, particularly at the grassroots and lower government levels, had some substantial disadvantages in this reorganization of power relations. They were the main supporting materials of the old system to be transformed, and any efforts on their part to hold on to power with the excuse of maintaining political leadership ran a risk of being interpreted as opposition to reform and an attempt to restore the overconcentration of power that was indicated as one of the sources of past Party failures. As old problems causing alienation between Party leaders and cadres faded away, new ones emerged. One was political corruption, which has grown almost out of control in recent years. In a word, the lingering central distrust of local cadres dampened the latter's hope for the reinstatement of their past hegemony.

In our assessment of China's prospects for a democratic transition based on the restructuring of authority, a major challenge is properly evaluating the citizens' role. Without question, for all the Party sponsorship of reform, citizen initiative has not been irrelevant to or completely absent in the enlargement of legislative authority and its enhanced representativeness. Employees' participation in workplace democratization was passionate from the very beginning. At government levels the general citizen indifference to congressional activities of the early 1980s was gradually replaced by a fresh political awareness and subsequent yearning for the protection of their legitimate civil rights that led to a surge of enthusiasm for participation in the elections of people's deputies—a key institutionalized channel through which ordinary citizens could bring their preferences to bear on the policy process. Also, through a reciprocal promotion mechanism, the popular initiative contributed to a more assertive exercise of the constitutionally conferred legislative authority. The intensified interactions between deputies and constituents provided another impetus to this process. The more strident voices in the legislature constitute an increasingly heavy pressure that the leadership has to confront, and it considerably narrows their policy options for future political development.

Nonetheless, we must not draw excessively optimistic conclusions. The bottom line of my discussions throughout this study is that for all the democratic achievements of China's political reform, it was by and large not a consequence of citizen initiative or growth of China's social democratic forces. Rather, it was to a larger extent a successful execution of the plans of Deng Xiaoping and his allies. In the first place, the political reform (which here refers exclusively to its second phase, after 1986) did not result as much from social pressure for political liberalization and democratization as from the leadership's own policy agenda, whose top priority was pushing through market reform. In that particular situation, political restructuring was not the only option, because the Party leadership could, like their predecessors in communist Eastern Europe and the Soviet Union during the 1960s, either slow down economic reform or revert to other measures that did not involve tinkering with the political structure. For that matter, one has to commend Deng for his resolve to carry through market reform, as well as his courage to pay a political price for it.

But Deng's freedom in choosing among the courses of action and his courage also suggested that he was in a rather secure position to control the entire reform process. With impressive political skills, he alternately played the "citizen card"—that is, the legislature as the "highest organ of state power"—and the "party (committee) leadership card" through a strategy of alignment, dealignment, and realignment among the three major relevant forces: the central leadership, local and grassroots cadres, and ordinary people. At local levels the leaders in Beijing attempted to work out a certain balance of power between the Party committee and the people's congress, ready to tip the scale to either side according to the situational needs. This divide-balance-control strategy that served to prevent either side from becoming arbitrary, despotic, and out of the center's control seems to have contributed substantially to the apparent success of China's market reform. It provides at least part of the explanation for why the Chinese regime succeeded where other socialist states failed.

Fundamental Limits of Reform Strategy

China's political and economic reforms alike are transitional, unstable, and subject to many unpredictable variables. It would be a fundamental mistake to think that the Chinese reform as it stands has escaped the logic of the communist system's fusion of politics and economics and created a new type of polity. Put another way, Deng was far from finding a final solution to the structural dilemma that mainly involved the status of Party apparatus and cadres in an increasingly complex society in which the growth of market forces and the capitalist mode of production had been rapidly destroying the economic foundation of China's existing political system.[2] As we have seen, although Deng was without doubt the original force driving political reform, he had been extremely cautious not to send any signals or permit any measures that might undermine the communist normative order. In his efforts to perpetuate the one-party system by repairing some of its structural "flaws," Deng placed strict limitations on the depth and breadth of political reform so that the "democratic" process would not diminish Party influence decisively. Despite all the "democratic" facades, therefore, there were very few, if any, competitions among the elites or organizations with differing ideologies, platforms, and political orientations. The articulation and pursuit of individual and group interests were sharply circumscribed and kept far from macropolitics. The supreme party leadership principle and the prohibition of political opposition placed even an assertive (local) congress in an inherently weak position in its potential confrontation with a Party apparatus. For that matter, the alignment between Party leaders and citizens (who had a certain representation in the legislature) had to take on a fragile and opportunistic, if not hypocritical quality.

Although the leadership's efforts to develop social support through reforms achieved some success, Deng could not fail to recognize, especially after Tiananmen, that Party cadres remained the mainstay of his regime. Thus, substantial power resources had to be left in the hands of Party cadres, selected by Party authorities and kept out of the reach of the mass public. The Party center needed this so-called organizational guarantee of party leadership to prevent mass participation from going beyond prescribed political and ideological limits. Among the power resources left at the disposal of Party apparatus, the crucial one was its considerable institutionalized influence over the election of government officials and congressional leaders and, to a lesser extent, people's deputies. In his report to the thirteenth Party congress, Zhao Ziyang said the most important function of Party committees was "to recommend cadres for key posts in local state organs." Presumably fearful that this function might not get enough public attention, a propaganda manual highlighted its significance and asserted that cadres/officials (as a tradition the two terms were often not clearly distinguished in China's political parlance) were a decisive factor in the implementation of the political line. "The Party must recommend its brilliant members to government posts. Through their activities in organs of state power, the Party line and policy will be executed."[3]

In theory the right to nominate candidates for chief government and congressional posts is shared equally by Party cadres and deputies. What is more, nominees must go through legal procedures and are subject to legislative ratification (competitive elections). But in reality these "democratic" mechanisms did not work to magnify the role of deputies to a significant degree in many areas. As indicated in Chapter 4, in practice the Party committee was usually the major nominator. And deputies tended either to underutilize their right to nominate or abuse it to make their nominees less electable. In contrast to its display of enthusiasm for the "democratic" election of people's deputies, the Party center never sincerely encouraged a larger legislative initiative in the elections and appointments of chief government officials. The organizational strength of the Party apparatus was reflected in the fact that most of the final candidates were Party nominees, and they were also more competitive, insofar as the election results showed, as compared with those spontaneously nominated by deputies. In most areas the method of exact-number election was adopted for chief government and congressional posts to ensure the election of Party nominees.

Party committee influence over appointments to cabinet posts was even greater than over the elections of government chiefs. Government chiefs usually did not have their own followers. After the Party-government separation, the government chief generally occupied the second place in the Party committee (i.e., first deputy Party secretary). To show Party organizations' superiority to governments on the personnel issue, the Party committee could submit candidates for cabinet posts in its own name directly to the SCPC for approval without even consulting elected government chiefs—though of course this was only symbolic, given a government chief's own Party position. This contrasted sharply with the policymaking procedures in which the proposals made by the Party committee had to be accepted by the government first and then submitted in the latter's name to the people's congress or SCPC.

Without question, legislative vetoes could produce disturbing results, but they could not undermine Party control significantly. First, compared with legislative approvals, the number of rejections was small after all. Second, the legislature, somewhat like the U.S. Congress, did not recommend candidates for cabinet posts; they just chose from among the Party nominees. In fact the legislative challenge to the candidacy of Party nominees could hardly be very strong because it was the prerogative of Party apparatus to examine the personal files of candidates. This Party prerogative is never explicitly stipulated but has been a common practice with the endorsement of the Party center. Known as *dang guan ganbu* (the Party controls cadres/officials), the principle embodied a typical tactic of the Party center that made organizational control a priority but took care not to let it damage the "democratic" appearance of reform.

The leadership's attempt to retain Party cadre clout over elections of officials and higher-level people's deputies was further exposed by its consistent refusal to extend direct elections from the county to higher levels, as well as to government officials. In state-owned enterprises, institutions, and so on, democratic election of directors, though a reality in many places, was never institutionalized or legally enforced. In such work units, local authorities were left to decide whether the heads should be freely elected or directly appointed.

Deng intended popular supervision to serve a quite limited purpose. For all the impressions reform may generate, Party cadres have never been placed under complete public control. Instead, with the antireform tendency of Party cadres constrained, Deng allowed them to remain strong enough to cope with any challenge to the regime. But the Deng regime could not play this balancing game indefinitely. Since a system of checks and balances without political opposition did not and could not work efficiently, it gave rise to widespread political corruption that triggered the Tiananmen prodemocracy movement in 1989 and for two reasons is likely to cause an even more profound regime crisis.

First, the appointment of Party cadres excludes citizen participation. Indeed since the late 1980s the Party machine itself has become more "democratic" in the sense that ordinary Party members have gained a greater say in the selection of Party cadres.[4] But the "democratization" has not gone far enough to allow Party members to decide the basic Party line or any major issues. Intra-Party grievances were illustrated by the large number of demonstrators with Party membership during April–June 1989 who did not think they could keep democratic control over the central decisionmaking. In any case, the elections of Party leaders and cadres were by and large the business of its members. After the separation of the Party from government, there were no direct institutional relationships between the Party committee and the people's congress. To supervise Party apparatus and cadres was not the "legitimate" responsibility of deputies. In theory Party cadres were subject only to intra-Party disciplinary supervision unless their conduct constituted a grave criminal offence. Second, since intra-Party procedures for the nomination of candidates for top government offices were not transparent, Party cadres had a good chance to recommend their cronies as candidates for profitable government offices in the name of the Party, regardless of the professional criteria and qualifications.[5] Given the legislature's inadequate capacity of looking into nominees' backgrounds and its general tendency to evade confrontation, the citizen role in that process was weak.

Political Corruption and China's Democratic Prospects

Given the prominence of the issue of political corruption in my discussion of China's democratic transition, it is not appropriate to relate it simply and solely to the lack of effective institutional supervision. Only through an examination of the deep historical, social, and structural roots of corruption in the Chinese context can we recognize the inherent limitations of political reform and see why corruption may become a catalyst for greater democratic transformation of the Chinese system.

Why Political Corruption Fails to Be Curbed

A variety of studies suggest that personalistic patron-client relationships characterize the sociopolitical structure of many peasant societies and also some industrial societies.[6] Clientelism is a particularly prominent feature of politics in the societies of Asia; China is certainly no exception.[7] In his comparative study of political corruption, James Scott shows how patron-client networks may easily bring about corrupt practice, especially in a nonelectoral system.[8] In China corruption is not just a consequence of patronage politics. It represents a somewhat "legitimate" bureaucratic tradition that was inherited during the Republican period (1911–1949) and culminated in the late 1940s.[9] It cost the Kuomintang regime popular support and contributed a great deal to the communist victory in 1949.

Political corruption was thus by no means a uniquely communist phenomenon in China. On the contrary, the CCP earned much credit during the 1950s and 1960s for its efforts in curbing cadre corruption.[10] During the post-Mao period, however, the intra-Party structural restraining mechanisms either decayed or malfunctioned with the dwindling Party role in the political-economic life and the loosened Party control over Chinese society. In China's transition from central planning to a market-oriented economy, Party cadres were "contaminated" by money worship that pervaded the whole society. Moreover, the transition generated the typical "politically oriented capitalism" that, according to Scott, involved the state's granting privileged opportunities for profit."[11]

After China's market reforms took off in urban areas in 1984, the transactions between power and wealth multiplied. What emerged was, to use Connie Meaney's words, not a true market but rather "a plethora of networks protected by cadres and bureaucrats, acting in secret."[12] As the Party machine lost its internal strength in curbing corruption, the one-party system displayed certain fundamental structural flaws. In the first place, there was no freedom of press to publicize corruption scandals, as it would tarnish the Party image.[13] Thus, in China many cases of corruption were exposed to the authorities not by public reports but by letters of accusation, many of which were written anonymously. They were addressed to Party committees, governments, and, increasingly, judicial organs and congresses.[14]

Prompted by these letters, teams set out to investigate the alleged corruption. Who undertook this task was critical. From some cases made known to the public, one feature stood out: People's congresses and deputies were excluded from investigations of the conduct of not only Party cadres but also government officials.[15] In one case the Party committee decided the removal of a government official from office. Judicial organs participated in the whole process but were hardly independent despite leaders' claims to the contrary and suggestions in academic works.[16] In practice, judicial offices—more often than government departments—asked Party committees for instructions in cases of corruption, especially if the cases implicated senior cadres or officials. In short, it was normally Party cadres who dominated investigations of alleged misconduct.

Such domination placed Party cadres in a position to (1) decide for themselves what kind of evidence was to be kept confidential and what exposed to the public or offered to congresses and (2) protect their clients if necessary or possible. Considering the intricate personal connections usually involved in the appointment of a cadre or official, very few cases of corruption could be treated in isolation. Most implicated numerous people, including the power-holders and those who joined the investigation team. The publicly exposed cases of corruption quite likely represented only the tip of an iceberg. Party cadres would think it in their best interest to protect their accused clients or patrons if they could, and if they couldn't, they isolated the cases and turned big problems into small ones. [17]

Can Corruption Be a Catalyst for Democratization?

I do not mean to imply that democratization will provide a panacea for over-coming political corruption. For all its apparent superiority, a democratic system is not a guarantee of the elimination of corruption.[18] But the above discussion is intended to suggest that the insufficient legislative clout over appointments of Party cadres and elections of government officials, as well as the Party apparatus's de facto monopoly of the right to investigate cadre and official misconduct, among other things, tends to place political corruption out of anybody's control. And it exposes the Achilles' heel of a one-party system that denies any partial solution. As the Tiananmen demonstration of 1989 best illustrates, rampant corruption could be handily turned into a highly ex-plosive issue and considerably enhance social pressure for political change.[19] Despite the endeavor by students and scholars (who constituted the minority of the demonstrators) to highlight human rights abuses, the issue of corruption was evidently the major focus of popular indignation. The students' skill-ful politicization of the corruption issue led many citizens, rightly or wrongly, to attribute inflation and the deterioration of their livelihoods to bureaucratic corruption, and hence drew numerous Beijing residents into the protest. "The issue of cadre corruption and privilege," as Meaney observes, "was probably the single most prominent issue uniting student demonstrators and the hun-dreds of thousands of Beijing residents who showed support for them."[20]

Aware of the dangerous political consequences of corruption, the leader-ship in Beijing attempted to cope with it by means of Party disciplinary ac-tions. After Tiananmen, Party leaders repeatedly stressed that the anticorrup-tion struggle would decide the life or death of the Party and state.[21] In July 1989 the Politburo launched a nationwide campaign to eliminate corruption.[22] In the five years up to January 1993, more than 730,000 Party members were charged with corruption, including 1,600 high-ranking Party cadres and 1,500 local cadres.[23] The efforts to strengthen intra-Party control, combined with the post-massacre anti-inflation policy and economic boom, did seem to produce some short-term positive effects. But so long as important power resources re-main in the hands of Party cadres whose selection had little or no popular base, it is almost impossible for the "cadres-check-cadres" mechanisms to work ef-fectively, particularly in the transitional stage of economy, as local Party orga-nizations are turning into corruptive political machines. In his report to the fifteenth Party congress in October 1997, Jiang Zemin acknowledged implicitly that the Party was losing the battle against corruption. He called anticorruption a "grave political struggle" that would determine the Party's fate.[24]

The failure to overcome corruption and its potential threat to the regime is compelling central decisionmakers to confront two difficult choices. They may choose to maintain the status quo—that is, to let great power resources remain at the disposal of Party cadres who are not only out of legislative control but cannot be effectively subjected to intra-Party surveillance—and wait for corruption to evolve into a profound sociopolitical crisis that will ultimately destroy the communist regime.[25] Or they may elevate citizen participation and representation to a higher level to place Party cadres under tighter public control. But this choice would unavoidably undermine the Party cadre capacity to defend the regime in case of a sociopolitical crisis, threatening the very foundation of Party hegemony. In either case, the Chinese system cannot be stabilized where it stands now. Stated another way, the economic and political reforms since the 1970s—for all their successes and achievements—have failed to get China's political system out of its fundamental structural dilemma.

*   *   *

It is difficult to determine a timetable for China's democratic transition based on the political development thus far, simply because of the many unpredictable variables. But the study of political reform may have landed us in a more satisfactory spot to predict how China is most likely to evolve in the years ahead. It is beyond dispute that the restructuring of political power in China has paved a path to a democratic form of government. And indeed China's political system has come a long way from the Maoist totalitarian rule to arrive almost at the last defensive line of a dictatorial regime. The one-party dictatorship has been considerably debilitated, the institutional changes having removed much of its foundation. The signs of the decline of Party hegemony in Chinese society actually came into view as early as 1989, when Party organizations and cadres in many regions were unable to dissuade the citizens under their jurisdiction from taking to the streets.

The past two decades also provided Chinese citizens with a training ground for democracy. Citizens became familiar with the representative, albeit not yet genuinely democratic, procedures and learned how to use legal rights to protect themselves. This learning process combined with a heightened degree of popular participation in the governmental process through institutionalized channels, or, more specifically, through the election of the people's representatives to congresses. To be sure, many citizens and their deputies have yet to take greater advantage of legislative mechanisms, and their expectations of a democratic system seem to remain modest, confined to day-to-day material gains rather than broader political and ideological issues. But this should not be a reason for pessimism, as popular demands are incremental by nature. Tiananmen shows that once citizens become aware that the civil rights to achieve what they desire are unavailable, they will call for changes in the political system.

Above all, China's reform strengthened representative institutions, the hallmark of democracy. Even in Western democracies, it took a long, long time to develop and legitimate such institutions. Thanks to the nature of the institutional progress, it would be difficult, if not impossible, to withdraw the political rights Chinese citizens have gained and exercised through legislative channels without placing the leadership's legitimacy in jeopardy.

The possibility of the people's congress emerging as a real democratic representative institution will depend on the overall democratization of China's political system. In this connection, two developments seem highly relevant. First, recent elections and legislative politics suggest that the vertical conflict within the Party has assumed a new dimension and is taking a more "dangerous" direction. Regional leaders and local cadres are learning to exploit "democratic elections" and the "respect" for the (local) popular will to defy the Party center in search of greater regional autonomy. The context of a more predominant market economy makes it increasingly critical for local authorities to protect parochial interests. As we have seen, this local protectionism has become the focus of recent central-local antagonism in national and provincial legislative politics. Although regionalism can in no way be associated with the issue of "bourgeois liberalism," it may serve to transform the legislature—the NPC in particular—into a more representative (of local interest) and more autonomous institution, and this development will create a political environment that favors the rise of political pluralism.

Second, market reform has transformed China's class structure and led to social stratification and polarization. There are signs that the people's congress may soon feel the impact caused by the diversification of social group or class interests. On the one hand, the rising entrepreneurial "middle" class is seeking representation in state organs to protect its newly acquired wealth and to influence government policy. Although the percentage of this new class in the population will perhaps remain very small, its wealth, as the democratic history of Western Europe manifests, will make its political influence disproportionally great. On the other hand, market reform has accelerated the socioeconomic polarization in which the losers and the deprived appeal for the egalitarian redistribution of wealth through state intervention. Thus, the relationship between rich and poor in Chinese society is taking on the quality of class conflict. The legislature is being turned into a battlefield not just for territorial interest but also for class interest. The societal restructuring would give the legislative representation political and ideological implications and provide a base for the formation of political opposition.

These developments in Chinese politics seem to augur well for a constitutional evolution toward democracy. But if Chinese democracy may be at hand and may offer a final solution to China's political dilemma, the Party center obviously still holds the key to the timing of democratization. The rise of territorial politics and class politics may not be taken as sufficient conditions for a democratic breakthrough. Other variables that would help determine the democratic process include the personalities and political orientations of Party leaders, how they evaluate the consequences of democratization and its lessons in the former Soviet Union and Eastern Europe, how they calculate the probability of a communist victory in a free election, and how strong their desire is to be accepted by the international community through democratic legitimacy. All these factors deserve further research.

Notes

1. "There were, and remain, strong indications that legislatures in most communist states do not legislate," Nelson observes. "Where they come closest, in Yugoslavia and Poland, their activities appear to have impact only at the periphery of 'rulemaking.'" See Nelson, "Editor's Introduction." Welsh also argues that other than in Yugoslavia, "examples of parliamentary rejection of party- or government-sponsored legislative proposals are almost non-existent." Welsh, "The Status of Research."

2. Though elaborated more than twenty years ago, Lowenthal's identification of a fourfold challenge to single-party regimes in the process of transition is still applicable to the Chinese case. The first challenge is how to adapt structurally and politically to the requirements of an efficient and rational industrial order. Lowenthal, "On 'Established' Communist Party Regimes."

3. Of course it did not forget to add that the Party must respect legal procedures: "We cannot substitute direct appointments for elections." Chen Yizi and Chen Jinfu (Bianxiezu), eds., *Zhengzhi*, p. 33.

4. Theoretically, even the masses could exert some influence. On January 28, 1986, the Central Committee announced some major principles for the appointments of Party cadres and demanded stringent adherence to them in practice. Among these principles was that the masses could nominate and recommend candidates by methods like the public opinion poll and secret ballot. "Under normal circumstances," it said, "the opinion of the majority [of the masses] should be respected. It is inappropriate to nominate those who fail to win support of the majority in their work units or regions." This suggestion was immediately qualified: "But the selection of candidates cannot be simply decided by how many votes they got from the masses." *RMRB*, February 2, 1986.

5. In fact Deng bore responsibility for this situation. In a 1980 speech he urged veteran cadres to pick their successors personally. He made it clear that the "primary task" of veteran cadres who were going to retire "is to help the Party organizations find worthy successors to work for our cause." Deng Xiaoping, *Selected Works,* pp. 302–325.

6. See Almond and Powell, *Comparative Politics,* ch. 8. "Typically," as they suggest, "these structures involved a diffuse pattern of exchange of goods and services between patrons and clients" (p. 203).

7. For a more detailed discussion, see Scott, "Patron-Client Politics"; Doronila, "The Transformation"; P. Cheng, "Political Clientelism."

8. See Scott, *Comparative Political Corruption,* chs. 3, 4. For one thing, as Scott suggests, seeking office for one's clients regardless of their qualifications is an integral part of patron-client loyalties. Clients tend to view the power and property associated with office as part of their personal domains—domains to be used in the pursuit of private and/or clique gain (pp. 44, 65).

9. As Moore argues, in any preindustrial society it was difficult to extract enough resources from the population to pay salaries to a large-scale bureaucracy. "The Chinese solution [to this problem] was to permit more or less open corruption." Moore, *Social Origins,* p. 172.

10. The Chinese system of the 1950s displayed some strength in controlling corruption. During that period the intra-Party supervisory system seemed to function effectively; severe punishment further deterred corruption. A highly centralized planning economy also provided cadres and officials with few opportunities for corruption.

11. Scott's study indicates a pattern of corruption common to Stuart England and many contemporary underdeveloped nations. During the period when commercial wealth had to depend on the favor and protection of government, the "capitalists" are often government officials because they are best placed to take advantage of the opportunities for profit-making. Other "capitalists" must seek patronage or favor from officials, mostly through bribery. See Scott, *Comparative Political Corruption,* chs. 3, 4.

12. "In particular, the dual economy of plan and market that emerged after the reforms greatly expanded opportunities for profiteering and speculation," Meaney comments. "Market reform left critical areas, notably prices, under state control. This created a kind of hybrid, two-track economy of plan and market, in which those with official connections could benefit from disparities in prices, inside information, and access to goods." See Meaney, "Market Reform," p. 126.

13. Liu Binyan, a prestigious Chinese journalist and currently a dissident in exile, was well known for reporting political corruption. Unfortunately, almost every report of his got him (and very often the publisher, too) into trouble. In most cases he was accused of "distorting or fabricating the facts." Moreover, these accusations were brought against him in the name of the local Party committee or the government. In an interview Liu acknowledged the enormous risks involved in publishing critical reports because these "offend some people's interests." According to Liu, many reporters lost their jobs and had to transfer to other professions after they wrote and published reports powerholders did not like. Jiang Yaochun, "Liu Binyan's Interview."

14. Obviously, the leadership preferred accusation letters to reveal corruption, presumably because this form avoided hurting the Party's image and left the authorities flexibility to handle the cases. Zhang Suofei, "Zhang Siqing Says."

15. Xing Shuliang, "The Decay of Power"; Ma Lin, "From Governor to Prisoner"; Zhu Xiangshan, "A Report."

16. The 1982 constitution provides that the heads of courts and procuratorial organs be elected by and responsible to their respective people's congresses (articles 62 and 101). In reality, however, congressional control over courts and procuratorial organs was even weaker than over the government (au. int.).

17. This was clearly manifested in the case of Zhang Wenli, an official in a county government who had to be dismissed by the next higher authorities. Under normal circumstances, the county head who appointed Zhang and the county congress that approved the appointment were fully authorized to remove Zhang. But in this instance "some of the county leaders have committed corruption and bribery themselves. Some have benefited a great deal from Zhang's crime. They supported and protected Zhang publicly or privately and made the investigation [by the next higher authorities]

very difficult." When higher authorities sent a team to investigate the corruption of a bureau director of a county in Hebei Province, more than 800 people bore false witness to protect him. Jiang Yaochun, "Liu Binyan's Interview."

18. Democracy could not eliminate political corruption, just as it could not eliminate clientelism. But in a competitive electoral context, corruption frequently assumes somewhat different form, and the benefit has to be disbursed more widely in the society. As Scott indicates, the quest for broad popular support entails being more responsive to more of the political demands coming from the society. Scott, *Comparative Political Corruption,* chs. 6, 7.

19. The demonstrations in spring 1989 were essentially more a popular protest against political corruption than a movement for democracy in its real sense, although many people tend to emphasize its democratic implications. An eyewitness account by Simmie and Nixon when the movement came to a climax is quite suggestive. "In Beijing, attacks on the Chinese leadership became increasingly vicious," they wrote, "but many groups of demonstrators carried portraits of Zhou Enlai. It was a sign of their love and respect for the late premier, and a pointed display of their lack of respect for Li Peng. Pictures and badges of Mao Zedong were also dusted off." Simmie and Nixon, *Tiananmen Square,* p. 121. Similar accounts can also be found in Thomas, *Chaos,* chs. 12–21. Zhang Boli, one of the major organizers of the 1989 demonstrations, was frequently asked a question after he came into exile in the United States: Why did the prodemocracy movement succeed in Eastern Europe but fail in China? Aside from a variety of differences between Eastern Europe and China, he replied, "the most important reason was that we never made an appeal to overthrow the communist rule, did not even demand an end to the one-party dictatorship." Zhang Boli, "I Dare."

20. Meaney, "Market Reform," p. 125.

21. Jiang Zemin's speech to the conference of the heads of the Party's organizational departments held in late August 1989. *RMRB,* August 22, 1989.

22. *RMRB,* August 15, 1989.

23. Quoted in *SJRB,* February 2, 1993.

24. Cao Xiao, "Wei Jianxing."

25. The Tiananmen movement suggests that citizens do not have to believe in true democratic values before they take to the streets for more democratization. They may be driven simply by their perception of the Party's incompetence to solve the problems that affect their personal welfare. When the solution to these problems requires further institutional reforms, a real systemic crisis may occur.

Abbreviations

BJRB	*Beijing Ribao* (Beijing daily), published by the Beijing Municipal Party Committee
CCP	Chinese Communist Party
CL	*Chao Liu* (Tide monthly), Hong Kong
CM	*Cheng Ming* (Contend), monthly, Hong Kong
CPLG	Central Political-Legal Group
CPPCC	Chinese People's Political Consultative Conference
CSIC	Capital Steel and Iron Company
DX	*Dong Xiang* (Trend), monthly, Hong Kong
DXLT	*Dangxiao Luntan* (Party school tribune), monthly, published by the Central Party School, Beijing
DYLC	*Dongyue Luncong* (Dongyue tribune), bimonthly, published by Shandong Province's Academy of Social Sciences
FDRS	factory director responsibility system
FX	*Fa Xue* (Law science monthly), published by the Eastern China Institute of Politics and Law, Shanghai
FXJK	*Faxue Jikan* (Law science quarterly), published by the Southwestern Institute of Politics and Law, Chongqing
FXPL	*Faxue Pinglun* (Law review), bimonthly, published by Wuhan University
FZJS	*Fazhi Jianshe* (Building of legal system), bimonthly, published by China's Ministry of Justice, Beijing
FZRB	*Fazhi Ribao* (Legal daily), published by China's Ministry of Justice, Beijing
GGZS	*Gaige Zhisheng* (Voice of reform), monthly, published by the Commission on Economic Reforms of Liaoning Province
GJJ	*Guang Jiao Jing* (Wide angle), monthly, Hong Kong

GMRB	*Guangming Ribao* (Enlightenment daily), published by the CCP Ministry of Propaganda, Beijing
GRRB	*Gongren Ribao* (Workers' daily), published by the National Trade Union, Beijing
GYYJ	*Gongyun Yanjiu* (Study of labor movement), semimonthly, published by the National Trade Union, Beijing
HDX	*Hangzhou Daxue Xuebao* (Journal of Hangzhou University—edition of social sciences), bimonthly, Zhejiang
HQ	*Hongqi* (Red flag), monthly 1958–1979, semimonthly 1980–1988, published by the CCP Central Committee, became *QS* (*Qiushi*) in 1988
JBYK	*Jingbao Yuekan* (The mirror monthly), Hong Kong
JFJB	*Jiefangjun Bao* (Liberation Army daily), published by the General Political Department, PLA
JFYB	*Jiefang Yuebao* (Emancipation monthly), Hong Kong
JJGL	*Jingji Guanli* (Economic management), monthly, published by the Institute of Industrial Economy, the Chinese Academy of Social Sciences, Beijing
JJRB	*Jingji Ribao* (Economic daily), published by the State Council, Beijing
JLRB	*Jilin Ribao* (Jilin daily)
JSND	*Jiushi Niandai* (The nineties), monthly, Hong Kong
JWT	*Jingji Wenti Tansuo* (Exploration of economic problems), monthly, published by the Research Institute of Economy of Yunnan
JYX	*Juece yu Xinxi* (Decisionmaking and information), monthly, published by the Research Center for Decisionmaking and Information in Wuhan, Hubei
KFZZ	*Kaifang Zazhi* (Open magazine), monthly, Hong Kong
KSZY	*Kexue Shehui Zhuyi Yanjiu* (Study of scientific socialism), monthly, Beijing
KZYJ	*Kongzi Yanjiu* (Study of Confucius), quarterly, Shandong
LLTS	*Lilun Tansuo* (Theoretical exploration), bimonthly, published by the Provincial Party School of Shanxi
LLXX	*Lilun Xuexi* (Theoretical study), monthly, Anhui
LPC	local people's congress
LWZK	*Liaowang Zhoukan* (Outlook weekly), published by New China (Xinhua) News Agency, Beijing
LZXK	*Lanzhou Xuekan* (Journal of Lanzhou Academia), bimonthly, Gansu
MB	*Ming Bao* (Mingbao daily), Hong Kong
MBYK	*Mingbao Yuekan* (Mingbao monthly), Hong Kong

MYF	*Minzhu yu Fazhi* (Democracy and law), monthly 1979–1995, semimonthly since 1995, published by the Chinese Association of Law Science, Shanghai
MZZG	*Minzhu Zhongguo* (Democratic China), bimonthly, published by the Federation of Democratic China (a Chinese overseas opposition party), New Jersey
NGT	*Nongcun Gongzuo Tongxun* (Newsletter on rural work), monthly, Beijing
NPC	National People's Congress
NPCSC	Standing Committee of the National People's Congress
PLA	People's Liberation Army
PRC	People's Republic of China
QB	*Qiao Bao* (Overseas daily), Chinese daily, New York
QI	*Qiusuo* (Search), bimonthly, published by Hunan Province's Academy of Social Sciences
QISH	*Qian Shao* (Frontline magazine), monthly, Hong Kong
QS	*Qiushi* (Seeking truth from facts), semimonthly, published by the CCP Central Committee, Beijing
QY	*Qun Yan* (Popular tribune), monthly, published by the Central Committee of China Democratic League, Beijing
QYGL	*Qiye Guanli* (Enterprise management), monthly, published by the Chinese Association for Enterprise Management, Beijing
QYJ	*Qi Ye Jia* (Entrepreneur), semimonthly, Wuhan
RMRB	*Renmin Ribao* (People's daily), published by the CCP Central Committee, Beijing
SCPC	standing committee of the (local) people's congress
SHKX	*Shehui Kexue* (Social sciences), bimonthly, published by the Shanghai Academy of Social Sciences
SJRB	*Shijie Ribao* (World journal), daily, New York
SKY	*Shehui Kexue Yanjiu* (Social science research), bimonthly, published by Sichuan Province's Academy of Social Sciences
SXRB	*Shanxi Ribao* (Shaanxi daily)
SZY	*Shehui Zhuyi Yanjiu* (Study of socialism), bimonthly, published by the Research Institute of Scientific Socialism, Central China Teachers University, Wuhan
TA	*Tanso* (Quest), monthly, New York
TS	*Tan Suo* (Exploration), bimonthly, published by the Second Provincial Party School of Sichuan
WHB	*Wen Hui Bao* (Wenhui daily), Hong Kong
XDJT	*Xiandai Jiating* (Modern family), monthly, published by the Women's Federation of Shanghai
XGC	*Xin Guan Cha* (New observer), semimonthly, Beijing

XHYB	*Xin-Hua Yuebao* (Xinhua monthly), published by New China (Xinhua) News Agency, Beijing
XZD	*Xinwen Ziyou Daobao* (Press freedom guardian), Chinese newspaper published in the United States
ZGSB	*Zhongguo Shibao* (China times), daily, Taiwan
ZGSBZK	*Zhongguo Shibao Zhoukan* (China times weekly), Taiwan
ZGZC	*Zhongguo Zhichun* (China spring), monthly, New York
ZLB	*Zhongguo Laodong Bao* (China labor daily), Beijing
ZSFZ	*Zhishi Fenzi* (The Chinese intellectual), quarterly, New York
ZSZ	*Zhongguo Shibao Zhoukan* (China times weekly), New York
ZYF	*Zhengzhi yu Falü* (Political science and law), bimonthly, published by the Institute of Law, Shanghai Academy of Social Sciences
ZYRB	*Zhongyang Ribao* (Central daily news), published by the Central Headquarters of the Kuomintang, Taiwan
ZYZ	*Zhengzhixue Yanjiu Ziliao* (Research materials of political science), quarterly, Hubei
ZZTG	*Zhongguo Zhengzhi Tizhi Gaige* (Reform of China's political structure), bimonthly, published by the Association for Research on Reform of China's Political Structure, Beijing
ZZXYJ	*Zhengzhixue Yanjiu* (Studies in political science), monthly, published by the Chinese Association of Political Science, Beijing

Bibliography

English-Language References

Alford, William P. "Double-edged Swords Cut Both Ways: Law and Legitimacy in the People's Republic of China." *Proceedings of the American Academy of Arts and Sciences,* 122, 2 (Spring 1993), 45–69.

Almond, Gabriel A., and Powell, G. Bingham, Jr. *Comparative Politics—System, Process, and Policy.* Boston: Little, Brown, 1978.

Andors, Stephen. *China's Industrial Revolution: Politics, Planning and Management, 1949 to the Present.* New York: Pantheon Books, 1977.

Barnett, A. Doak. *Cadres, Bureaucracy, and Political Power in Communist China.* New York: Columbia University Press, 1967.

Baum, Richard. "China After Deng: Ten Scenarios in Search of Reality." *China Quarterly,* 145 (March 1996), 153–175.

————. *Burying Mao: Chinese Politics in the Age of Deng Xiaoping.* Princeton: Princeton University Press, 1994.

————. "Modernization and Legal Reform in Post-Mao China: The Rebirth of Socialist Legality." *Studies in Comparative Communism,* 29, 2 (Summer 1986), 69–104.

Beer, Samuel H. *British Politics in the Collectivist Age.* New York: Vintage Books, 1965.

Benewick, Robert. "Political Institutionalisation at the Basic Level of Government and Below in China." In Gordon White, ed. *The Chinese State in the Era of Economic Reform: The Road to Crisis.* Armonk, NY: M. E. Sharpe, 1991, 243–264.

Bialer, Seweryn. *Stalin's Successors: Leadership, Stability, and Change in the Soviet Union.* Cambridge: Cambridge University Press, 1980.

Blecher, Marc. "The Contradictions of Grass-Roots Participation and Undemocratic Statism in Maoist China and Their Fate." In Brantly Womack, ed. *Contemporary Chinese Politics in Historical Perspective.* New York: Cambridge University Press, 1991, 129–152.

Blondel, Jean. *Comparative Legislatures.* Englewood Cliffs, NJ: Prentice-Hall, 1973.

Bova, Russell. "Political Dynamics of the Post-Communist Transition: A Comparative Perspective." *World Politics,* 44 (October 1991), 113–138.

Brady, James P. *Justice and Politics in People's China: Legal Order or Continuing Revolution?* New York: Academic Press, 1982.

Brugger, William. *Democracy and Organisation in the Chinese Industrial Enterprise (1948–1953).* Cambridge, UK: Cambridge University Press, 1976.

Brugger, William, and Kelly, David. *Chinese Marxism in the Post-Mao Era.* Stanford, CA: Stanford University Press, 1990.

Brus, Wlodzimierz. "Marketisation and Democratisation: The Sino-Soviet Divergence." *Cambridge Journal of Economics,* 17, 4 (December 1993), 423–440.

Buchholz, Arnold. "Perestroika and Ideology: Fundamental Questions as to the Maintenance of and Change in the Soviet System." *Studies in Soviet Thought,* 36, 3 (October 1988), 149–168.

Bunce, Valerie. "Comparing East and South." *Journal of Democracy,* 6, 3 (July 1995), 87–100.

Burns, John P. "China's Governance: Political Reform in a Turbulent Environment." *China Quarterly,* 119 (September 1989), 481–517.

————, ed. *The Chinese Communist Party's Nomenklatura System: A Documentary Study of Party Control of Leadership Selection, 1979–1984.* Armonk, NY: M. E. Sharpe, 1989.

Burns, John P., and Rosen, Stanley, eds. *Policy Conflicts in Post-Mao China: A Documentary Survey with Analysis.* Armonk, NY: M. E. Sharpe, 1986.

Burton, Charles. *Political and Social Change in China Since 1978.* Westport, CT: Greenwood Press, 1990.

Butterfield, Fox. "In Peking Election, Ballot Is Secret, Campaign Is Hot." *New York Times,* November 29, 1980.

Byrd, William A. *The Market Mechanism and Economic Reforms in China.* Armonk, NY: M. E. Sharpe, 1991.

————. "Chinese Industrial Reform, 1979–89." In William A. Byrd, ed., *Chinese Industrial Firms Under Reform.* New York: Oxford University Press, 1992, 1–32.

————. "The Impact of the Two-Tier Plan/Market System in Chinese Industry." In Bruce L. Reynolds, ed., *Chinese Economic Reform: How Far, How Fast?* San Diego, CA: Academic Press, 1988, 5–18.

Chamberlain, Heath B. "Party-Management Relations in Chinese Industries: Some Political Dimensions of Economic Reform." *China Quarterly,* 112 (December 1987), 631–660.

Chang, Parris H. *Power and Policy in China.* University Park: Pennsylvania State University Press, 1975.

Cheng, Chu-yuan. *Behind the Tiananmen Massacre: Social, Political and Economic Ferment in China.* Boulder, CO: Westview Press, 1990.

Cheng, Peter P. "Political Clientelism in Japan." *Asian Survey,* 28, 4 (April 1988), 471–483.

Chevrier, Yves. "Micropolitics and the Factory Director Responsibility System, 1984–1987." In Deborah Davis and Ezra F. Vogel, eds., *Chinese Society on the Eve of Tiananmen: The Impact of Reform.* Cambridge: Harvard University Press, 1990, 109–133.

Ch'i, Hsi-sheng. *Politics of Disillusionment: The Chinese Communist Party Under Deng Xiaoping, 1978–89.* Armonk, NY: M. E. Sharpe, 1991.

"CPC to Boost Ideological Work." *Beijing Review,* 32, 31 (July 31, 1989), 5.

Dahl, Robert. *A Preface to Economic Democracy.* Berkeley: University of California Press, 1985.

————. *Polyarchy: Participation and Opposition.* New Haven: Yale University Press, 1971.

————. *Who Governs?* New Haven: Yale University Press, 1961.

————. *A Preface to Democratic Theory.* Chicago: University of Chicago Press, 1956.

"Decision of the Central Committee of the Communist Party of China on Reform of the Economic Structure." Adopted by the twelfth Central Committee of the Communist Party of China at its third plenary session on October 20, 1984. *Beijing Review,* 27, 44 (October 29, 1984), documents section.

Deng Xiaoping. *Fundamental Issues in Present-Day China.* New York: Pergamon Press, 1987.

————. *Selected Works of Deng Xiaoping (1975–1982).* Beijing: Foreign Languages Press, 1984.

————. "Greeting the Great Task." *Beijing Review,* 42 (October 20, 1978), 5–8.

Di Palma, Giuseppe. *To Craft Democracies.* Berkeley: University of California Press, 1990.

Diamond, Larry. "Is the Third Wave Over?" *Journal of Democracy,* 7, 3 (July 1996), 20–37.

Diamond, Larry; Linz, Juan J.; and Lipset, Seymour Martin, eds. *Democracy in Developing Countries: Asia.* Boulder, CO: Lynne Rienner Publishers, 1989.

Dicks, Anthony. "The Chinese Legal System: Reforms in the Balance." *China Quarterly,* 119 (September 1989), 540–576.

Dittmer, Lowell. *China Under Reform.* Boulder, CO: Westview Press, 1994.

————. "Patterns of Elite Strife and Succession in Chinese Politics." *China Quarterly,* 123 (September 1990), 405–430.

————. "The Origins of China's Post-Mao Reforms." In Victor C. Falkenheim, ed., *Chinese Politics from Mao to Deng.* New York: Paragon House, 1989, 41–65.

Doronila, Amando. "The Transformation of Patron-Client Relations and Its Political Consequences in the Philippines." *Journal of Southeast Asian Studies,* 16, 1 (March 1985), 99–116.

Easton, David. *A System Analysis of Political Life.* New York: John Wiley & Sons, 1965.

Eckstein, Harry. "A Culturalist Theory of Political Change." *American Political Science Review,* 82, 3 (September 1988), 789–804.

Elster, Jon. *Making Sense of Marx.* New York: Cambridge University Press, 1985.

Fainsod, Merle. *How Russia Is Ruled.* Cambridge: Harvard University Press, 1965.

Fairbank, John King. *China: A New History.* Cambridge: Belknap Press of Harvard University Press, 1992.

Falkenheim, Victor C., ed. *Citizens and Groups in Contemporary China.* Ann Arbor: Center for Chinese Studies, University of Michigan, 1987.

Fewsmith, Joseph. *Dilemmas of Reform in China: Political Conflict and Economic Debate.* Armonk, NY: M. E. Sharpe, 1994.

Fleron, Frederic J., Jr., ed. *Communist Studies and the Social Sciences: Essays on Methodology and Empirical Theory.* Chicago: Rand McNally, 1969.

Forster, Keith. "The Reform of Provincial Party Committees in China—The Case of Zhejiang." *Asian Survey,* 24, 6 (June 1984), 618–636.

Friedman, Edward, ed. *The Politics of Democratization: Generalizing East Asian Experiences.* Boulder, CO: Westview Press, 1994.

Friedrich, Carl J., ed. *Totalitarianism.* Cambridge: Harvard University Press, 1954.

Friedrich, Carl J., and Brzezinski, Zbigniew K. *Totalitarian Dictatorship and Autocracy.* New York: Praeger, 1965.

Glassman, Ronald M. *China in Transition: Communism, Capitalism, and Democracy.* New York: Praeger, 1991.

Goldman, Merle. *Sowing the Seeds of Democracy in China: Political Reform in the Deng Xiaoping Era.* Cambridge: Harvard University Press, 1994.

Goldman, Merle, with Cheek, Timothy, and Hamrin, Carol Lee, eds. *China's Intellectuals and the State: In Search of a New Relationship.* Cambridge: Council on East Asian Studies, Harvard University, 1987.

Goldman, Stuart. "The New Soviet Legislative Branch." In Robert T. Huber and Donald R. Kelley, eds., *Perestroika-Era Politics: The New Soviet Legislature and Gorbachev's Political Reforms.* Armonk, NY: M. E. Sharpe, 1991, 51–75.

Goldrich, Daniel. *Sons of the Establishment: Elite Youth in Panama and Costa Rica.* Chicago: Rand McNally, 1966.

Goldstein, Steven M. "China in Transition: The Political Foundations of Incremental Reform." *China Quarterly,* 144 (December 1995), 1105–1131.

Goodman, David S. G., ed. *Groups and Politics in the People's Republic of China.* Armonk, NY: M. E. Sharpe, 1984.

Goodman, David S. G., and Segal, Gerald, eds. *China in the Nineties: Crisis Management and Beyond.* New York: Oxford University Press, 1991.

Gross, Bertram M. *The Managing of Organizations.* 2 vols. New York: Free Press, 1964.

Gurr, Ted R. *Why Men Rebel.* New Jersey: Princeton University Press, 1970.

Habermas, Jürgen. *The Structural Transformation of the Public Sphere: An Inquiry into a Category of Bourgeois Society.* Cambridge: MIT Press, 1989.

Halpern, Nina P. "Economic Reform, Social Mobilization, and Democratization in Post-Mao China." In Richard Baum, ed., *Reform and Reaction in Post-Mao China—The Road to Tiananmen.* New York: Routledge, 1991, 38–59.

Hamrin, Carol Lee. *China and the Challenge of the Future: Changing Political Pattern.* Boulder, CO: Westview Press, 1990.

Harding, Harry. *China's Second Revolution: Reform After Mao.* Washington, DC: Brookings Institution, 1987.

———. "Political Development in Post-Mao China." In A. Doak Barnett and Ralph N. Clough, eds., *Modernizing China: Post-Mao Reform and Development.* Boulder, CO: Westview Press, 1986, 13–37.

———. *Organizing China: The Problem of Bureaucracy, 1949–1976.* Stanford, CA: Stanford University Press, 1981.

Hasegawa, Tsuyoshi. "The Connection Between Political and Economic Reform in Communist Regimes." In Gilbert Rozman, with Seizaburo Sato and Gerald Segal, eds., *Dismantling Communism: Common Causes and Regional Variations.* Baltimore: Johns Hopkins University Press, 1992, 59–117.

Hewett, Ed A., and Winston, Victor H., eds. *Milestones in Glasnost and Perestroika: The Economy.* Washington, DC: Brookings Institution, 1991.

Hine, David. *Governing Italy: The Politics of Bargained Pluralism.* Oxford: Oxford University Press, 1993.

Holmes, Leslie. *The End of Communist Power.* New York: Oxford University Press, 1993.

Hough, Jerry. *Russia and the West: Gorbachev and the Politics of Reform.* New York: Simon and Schuster, 1988.

———. "The Soviet System: Petrification or Pluralism?" *Problems of Communism,* 21 (1972), 35–45.

Hough, Jerry, and Fainsod, Merle. *How the Soviet Union Is Governed.* Cambridge: Harvard University Press, 1979.

Huntington, Samuel P. *The Third Wave: Democratization in the Late Twentieth Century.* Norman: University of Oklahoma Press, 1991.

————. "Will More Countries Become Democratic?" *Political Science Quarterly,* 99, 2 (Summer 1984), 217–218.

————. *Political Order in Changing Societies.* New Haven: Yale University Press, 1968.

Jan, George P., ed. *Government of Communist China.* San Francisco: Chandler, 1966.

Jia, Hao, and Lin, Zhimin, eds. *Changing Central-Local Relations in China: Reform and State Capacity.* Boulder, CO: Westview Press, 1994.

Jowitt, Ken. "The Leninist Extinction." In Daniel Chirot, ed. *The Crisis of Leninism and the Decline of the Left.* Seattle: University of Washington Press, 1991.

Kallgren, Joyce K., ed. *Building a Nation-State: China After Forty Years.* Berkeley: Institute of East Asian Studies, University of California, 1990.

Karl, Terry Lynn. "Dilemmas of Democratization in Latin America." *Comparative Politics,* 23 (October 1990), 1–21.

Karl, Terry Lynn, and Schmitter, Philippe C. "From an Iron Curtain to a Paper Curtain: Grounding Transitologists or Students of Postcommunism." *Slavic Review,* 54, 4 (Winter 1995), 965–978.

Karnow, Stanley. *Mao and China: A Legacy of Turmoil.* New York: Penguin Books, 1990.

Keith, Ronald C. *China's Struggle for the Rule of Law.* New York: St. Martin's Press, 1994.

Kelliher, Daniel. *Peasant Power in China: The Era of Rural Reform, 1979–1989.* New Haven: Yale University Press, 1992.

Kim, Kyung-won. "Marx, Schumpeter, and the East Asian Experience." In Larry Diamond and Marc F. Plattner, eds., *Capitalism, Socialism and Democracy Revisited.* Baltimore: Johns Hopkins University Press, 1993, 11–25.

Kraus, Richard. "The Chinese State and Its Bureaucrats." In Victor Nee and David Mozingo, eds., *State and Society in Contemporary China.* Ithaca, NY: Cornell University Press, 1983, 132–147.

Lakoff, Sanford. *Democracy: History, Theory, Practice.* Boulder, CO: Westview Press, 1996.

Lampton, David M., ed. *Policy Implementation in Post-Mao China.* Berkeley: University of California Press, 1987.

Lane, Robert E. *Political Ideology: Why the American Common Man Believes What He Does.* New York: Free Press, 1962.

LaPalombara, Joseph. *Democracy, Italian Style.* New Haven: Yale University Press, 1987.

————, ed. *Bureaucracy and Political Development.* Princeton: Princeton University Press, 1963.

Latham, Richard J. "The Implications of Rural Reforms for Grass-roots Cadres." In Elizabeth J. Perry and Christine Wong, eds., *The Political Economy of Reform in Post-Mao China.* Cambridge: Council on East Asian Studies, Harvard University, 1985, 157–173.

Lee, Hong Yung. *From Revolutionary Cadres to Party Technocrats in Socialist China.* Berkeley: University of California Press, 1991.

Lenin, V. I. "Original Version of the Article 'The Immediate Tasks of the Soviet Government.'" In V. I. Lenin, *Collected Works of Lenin.* Moscow: Progress Publishers, 1964, vol. 27, 212.

Lewin, Moshe. *The Gorbachev Phenomenon.* Berkeley: University of California Press, 1989.

Lieberthal, Kenneth. *Governing China: From Revolution Through Reform.* New York: W. W. Norton & Company, 1995.

Lieberthal, Kenneth, and Lampton, David M., eds. *Bureaucracy, Politics, and Decision Making in Post-Mao China.* Berkeley: University of California Press, 1992.

Lieberthal, Kenneth, and Oksenberg, Michel. *Policy Making in China: Leaders, Structures, and Processes.* Princeton: Princeton University Press, 1988.

Lindblom, Charles. *Politics and Markets: The World's Political-Economic Systems.* New York: Basic Books, 1977.

Linz, Juan. "Totalitarian and Authoritarian Regimes." In Fred I. Greenstein and Nelson W. Polsby, eds., *Handbook of Political Science.* Reading, MA: Addison-Wesley, 1975, 175–252.

Loewenberg, Gerhard, and Patterson, Samuel C. *Comparing Legislatures.* Boston: Little, Brown, 1979.

Lowenthal, Richard. "On 'Established' Communist Party Regimes." *Studies in Comparative Communism,* 7, 4 (Winter 1974), 335–358.

Lu Yun. "China Speeds Up Democratization." *Beijing Review,* 30, 16 (April 20, 1987), 14–20.

Lubman, Stanley, ed. *China's Legal Reform.* New York: Oxford University Press, 1996.

MacFarquhar, Roderick, ed. *The Politics of China: The Eras of Mao and Deng.* 2nd ed. New York: Cambridge University Press, 1997.

————. *The Origins of the Cultural Revolution, 2: The Great Leap Forward, 1958–1960.* New York: Columbia University Press, 1983.

————. *The Origins of the Cultural Revolution, 1: Contradictions Among the People, 1956–1957.* New York: Columbia University Press, 1974.

McCormick, Barrett L. "China's Leninist Parliament and Public Sphere: A Comparative Analysis." In Barrett McCormick and Jonathan Unger, eds., *China After Socialism.* Armonk, NY: M. E. Sharpe, 1996, 29–53.

————. *Political Reform in Post-Mao China: Democracy and Bureaucracy in a Leninist State.* Berkeley: University of California Press, 1990.

————. "Leninist Implementation: The Election Campaign." In David M. Lampton, ed., *Policy Implementation in Post-Mao China.* Berkeley: University of California Press, 1987, 383–413.

McCormick, Barrett, and Kelly, David. "The Limits of Anti-Liberalism." *Journal of Asian Studies,* 53, 3 (August 1994), 804–831.

McMillan, John, and Naughton, Barry. "How to Reform a Planned Economy: Lessons from China." *Oxford Review of Economic Policy,* 8, 1 (Spring 1992), 130–143.

Meaney, Connie Squires. "Market Reform and Disintegrative Corruption in Urban China." In Richard Baum, ed., *Reform and Reaction in Post-Mao China—The Road to Tiananmen.* New York: Routledge, 1991, 124–142.

Meisner, Maurice. *Mao's China and After—A History of the People's Republic.* New York: Free Press, 1986.

Mény, Yves. *Government and Politics in Western Europe.* Oxford: Oxford University Press, 1993.

Mernissi, Fatima. *Islam and Democracy.* Reading, MA: Addison-Wesley, 1992.

Mezey, Michael. *Comparative Legislatures.* Durham, NC: Duke University Press, 1979.

Mill, John Stuart. *On Liberty.* Ed. D. Spitz. New York: W. W. Norton & Company, 1975.

Mills, Harriet C. "Thought Reform: Ideological Remolding in China." In George P. Jan, ed., *Government of Communist China.* San Francisco: Chandler, 1966, 486–498.

Mills, Miriam K., and Nagel, Stuart S., eds. *Public Administration in China*. Westport, CT: Greenwood Press, 1993.

Mishler, William, and Rose, Richard. "Support for Parliaments and Regimes in the Transition Toward Democracy in Eastern Europe." *Legislative Studies Quarterly,* 19, 1 (February 1994), 5–32.

Moody, Peter R., Jr. *Political Opposition in Post-Confucian Society*. New York: Praeger, 1988.

Moore, Barrington, Jr. *Social Origins of Dictatorship and Democracy: Lord and Peasant in the Making of the Modern World*. Boston: Beacon Press, 1966.

Nathan, Andrew J. "China's Constitutionalist Option." *Journal of Democracy,* 7, 4 (October 1996), 43–57.

———. *China's Crisis: Dilemmas of Reform and Prospects for Democracy*. New York: Columbia University Press, 1990.

———. *Chinese Democracy*. Berkeley: University of California Press, 1986.

Nathan, Andrew J., and Shi, Tianjian. "Cultural Requisites for Democracy in China: Findings from a Survey." *American Academy of Arts and Sciences,* 122, 2 (Spring 1993), 95–123.

Nee, Victor, and Mozingo, David, eds. *State and Society in Contemporary China*. Ithaca, NY: Cornell University Press, 1983.

Nelson, Daniel N. "Editor's Introduction: Communist Legislatures and Communist Politics." *Legislative Studies Quarterly,* 5, 2 (May 1980), 161–173.

———, ed. *Local Politics in Communist Countries*. Lexington: University of Kentucky Press, 1980.

Nodia, Ghia. "How Different Are Postcommunist Transitions?" *Journal of Democracy,* 7, 4 (October 1996), 15–29.

Nolan, Peter. *State and Market in the Chinese Economy: Essays on Controversial Issues*. London: Macmillan, 1992.

O'Brien, Kevin J. "Rightful Resistance." *World Politics,* 49 (October 1996), 31–55.

———. "Agents and Remonstrators: Role Accumulation by Chinese People's Congress Deputies." *China Quarterly,* 138 (June 1994), 359–380.

———. "Chinese People's Congresses and Legislative Embeddedness: Understanding Early Organizational Development." *Comparative Political Studies,* 27, 1 (April 1994), 80–107.

———. *Reform Without Liberalization: China's National People's Congress and the Politics of Institutional Changes*. New York: Cambridge University Press, 1990.

———. "Legislative Development and Chinese Political Change." *Studies in Comparative Communism,* 32, 1 (Spring 1989), 59.

O'Brien, Kevin J., and Li, Lianjiang. "Chinese Political Reform and the Question of 'Deputy Quality.'" *China Information,* 8, 3 (Winter 1993–1994), 20–31.

O'Brien, Kevin J., and Luehrmann, Laura M. "Institutionalizing Chinese Legislatures: Trade-offs Between Autonomy and Capacity." *Legislative Studies Quarterly,* 23, 1 (February 1998), 91–108.

Odom, William E. "Soviet Politics and After: Old and New Concepts." *World Politics,* 45 (October 1992), 66–98.

O'Donnell, Guillermo, and Schmitter, Philippe. *Transitions from Authoritarian Rule: Tentative Conclusions About Uncertain Democracies*. Baltimore: Johns Hopkins University Press, 1986.

Ogden, Suzanne, et al., eds. *China's Search for Democracy: The Student and Mass Movement of 1989*. Armonk, NY: M. E. Sharpe, 1992.

Oi, Jean C. *State and Peasant in Contemporary China: The Political Economy of Village Government*. Berkeley: University of California Press, 1989.

Olson, David M. *The Legislative Process: A Comparative Approach.* New York: Harper & Row, 1980.

"On Questions of Party History—Resolution on Certain Questions in the History of Our Party Since the Founding of the People's Republic of China." Adopted by the Sixth Plenary Session of the Eleventh Central Committee of the Communist Party of China, June 27, 1981. *Beijing Review,* 27 (July 6, 1981), 10–39.

Pei, Minxin. *From Reform to Revolution: The Demise of Communism in China and the Soviet Union.* Cambridge: Harvard University Press, 1994.

Peng Zhen's Report to the fifth session of the Fifth NPC on November 26, 1982. *Beijing Review,* 25, 50 (December 13, 1982), 9–23.

Perry, Elizabeth J., and Wong, Christine, eds. *The Political Economy of Reform in Post-Mao China.* Cambridge: Council on East Asian Studies, Harvard University, 1985.

Polanyi, Karl. *The Great Transformation: The Political and Economic Origins of Our Time.* Boston: Beacon Press, 1944.

Polsby, Nelson W. "Legislature." In Fred I. Greenstein and Nelson W. Polsby, eds., *Handbook of Political Science,* vol. 5. Reading, MA: Addison-Wesley, 1975, 258–259.

Powell, G. Bingham, Jr. *Contemporary Democracies: Participation, Stability, and Violence.* Cambridge: Harvard University Press, 1982.

Pravda, Alex. "Elections in Communist States." In Stephen White and Daniel Nelson, eds., *Communist Politics: A Reader.* Houndmills, UK: Macmillan, 1986, 27–54.

PRC Yearbook, 1989, 1994. Beijing: PRC Yearbook, 1989, 1994.

"Provisional Regulations Concerning Congresses of Workers and Staff Members in State-Owned Industrial Enterprises." Promulgated by the Central Committee and the State Council on June 15, 1981. *Beijing Review,* 36 (September 7, 1981), 16–19.

Przeworski, Adam. "Some Problems in the Study of the Transition to Democracy." In Guillermo O'Donnell, Philippe Schmitter, and Laurence Whitehead, eds., *Transitions from Authoritarian Rule: Comparative Perspectives.* Baltimore: John Hopkins University Press, 1986, 47–63.

Przeworski, Adam, and Teune, Henry. *The Logic of Comparative Social Inquiry.* New York: Wiley-Interscience, 1970.

Pye, Lucian. "Political Science and the Crisis of Authoritarianism." *American Political Science Review,* 84, 1 (March 1990), 3–19.

————. *Asian Power and Politics: the Cultural Dimensions of Authority.* Cambridge: Harvard University Press, 1985.

————. *The Dynamics of Chinese Politics.* Cambridge, MA: Oelgeschlager, Gunn & Hain, 1981.

"Reshuffle of State Leading Personnel." *Beijing Review,* 37 (September 15, 1980), 3.

Reynolds, Bruce L., ed. *Chinese Economic Reform: How Far, How Fast?* San Diego: Academic Press, 1988.

Rigby, T. H. "Traditional, Market, and Organizational Societies and the USSR." *World Politics,* 16 (July 1964), 539–557.

Riggs, F. W. "Legislative Structures: Some Thoughts on Elected National Assemblies." In Allan Kornberg, ed., *Legislatures in Comparative Perspective.* New York: David McKay, 1973.

Riskin, Carl. *The Political Economy of Chinese Development Since 1949.* New York: Oxford University Press, 1986.

Roeder, Philip G. *Red Sunset: The Failure of Soviet Politics.* Princeton: Princeton University Press, 1993.

Rosenbaum, Arthur Lewis, ed. *State and Society in China: The Consequences of Reform*. Boulder, CO: Westview Press, 1992.

Rowen, Henry S. "The Short March: China's Road to Democracy." *National Interest* (Fall 1996), 61–70.

Rueschemeyer, Dietrich; Stephens, Evelyne Huber; and Stephens, John D. *Capitalist Development and Democracy*. Cambridge: Polity Press, 1992.

Sartori, Giovanni. *The Theory of Democracy Revisited*. Chatham, NJ: Chatham House, 1987.

Scalapino, Robert A. *The Politics of Development: Perspectives on Twentieth-Century Asia*. Cambridge: Harvard University Press, 1989.

Schmitter, Philippe C., with Karl, Terry Lynn. "The Conceptual Travels of Transitologists and Consolidologists: How Far to the East Should They Attempt to Go?" *Slavic Review,* 53, 1 (Spring 1994), 173–185.

Schumpeter, Joseph. *Capitalism, Socialism and Democracy*. New York: Harper & Row, 1950.

Schurmann, Franz. *Ideology and Organization in Communist China*. Berkeley: University of California Press, 1966.

Scott, James C. *Domination and the Arts of Resistance: Hidden Transcripts*. New Haven: Yale University Press, 1990.

————. *Comparative Political Corruption*. Englewood Cliffs, NJ: Prentice-Hall, 1972.

————. "Patron-Client Politics and Political Change in Southeast Asia." *American Political Science Review,* 66 (March 1972), 81–113.

Seymour, James D., ed. *The Fifth Modernization—China's Human Rights Movement, 1978–1979*. Stanfordville, NY: Earl M. Coleman Enterprises, 1980.

Shi, Tianjian. *Political Participation in Beijing*. Cambridge: Harvard University Press, 1997.

Shirk, Susan. *The Political Logic of Economic Reform in China*. Berkeley: University of California Press, 1993.

————. "The Politics of Industrial Reform." In Elizabeth J. Perry and Christine Wong, eds., *The Political Economy of Reform in Post-Mao China*. Cambridge: Council on East Asian Studies, Harvard University, 1985, 195–221.

Shue, Vivienne. *The Reach of the State: Sketches of the Chinese Body Politic*. Stanford, CA: Stanford University Press, 1988.

Simmic, Scott, and Nixon, Bob. *Tiananmen Square—An Eyewitness Account of the Chinese People's Passionate Quest for Democracy*. Vancouver: Douglas & McIntyre, 1989.

Skilling, H. Gordon. "Interest Groups and Communist Politics Revisited." *World Politics,* 36 (October 1983), 24–27.

Skilling, H. Gordon, and Griffiths, Franklyn, eds. *Interest Groups in Soviet Politics*. Princeton: Princeton University Press, 1971.

Smith, Gordon. *Politics in Western Europe: A Comparative Analysis*. 5th ed. New York: Holmes & Meier, 1989.

Snow, Edgar. *The Long Revolution*. New York: Random House, 1972.

Solinger, Dorothy J. *China's Transition from Socialism: Statist Legacies and Market Reforms*. Armonk, NY: M. E. Sharpe, 1993.

————. "The Fifth National People's Congress and the Process of Policymaking: Reform, Readjustment, and the Opposition." *Issue and Studies,* 18, 8 (August 1982), 63–106.

Spence, Jonathan D. *The Search for Modern China*. New York: W. W. Norton & Company, 1990.

Starr, John Bryan. *Continuing the Revolution: The Political Thought of Mao.* Princeton: Princeton University Press, 1979.

Steinberg, David I. "The Republic of Korea: Pluralizing Politics." In Larry Diamond, Juan J. Linz, and Seymour Martin Lipset, eds., *Politics in Developing Countries: Comparing Experiences with Democracy.* Boulder, CO: Lynne Rienner Publishers, 1995, 369–415.

Tacheron, Donald G., and Udall, Morris K. *The Job of the Congressman: An Introduction to Service in the US House of Representatives.* 2nd ed. Indianapolis: Bobbs-Merrill, 1970.

Tanner, Murray Scot. "How a Bill Becomes a Law in China: Stages and Processes in Lawmaking." In Stanley Lubman, ed., *China's Legal Reform.* Oxford: Oxford University Press, 1996, 39–64.

―――. "The Erosion of Communist Party Control over Lawmaking in China." *China Quarterly,* 138 (June 1994), 381–403.

―――. "Organizations and Politics in China's Post-Mao Law-Making System." In Pitman B. Potter, ed., *Domestic Law Reforms in Post-Mao China.* Armonk, NY: M. E. Sharpe, 1994, 56–93.

Teiwes, Frederick C. *Politics and Purges in China: Rectification and the Decade of Party Norms, 1950–1965.* Armonk, NY: M. E. Sharpe, 1993.

Thomas, Gordon. *Chaos Under Heaven—The Shocking Story of China's Search for Democracy.* New York: Birch Lane Press, 1991.

Tien, Hung-Mao. "Transformation of an Authoritarian Party State: Taiwan's Development Experience." In Tun-jen Cheng and Stephan Haggard, eds., *Political Change in Taiwan.* Boulder, CO: Lynne Rienner Publishers, 1992, 33–55.

Tilly, Charles, ed. *The Formation of National States in Western Europe.* Princeton: Princeton University Press, 1975.

Tocqueville, Alexis de. *Democracy in America.* 2 vols. New York: Vintage Books, 1945.

Townsend, James R. *Political Participation in Communist China.* Berkeley: University of California Press, 1968.

Townsend, James R., and Womack, Brantly. 3rd ed. *Politics in China.* Boston: Little, Brown, 1986.

Tsou, Tang. *The Cultural Revolution and Post-Mao Reforms: A Historical Perspective.* Chicago: University of Chicago Press, 1986.

Unger, Jonathan. "The Decollectivization of the Chinese Countryside: A Survey of Twenty-eight Villages." *Pacific Affairs,* 58 (Winter 1985–1986), 585–607.

Vanneman, Peter. *The Supreme Soviet: Politics and the Legislative Process in the Soviet System.* Durham, NC: Duke University Press, 1977.

Wahlke, John C. "Policy Demands and System Support: The Role of the Represented." *British Journal of Political Science,* 1 (July 1971), 271–290.

Wakeman, Frederic, Jr. "A Note on the Development of the Theme of Bureaucratic-Monarchic Tension in Joseph R. Levenson's Work." In Maurice Meisner and Rhodes Murphey, eds., *The Mozartian Historian: Essays on the Works of Joseph Levenson.* Berkeley: University of California Press, 1976, 123–133.

Walder, Andrew G. "Urban Industrial Workers: Some Observations on the 1980s." In Arthur Lewis Rosenbaum, ed., *State and Society in China: The Consequences of Reform.* Boulder, CO: Westview Press, 1992, 103–120.

―――. "Factory and Manager in an Era of Reform." *China Quarterly,* 118 (June 1989), 242–264.

Wang, James C. F. *Contemporary Chinese Politics: An Introduction.* 5th ed. Engle-wood Cliffs, NJ: Prentice-Hall, 1995.

Wasserstrom, Jeffrey N., and Perry, Elizabeth. *Popular Protest and Political Culture in Modern China.* Boulder, CO: Westview Press, 1994.

Watson, Andrew. *Economic Reform and Social Change in China.* London: Routledge, 1992.

Webb, Sidney, and Webb, Beatrice. *Industrial Democracy.* London: Longmans, Green, 1926.

Weber, Max. *Economy and Society.* Trans. Gunther Roth and Clauss Wittich. New York: Bedminster Press, 1978.

Weiner, Myron, and LaPalombara, Joseph. "The Impact of Parties on Political Devel-opment." In Joseph LaPalombara and Myron Weiner, eds., *Political Parties and Po-litical Development.* Princeton: Princeton University Press, 1966, 399–435.

Welsh, William A. "The Status of Research on Representative Institutions in Eastern Europe." *Legislative Studies Quarterly,* 5, 2 (May 1980), 275–308.

Wheare, K. C. *Legislatures.* London: Oxford University Press, 1963.

White, Gordon. *Riding the Tiger: The Politics of Economic Reform in Post-Mao China.* London: Macmillan, 1993.

————, ed. *The Chinese State in the Era of Economic Reform: The Road to Crisis.* Armonk, NY: M. E. Sharpe, 1991.

White, Lynn T., III. *Policies of Chaos: The Organizational Causes of Violence in China's Cultural Revolution.* Princeton: Princeton University Press, 1989.

White, Stephen. "Some Conclusions." In Daniel Nelson and Stephen White, eds., *Communist Legislatures in Comparative Perspective.* London: Macmillan, 1982, 191–196.

————. "The USSR Supreme Soviet: A Developmental Perspective." In Daniel Nelson and Stephen White, eds., *Communist Legislatures in Comparative Perspec-tive.* London: Macmillan, 1982, 247–274.

Wiegel, George. "Catholicism and Democracy." In Brad Robert, ed., *The New Democ-racies.* Cambridge: MIT Press, 1990.

Wilson, Amy Auerbacher; Greenblatt, Sidney Leonard; and Wilson, Richard W., eds. *Methodological Issues in China Studies.* New York: Praeger, 1983.

Womack, Brantly, ed. *Contemporary Chinese Politics in Historical Perspective.* New York: Cambridge University Press, 1991.

————. "The 1980 County-level Elections in China: Experiment in Democratic Modernization." *Asian Survey,* 22, 3 (March 1982), 261–277.

Wong, Christine. "Between Plan and Market: The Role of the Local Sector in Post-Mao China." *Journal of Comparative Economics,* 11 (1987), 385–398.

Xin, Qi. *China's New Democracy.* Hong Kong: Cosmos Books, 1979.

Young, Christopher. "The Strategy of Political Liberalization: A Comparative View of Gorbachev's Reforms." *World Politics,* 45 (October 1992), 47–65.

Zhao Ziyang. "Report on the Work of the Government (Delivered at the 5th Session of the Sixth NPC on March 25, 1987)." *Beijing Review,* 30, 16 (April 20, 1987).

————. "Report on the Work of the Government (Delivered at the 2nd Session of the Sixth NPC on May 15, 1984)." *Beijing Review,* 24 (June 11, 1984), documents section.

Zheng, Shiping. *Party vs. State in Post-1949 China: The Institutional Dilemma.* New York: Cambridge University Press, 1997.

Zhou Ping. "An Important Step Towards Democratic Management." *Beijing Review,* 36 (September 7, 1981), 14–16.

Chinese-Language References

"Admit Brilliant Intellectuals into the Party on a Large Scale." *RMRB,* March 15, 1985.

Ai Kesi. "The Conservatives Control the NPC Standing Committee." *CM,* 109, 11 (November 1986), 68–69.

Ao Feng. "NPC Deputies Pose Indirect Challenges to Jiang Zemin." *CM,* 4 (April 1995), 48–49.

Bai Dehua. "The [NPC] Deputies Proposed Party-Government Separation." *ZGSB,* March 21, 1998.

Beijing Shiwei Lilunbu (Department of Theoretical Research, Municipal Party Committee of Beijing), ed. *Xinshiqi Dangde Jianshe* (Party-building in the new period). Beijing: Beijing Shifan Xueyuan Chubanshe, 1987.

Beijing Tezhonggang Chang (Beijing Special Steel Plant). "Support the Workers as Masters Wholeheartedly." *QYGL,* 1 (January 1982), 23–24.

"Bo Xilai Was Reelected Dalian Mayor." *MB,* January 14, 1998, A13.

Bulletin of the NPC Standing Committee of the People's Republic of China, 2, April 15, 1988.

Bulletin of the NPC Standing Committee of the People's Republic of China, 7, December 20, 1986.

Bulletin of the State Council of the People's Republic of China, 36, January 10, 1986, 1171–1176.

Cai Dingjian. "Are China's People's Congresses Still Rubber Stamp?" *JBYK,* 248, 3 (March 1998), 28–29.

———. "The Legislative Supervision Must Be Given Top Priority." *MYF,* 233, 24 (December 20, 1996), 34.

Cao Qirui, Huang Shixiao, and Guo Dacai, eds. *Difang Renda Daibiao shi Zenyang Kaizhan Gongzuo De* (How local people's deputies work). Beijing: Zhongguo Minzhu Fazhi Chubanshe, 1996.

Cao Xiao. "Wei Jianxing Has New Points of View Against Corruption." *JBYK,* 247, 2 (February 1998), 38–39.

Cao Zhi. "Improve and Strengthen Party Leadership in Enterprises." *HQ,* 14 (July 16, 1985), 13–17.

"The CCP Central Committee's Notice Regarding the Further Strengthening and Improvement of Party-Building in State-owned Enterprises." *FZRB,* March 11, 1997.

Chang Qing. "The Percentage of Votes Declined in Guangxi People's Congress." *DX,* 90, 2 (February 1993), 34.

Chen Bingquan. "A Great Reform of Enterprise Leadership System in Our Country." *HQ,* 9 (May 1, 1985), 20–23.

Chen Hongyi. "1993: A New Term of China's Organs of State Power at Five Levels." *LWZK* (overseas edition), 7 (February 15, 1993), 3–4.

Chen Jing, Wang Longjaing, and Wei Xiaodong. "The Effects and Experience of Institutional Reforms in Ha'erbin." *ZZTG,* 2 (March 1989), 18–20.

Chen Junsheng. "Study New Conditions and New Experiences of Democratic Management of Enterprises." *GYYJ,* 15 (August 1, 1985).

Chen Pixian. "On the Supervisory Power of the People's Congress and Its Standing Committee (November 30, 1987)." In QRCBY, ed., *Zhonghua Renmin Gongheguo Renmin Daibiao Dahui Wenxian Ziliao Huibian, 1949–1990* (A collection of the documents and materials of the National People's Congress of the People's Republic of China, 1949–1990). Beijing: Zhongguo Minzhu Fazhi Chubanshe, 1990, 612–614.

Chen Xiaochun and Zhang Qinglin. "An Investigation on the Appointment System in Enterprises." *QYJ*, 9 (May 1, 1991), 36.

Chen Yizi. *Zhongguo: Shinian Gaige yu Bajiu Minyun* (China: Ten years of reform and democracy movement of 1989). Taipei: Lianjing Chuban Shiye Gongsi, 1990.

Chen Yizi and Chen Jinfu (Bianxiezu), eds. *Zhengzhi Tizhi Gaige Jianghua* (A talk on the reforms of the political structure). Beijing: Renmin Chubanshe, 1987.

Chen Yun. *Chen Yun Wenxuan, 1956–1985* (Selected works of Chen Yun, 1956–1985). Beijing: Renmin Chubanshe, 1986.

————. "Speech at the Sixth Session of the Central Commission for Discipline Inspection." *RMRB*, September 27, 1985.

Chen Zhinong. "The CCP Strengthens Its Control over the NPC." *JSND*, 339, 4 (April 1998), 28–29.

Chen Ziming. "Who Is the Person Condemned by History?" *XZD*, June 28, 1991.

Cheng Lishun and Chen Gang. "The Status Quo of the Separation of the Party from Government at the Level of Township." *LLXX*, 6 (June 1989), 44–45.

Cheng Xiangqing. "The Supervision of the People's Congress and 'Checks and Balances.'" *FZRB*, May 29, 1997.

————. "We Must Summarize the Experience of LPC Supervision." *FZRB*, March 13, 1997.

Cheng Zihua's Report on the Nationwide Direct Election. *RMRB*, August 4, 1980.

Chi Fulin and Huang Hai, eds. *Deng Xiaoping Zhengzhi Tizhi Gaige Sixiang Yanjiu* (A study of Deng Xiaoping's thinking of political structural reform). Beijing: Chun Qiu Chubanshe, 1987.

Chi Huiling and Jia Weizhuan. "Democratic Management Must Be Stressed Under the FDRS." *QYGL*, 10 (October 1986), 7–8.

Cui Lan. "No. 32 Lecture: The Management Must Be Democratized." *QYGL*, 7 (July 1992), 45–47.

Dai Huaying. "Only If the Status of the Workers as Masters Is Guaranteed Can They Play the Masters' Role." *QYJ*, 12 (June 15, 1991), 22.

Deng Xiaoping. *Deng Xiaoping Wenxuan, Disanjuan* (Selected works of Deng Xiaoping, vol. 3). Beijing: Renmin Chubanshe, 1993.

The Document of the Standing Committee of the Provincial People's Congress of Guangdong. Guangdong: General Office of the Standing Committee of the Provincial People's Congress of Guangdong, December 1986.

Dong Hu. "Chinese Politics Is Vacillating." *CM*, 117, 7 (July 1987), 11–12.

Dong Taifang. "The Significance of Li Shuxian Being Elected as a People's Deputy." *ZGZC*, 50 (August 1987), 61–62.

Dong Xusheng. "Li Shuxian, Fang Lizhi's Wife, Joined the Election Campaign and Won High Percentage of Votes." *ZGZC*, 49 (July 1987), 58.

Du Yuelin et al. *Zenyang Xuanju Chejian Zhuren, Gongduan Duanzhang he Banzu Zuzhang* (How to elect workshop directors, section chiefs and group heads). Guangdong: Renmin Chubanshe, 1979.

Duan Muzheng. "On the Improvement of the Quality of People's Deputies." *QY,* 9 (September 1989), 13–17.

Feng Bowei. "Seriously Carry Out the Enterprise Law and Promote Democratic Management of Enterprise." *QYGL*, 1 (January 1991), 32–33.

Feng Hui and Hu Shengsheng. "A Demonstration of Increasing Democratization and Openness of Chinese Politics." *MYF*, 7 (July 1987), 5–6.

Feng Weitian. "They Are Worthy of the Envoys of the People." *MYF*, 9 (September 1988), 17–18.

"The First Democratically Elected University President." *BJRB*, reprinted in *QB*, April 8, 1995, 26.

Ge Fengchen. "Deng Xiaoping Uses the Army to Run the Country." *JFYB*, 4 (April 1988), 19–21.

Ge Shufan. "Is the NPC Still a Rubber Stamp?" *JFYB*, 4 (April 1988), 21–22.

Gu Ming. "Why Is It Necessary for a Socialist State to Formulate a Bankruptcy Law?" *JJRB*, November 11, 1986.

Gu Wenhong and Shan Guoxing. "An Investigation of the Democratically Elected Leaders in State Enterprises." *MYF*, 211, 2 (January 21, 1996), 16–18.

Guan Zaiyuan and Zhang Jianguo. "Let the Workers Be in Masters' Position." *QYGL*, 10 (October 1991), 25–27.

Guo Daohui. *Zhongguo Lifa Zhidu* (The legislative system in China). Beijing: Renmin Chubanshe, 1988.

Guo Guangdong. "Voters' Mentalities, Deputies' Perspectives and the Electoral System." *FX*, 7 (July 1997), 4–6.

Guo Sheng. "The Anti-Mao Tendency in the Revision of the Constitution." *JFYB*, 4 (April 1988), 24–26.

Guojia Tongjiju (State Bureau of Statistics), ed. *Zhongguo Gongye Jingji Tongji Nianjian, 1989* (Statistical yearbook of China's industrial economy, 1989). Beijing: Zhongguo Tongji Chubanshe, 1990.

Guowuyuan Fazhiju (Bureau of Legal System, State Council), ed. *Zhonghua Renmin Gongheguo Xinfagui Huibian* (A collection of new laws and regulations of the People's Republic of China). Beijing: Zhongguo Fazhi Chubanshe, 1993, 1995.

Hangzhoushi Renda (Municipal People's Congress of Hangzhou), ed. *Zhongxin Chengshi Renda Gongzuo de Xinjinzhan* (The new progress of people's congress work in major cities). Beijing: Zhongguo Minzhu Fazhi Chubanshe, 1997.

Hao Wang. "A Report of Investigation on the Separation of the Party from Government." *ZZXYJ*, 1 (January 1989), 17–23.

Hao Weilian. "The Progress of China's Electoral Reform in the Past Fourteen Years." *LWZK* (overseas edition), 7 (February 15, 1993), 4–5.

He Daquan. "Some Difficult Problems Must Be Solved in the Separation of the Party from Government." *DXLT*, 3 (March 1989), 49–50.

He Ping. "The Execution of Chinese Laws and Human Rights." *CM*, 161, 5 (May 1991), 36–42.

―――. "Writing the History of China's Freedom of Press." *TA*, 76 (April 1990), 56–58.

Hong Chenghua and Guo Xiuzhi, eds. *Zhonghua Renmin Gongheguo Zhengzhi Tizhi Yange Dashiji 1949–1978* (A chronicle of the evolution of the political structure of the People's Republic of China, 1949–1978). Beijing: Chun Qiu Chubanshe, 1987.

Hongqi Zazhi Bianjibu Zhengzhishi (Department of Politics, Editorial Board of Hongqi), ed. *Xinshiqi Dangde Jianshe de Guanghui Wenxian* (Brilliant literature on party-building in the new period). Beijing: Hongqi Chubanshe, 1983.

Hou Dinghe. "On the Scientific Separation of the Party Committees from Management and Their Perfect Combination in Enterprises." *DXLT*, 5 (May 1989), 24–27.

Hou Zhaoxun. "The Elections of People's Congresses Proceed Smoothly." *FZRB*, March 2, 1998, 1.

"How Does the Party Committee in the Beijing Knitting Wool Factory Exercise Ideological and Political Leadership?" *QYGL*, 8 (August 1987), 17.

HQ editorial. *HQ*, 4 (April 1968), 5–12.

Hu Guohua. "The New Milestone in the Establishment of Democratic Politics in Our Country." *LWZK*, 13 (March 28, 1988), 4–6.

Hu Guozhang. "The Tendency of De-professionalization of Leading Party Cadres in Enterprises." *ZZTG*, 3 (May 1989), 59–61.

Hu Manhong and Zhang Hong. "To Accept the Supervision of People's Deputies and Do a Good Job in Public Security." *MYF*, 17 (September 1995), 32.

Hu Nan. "The Lobbyist 'Cao Bankruptcy.'" *ZGZC*, 98 (July 1991), 39–42.

Hu Quan. "To Be Fair to Professional Party Cadres." *LWZK*, 6 (February 8, 1988), 13.

Hu Tugui. "The NPC Should Make Full Use of Its Legislative Power." *FX*, 2 (February 1995), 8–9.

Hu Zuogen, Zhang Shusheng, Chen Guangping, and Ding Zhenxiang. "The Self-Perception of Enterprise Employees." *QYJ*, 5 (March 1, 1992), 32.

Hua Ding. "Cast Away the 'Sense of Loss' and Strengthen Responsibility." *LWZK*, 45 (November 9, 1987), 1.

Huang Bailian. *Ezhi Fubai: Minzhu Jiandu de Chengxu yu Zhidu Yanjiu* (Curb corruption: A study of the procedures and system of democratic supervision). Beijing: Renmin Chubanshe, 1997.

Huang Ho et al., eds. *Kai Tuo: Beida Xuanju Wenxian Huibian* (Open up the path: The documents of election in Peking University). Hong Kong: Tianyuan Publishers, 1990.

Huang Liqun and Jiang Guofang. "The Standing Committees of People's Congresses Should Take Part in Examination of Officials' Records." *FX*, 10 (October 1987), 5–8.

Huang Zexiao. "Objection to the Recall of the Vice Governor in the Second Session of the 7th Provincial People's Congress of Hunan." *MYF*, 9 (September 1989), 41.

Hunan Shengwei Yanjiushi (Research Institute of the Provincial Party Committee of Hunan). "To Promote Reforms of Political Structure in Enterprises." *ZZTG*, 3 (May 1989), 48–50.

HZXK (Huadong Zhengfa Xueyuan Keyanbu: Department of Scientific Research, East China Institute of Political Science and Law), ed. *Faxue Lunwenji* (Collected papers on laws). Shanghai: Shanghai Shehui Kexueyuan Chubanshe, 1987.

Jian Jun. "A Long Road: From the 'April 5' to the 'June 4.'" *ZGZC*, 83 (April 1990), 6–9.

———. "The 1980 Elections in Peking University." *ZGZC*, 84 (May 1990), 31–35.

Jiang Huaxuan and Zhang Weiping, eds. *Zhongguo Gongchandang Huiyi Gaiyao* (A general survey of CCP conferences). Shenyang, Liaoning: Shenyang Chubanshe, 1991.

Jiang Yaochun. "Liu Binyan's Interview with the Reporter." *MYF*, 9 (September 1986), 12–13.

Jiang Yaochun and Ma Yijun. "Reports on Chinese Democracy." *MYF*, 5 (May 1988), 8–16.

Jiang Zemin. "Strive to Build the Party into a Stronger Vanguard of the Working Class (December 29, 1989)." *RMRB*, July 1, 1990.

Jiang Zemin's speech to the conference of the heads of departments of organization held in late August 1989. *RMRB*, August 22, 1989.

Jiao Shiying. "A Study of the Separation of the Party from Government at the Local Level." *SZY*, 2 (March 1988), 11–14.

Jin Zhong. "Zhao Ziyang and China's Political Reform—Interviews with Dr. Wu Guoguang." *KFZZ*, 5 (May 1997), 31–39.

Jin Ziyan. "Why Is the Percentage of Votes for Li Peng Not High?" *MB*, March 17, 1998, A13.

Jing Dong. "The Party Cannot Substitute for the Government." *HQ*, 21 (November 1, 1980), 5–8.

Joint editorial of *RMRB, HQ,* and *JFJB.* "Study the Documents Well and Grasp the Key Link." *HQ,* 3 (March 1977), 15–18.

Kang Yonghe. "Democratically Elect Heads of the Basic-level Units." *HQ,* 12 (December 1979), 66–68.

"Labor-Capital Relations in China's Foreign-Invested Enterprises." Published in *ZGS-BZK,* 116 (March 20–26, 1994), 8–16.

Lang Fang. "Why Was Jiang Chunyun Deposed Halfway?" *DX,* 152, 4 (April 15, 1998), 25–28.

Li Chun. "Some Ideas on the Separation of the Party from Government." *LLTS,* 3 (May-June 1989), 44–47.

Li Jiating. "Establish and Improve the Mechanisms for Internal Competitions in Enterprises." *QS,* 10 (May 16, 1993), 25–27.

Li Nanhua. "Appraisal: An Effective Method of Strengthening the Legislative Supervision." *LWZK,* 737, 10 (March 9, 1998), 23.

Li Shen. "Adjust the Mentality of Professional Party Cadres." *QYGL,* 6 (June 1989), 11–12.

Li Shenkuan, ed., *Qianjin Zhongde Shiji Renda* (Municipal people's congresses in progress). Beijing: Zhongguo Minzhu Fazhi Chubanshe, 1997.

Li Yongchun and Luo Jian, eds. *Shiyijie Sanzhong Quanhui yilai Zhengzhi Tizhi Gaige de Lilun yu Shijian* (The theory and practice of political reform since the third plenum of the eleventh Central Committee). Beijing: Chun Qiu Chubanshe, 1987.

Li Yu. "The People's Congress: The CCP's Instrument." *CM,* 183, 3 (March 1993), 53–56.

Li Zhuxing. "The Voting System of the People's Congress and Its Reform." *FX,* 11 (November 1986), 2–6.

Li Zijing. "Jiang Zemin Prohibits Any Mention of Political Reform." *DX,* 151, 3 (March 1998), 14–15.

————. "Mao and Zhou Got Votes in the Elections of the Two Conferences." *CM,* 246, 4 (April 1998), 22.

————. "Stick and Carrot to Prevent Losing Control over the Two Conferences." *CM,* 233, 3 (March 1997), 23–24.

————. "The NPC Turmoil Disturbs the Party." *CM,* 5 (May 1995), 13–14.

Liang Qiongfang. "Three Suggestions on the Improvement of the Electoral System." *SZY,* 4 (July–August 1988), 17–18.

Liao Gailong, ed. *Zhongguo Zhengzhi Tizhi Gaige de Lilun Tantao* (A theoretical exploration of China's reform of the political structure). Shenyang: Liaoning Daxue Chubanshe, 1987.

Liao Gailong, Zhao Baoxu, and Du Qinglin, eds. *Dangdai Zhongguo Zhengzhi Dashidian, 1949–1990* (Encyclopedia of major political events in contemporary China, 1949–1990). Changchun: Jilin Wenshi Chubanshe, 1991.

Liao Guanxian. "Can the County Head Be Appointed Without [Election by] the People's Congress?" *MYF,* 5 (May 1983), 5.

Liu Chong. "The Electoral System of Congresses Suits China's Conditions: Reports from Guangzhou." *WHB,* March 21, 1998.

Liu Hailiang, ed. *Zhongguo Difang Fazhi Jianshe* (The building of local legal system in China). Beijing: Zhongguo Minzhu Fazhi Chubanshe, 1996.

Liu Han. *Minzhu yu Zhuanzhi* (Democracy and dictatorship). Beijing: Falü Chubanshe, 1987.

Liu Jiang. "The 8th NPC Has New Features in Personnel Matters." *JBYK,* 3 (March 1993), 28–31.

—————. "The Second Plenum Decides the Matters Concerning the 8th NPC and CPPCC." *JBYK*, 4 (April 1993), 24–27.

Liu Jun. "Rely on the Workers' Congress in Running Socialist Enterprises." *QYGL*, 1 (January 1982), 27–28.

Liu Li, ed. *Zhonghua Renmin Gongheguo Guojia Jigou* (The state institutions of the People's Republic of China). Ha'erbin, Heilongjiang: Ha'erbin Chubanshe, 1988.

Liu Liantie. "Stabilize the Ranks of Party Cadres and Strengthen Ideological Work." *QYJ*, 2 (January 15, 1990), 26–27.

Liu Xia. "Reform of the Political Structure and the Quality of People's Deputies." *FZJS*, 5 (September 1987), 20–22.

Liu Yingxing. "An Important Issue Concerning the Structuring of Standing Committees of Local People's Congresses." *ZYZ*, 3 (Autumn 1988), 20–22.

Lu Cheng and Zhu Gu. "Earnestly Guarantee the People's Democratic Rights." *HQ*, 17 (September 1, 1980), 9–11.

Lu Jindong. "Analyze the Issue of Joint Party-Government Documents from a Legal Perspective." *FX*, 1 (January 1997), 3.

Lu Ren. "'The Merger of Party and Government' and 'Separation of Government from Enterprises.'" *JBYK*, 3 (March 1993), 36–38.

Luo Bing. "Jiang and Zhu Are Blamed for Violating the Constitution." *CM*, 249, 7 (July 1998), 10–11.

—————. "Jiang Zemin and Zhu Rongji Jointly Cope with Regional Leaders." *DX*, 152, 4 (April 1998), 8–9.

—————. "Qiao Shi Criticized the Political System in His South China Tour." *DX*, 150, 2 (February 1998), 12–13.

—————. "Tian Jiyun's Speeches Stirred Up Troubles." *CM*, 210, 4 (April 1995), 6–9.

—————. "The Change of Personnel at the Highest Level of the CCP." *CM*, 82, 8 (August 1984), 23–25.

Luo Bing and Li Zijing. "Why So Many Shells at the NPC Session?" *CM*, 198, 4 (April 1994), 9–11.

—————. "The Noise Behind the NPC Scenes." *CM*, 186, 4 (April 1993), 23–24.

—————. "Spectacles of the Nationwide Elections." *DX*, 91, 3 (March 1993), 8–10.

Luo Shugang and Liu Jinxiu. "The Shock of Competitive Elections." *QS*, 2 (July 16, 1988), 36–39.

LWZK Jizhe (*LWZK* correspondent). "Observe the Democratization Process from China's Elections of Provincial People's Congresses and Governments." *LWZK* (overseas edition), 10 (March 7, 1988), 3.

Ma Lin. "From Governor to Prisoner." *MYF*, 6 (June 1987), 11–15.

Ma Shouliang. *Dangzheng Guanxi de Lishi Kaocha he Gaige Qushi* (A historical study of the party-government relationship and the tendency of reform). Hangzhou: Zhejiang Renmin Chubanshe, 1988.

Mao Yongxiong. "A New Beginning—Report on the Publicity Given to the Candidates for Shanghai's Leadership." *XDJT*, 8 (August 1988), 10–13.

Maoming Shiyou Gongsi (Maoming Oil Company). "The Conception Concerning Political and Ideological Work Must Be Changed." *QS*, 13 (July 1, 1993), 39–41.

Mei De'ying. "On the Direct Election of People's Deputies at the Level of Urban Districts." *ZYZ*, 1 (Spring 1988), 22–24.

Meng Xiangxi. "The Thinking About the Exercise of Political Leadership by Local Party Committees." *ZZTG*, 3 (May 1989), 43–47.

Min Qi. *Zhongguo Zhengzhi Wenhua: Minzhu Zhengzhi Nanchan de Shehui Xinli Yinsu* (China's political culture—Social mentality that impedes political democratization). Kunming: Yunnan Renmin Chubanshe, 1989.

Mu Qing. "What Does It Mean to Cast Negative Votes?" *CL,* 15 (May 15, 1988), 16–18.

MYF Pinglunyuan (*MYF* commentator). "The Party Must Conduct Its Activities Within the Limits Permitted by the Constitution and the Laws." *MYF,* 9 (September 1982), 2.

Nie Gaomin, Li Yizhou, and Wang Zhongtian, eds. *Dangzheng Fenkai Lilun Tantao* (A theoretical exploration of the party-government separation). Beijing: Chun Qiu Chubanshe, 1987.

Ning Yongkang et al. "The Procedures and Process of Institutional Reforms in Zigong City." *ZZTG,* 2 (March 1989), 20–24.

Pan Bo'wen. "The Direct Election and Nomination of Candidates for People's Deputies." *ZYF,* 2 (March 1989), 19–20.

Peng Weixiang. "A Witness to the NPC Election." *WHB,* March 17, 1998, A1.

Peng Zhen. *Lun Xinzhongguo de Zhengfa Gongzuo* (On the work of politics and law of new China). Beijing: Zhongyang Wenxian Chubanshe, 1992.

————. *Lun Xinshiqi de Shehui Zhuyi Minzhu yu Fazhi Jianshe* (On the building of socialist democracy and legal system during the new period). Beijing: Zhongyang Wenxian Chubanshe, 1989.

Proceedings (*hui kan*) of the Standing Committee of the [tenth] Municipal People's Congress of Wuxi, 8–9, April 20, 1989.

Pu Xingzu, Ding Rongsheng, Sun Guanhong, and Hu Jinxing. *Zhonghua Renmin Gongheguo Zhengzhi Zhidu* (The political system of the People's Republic of China). Hong Kong: Joint Publishing H. K. Co., 1995.

QRCBL (Quanguo Renda Changweihui Bangongting Lianluoju: Liaison Bureau of the General Office of the NPC Standing Committee). "The Reasons for Disapproval of the Candidates for Government Offices by the Standing Committees of the People's Congresses in 27 Provinces." October 1988.

————, ed. *Xuanju Wenjian Huibian* (Collected election documents). July 1988.

QRCBY (Quanguo Renda Changweihui Bangongting Yanjiushi: Research Institute of the General Office of the NPC Standing Committee), ed. *Difang Renda Xingshi Zhiquan Shili Xuanbian* (Selected cases of local people's congresses' exercise of their functions). Beijing: Zhongguo Minzhu Fazhi Chubanshe, 1996.

————, ed. *Difang Renda shi Zenyang Xingshi Zhiquande?* (How local people's congresses exercise their power). Beijing: Zhongguo Minzhu Fazhi Chubanshe, 1992.

————, ed. *Renmin Daibiao Dahui Zhidu Luncong* (Essays on the people's congress system), vol. 1. Beijing: Zhongguo Minzhu Fazhi Chubanshe, 1992.

————, ed. *Renmin Daibiao Dahui Zhidu Jianshe Sishinian* (The forty years of structuring of the people's congress system). Beijing: Zhongguo Minzhu Fazhi Chubanshe, 1991.

————, ed. *Lun Woguo Renmin Daibiao Dahui Zhidu de Jianshe* (On the buildup of the people's congress system in our country). Beijing: Zhongguo Minzhu Fazhi Chubanshe, 1990.

————, ed. *Zhonghua Renmin Gongheguo Renmin Daibiao Dahui Wenxian Ziliao Huibian, 1949–1990* (A collection of the documents of the PRC National People's Congress, 1949–1990). Beijing: Zhongguo Minzhu Fazhi Chubanshe, 1990.

————, ed. *Lun Renda Jiqi Changweihui de Jianduquan* (On the supervisory power of the people's congress and its standing committee). Beijing: Falü Chubanshe, 1988.

QRFW (Quanguo Renda Fazhi Weiyuanhui: NPC Legal Committee). "The Conditions and Legal Problems of the 1988 Elections in Various Provinces, Autonomous Regions, and the Municipalities Under the Direct Jurisdiction of the Central Government." In *No. 12 Document (fa gong guo zi)*, March 22, 1988.

Qu Naiyu. "Correctly Handle the Relationship Between the Director and the Workers' Congress." *QYGL,* 1 (January 1982), 25–26.

QXZXB (Quanguo Xianji Zhijie Xuanju Bangongshi: Office for Nationwide Direct Election at the County Level), ed. *Diyijie Quanguo Xianji Zhijie Xuanju Wenjian Huibian* (Collected documents concerning the first nationwide direct election at the county level). Beijing: Falü Chubanshe, 1984.

QZGY (Quanguo Zonggonghui Gongyun Yanjiushi: Research Institute of Labor Movement, National Trade Union), ed. *Minzhu Duihua de Lilun yu Shijian* (The theory and practice of democratic dialogue). Beijing: Gongren Chubanshe, 1988.

QZHHAD (Quanguo Zonggonghui fu Hunan, Hubei he Anhui Diaochazu: Investigation Team of the National Trade Union to Hunan, Hubei, and Anhui Provinces). "A Preliminary Study of Some Issues on Enterprise Management." *GYYJ,* 19 (October 1, 1985).

QZZY (Quanguo Zonggonghui Zhengce Yanjiushi: Policy Research Institute of the National Trade Union). *Qiye Minzhu Guanli de Lilun Lishi yu Shijian* (The theory, history, and practice of democratic management of enterprises). Beijing: Jingji Guanli Chubanshe, 1986.

"Regulations Concerning the Change of Managing Mechanisms of State Enterprises." *QYGL,* 9 (September 1992), 3–11.

"Report on the Dismissal of the Vice Governor by the Provincial People's Congress of Hunan." *MYF,* 6 (June 1989), 16.

"Right and Wrong of the NPC and CPPCC." *JSND,* 220 (May 1988), 62.

RMRB Pinglunyuan (*RMRB* commentator). "'The Party Secretary Forming the Cabinet' Must Be Resolutely Prohibited." *RMRB,* April 3, 1995.

————. "Local Party Committees Should Defend the Central Authority Conscientiously." *RMRB,* December 26, 1994.

————. "Defending Professional Party Cadres." *RMRB,* January 11, 1988.

Ruan Jianming. "The Suggestions for Arousing Employees' Initiative." *QYJ,* 17 (September 1, 1991), 42.

Ruan Jihong. "Some Aspects of the Election of People's Deputies in Guangzhou Area." *MB,* March 23, 1998, B10.

SDMG (Shanghai Di'er Mianfang Gongsi: Shanghai Number 2 Textile Company). "Accelerate Development by Changing Managing Mechanisms." *JJGL,* 10 (October 1993), 51–53.

Shen Jiali. "When Will the Controversy over the Dismissal and Appointment of Directors Be Set at Rest?" *MYF,* 9 (September 1994), 22–23.

Shen Jiali et al. "Re-create Brightness with Honesty—Special Reports for the Two Conferences." *MYF,* 7 (April 1995), 5–8.

Shu Zhan. "Competitive Election Is a Reform Too." *XGC,* 1 (January 1, 1988), 17–18.

SMBG (Shanghai Maojin Beidan Gongsi: Shanghai Towel and Sheet Company). "How to Handle the Relationship Between the Party Secretary and the Director After Labor Is Divided." *JJGL,* 4 (April 1983), 49–53.

SSDWSDLD (Shandong Shengwei Dangxiao he Weifang Shiwei Dangxiao Lianhe Diaochazu: Joint Investigation Team of the Party School of the Provincial Party Committee of Shandong and the Party School of the Municipal Party Committee of Weifang). "Focus on the Changes of the Functions and Do a Good Job in Institutional Reforms—Investigation on the Institutional Reforms in Weifang City." *ZZXYJ,* 1 (January 1989), 70–74.

SSKZ (Sichuansheng Shehui Kexueyuan Zhengzhixuesuo: Institute of Political Science of Sichuan Province's Academy of Social Sciences). "Improve the System of Electing People's Deputies Through Reform." *SKY,* 6 (November 1988), 20–25.

Sun Chao and Xu Xianghua. "A Thought for Strengthening the Ability to Discuss Political Affairs of the Members of Standing Committees of Local People's Congresses." *FX,* 4 (April 1987), 5–7.

————. "Eliminate the Administrative Imprint of Standing Committees of Local People's Congresses." *FX,* 10 (October 1986), 15–17.

Sun Liming. "On Socialist Competition." *TS,* 1 (March 1989), 22–23.

Sun Zhenyuan. "Place Focal Point of the Work on Workshops." *QYGL,* 2 (February 1992), 30–32.

Tang Tingfen. "On the Party's Exercise of Political Leadership Through the People's Congress." *SZY,* 5 (September 1988), 29–32.

Tao Jiuyuan. "The Thinking About Party Organizations' Participation in Decision Making on Major Issues in Enterprises." *QS,* 15 (August 1, 1993), 44–45.

Tao Jun. "An Analysis of the Sixth NPC." *CM,* 69, 7 (July 1983), 51–53.

Tian Jiyun's Speech to the Guangdong Delegation of NPC Deputies on March 16, 1995. *QB,* March 17, 1995, 5.

Tian Zhen. "People's Deputies Suggest Direct Elections [of Government Officials]." *CM,* 192, 10 (October 1993), 28–30.

Tie Li. "The Party Leads the People and the People Supervise the Party." *FX,* 12 (December 1995), 2–3.

Tu Li. "The Hong Kong NPC Deputies Representing the Party Spirit." *DX,* 90, 2 (February 1993), 58–59.

Wafang Zhouchengchang Dangwei (CCP Committee in the Wafang Bearing Factory). "Increase the Vigor of Enterprise Party Organizations in Production and Management." *QS,* 14 (July 16, 1993), 40–43.

Wan Sha. "To Whom Should the People's Deputy with Party Membership Be Responsible First?" *DXLT,* 5 (May 1989), 30–32.

Wang Chongming and Yuan Ruiliang. *Zhonghua Renmin Gongheguo Xuanju Zhidu* (The electoral system of the People's Republic of China). Beijing: Zhongguo Minzhu Fazhi Chubanshe, 1990.

Wang Hongchang. "Economic Democracy Is the Important Content of Enterprise Reforms." *GRRB,* January 8, 1993.

Wang Jinzhong. "The Workers and Workers' Congresses." *QYGL,* 6 (June 1988), 26–28.

Wang Jue. "The New Wind of Democratic Politics." *HQ,* 8 (April 16, 1988), 28–29.

Wang Kejia. "Hu Jiwei Is in a Difficult Situation." *TA,* 77 (May 1990), 72–74.

Wang Shuhua. "Don't Substitute Transfer Orders for Votes." *ZYZ,* 1 (Spring 1988), 18–21.

Wang Xinxue. "Comments and Thinking on the Ten-Year Reforms of Our Country's Electoral System." *SZY,* 6 (November–December 1988), 26–28.

Wang Youjin. "The Right and Wrong of the Xi Yang Case." *JBYK,* 11 (November 1993), 22–24.

Wang Youqun. "Can LPCs Supervise Concrete [Legal] Cases?" *QY,* 102, 9 (September 1993), 12–13.

Wang Yuyan. "Local Forces Demonstrate to the Party Center." *SJRB,* March 18, 1995, A18.

Wang Zhengxiang and Zhang Jinhai, eds. *Zhongguo Jingji yu Zhengzhi Tizhi Gaige de Jiben Wenti* (The basic issues concerning the reform of China's economic and political structures). Beijing: Zhongguo Tiedao Chubanshe, 1990.

Wang Zhenhai and Han Xijiang. "On the Organizational Building of the Current Villagers' Committees." *ZYF,* 5 (September 1988), 7–10.

Wu Changqi and Chen Jiyu, eds. *Difang Renda Zhidu* (Local people's congress system). Hefei, Anhui: Anhui Jiaoyu Chubanshe, 1994.

Wu Jian. "Arouse the Initiative of Enterprise Managers." *QS,* 6 (March 16, 1993), 42–43.

Wu Jiang. "Some Supplements on Hu Yaobang's Resignation and the Relations Between Him and Zhao Ziyang." *JBYK,* 5 (May 1997), 60–62.

————. *Shi Nian De Lu: He Hu Yaobang Xiangchu de Rizi* (The path of the past 10 years: The days with Hu Yaobang). Hong Kong: Mirror Post Cultural Enterprises, 1996.

Wu Kangmin. *Renda Huiyilu* (The memoirs about the NPC). Hong Kong: Ming Bao Chubanshe, 1990.

Xiang Ping. "Legal Recall Is Beyond Reproach." *MYF,* 11 (November 1989), 10–11.

Xiao Huazhang. "Fully Arouse Employees' Labor Initiative in the Reform." *QYGL,* 7 (July 1989), 43–45.

Xiao Tie. "On the Institutional Guarantee of People's Deputies' Performance of Their Duties." *FXPL,* 6 (December 1994), 8–12.

Xie Qichen. "A Second Comment on Indirect Election." *TS,* 2 (March 1989).

Xie Qingkui, Yan Jirong, and Zhao Chenggen, *Zhongguo Zhengfu Tizhi Fenxi* (An analysis of the structure of Chinese government). Beijing: Zhongguo Guangbo Dianshi Chubanshe, 1995.

Xie Qingkui, Chen Shuhong, Fu Xiong, and Lin Zhaowu. *Xian Zhengfu Guanli: Wanning Xian Diaocha* (The management of county government: An investigation in Wanning City). Beijing: Zhongguo Guangbo Dianshi Chubanshe, 1994.

Xing Shuliang. "The Decay of Power—A Report on He Yuantang's Abuse of Power for Private Gain." *MYF,* 6 (June 1987), 17–19.

Xiong Fu. "On Democratic Management." *DYLC,* 4 (July 1983), 3–9.

Xu Bing. "The Workers' Status as Masters Must Be Embodied in the FDRS." *HQ,* 4 (February 16, 1985), 3–6.

————. "A Study of the Administrative Reform of State-Owned Enterprises." *GYYJ,* 19 (October 1984), 5–7.

Xu Chongde, ed. *Zhongguo Xianfa* (China's constitutions). Beijing: Zhongguo Renmin Daxue Chubanshe, 1996.

————, ed. *Renmin Daibiao Bibei* (Required reading of people's deputies). Beijing: Renmin Chubanshe, 1987.

————. "How Many New Developments Does the [Current] Electoral System of Our Country Include?" *FX,* 5 (May 1983), 14–17.

Xu Minhe, Hu Guohua, and Shao Quan. "Watch China's Democratization Process Through Two Congresses." *LWZK,* 16 (April 18, 1988), 4–7.

Xu Yaotong. "A Socialist Electoral System Should Permit Campaigning." *QI,* 3 (May 1989), 34–37.

Yan Jiaqi. "A Commentary on the Ninth NPC." *CM,* 246, 4 (April 1998), 22–24.

Yan Xiansheng. "The Investigation of Citizens' 'Sense of Constitutionality' in Our Country." *ZZXYJ,* 1 (January 1986), 69–73.

Yang Changjun. "Look for Higher-quality Deputies." *FZRB,* June 19, 1997.

Yang Fengchun, ed. *Zai Shengji Renda Gongzuo Gangweishang* (Working in provincial people's congresses). Beijing: Zhongguo Minzhu Fazhi Chubanshe, 1997.

Yang Li. "A Study of the Internal Democratic Mechanism of the People's Congress." *ZYF,* 4 (July 1988), 14–16.

Yang Minqing. *Zhongguo Da Xuanju* (Great elections in China). Changsha: Hunan Wenyi Chubanshe, 1989.

Yi Ming. "Is It Legitimate for the Party Secretary to Demand That Party Members Vote for the Candidates He Designates?" *MYF,* 5 (May 1980), 40–41.

Yu Chunsheng. "Comparative Study of Different Periods of Democratic Management of Enterprises in Our Country." *HDX,* 4 (July–August 1985), 30–37.

Yu Yannan. "Seriously Implement the Workers' Congress System." *HQ,* 20 (October 16, 1982), 38–41.

Yu Yunyao. "Thought on Strengthening and Improving Party Organizations in State Enterprises." *QS,* 13 (July 1, 1993), 36–39.

Yuan Baohua. "State Enterprises Must Solve the Problems Concerning the Relationship between Government and Enterprise." *JJGL,* 1 (January 1994), 5–6.

Yuan Guanghou. "Democratic Whirlwind in the Mountain City." *MYF,* 8 (August 1988), 2–4.

Yuan Mu. "Some Comments on the Economic Situation of 1986." *LWZK,* 52 (December 29, 1986), 12–15.

Yue Ming. "Regional Leaders Collectively Boycott the Application for the Olympic Games." *QISH,* 6 (June 8, 1993), 27–29.

ZDZTGYX (Zhongyang Dangxiao Zhengzhi Tizhi Gaige Yanjiu Xiaozu; The Research Group of Political Reforms, the Central Party School), ed. *Guanyu Zhengzhi Tizhi Gaige de Lilun Yanjiu* (A theoretical study of the reform of the political structure). Beijing: Hua Xia Chubanshe, 1987.

Zeng Heng and Zhong Ming. "On the Legal Supervision of Party Organizations by the Standing Committees of People's Congresses." *FXJK,* 1 (Spring 1987), 39–44.

ZFXYW (Zhongguo Faxuehui, Xianzheng Yanjiu Weiyuanhui; the Research Committee of Constitutionalism, the Chinese Association of Law), ed. *Xianfa yu Gaige* (Constitution and reforms). Chongqing: Qunzhong Chubanshe, 1986.

Zhang Boli. "I Dare Neither to Recall Nor to Forget." *ZYRB* (International Edition), August 3, 1992.

Zhang Fen. "History Will Do Justice to the June 4 [Event]: Extracts from Interviews with Zhao Ziyang." *ZGSB,* November 2, 1997, 3.

Zhang Gongchang et al. *Zenyang Danghao Qiye Dangwei Shuji* (How to be a good enterprise party secretary). Beijing: Zhonggong Zhongyang Dangxiao Chubanshe, 1985.

Zhang Huanguang and Su Shangzhi, eds. *Zhonghua Renmin Gongheguo Xingzhengfa Ziliao Xuanbian* (Selected materials concerning the PRC administrative decrees). Beijing: Qunzhong Chubanshe, 1984.

Zhang Mingshu. *Zhongguo Zhengzhiren: Zhongguo Gongmin Zhengzhi Suzhi Diaocha Baogao* (China's "political man": An investigation report of the political quality of Chinese citizens). Beijing: Zhongguo Shehui Kexue Chubanshe, 1994.

Zhang Mo. "Two Conferences Structure the Post-Deng System." *JBYK,* 4 (April 1993), 20–23.

Zhang Songquan. "The Election of People's Deputies Should Not Violate the Electoral Law." *MYF,* 5 (May 1983), 5.

Zhang Suofei. "Zhang Siqing Says: Deepen the Struggle Against Corruption and Bribery." *MYF,* 7 (July 1990), 8–9.

Zhang Weiguo. "Watch the Two Congresses—The Focus of China's Process of Political Democratization." *FX,* 5 (May 1989), 1–4.

Zhang Wenqi and Fang Xiangming. "The FDRS Must Be Based on the Workers' Status as Masters: An Investigation in the Lanzhou No. 2 Woolen Mill." *LZXK,* 2 (March 1985), 17–22.

"Zhang Youyu's Interview with the Reporter." *GMRB,* October 28, 1986.

Zhang Yun. "The Improvement of Party Members' Quality Is the Solid Basis of the Fundamental Improvement of Party Conduct." *HQ,* 10 (May 16, 1986), 3–14.

Zhang Zhigang and Cao Yuhai, eds. *Zuohao Difang Renda Gongzuo* (Do the work of local people's congresses well). Beijing: Qunzhong Chubanshe, 1990.

Zhao Baoxu, ed. *Minzhu Zhengzhi yu Difang Renda* (Democratic politics and local people's congresses). Xi'an: Shaanxi Renmin Chubanshe, 1990.

————, ed. *Zhengquan Jiegou yu Dangde Zhineng* (The structure of political power and the Party's functions). Xi'an: Shaanxi Renmin Chubanshe, 1990.

Zhao Ziyang. "On the Separation of Party and Government—Speech at the Preparatory Meeting of the Seventh Plenary Session of the Twelfth Party Central Committee (October 14, 1987)." *HQ,* 23 (December 1, 1987), 2–4.

————. "Speech at the Conference of Propaganda, Theoretical Study, Mass Communication and Party School Cadres." *RMRB,* July 10, 1987.

Zheng Haihang. "On the Unity of the Authority of Enterprise Chiefs and Workers' Democracy." *DYLC,* 5 (September 1986), 19–23.

Zhong Xingzhi. "Cries for Justice Echo in the Great Hall of the People." *ZGSBZK,* April 10–16, 1994, 54–55.

Zhongguo Gongchandang Daibiao Dahui Baogao Huibian (Collected reports of the CCP Conventions). Beijing: Zhongyang Dangxiao Chubanshe, 1982.

Zhonggong Zhongyang Wenjian Xuanbian (Selected documents of the CCP Central Committee). Beijing: Zhonggong Zhongyang Dangxiao Chubanshe, 1992.

Zhou Runhong. "Let LPCs Exercise Their Functions Independently." *MYF,* 7 (July 1989), 26.

Zhu Guanglei, ed. *Dafenhua Xinzuhe: Dangdai Zhongguo Shehui Gejieceng Fenxi* (Drastic divisions and new combinations: An analysis of various strata of contemporary Chinese society). Tianjin: Tianjin Renmin Chubanshe, 1994.

Zhu Jiazhen's (vice governor of Liaoning province) Speech. In *QYGL,* 5 (May 1990), 6–7.

Zhu Siming. "How to Be a Good People's Deputy." *QY,* 133, 4 (April 7, 1996), 14–15.

Zhu Xiangshan. "A Report About the Investigation of Zhang Wenli's Corruption and Bribery." *MYF,* 12 (December 1990), 20–24.

Zhuang Zhenhua and Zhou Jiquan. "Democratic Management Vitalizes the Enterprise." *SHKX,* 2 (March 1982), 51–54.

Zi Mu, ed., *Minzhu de Gousi* (Thinking over democracy). Beijing: Guangming Ribao Chubanshe, 1989.

Zu Boguang. "The Separation of the Party from Government Has Been Preliminarily Realized in the Institutions at All Levels of Ha'erbin City." *LWZK,* 6 (February 8, 1988), 4–5.

ZZSY (Zhonggong Zhongyang Shujichu Yanjiushi; The Research Institute of the CCP Central Secretariat), ed. *Dangde Shiyijie Sanzhong Quanhui Yilai Dashiji* (A chronicle of events since the Third Plenum of the Eleventh National Party Congress). Beijing: Hongqi Chubanshe, 1987.

ZZWY (Zhonggong Zhongyang Wenxian Yanjiushi The Research Institute of the Documents of the CCP Central Committee), ed. *Xinshiqi Dangde Jianshe Wenxian Xuanbian* (Selected documents concerning party-building in the new era). Beijing: Renmin Chubanshe, 1991.

————, ed. *Shi'erda Yilai Zhongyao Wenxian Xuanbian* (Selected important documents Since the Twelfth National Party Congress). Vol. 3. Beijing: Renmin Chubanshe, 1988.

Index

About the Book

This systematic study of China's structural transformation during the past two decades emphasizes the balance-of-power game so ably played by Deng Xiaoping and others among the post-Mao national leadership.

Chen argues that to prevent party cadre opposition to market restructuring—the nemesis of change in other communist states—national leaders manipulated legislative channels and party regulations to allow citizen participation in the implementation of reform programs. Opportunistic realignments at the political level, involving the central leadership, local party cadres, and ordinary citizens, brought "people power" into the policymaking process. That power, suggests Chen, may also presage China's constitutional evolution toward a democratic form of government.

Previously a research fellow at the Chinese Academy of Social Sciences, **An Chen** is assistant professor of political science at the National University of Singapore.